Entrepreneurship
Version 2.0

Laura Portolese, Jaclyn Krause, and Julie R. Bonner

FlatWorld

978-1-4533-4068-4

Entrepreneurship
Version 2.0

Laura Portolese, Jaclyn Krause, and Julie R. Bonner

Published by:

FlatWorld
292 Newbury Street
Suite #282
Boston, MA 02115-2832

© 2023 by Boston Academic Publishing, Inc. d.b.a. FlatWorld
All rights reserved. Your use of this work is subject to the License Agreement available at https://catalog.flatworldknowledge.com/legal.

No part of this work may be used, modified, or reproduced in any form or by any means except as expressly permitted under the License Agreement.

Gen: 202210171918

Brief Contents

About the Authors
Acknowledgements
Dedication
Preface

PART 1 The Idea
Chapter 1 What Is Entrepreneurship?
Chapter 2 Understanding the Basics of Business
Chapter 3 How Do I Determine a Good Idea and Opportunity?

PART 2 Entrepreneurship Planning
Chapter 4 How Do I Write a Marketing Plan?
Chapter 5 How Do I Perform Financial Analysis?
Chapter 6 How Do I Write an Operational Plan?
Chapter 7 How to Write a Management Plan
Chapter 8 How to Put Together a Business Plan

PART 3 Entrepreneurship Execution
Chapter 9 How Do I Manage Change?
Chapter 10 Handling Human Resources

PART 4 Growing and Sustaining Your Business
Chapter 11 How Do I Grow My Business?
Chapter 12 Planning for the Future
Appendix A Start Your Business Resources
Appendix B Social Media Marketing
Index

Contents

About the Authors		1
Acknowledgements		3
Dedication		5
Preface		7
PART 1	The Idea	11
Chapter 1	**What Is Entrepreneurship?**	13
1.1	Entrepreneurs and Entrepreneurship—Defining What We Mean by Small Business	15
	The Difference Between a Small Business and an Entrepreneurial Venture	18
1.2	How Small Businesses Helped Shape America	20
	A Brief History of Small Business Ownership—the American Dream	20
	The Value of Small Businesses to the American Economy	22
	The Internet Revolution and Business	23
	Major Entrepreneurial Theories	24
1.3	Why Start Your Own Business?	26
1.4	Dispelling the Myths about Small Business Ownership: It's a Lot of Work!	29
	The Global Pandemic: COVID-19	30
1.5	Test Your Skills: Applied Case	31
	Gina's Party Planning	31
1.6	Endnotes	32
Chapter 2	**Understanding the Basics of Business**	33
2.1	Business Ownership Models	34
	Sole Proprietorship	35
	Partnerships	36
	Corporations	36
	Cooperatives	38
2.2	Service Businesses vs. Product Businesses	41
	Do You Sell a Product, Service, or Both?	41
	Are You a Product-Producing or Service-Producing Business?	42
2.3	Franchising	42
	Different Ways to Obtain a Business	43
	Advantages of Franchise Ownership	43
	The Importance of Protecting the Brand	44
	Risks of Owning a Franchise	45
2.4	Self-Employment vs. Entrepreneurship	46

		What Does It Mean to be Self-Employed?	46
		Is Someone Who Is Self-Employed an Entrepreneur?	47
	2.5	The Characteristics and Mindset of an Entrepreneur	48
		The Small Business Owner vs. the Entrepreneur	49
		How Are They the Same?	50
		Myths about Entrepreneurs	50
	2.6	Test Your Skills: Applied Case	52
		Striking Out on Your Own	52
	2.7	Endnotes	53
Chapter 3		**How Do I Determine a Good Idea and Opportunity?**	**55**
	3.1	The Timmons Framework	56
		Opportunity	57
		Resources	57
		Team	57
	3.2	Generating a Good Idea	59
		Characteristics of a Good Idea Generation Process	59
		Passion vs. Hobby vs. Real Business Idea	60
		Idea Generation Methods	61
	3.3	Evaluating the Idea: Opportunity Assessment Plans	65
		The Stages of Successful Ideation	65
		Opportunity Assessment Plans	66
	3.4	Nailing Down the Idea: Planning for Product or Service Development	68
		Product Lifecycle	69
		Types of Innovation	70
		Product Planning and Development Process	71
	3.5	Test Your Skills: Applied Case	73
		Maria's Cakes and the Product Development Process	73
	3.6	Endnotes	74
PART 2		**Entrepreneurship Planning**	**75**
Chapter 4		**How Do I Write a Marketing Plan?**	**77**
	4.1	Market Research Methods	78
		Secondary Research	79
		Primary Research	80
		Market Research Steps	81
	4.2	Target Markets	83
		Demographics	84
		Geographic Segmentation	86
		Price Segmentation	86
		Psychographic or Lifestyle Segmentation	86
		Behavioral Segmentation	87
		Buyer Behavior	87
	4.3	The Marketing Mix	89
		Product (or Service)	90

		Price	90
		Place	91
		Promotion	92
	4.4	Writing the Marketing Plan	94
		Situation Analysis	94
		Goals and Objectives	95
		Target Market	96
		Pricing and Place	97
		Promotional Strategies	97
		Budget	97
	4.5	Test Your Skills: Applied Case	98
		LaPorchea's Dog Walking and Promotion	98
	4.6	Endnotes	98
Chapter 5		How Do I Perform Financial Analysis?	99
	5.1	Funding Source Options	100
		What Is Your Personal Credit Score?	101
		What Are Funding Sources?	102
	5.2	How Do I Estimate Needed Funding?	104
		Where Can You Research Financial Information?	105
		How Do I Identify Fixed Assets and Monthly Expenses?	106
		How Do I Differentiate Operating Expenses from the Cost of Goods Sold?	108
		How Do I Identify the Fixed Costs of My Business vs. the Variable Expenses?	110
		How Do I Determine My Cash Cycle?	110
	5.3	How Do I Read Financial Statements?	114
		Income Statement	115
		Balance Sheet	118
		Revisit the Opening Case	119
		Cash Flow Statements	120
		Accountability	121
	5.4	How Do I Perform A Break-Even Analysis?	122
		Identify Your Fixed and Variable Costs and the Price of Your Product	122
		Plug the Information into the Break-Even Formula	123
	5.5	How Do I Write a Financial Plan?	124
		How to Write the Financial Plan	124
		How to Evaluate Your Accounting Partner	125
	5.6	Test Your Skills: Applied Case	127
		A Handyman Story	127
	5.7	Endnotes	128
Chapter 6		How Do I Write an Operational Plan?	129
	6.1	Location	130
		How to Assess Your Needs for a Location	130
		Selecting a Manufacturing Location	132
	6.2	Facilities and Equipment	133
		Space Requirements	134

		Assessing Equipment Needs for Your Location Through Buying or Leasing	135
	6.3	Employees and Insurance	136
		Personnel Decisions in the Operations Plan	136
		Insurance Considerations for Employees and Facilities	137
	6.4	Suppliers, Supplier Management, and Cost Decisions	138
		Selecting Suppliers	139
		Supplier Management	140
		Cost Decisions	140
	6.5	Writing the Operational Plan	142
		Putting It All Together	142
	6.6	Test Your Skills: Applied Case	143
		Jill's Manufacturing	143
	6.7	Endnotes	144
Chapter 7	**How to Write a Management Plan**		**145**
	7.1	Building a Team	146
		Skill Assessment	146
		Internal Team	148
		External Team	149
		Management vs. Leadership	150
	7.2	Organizational Structures	151
		Selecting an Organizational Structure	152
		Choosing an Organizational Structure	155
	7.3	Writing the Organization and Management Plan	156
		Team Bios and Roles	156
		Organizational Structure	157
		Succession Plan	158
	7.4	Test Your Skills: Applied Case	161
		Stella's Stellar Salesperson	161
	7.5	Endnotes	162
Chapter 8	**How to Put Together a Business Plan**		**163**
	8.1	Formal vs. Informal Business Plans: When You Need Each	164
	8.2	The Components of a Business Plan: From the Executive Summary through the Appendix	166
		Business Plan Organization	167
		Business Plan Sections	167
	8.3	Resources to Help You Prepare Your Plan and Obtain Funding	170
		Loans vs. Grants vs. Investors	171
		Sources for Obtaining Loans	171
		Sources for Obtaining Grants	172
		Sources for Obtaining Investors	173
		How the Small Business Administration Can Help	175
		Additional Resources	175
	8.4	Presenting the Plan to Potential Investors	176
		Preparing for the Business Presentation	177

		Preparing a PowerPoint Presentation of Your Business Plan	178
		Reviewing Contracts, Agreements, and other Loan Documents	179
	8.5	Test Your Skills: Applied Case	180
		Ahmed's Gasoline Additive	180
	8.6	Endnotes	181

PART 3   Entrepreneurship Execution   183

Chapter 9   How Do I Manage Change?   185

	9.1	Understanding Factors that Impact the Business	186
		SWOT Analysis	186
	9.2	External Factors	190
		Political	191
		Economic	191
		Social	192
		Technological	193
		Legal	193
		Ethical/Environmental	194
		Using SWOT and PESTLE for Strategic Planning	195
	9.3	Internal Factors	196
		Employees and Company Culture	197
		Stakeholder Management	198
		Vendor and Supplier Management	200
	9.4	Additional Considerations for Managing Change	201
		Should You Hire an Attorney?	202
		Time Management	202
		Leadership and Interpersonal Skills	204
		Crisis Situations and Planning Before Change Occurs	205
	9.5	Test Your Skills: Applied Case	207
		The Millers Supply Chain Problems	207
	9.6	Endnotes	208

Chapter 10   Handling Human Resources   209

	10.1	Recruitment, Selection, and Hiring Process	210
		Recruitment	210
		Selection	213
		Legal Considerations in Hiring and Beyond	216
	10.2	Training and Development	220
		Training Steps	220
	10.3	Compensation	223
		Purpose of Compensation	223
		Considerations in Compensation	224
		Types of Compensation	224
	10.4	Other HR Considerations	226
		Employee Performance Management	226
		Performance Issue Model	228

		Performance Evaluations		229
		Remote Workforces		230
	10.5	Test Your Skills: Applied Case		231
		Shannon Lopez and Human Resource Planning		231
	10.6	Endnotes		232

PART 4 — Growing and Sustaining Your Business — 233

Chapter 11 — How Do I Grow My Business? — 235

11.1	External Sources of Growth		236
	Joint Ventures		237
	Venture Capital		237
	Initial Public Offering (IPO)		238
	Acquisitions		238
	Mergers		238
	International Considerations		239
11.2	Internal Sources for Growth		240
	Expansion of Products and Services		241
	Referrals and Subscriptions		241
	Expand Your Market		241
	Cut Costs and Loser Products		242
	Duplicate Yourself		242
11.3	Models for Innovation and Growth Management		244
	Innovation Strategies		244
	Growth Management		246
11.4	Test Your Skills: Applied Case		247
	Ebony's Dog Grooming Business		247
11.5	Endnotes		248

Chapter 12 — Planning for the Future — 249

12.1	Succession Planning		250
	Why Succession Planning?		250
	Selling Your Business		251
	Transfer the Business to Family		253
	Dissolving the Business		254
12.2	The Future of Entrepreneurship		256
	Ethics		256
	Social Entrepreneurship		258
	Other Trends in Entrepreneurship		259
12.3	Test Your Skills: Applied Case		261
	Noah Miles and Succession Planning		261
12.4	Endnotes		262

Appendix A — Start Your Business Resources — 263

A.1	Entrepreneurship Planning		263
	Entrepreneurship Self-Assessment		263
	Start Your Business Resources		263

| | | Business Model Canvas Template | 263 |
| | | Business Plan Templates | 264 |

Appendix B Social Media Marketing — 265

    B.1 A Brief Look at Using Social Media to Market Your Business — 265
        What Is Social Media Marketing? — 265
        Advantages of Using Social Media Marketing — 265
        How to Leverage Social Media to Market Your Business — 266

Index — 269

About the Authors

Laura Portolese

Laura Portolese (Doctorate, Argosy University) is the author or co-author of four books with FlatWorld (*Human Resource Management, Human Relations, The Art of Supervision and Leadership,* and *Consumer Behavior Today*). Professor Portolese holds a Master of Business Administration from City University and a Doctorate of Business Administration from Argosy University. She teaches in the Department of Information Technology and Administrative Management, part of the Central Washington University's College of Education and Professional Studies. Before beginning her teaching career, Professor Portolese worked for several organizations in management and operations. She's also an entrepreneur who has performed consulting work for companies such as Microsoft.

Jaclyn A. Krause

Jackie Krause (Ph.D., Walden School of Management) earned her degree in applied management and information sciences. She possesses thirty-five years of comprehensive and progressive experience in information technology work including network administration, application design and development including web-based applications, website development, information systems analysis, design, and architecture, and information technology project management. Professor Krause has been an academic department chair responsible for supervising the activities of forty-five full-time and adjunct faculty in the School of Information Systems and Technology. She is also an IT professional who has been embedded within business units and has supervised faculty and help desk staff, led teams of system administrators, and led multi-discipline, cross-functional project teams as a project manager.

Julie R. Bonner

Julie Bonner (Doctorate, University of Phoenix) earned her degree in management. She has consulted extensively for large clients in the aerospace, consumer products, and gaming industries providing services in accounting and information systems design.

Acknowledgements

We would like to thank all of the reviewers for their contributions to this book. Their ideas, feedback, and suggestions helped make this book unprecedented. We thank them personally for their insight, and we hope we have a chance to shake their hands in person one day.

- Chandra D. Arthur, MBA, MAFM, Cuyahoga Community College
- Dr. April Bailey, St. Petersburg College
- Christopher Boucher, University of New England
- Gina Deschamps, DBA, Endicott College
- Vishal K. Gupta, University of Alabama
- Kyungmoon Kim, West Virginia University Institute of Technology
- Ben Kish, Blue Ridge Community College
- Dr. Mark Matheson, Southern Virginia University
- Robert (Chip) Matthews, Sam Houston State University
- Leann Mischel, PhD. Coastal Carolina University
- Dr. Mary Jackson Pitts, Arkansas State University
- Dr. Andrea Smith-Hunter, Siena College
- Matthew Wilson, Delaware Technical Community College
- Zhe Zhang, Eastern Kentucky University

The team at FlatWorld is the best in the business. We appreciate Sean Wakely for his enthusiasm for this project, Briana Leonard for her coordination of the project, and the rest of the FlatWorld team for their contributions. We would also like to thank the FlatWorld staffers whom we've never met—those who render drawings, edit content, and otherwise ensure the quality of the text.

We would like to thank our family and friends for supporting our efforts during such a huge undertaking.

We would also like to thank the professors who adopt this book and the students who use it. We hope it will serve as an excellent resource for all of your future endeavors.

Dedication

Laura would like to dedicate this book to her outstanding co-authors and colleagues, Jackie and Julie. This book is also dedicated to Lori and Laurie, colleagues in the Information Technology and Administrative Management department at Central Washington University. Laura would further like to dedicate this book to her friends and family.

Jackie would like to dedicate this book to her amazing co-authors, Laura and Julie, who made working on this book a joy. She would also like to dedicate it to her colleagues Lori and Laurie in the Information Technology and Administrative Management department at Central Washington University, for their unwavering support and encouragement. Finally, she dedicates this book to her husband, Bernie, who is always a source of encouragement and support in all that she does.

Julie would like to dedicate this book to her amazing co-authors, Laura and Jackie. In addition, many thanks go to Lori in the Information Technology and Administrative Management department at Central Washington University, for her insight and support as a colleague. Finally, Julie wants to thank her spouse, Alex, for supporting her career aspirations and making her laugh on a daily basis.

Preface

Thank you for using Portolese, Bonner, & Krause's *Entrepreneurship* v2.0. We think you will enjoy its conversational style, multimedia content, and wealth of information.

Whether you are an instructor or a student, by using this book, you are becoming a part of the low-cost textbook revolution! Instructors can customize this book by rearranging, adding, deleting, or editing its content. We are using technology to make textbooks less expensive and more relevant for our students.

The goal of this book is to provide accessible and practical content for students hoping to start their own businesses at some point in their careers. Even if this isn't your goal as a student, this text will provide you with a basis for innovative thinking that can be applied to any field you find yourself working in.

Other unique features of this book include . . .

- A focus on service-oriented businesses
- Small-business examples that make concepts engaging and relatable
- Multimedia content in every chapter to engage visual learners
- Captivating opening cases focused on smaller businesses and start-ups
- "What Would You Do?" callout boxes that pose real-life challenges and questions to readers
- "Leveraging" callout boxes that explain how to leverage outside resources to make business decisions
- Interactive end-of-chapter activities

These pedagogical components and features make the book easy to read and understand, while still maintaining an academic focus.

Organization

The organization of this book is intuitive and follows the process entrepreneurs go through to start a new business.

The first part of the book, called "The Idea," addresses the basics of entrepreneurship in Chapter 1. Chapter 2 focuses on the basics of business, presenting baseline information that will be important to understanding the next steps of developing a business. Chapter 3 presents methods for generating business ideas, as well as strategies for narrowing those ideas and focusing on the one with the most potential.

The second part of the book, called "Entrepreneurship Planning," teaches readers how to develop the business plan they'll need to obtain funding for a new business venture. Chapter 4 focuses on marketing analysis, Chapter 5 on understanding the financials of a business, and Chapter 6 on the operational aspects of a business. Chapter 7 addresses the management aspects of a business, and Chapter 8 discusses how to assemble the business plan and market the business idea.

The third part of the book, which includes Chapter 9 and Chapter 10, addresses "Entrepreneurship Execution." This section covers planning, managing change, and dealing with various internal and external factors involved in starting a business.

The fourth and final section of the book, "Growing and Sustaining Your Business," addresses how to grow a business in Chapter 11 and how to plan for the future of a business in Chapter 12.

Features

Each chapter contains a number of innovative features to engage students:

- Opening cases: The opening case at the beginning of each chapter introduces the content of the chapter by presenting a specific small business case. Insight from these cases will provide useful baseline knowledge for the rest of the chapter.
- Learning objectives by section: Instead of presenting a long list of learning objectives at the beginning of each chapter, we divide learning objectives by section and define key terms for every section in the book.
- "How Would You Handle It?": These scenarios will help students develop the critical thinking skills necessary for solving entrepreneurial problems.
- Multimedia: Use of multimedia content in each chapter allows readers to identify visually with specific concepts presented in the chapter.
- Figures: Clear and focused visuals in each chapter illustrate key strategic concepts in entrepreneurship.
- Interactive activities: Every chapter includes interactive activities. These activities guide readers through the development of a business plan, while teaching the critical thinking and teamwork skills necessary for a successful business venture.

What's New in Version 2.0

Any revision of a book since 2020 has to address the impact of the global pandemic of COVID-19. The pandemic that spread worldwide impacted all organizations and employees and has had profound effects on the business world. In entrepreneurship, the pandemic shows that entrepreneurs cannot predict the changes that may come along in the business world. Yet, every entrepreneur has to be creative and think on their feet. Therefore, every chapter of the book is updated with considerations introduced by COVID-19 to the workplace. While COVID-19 is still impacting businesses large and small, and the effects of the pandemic are ever-evolving, the additions to the book give you some ideas about how to handle structural shifts in the entrepreneur's world.

In addition, while COVID-19 has had an enormous influence on everyone, including small business owners, the following changes have also been introduced in version 2.0:

- Appendix A: A new mini-chapter that provides students with resources and tools to help them start their businesses. This appendix addresses the business model canvas and business plan templates and provides self-assessments to help students identify skills and abilities to make their business plan a success.
- Appendix B: A new mini-chapter on Social Media Marketing is included where students are guided through the process of leveraging the power of social media for their new business venture.
- COVID-19 is addressed in each chapter to help students think about the impacts of major external events and how to respond effectively to these challenges and plan for contingencies.

- Every chapter has been revised for new and updated research, data, and statistics.
- End-of-chapter cases have been added to aid students in applying practical skills learned to real scenarios.

Supplements

Entrepreneurship v2.0 is accompanied by a robust supplements program that augments and enriches both the teaching and student learning experiences. The authors personally prepared all of the supplements to ensure accuracy and to ensure full alignment with the book's narrative. Faculty should contact their FlatWorld sales representative or FlatWorld support at support@flatworld.com for more information or to obtain access to the supplements upon adoption.

Sample Syllabi

Sample syllabi based on either 16-week or 10-week terms provide useful templates that help new adopters transition from their current course textbook to Human Resource Management. Faculty can download the syllabi from the FlatWorld website or they can be obtained by contacting your local FlatWorld representative or FlatWorld support (support@flatworld.com).

Instructor's Manual

The Instructor's Manual (IM) includes Learning Objectives and an outline for each chapter. The IM also features possible responses to case discussion questions which encourage students to more deeply engage with course material.

PowerPoint Slides

PowerPoint Slides organized by chapter include a concise and thorough outline, a list of Learning Objectives, and figures and tables contained in the text. These slides work well for both face-to-face and online learning environments, enliven lectures, and stimulate class discussions. Adopters can use the slides as composed to support lectures or customize and build upon them to suit their particular teaching goals.

Test Item File

The Test Item File (TIF) includes more than fifty questions per chapter in multiple-choice, fill-in-the-blank, and essay-question formats. All answers are provided, including possible responses to the essay questions. The items have been written specifically to reinforce the major topics covered in each chapter and to align with FlatWorld Homework and in-text quiz items. The Test Item File questions are also available in pre-formatted form for easy export into popular learning management systems such as Canvas or Blackboard.

Test Generator—Powered by Cognero

FlatWorld is pleased to provide a computer-generated test program powered by the leading assessment provider Cognero to assist instructors with selecting, randomizing, formatting, loading online, or printing exams. Please contact your local FlatWorld representative or FlatWorld support (support@flatworld.com) for more information or to request the program.

FlatWorld Homework

FlatWorld Homework is provided in an easy-to-use interface. Multiple choice, fill-in-the-blank, matching, and other question types are available for use and are all auto-gradable. Students who utilize the homework questions should see their performance improve on examinations that are given using the Test Item File questions that accompany this book.

Online Quizzes and Flashcards

Autograded Quiz questions and Flashcards for student self-evaluation are organized by chapter and section and embedded in the online version of the book. Students can use the Quizzes and Flashcards to test their comprehension by section as they read and learn, once they have completed a chapter, or for test review.

We are confident that you will enjoy reading this book as much as we enjoyed writing it for you, the instructors, professors, and students. Please feel free to send us a personal email if you have questions or comments about the text. Best wishes for a great semester or quarter!

Laura, Ellensburg, WA, laura.portolese@cwu.edu

Julie, Seattle, WA, julie.bonner@cwu.edu

Jackie, Ellensburg, WA, jaclyn.krause@cwu.edu

PART 1
The Idea

Source: © Shutterstock, Inc.

CHAPTER 1
What Is Entrepreneurship?

Case Study—Jane Quilts

Jane always loved sewing. Quilting, to be precise. Although Jane learned to sew at a young age, she never really enjoyed making clothes for herself or others. Jane's mom loved to quilt. When she was in her early twenties, she went to a quilting exhibition with her mom and was hooked. She loved the idea of taking large pieces of fabric, cutting them into smaller pieces, and then sewing them back together to make works of art. It seemed so impractical, but so satisfying.

Although Jane started quilting for family and friends, her passion soon grew. She bought sewing machines and quilting supplies as time and resources became available. To expand her hobby, Jane would offer to finish quilts for other hobbyists that either lost interest or simply did not have the time.

Source: © Shutterstock, Inc.

Finishing a quilt involves a tying off process in which the pieced top is joined with the backing material by "sandwiching" a batting material in between the two. Then, all three layers need to be joined in some manner so that they stay as one unit. This process can be done in several different ways, but the most beautiful, longest lasting, and most effective, is by using a long-arm quilting machine. It can also be the most expensive and Jane did not own one of these machines . . . yet.

Jane knew that investing in a long-arm quilting machine for her own projects was a luxury, but if she used the long-arm machine to finish not only her quilts, but those for other quilters, she might be able to offset the cost of the machine. Initially, Jane set out to make enough money professionally by finishing other people's quilts to pay for her hobby. Because Jane lived in a small, rural area of Washington state, she knew finding clientele might be a challenge. There were three quilt guilds within a fifty-mile radius which could be used to feed her new business. This seemed reasonable so Jane decided to proceed; she figured she didn't need a lot of business to accomplish her goals. After research of what others were charging for similar services, Jane would need to complete five or six quilts a month to help cover her costs.

Finally, Jane was able to buy a big, beautiful, expensive long-arm machine. To get started, Jane placed her long-arm machine in her garage. She taught herself to use the machine by quilting several samples. This allowed her a way of demonstrating her work to her customers. As she established her business, customers would drop off quilts for her to complete. This proved an enjoyable and profitable supplement to her hobby. As her business grew, she became known as Jane Quilts.

During her first year, Jane was mainly focused on investing most of her profits back into the business, paying off equipment, developing a web presence, and buying another new quilting machine. Soon Jane decided to expand her quilting business to accepting new quilt orders online. She worked with a local web developer to create a website that allowed customers to purchase her services and ship their quilts directly to their doorstep. Jane offered a two-day rush service for those that needed fast turnaround. It only took a year before Jane found that she had enough work to keep two quilting machines running most days. As she expanded, so did her services.

As her web business grew, Jane began to focus on a social media presence that included Facebook, Instagram, and YouTube. This caused more demand and likewise, some difficult decisions. Jane needed to expand out of her garage or extend lead times for her customers. She knew expanding lead times would be disappointing but expanding also had several risks. Confident that the business would turn a profit in the next few years, this could have also meant moving into a different, larger space and hiring and training staff that could work as well and thoughtfully on customer quilts as she did. Jane voiced her concerns regarding this move with her followers, unsure if she should limit how big her business grew. After all, this was just a way for her to pay for her hobby.

Jane Quilts is one example of a passion for a hobby that has turned into a thriving enterprise. Whether you want to start a small business to supplement your income, to further your passion, to work from home, or to serve as a stepping stone to a larger, even national business enterprise, it's important to understand all the different aspects defining your small business. Jane is definitely an entrepreneur . . . but what, exactly, does that mean? What is entrepreneurship itself?

Many dream of owning their own business or being their own boss. Whether your dream is to start a small local bakery, open a consulting firm, turn your hobby into full-time job, or launch the next big internet sensation, it's not enough to have an idea. You need to know how to transform the idea into a viable business enterprise. Additionally, you need to know how to run and grow your business into a successful enterprise. You need to know *how to be an entrepreneur*.

In this text, we will explore entrepreneurship by looking at the many aspects that are involved in starting, growing, managing, and maintaining a successful small business. We'll also look at what it means to take your business to the next level.

Ready? Then let's get started.

1.1 Entrepreneurs and Entrepreneurship—Defining What We Mean by Small Business

Learning Objectives

1. Identify different types of small businesses.
2. Differentiate between a small business and an entrepreneurial venture.

In this section, we will look at small businesses, small business owners, entrepreneurs, and entrepreneurial ventures.

So, who is an entrepreneur? What is entrepreneurship? It is common to see these terms used interchangeably with "small business owner" and "small business." When used like this, they mean the same thing: starting a business venture. When you look at the terms more closely, though, they have specific definitions.

In the simplest sense, an **entrepreneur** is the individual or individuals who start a new business venture, while **entrepreneurship** is the activity of starting or building a business venture. When talking about entrepreneurship, we are talking about starting some business. Most businesses start out as small businesses and, with hard work and effort, grow into thriving enterprises. But what types of businesses are considered *small*—and does the type of business matter?

entrepreneur
An individual or individuals engaged in the formation and start-up of an innovative small business enterprise.

entrepreneurship
The act of starting a small business enterprise.

Source: © Shutterstock, Inc.

There are many types of small businesses. The Small Business Administration defines a small business by its size (the number of employees and the annual income) based on the industry in which it operates. For example, a small, independently owned bakery that employs five people, both full and part time, would qualify as a small business. An independently owned and operated manufacturing company that employees 225 people would *also* qualify as a small business, however.[1]

Let's look at some small business examples:[2]

FIGURE 1.1 The Many Types of Small Businesses

- Home-based
- Storefront
- Food service
- Franchise
- Agency
- Consulting/Contracting
- Professional services
- Online retailer

Small Business Types

Source: Laura Portolese et al.

- **Home-based**

    A business located primarily in the owner's home may be large or small and may have one or many employees. Often these businesses may start out as a hobby and grow into a full-time business venture. Similarly, home-based businesses may move into more appropriate spaces as they grow. Examples of home-based businesses include cleaning and repair services, writing and editorial services, event planning, home inspection, and interior decorating. Home-based businesses save money because there is no need to rent office or other facility space. Additionally, eliminating the time it takes to commute to work can mean a gain in productive work hours. Running a business from home requires self-discipline, as there are many potential distractions and competing demands for your time. Starting a home-based business is nonetheless a good first step that allows you to minimize your initial startup costs.

- **Online retailers**

    These internet businesses typically are run fully online and may offer goods or services. Many online retailers start as home-based businesses. However, depending on the goods or services offered, appropriate office space may be required. This is especially true of online retailers requiring significant space for inventory, or service-based businesses that may have several employees. It is often very easy and inexpensive to start an online storefront. Examples of online retailers include those for specialized products such as dog food and pet supplies, craft supplies, clothing, custom furniture, hand-made items such as jewelry, cards, handbags, etc.

- **Storefronts**

    Often when we think of a small business, we think of the local "mom-and-pop" store on Main Street, USA. Many storefront businesses are family owned and operated. Usually (but not always) these businesses are single stores selling either goods or services. Some examples of storefront businesses include hairdressers/beauty salons, tire stores, lumber and hardware stores, nurseries, convenience stores, and child-care providers, to name a few.

- **Food service**

    Examples of food service businesses include restaurants, coffee shops, take-out locations, catering services, and related businesses. Often these businesses are family owned and offer unique, specialized cuisine. In recent years, food trucks have become a popular form of food service small business, serving a variety of gourmet fast food.

- **Professional services**

    Businesses such as building contractors and architects, plumbers, electricians, pest control, and carpet cleaners are just a few examples of professional trade services. Other examples of professional services include doctors, dentists, lawyers, and accountants. Some professional services may be home-based businesses. These businesses may be **sole proprietorships** and may have a small number of employees.

- **Franchises**

    One way to start a small business is to purchase a franchise, which allows the owner to sell products or services from a known entity. Franchise businesses frequently offer national advertising and custom support for their franchisees. A few well-known examples of franchise opportunities are McDonalds, Subway, Supercuts, ServPro, and Anytime Fitness. We will look at franchises in more detail in Chapter 2.

- **Consulting/contracting firms**

    One popular way in which individuals decide to leave corporate life and work for themselves is by starting a consulting or contracting business. Consultants may work from home or from another office space. These may be knowledge-based businesses where the commodity sold is experience or expertise. Examples of consulting businesses include pro-

> **sole proprietorships**
> The simplest form of business in which there is a single business owner.

ject and risk managers, real estate appraisers, computer analysts/programmers/developers, web designers, and marketing and media designers.

- **Agencies, including insurance, investment, and real estate**

    Agencies employ agents who broker the sales of specific goods or services. For example, insurance agents help you find the best insurance to fit your needs, investment brokers help you manage your money investments, and real estate agents help you buy or sell a home or other real estate property. Agents act as representatives for buyers and sellers of goods and services. There are several other examples of agents, but those listed here are the most common. Agents also may be franchisees, selling a specific insurance brand or representing a national agency.

Zane's Cycles

Chris Zane started fixing bikes at age twelve. By the time he was a junior in high school, Zane had started his own bike shop. In this video, he tells his story, and explains what he brings to the industry, in his own words.

View in the online reader

The Difference Between a Small Business and an Entrepreneurial Venture

We have looked at several examples of small businesses. Is there a difference between a small business and an entrepreneurial venture? There are several differences, in fact—and some similarities.

The differences between an entrepreneurial venture and a small business can be both subtle and complex. Most agree that both small businesses and entrepreneurial ventures start off with many of the same steps: planning, effort, and (of course) funding. So what makes them different?

One distinct difference is that small businesses deal with products—goods or services—that are *known*, whereas entrepreneurial ventures tend to seek *new and* **innovative** opportunities.[3] When entering into a new and innovative area, **risk** may be unknown, whereas small businesses tend to have a good understanding of the risks from the beginning of the venture. Another difference is that small businesses tend to *stay* small, whereas entrepreneurships are intended to grow quickly while seeking rapid rewards. It is possible that the entrepreneurial venture will be a start-up that, once viable, may be sold for significant profits.

Entrepreneurs may start small businesses, but not all small business owners are entrepreneurs. Many small business owners become business owners through acquiring an existing small

innovative

A term referring to new and original ideas. Often these ideas become new products and services.

risk

A situation or condition that may expose a business to harm or loss, often financial.

business or inheriting a family business. Commissioned agents, such as real estate agents, insurance agents, and investment agents represent small business ownership, but they are not entrepreneurial ventures. Similarly, owning a franchise selling goods and services does not qualify the owner as an entrepreneur. While there are many similarities to entrepreneurship, such as the risk, franchise ownership is not considered entrepreneurship because the goods and services are already available commodities.[4] Franchisees are not creating new products or services that are not already available in the marketplace.

> ### Leveraging: When a Family Business Becomes an Entrepreneurial Venture
>
> There are times when a small business might grow into an entrepreneurial endeavor. Colgate is one such business. Colgate was a small, family-owned business that become an exciting and innovative company in the early 1900s. Originally started as a soap and candle company in the 1800s, the Colgate Company made a significant change in direction when the company's founder, William Colgate, died. Under William's son, Samuel, Colgate began selling toothpaste in a jar in the 1870s. By the 1890s, this had become toothpaste in a tube. Meanwhile, B. J. Johnson developed a new soap containing both palm and olive oil which he called Palmolive. Both innovators were bringing new products to market independently. They eventually merged, forming Colgate-Palmolive, a global conglomerate offering brands such as Murphy's Oil soap, Hill's Science Diet pet food, Tom's of Maine, Ajax, Irish Spring, and Speed Stick. Through continued innovation and effort, this once family-run business became an entrepreneurial enterprise.

Now that we have defined some terms that are identified with entrepreneurship, it's a good time to discuss the focus of this textbook—and how you can use the information provided within these pages. This book is intended to help you explore small business start-up and ownership. These businesses may be small and traditional, or they may be entrepreneurial ventures. They may be storefronts or they may be online.

We will also look at what is needed to start a business from the ground up, as well as what it takes to grow, market, manage, and develop such enterprises. Although we recognize there are differences between entrepreneurs and small business owners, we will look at both with a similar focus. When appropriate, we will describe the differences that might be important. Finally, we realize that all business ventures involve *some* risk, so we will try to help you navigate those risks.

Key Takeaway

- Small businesses are the engine of America; they represent the American dream.

Interactive Activity

1. Are you ready to be an entrepreneur? Take this quiz located at Entrepreneur's website and be prepared to discuss your results. What was the biggest surprise in your findings? Identify three things that you might do to be better prepared for entrepreneurship.

1.2 How Small Businesses Helped Shape America

Learning Objectives

1. Explain the history of small businesses in America.
2. Explain how small businesses affect the American economy.

small business

An independently owned and operated company that conforms to the guidelines set by the U. S. Small Business Administration for size and number of employees.

entrepreneurial ventures

The result of starting a small business enterprise.

In Section 1, we defined some terms concerning **small businesses** and **entrepreneurial ventures**. In this section, we will look at the history of small business in the United States and see just how important these businesses are to the economic well-being of our country.

A Brief History of Small Business Ownership—the American Dream

The American dream[5] has been defined as one in which, through hard work and effort, success can be achieved. During the seventeenth and eighteenth centuries, early American settlers became landowners, farmers, and ranchers. Early businesses were family farms. Back then, families had to produce the materials needed for life on the farm.[6] The large variety of items needed included such things as soap, candles, clothing, bedding, utensils and cookware, shoes, tools, and other necessities. Often, families would sell some of the items they made to other families. Trading became a way of life.

Source: Drew Horne/Shutterstock.com

As towns formed, more business localized. Small merchants and craftsman could service larger numbers of the town's citizenry. As transportation into and between towns became more accessible, the general store became the hub for obtaining goods.

During the nineteenth century, the **industrial revolution** changed the way we work. Towns became larger. Goods that might have been produced by hand were now produced by machine. Large manufacturing facilities replaced small enterprises. Some families left farming. During the twentieth century, many family farms were bought by large corporations. The production of our food changed. Toward the end of the twentieth century, work moved from labor-based jobs to **knowledge-based jobs**.

> **industrial revolution**
> The time between the 17th and 18th century, which introduced machinery, gas powered equipment, and locomotive transportation. The Industrial Revolution began in Great Britain in the late 1700s and spread to America in the 1820s. Jobs moved from agriculture to factories.

> **knowledge-based jobs**
> Sometimes referred to as "white collar jobs," these are jobs in which individuals use their minds rather than engage in physical labor. Some examples of knowledge-based jobs include computer programmers/developers, writers, doctors, pharmacists, engineers, accountants, and attorneys.

What Would You Do?

Erin Baker began selling wholesome, quality breakfast cookies from a jar on the counter at a local health food store. She rented kitchen space from a local county fairground to bake her cookies, making deliveries to local stores on her Schwinn bicycle. Her cookies were popular with the customers. One day, however, a customer called asking about nutritional information. Once it became common knowledge that Erin's cookies were only two Weight Watcher points, her company exploded.

In 1999 Erin Baker's company grew from two employees to 100. When Weight Watchers changed their point system, however, Erin's cookies fell out of favor. The company lost a chunk of its customer base, but Erin changed her process by taking her cookies back to basics. She focused on wholesome, fresh ingredients and marketed "the best breakfast cookie on the market." Today, Erin Baker's Wholesome Baked Goods is housed in a large, 15,000-square-foot facility. The company sells its food products all over the country.[7]

What would you do if a significant percentage of your customers disappeared? How might you reinvent your business?

The middle of the twentieth century saw the invention of the personal computer. By the 1980s, personal computers were everywhere.[8] Small businesses benefited from the computer, as these devices allowed businesses to process information faster and with greater accuracy.

When small networks developed, businesses could transmit data and communicate with other businesses and their customers much faster and more efficiently. As personal computers flourished, the **internet** became available to the masses, ushering in such communication technologies as electronic mail (email), instant messaging, and web conferencing. During the early twenty-first century, cellular communication became ubiquitous. Communication between businesses and their customers became instantaneous, lowering costs and allowing businesses to serve customers with greater speed and accuracy. The new technologies also allowed businesses to reach a global customer base.

> **internet**
> A global network of networks that allows computers from all over the world to communicate with one another.

Today, we see the technological advances of the late twentieth century and early twenty-first century readily available to small businesses, transforming how business is conducted. Today there are many types of businesses that could not have existed before these technologies became common. The internet has spawned hundreds of storefronts. Through these e-commerce websites, individuals can buy and sell goods and services. Popular online marketplaces like eBay and Etsy allow individuals and businesses alike to reach customers worldwide. PayPal, Amazon, and Google, to name a few, all offer payment transaction services for individuals and businesses, through which money can be exchanged safely and securely online.

The Industrial Economy, a Crash Course in U.S. History #23

This video presents the rise of the industrial era from the Civil War to today.

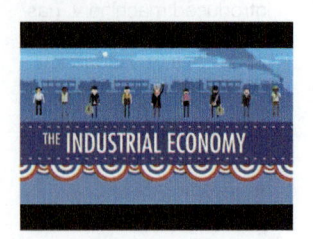

View in the online reader

economy

Refers to the wealth and resources of a country or area and may refer to the complicated activities of the production and consumption of goods and services.

gross domestic product (GDP)

A measurement of a country's economy that refers to the total value of all goods produced and services provided.

The Value of Small Businesses to the American Economy

Small businesses are a major force in the **economy** of the United States.[9] They may for as much as 50 percent of the country's **gross domestic product (GDP)**. Small businesses create jobs, encourage innovation, and help millions realize independence and financial success. Many businesses that started out small have become major enterprises, such as Microsoft, Apple, Walmart, Dell, Google, Amazon, and PayPal.

According to the Small Business Administration,[10] small businesses have a big impact on the economy. In 2013, there were approximately 28.8 million small businesses in America, accounting for 54 percent of all sales in the United States. To put this into perspective, small businesses account for 99.9 percent of all firms in the United States. Of these businesses, 600,000 are franchised small businesses, accounting for roughly 40 percent of all sales. In addition to sales, 48 percent of all private sector jobs are in small businesses, representing approximately 8 million in retail sales.

FIGURE 1.2 Small Business Contributions by the Numbers

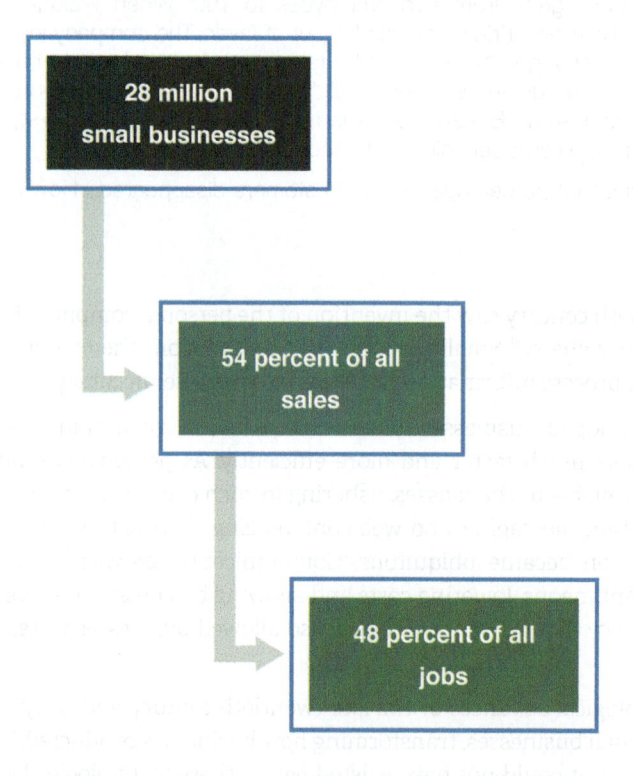

- 28 million small businesses
- 54 percent of all sales
- 48 percent of all jobs

Source: Laura Portolese et al.

When we look at who owns small businesses,[11] we see that 9.9 percent are owned by women, 29.3 percent are owned by minoritized people, and 9.3 percent are owned by veterans. Approximately one-fifth of all small businesses are family-owned. About 50 percent of all small businesses are home-based businesses, with 60 percent of all firms having no employees. Finally, approximately 30 percent to 50 percent of all commercial space is dedicated to small businesses.

Small businesses account for about 63 percent of all net new jobs.[12] This may be a direct result of long-term unemployment that resulted from the recession of 2007 to 2009. Many new small businesses are in the high-tech arena, such as:

- data processing and hosting;
- pharmaceutical and medicine manufacturing;

- computer systems design;
- measurement and instrument manufacturing;
- aerospace parts and products manufacturing;
- scientific research and development;
- software publishing;
- architecture and engineering;
- semiconductor and peripheral manufacturing;
- computer and peripheral manufacturing; and
- communications equipment manufacturing.

The Internet Revolution and Business

As we discussed previously, the internet has played an important role in developing the new e-commerce marketplace for goods and services. Many innovations have spawned from the internet, making it easy for anyone to do business online. For example, Amazon offers entrepreneurs a platform for selling their goods through Amazon Services. Small or large businesses can take advantage of the reach Amazon offers. Additionally, there are many web hosting services offering quick and easy solutions to create e-commerce websites and accept payments over the web. Some of the most popular options for hosting e-commerce sites include Wix, GoDaddy, Shopify, and BigCommerce. Each of these options allow the user to implement a shopping cart and take online payments through various payment vendors. For those who want to sell both online and face-to-face with customers, merchants can accept credit cards via mobile apps on their cell phones. Current service providers include Square, PayPal, Flint, and PayAnywhere. It is possible to integrate e-commerce with mobile credit card services, the merchant to capture data transactions seamlessly regardless of platform.

Online commerce is not the only way in which the internet has facilitated innovation and success in business. Some examples of monetizing the internet include . . .

How Important Are Small Businesses?
As you watch this video, think of a small business you know. What is the impact of that business on your local community, your state, and the U.S. economy?

View in the online reader

Mark Zuckerberg—Facebook

Facebook was started in the Harvard University dorm room of founder Mark Zuckerberg in 2004. It quickly rose to become the leading social media platform for connecting friends and family. Facebook was originally intended to connect university students. As the site's popularity grew, Zuckerberg opened Facebook to other universities and, eventually, the public.

With the introduction of the news feed—a real-time stream of information from Facebook members—the platform experienced explosive growth. To pay for this free technology, Facebook sold advertising. It wasn't just any advertising, however. With Google, Facebook developed the ability to provide customized advertising specific to the user's interests and browsing habits. For example, if you just browsed Amazon for a pair of black shoes, customized advertisements for black shoes from Amazon would appear in your Facebook news feed. While some consider this type of data gathering intrusive, the technology nonetheless became a game changer in online advertising.

Sergey Brin and Larry Page—Google

Sergey Brin and Larry Page met while graduate students at Stanford University in 1995. Together, they realized there was a need for an efficient way to find information on the internet. A year later, the two developed BackRub, a search engine that utilized page ranking to return results based on the search terms users entered. This was an entirely new way of returning search results. Pages were ranked on importance based on the number of Internet links found leading back to the source. Like Facebook, Brin and Page started BackRub from their dorm. The company quickly outgrew this location. It became Google, which represents a one followed by one hundred zeros. By 1999, the company was off and running, moving multiple times into larger and larger facilities. Its current headquarters, known as the GooglePlex, is in Mountain View, California.

As with Facebook, Google earns income from advertising. Through Google's AdWords, businesses can offer advertising at the time the user is searching Google for content. Businesses do not pay until the user clicks on the advertisement. This pay-per-click concept was unheard of at the time it was first offered. It gives businesses of all sizes the opportunity to reach potential customers through the internet.

Today, Google provides a variety of services to its users. Many of these services are free, such as Gmail, YouTube, Google Maps, Google Docs, Google Photos, Google Drive, and the Google Chrome browser. Some of Google's paid services include Google Fiber, Google Fi (mobile phone service), and Google Wallet (payment services). Most of Google's income still comes from advertising, however.

Mark Cuban—Broadcast.com

Before Pandora and iHeartRadio, there was AudioNet, an audio streaming service that Mark Cuban started in 1995. He and many others just wanted to listen to their favorite sports team over the radio when they were out of the broadcast area. The idea of streaming radio stations over the internet was born. As the service gained popularity, AudioNet was renamed Broadcast.com in 1998. Soon, the founders began looking at streaming video over the internet. Long before YouTube or Netflix, Broadcast.com was offering a video streaming service.

By 1999, Broadcast.com had more than 550,000 users. It was purchased by Yahoo.com for $5.7 billion. Unfortunately, the service proved to be way ahead of its time. Slow bandwidth connections meant that video would freeze during playback, causing customers to leave the service. Although Yahoo shut down Broadcast.com in 2002, it was considered a pioneer in streaming media services, paving the way for those we enjoy today.

These ventures provide free services to millions, seemingly with no means of generating income. It was not until businesses began to see the incredible potential of advertising online through these spaces that the value of these services increased.

Major Entrepreneurial Theories

Entrepreneurs have long shaped the economic growth and history of America, but their role in society has not always been clear. Over the years, many management theorists have examined entrepreneurs and entrepreneurship, developing various theories to explain trends they were seeing in society. Table 1.1 highlights a few of the popular theories of entrepreneurship in a timeline format.

When the economy moved from farming to manufacturing, we began to see a greater push toward innovation in equipment and manufacturing processes. This development led many to view innovation from the perspective of the organization, meaning that individuals within organizations helped develop new ways of using materials, processes, or opportunities to develop new products and services. The spirit of entrepreneurial innovation soon migrated from organizations to individuals.

The Age of Great Invention sparked many new and exciting developments. These included electricity, light bulbs, railroad travel, steel production, streetcars, and electrical motors. Great inventors such as Carnegie, Edison, and the Wright brothers have changed our lives in powerful ways. As a result, management thinkers began to formulate theories to explain this growth in innovation and entrepreneurship.

TABLE 1.1 Entrepreneurial Theories that Have Shaped Our Understanding of Entrepreneurship

Theorist	Theory	Definition
Marshall (1890)	Entrepreneurship	Defines several characteristics of an entrepreneur, including good leadership skills, the ability to foresee supply and demand changes, and a willingness to take risks and act when needed. These factors may be influenced heavily by the economic conditions at the time.
Weber (late 1800s, early 1900s)	Sociological	Suggests that religion, and religious viewpoints, determine how one views entrepreneurship, the accumulation of wealth, and how one views a means to an end.
Knight (1921)	Risk-Bearing	Suggests that profit is the reward for taking risks during uncertainty. Also referred to as the Cost of Uncertainty theory.
Schumpeter (1934)	Innovation	Suggests that innovation and entrepreneurship are key factors in economic growth. Innovation, or creating something new, using new processes or methods, opening new markets, acquiring new supplies or suppliers, or developing new positions or structures will drive business success.
Drucker (1964)	Entrepreneurship	Suggests that entrepreneurs are always looking for opportunities for change and to exploit those opportunities where they are present. An individual who seeks to maximize opportunities.
Leibenstein (1968)	X-Efficiency	Refers to the degree to which resources within the firm are used inefficiently. Entrepreneurs seek to find opportunities to use resources more efficiently and in new ways.
Casson (1982)	Economic	Suggests that individuals engage in entrepreneurial pursuits based on the economic conditions around them. These include tax policies, availability of materials, infrastructure, technology, and favorable access to financing and market conditions.
McClelland (1987)	Human (Achievement) Motivation Theory	Different types of motivation impact individual performance. Those driven by achievement are more focused on the attainment of the goals than on the rewards that may be earned.
Kirtzner (1997)	Entrepreneurship	Suggests that alert individuals take advantage of opportunities that others don't see. Entrepreneurs are focused on the discovery of new opportunities.

Key Takeaways

- American history has included small businesses since inception, beginning with family farms, continuing through the industrial revolution and growing to the many high-tech companies that exist today.
- Technology—such as electronic communications, cellular communications, the personal computer, networked computers, and the internet—has profoundly impacted the way in which business is performed, allowing many small businesses to flourish and compete.

> **Interactive Activity**
>
> 1. In small groups, reflect on the challenges faced by many of the early settlers to America. Identify at least three ways in which the technology of the industrial revolution eliminated these challenges.

1.3 Why Start Your Own Business?

> **Learning Objectives**
>
> 1. Explain why someone would want to start a small business.
> 2. Identify the benefits of small business ownership.

Source: © Shutterstock, Inc.

Now that we have a good understanding of the types of small business, let's look at some of the many reasons why someone might choose to start a small business. Some small business owners want to work for themselves. Others want to make some extra income while managing family obligations. Still others seek financial independence or creative freedom. Some business owners seek to exploit their knowledge or skills while reaping the rewards for themselves. Finally, some wish to make a significant difference, whether that be through the innovation of new and exciting tools, technologies, or services, or through different ways of providing social services. Whatever the motivation for starting a small business, most individuals share similar desires. Entrepreneur Magazine identified the top fifty reasons why people decide to start their own business.[13] Here are a few:

- flexibility—able to work your own hours
- calling your own shots, making your own decisions
- setting your own deadlines
- working on projects you want to work on/selling products you want to sell
- pursuing your **passion**
- watching something you build from scratch become a reality
- helping people to improve their lives
- investing in yourself

passion

A strong emotion, excitement, or feeling of enthusiasm for doing something you enjoy.

FIGURE 1.3 Some of the Reasons Why People Decide to Start a Small Business

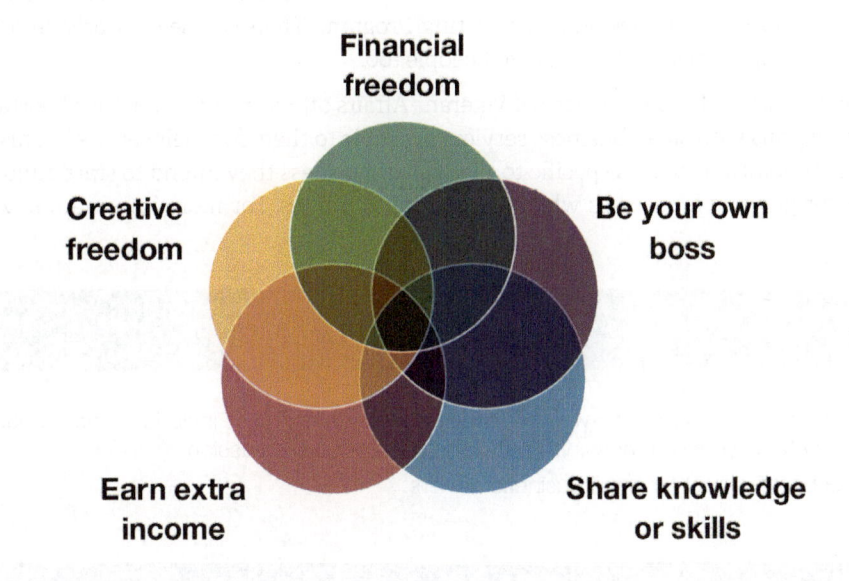

- Financial freedom
- Creative freedom
- Be your own boss
- Earn extra income
- Share knowledge or skills

Source: Laura Portolese et al.

Leveraging: A Ready and Willing Customer Base—Dell Computers

Michael Dell was fascinated with computers at a young age. At fifteen, he took apart an Apple computer just so he could see how it worked. In college, he began building computers to sell to fellow students at cheaper prices and with better service and support. Dell was convinced that if he could sell computers directly to customers and provide excellent customer support, he would be successful. In 1984, Dell introduced his computers to the masses. Today, Dell is consistently ranked among the top five best computer brands.[14]

Other good reasons[15] for starting a business include the tax benefits. Most items required to run your business are **tax deductible**, including (but not limited to):

- office, retail, or warehouse space either rented or purchased;
- equipment involved in the operations of the business or the manufacturing of items sold through the business;
- automobile expenses;
- legal, accounting, and other professional service fees;

tax deductible

Expenses incurred by the business which may be deducted when computing profit or loss, thereby lowering the overall tax liability owed by the business.

- advertising;
- phone, internet, and other communications expenses;
- software and computer equipment;
- travel and travel related expenses;
- insurance;
- gifts; and
- bad debts.

There are additional benefits for qualifying minoritized people who start a business. The Small Business Administration offers training, workshops, individual counseling, and management and technical guidance.[16] Mentor-protégé programs are also available for further support. Additionally, minority-owned businesses are encouraged to compete for government contracting opportunities. For more information, visit this website. Both the federal and state governments offer resources for small businesses owned by women. The Small Business Administration has resources for women seeking to compete in the Federal Contracting Program. There are several private organizations that want to help women and minoritized people too.

In addition, the U.S. Department of Veterans Affairs offers an entrepreneurial portal that helps connect veterans with small business services available to them for their service.[17] This portal connects veterans with resources specific to the type of business they intend to start, funding sources, and tips for growing a business while finding opportunities. For more information, visit the VA's website.

Use Entrepreneurship to Reinvent Yourself
As you watch the video, see if you can identify whether your business interests are different from your background and training. Are you seeking to reinvent yourself? Are you seeking to follow your passion?

View in the online reader

Key Takeaways

- There are several reasons why people start a business. These include financial freedom, the ability to be your own boss, flexibility, and pursuing one's passion.
- Tax benefits exist for small business owners.

Interactive Activities

1. Identify at least three things about which you are passionate. List several possible business opportunities for each of these areas.
2. Choose one business idea that you considered in the previous question, which you think you might be interested in pursuing as a small business. Investigate and identify existing businesses that would compete directly with your new business. Identify three possible ways in which to differentiate your business from the competition.
3. Identify your personal reasons for starting a business. List the top three reasons.

1.4 Dispelling the Myths about Small Business Ownership: It's a Lot of Work!

Learning Objective

1. Discuss both the positive and negative aspects of small business ownership.

While there are many great reasons to start a small business, it's important to understand that starting, growing, and running a small business is a lot of work, regardless of the form of business you undertake. A business is still, well, a *business*. It will require time, attention, and funding to get it off the ground and keep it operating. This means that there is work to do every day. New businesses often require long hours of commitment, exceeding those of a "regular job." There are **legal regulations**, **financial obligations**, tax implications, and many other challenges to the new business owner. This text will provide you with information you need to start and run a business, but understand that there are many challenges.

legal regulations
Laws that control the conduct and operations of the business, with which the business must abide.

financial obligations
The requirement to pay money owed by the business. Some forms of financial obligation include wages, taxes, loan debt, and payments to suppliers.

Source: © Shutterstock, Inc.

Carol Roth is the author of *The Entrepreneur Equation: Evaluating the Realities, Risks, and Rewards of Having Your Own Business*.[18] She is quick to remind those interested in starting a small business that, while they think they will "be their own boss," they may be mistaken. While small business owners enjoy some **autonomy**, they often answer to many "bosses." When one must pay employees' salaries or rely on employees to do important work for the business, then the employees become bosses of a sort. When a business relies on products or parts from vendors, then vendors also become bosses. Finally, let's not forget that customers are also bosses, with expectations and needs that your small business must fulfill. While some businesses allow you the luxury of deciding what clients or customers you accept, many do not. Consider the COVID-19 crisis and the losses small businesses suffered as a result of being forced to close by local and state govern-

autonomy
Refers to self-governing, self-directing, or being independent. Autonomy is the ability to determine one's own actions.

ments. In this case, the government is the boss, in a way! As romantic a notion as being your own boss might seem, be prepared for the hard work, long hours, and many authorities to whom you will answer along the way.

> **A Conversation with Elon Musk, CEO of Tesla Motors and SpaceX**
>
> In this long video, listen to Elon Musk discuss the many challenges he faced as he started and grew each of his businesses. There always seems to be something wrong!
>
> Elon Musk CEO of Tesla Motors and SpaceX — Khan Academy
>
> View in the online reader

The Global Pandemic: COVID-19

In the late fall of 2019, a global pandemic hit, the likes of which have not been seen since the Spanish Flu (H1N1) in 1918. The Coronavirus, or COVID-19 (SARS-CoV-2) impacted the world in several ways. Aside from the millions of people infected, people were forced to quarantine. Businesses shut down to deal with the virus and protect employees and the public. Schools were shut down. When possible, work and school were moved online and into homes. This impacted the availability of goods and services. Basic products were missing from the shelves while people were warned to stay home and to avoid infection. The supply chain suffered as businesses had trouble getting parts or raw materials to build.

During this time, online retailing exploded. However, products became scarce, and prices increased. Deliveries were slow. But all in all, people managed to get through the worst.

As of the writing of this new edition, the pandemic is still ongoing. Throughout this text, the authors will discuss the pandemic and ask how you might deal with some of the issues faced by business owners during this difficult time. Because the pandemic is ongoing, it is difficult to look at this from a purely historical perspective as to what *did* happen. However, we can think about what *might* happen, or more importantly, what *you* might do when faced with similar concerns.

Key Takeaways

- Small business owners typically work hard and put in a lot of hours starting, growing, and running their businesses.
- There are several myths about small business ownership. One of the most notable is the misconception that small business owners answer only to themselves.

Interactive Activity

1. Investigate a small business and interview the owners. Identify the three biggest challenges they face and make recommendations for managing those challenges.

1.5 Test Your Skills: Applied Case

Gina's Party Planning

During the summer of 2019, Gina began a party business. The business provided services for both children and adult parties such as birthdays, anniversaries, bridal and baby showers, to name a few. Especially popular were "princess" or "hero" parties, which included visits by your child's favorite princess or hero characters. In addition to parties, Gina provided yard signs that celebrated special occasions. Gina provided a full service that included cake, hors d'oeuvre, games, and equipment rental.

Source: © Shutterstock, Inc.

Then, the COVID-19 pandemic hit, just as Gina's business was taking off.

1. Should Gina pause her business and wait out the pandemic? Why? Why not?
2. If Gina continues with her business, what changes will she need to make to be relevant?
3. Identify at least three ways in which Gina could offer her services to potential clients.
4. Discuss various ways in which businesses similar to Gina's managed to stay active during the pandemic.

Endnotes

1. The U.S. Small Business Administration: SBA.gov. (2016, February 26). Table of Small Business Size Standards. Retrieved from: https://www.sba.gov/contracting/getting-started-contractor/make-sure-you-meet-sba-size-standards/table-small-business-size-standards
2. Duermyer, R. (2017, May 9). What is an Entrepreneur? Definition and Characteristics of an Entrepreneur. Retrieved from: https://www.thebalance.com/entrepreneur-what-is-an-entrepreneur-1794303
3. Seth, S. (n.d.). Entrepreneur vs. Small Business Owner, Defined. Retrieved from: http://www.investopedia.com/articles/investing/092514/entrepreneur-vs-small-business-owner-defined.asp
4. Lesonsky, R. (n.d.). Are Franchisees 'Really' Entrepreneurs? Retrieved from: https://www.allbusiness.com/are-franchisees-really-entrepreneurs-12357164-1.html
5. Amadeo, K. (2017, February 20). What Is the American Dream? Quotes and History. Retrieved from: https://www.thebalance.com/what-is-the-american-dream-quotes-and-history-3306009
6. Moffatt, M. (2017, March 27). The History of Small Business in the United States: A Look at American Small Business from the Colonial Era to Today. Retrieved from: https://www.thoughtco.com/history-of-small-business-in-the-us-1147913
7. Erin Baker's Wholesome Baked Goods. (n.d.). Our Story Begins with a Breakfast Cookie. Retrieved from: https://erinbakers.com/pages/about-us
8. Wikiversity. (2015, November 3). Introduction to Computers/Computer types. Retrieved from: https://en.wikiversity.org/wiki/Introduction_to_Computers/Computer_types
9. *Exploring business*. (2016). Minneapolis, MN: University of Minnesota Libraries of Publishing.
10. The U.S. Small Business Administration: SBA.gov. (n.d.). Small Business Trends. Retrieved from: https://www.sba.gov/managing-business/running-business/energy-efficiency/sustainable-business-practices/small-business-trends
11. *Frequently Asked Questions About Small Business*. (2016). Retrieved from: https://www.sba.gov/sites/default/files/advocacy/SB-FAQ-2016_WEB.pdf
12. *Frequently Asked Questions About Small Business*. (2016). Retrieved from: https://www.sba.gov/sites/default/files/advocacy/SB-FAQ-2016_WEB.pdf
13. Demers, J. (2015, February 23). 50 Reasons to Start Your Own Business. Retrieved from: https://www.entrepreneur.com/article/243145
14. Dell. (n.d.). Company Heritage. Retrieved from: http://www.dell.com/learn/us/en/uscorp1/about-dell-company-timeline?c=us&l=en&s=corp&cs=uscorp1
15. Mueller, K. P. (2010, March 4). 15 Small-Business Tax Deductions. Retrieved from: https://www.entrepreneur.com/article/205334
16. The U.S. Small Business Administration | SBA.gov. (n.d.). Minority-Owned Businesses. Retrieved from: https://www.sba.gov/starting-business/how-start-business/business-types/minority-owned-businesses
17. Office of Small & Disadvantaged Business Utilization - U. S. Department of Veterans Affairs. (n.d.). Veteran Entrepreneur Portal. Retrieved from: https://www.va.gov/osdbu/entrepreneur/index.asp
18. Roth, C. (2012). *The Entrepreneur Equation: Evaluating the Realities, Risks, and Rewards of Having Your Own Business*. Dallas, TX: BenBella Books.

CHAPTER 2
Understanding the Basics of Business

Case Study—Golden State Surplus

Lake Isabella is a small town located in the Kern River Valley of California. The Kern River Valley consists of several small towns, comprising a population of approximately 10,500 full-time residents. The valley region is known for tourism. Visitors flock to the area take advantage of the Kern River and Lake Isabella during the summer months, and Alta Sierra Ski Resort during the winter.

Source: © Shutterstock, Inc.

Golden State Surplus in Lake Isabella is an outfitter that sells a wide variety of clothing, shoes, jeans and western wear, boots, camping equipment, water sports equipment, fishing supplies, and other goods for both residents of and visitors to the Kern River Valley. In addition, Golden State Surplus sells military surplus items. The store serves a wide community from Ridgecrest to Bakersfield. It has a reputation for selling quality, hard-to-find items.

Joe Ciriello first purchased Golden State Surplus in 1986. He worked in his family's grocery store growing up and recalls that his father worked for someone else for many years before buying his own store. Joe also remembers that his father was happiest when working for himself. This influenced Joe's decision to leave the Los Angeles area and purchase his own store in Lake Isabella. At the time, Golden State Surplus was small—just 1,200 square feet. Joe has expanded the store twice since then. His current location is an 8,200-square-foot building right in the heart of town.

When Joe first purchased the store, he ran the business as a sole proprietor. As he expanded, he needed help in the form of capital. Forming a partnership with his brother Dan was one way to infuse the business with additional funding. When it came time to develop a formal business relationship, however, the brothers decided, on the advice of their attorney, that an S-corporation would be the best choice. This would protect their personal assets from the liabilities of the business. This model worked well for Dan and his family, who were now 50 percent owners of the business. Joe's motivation for forming a corporation was that, in his experience, he had seen too many partnerships that were not well thought out—and in which conflicts arose as a result. As he put it, "Everything is okay . . . until it isn't."

When asked how well the business ownership model worked for everyone involved, Joe explained that his family's first priority has always been, and always will be, that they are brothers first and business partners second. All major decisions are made collaboratively, with careful consideration for what is best for everyone. When there is a disagreement between the brothers, the resolution is always with regard to family first. For example, owing a mortgage on the building caused Joe stress. He and Dan decided to pay off the mortgage as quickly as possible. This allowed them to weather the rough economic downturn of 2007, which saw many small busi-

> nesses fail in the Kern River Valley. Joe admits that while the economy in the valley is improving, it was through good capitalization and a low debt load that Golden State Surplus has remained in business.

As we look at the basics of business in this chapter, we will examine various business ownership models, including the S-corporation established for Golden State Surplus. We will also look at service-based businesses as compared to product-based businesses, franchise ownership, self-employment, and the mindset and characteristics of an entrepreneur.

2.1 Business Ownership Models

Learning Objectives

1. Explain the four types of business ownership models: sole proprietorship, partnership, corporation, and cooperative.
2. Recommend the appropriate ownership model for the type of business.

In Chapter 1, we discussed many different types of businesses, including home-based, storefront, professional service, and agencies. In this section, we will look at different forms of business ownership and discuss how these can help or hurt the business owner. It is important to understand these ownership models, as there are both legal and tax implications for each.

Source: © Shutterstock, Inc.

Sole Proprietorship

The first and probably the most common form of small business ownership is that of **sole proprietor**. In this ownership model, there is a single business owner. While not a legal entity, this form of business ownership has significant impact on the business owner.[1] A sole proprietor is the individual who both reaps the rewards of the business and is responsible for all its **liabilities**. There is no **legal separation** between the individual and the business, even if the individual creates a **fictitious business name**, also known as a DBA, or "doing business as."

A benefit of this form of business ownership is simplicity. Often, business is conducted in the individual's name. Contracts can be signed, loans obtained, and property purchased all in the name of the business owner. Completing **tax returns** is simple in that the business owner typically completes a Schedule C addendum to their personal income tax filing. This accounts for the **business income** or **losses** and **expenses**.

Source: U.S. Department of the Treasury. Internal Revenue Service. (2021). *Profit or Loss From Business (Sole Proprietorship)*. Retrieved from https://www.irs.gov/pub/irs-pdf/f1040sc.pdf

There are, however, drawbacks to this ownership model. For example, when the business is sued, the owner is sued. Additionally, the business owner is responsible for all debts incurred as a result of the business. If the business closes, the owner must still pay all outstanding debts.

---

sole proprietor

The simplest form of business, in which the business has one owner.

liabilities

Legal claims against the business or its assets. These can include rents, wages, and payments to vendors, to name a few.

legal separation

A term used to describe the separation of business activities from personal responsibility.

fictitious business name

Often referred to as "doing business as" or DBA, is a name given to your business that separates the business identity from your own identity.

tax returns

The forms required of individuals, businesses, or corporations, which are used to determine tax liability. Tax returns often include many forms to identify income, expenses, and any tax owed or to be refunded to the entity.

business income

The money earned by the business after all liabilities have been paid.

losses

Decrease the income from the business. One common way to incur a loss is when money owed by customers is not paid. Other ways include losses from lawsuits or the sale of an asset for less than what is owed.

expenses

Debts incurred, money owed, or money paid to run the business.

Partnerships

partnership
A form of business ownership in which two or more individuals own a business.

The second form of business ownership is that of a **partnership**. In a partnership, two or more individuals share the management, liabilities, and profits of the business.[2] This is a legal form of business ownership and, while there are many forms of partnerships, the most common are general and limited. In a general partnership, all partners share in the responsibility, profit, and liabilities of the business (although not necessarily equally).

In a limited partnership, there may be both general and limited partners. General partners share the responsibility, but limited partners do not. Limited partners may be investors only. Typically they have no day-to-day responsibility for running the business.

There are some advantages to partnerships. For example, there may be multiple sources of startup capital available among the partners. In addition, because a partnership is a legal entity, different tax rules apply, requiring a separate tax return. Individual partners can claim their portion of the profits on their personal tax returns. Because of the legal nature of a partnership, individual owners are protected from the liabilities of the business. These liabilities include tax and other debt liabilities.

There are several considerations when forming a partnership. First, due to the legal nature of a partnership, it can be difficult and expensive to start. Next, it is important to consider how the day-to-day running of the business will be handled. For example, one partner may be especially good at marketing and growing the business, while the other is better at managing customers. This is a great way to separate some of the tasks of running the partnership. However, there are still several additional tasks that should be considered and assigned. Without a careful plan, the business could face problems. Additionally, because each partner may act independently on behalf of the business, a partner may incur business contracts, liability, debts, or other loans that all partners must accept.

Corporations

corporation
A form of business in which a group of people (shareholders) act as a single legal entity.

board of directors
Comprises elected officials who will act on behalf of the stockholders in a corporation. Members are elected by stockholders and serve a given term.

The third form of business ownership is a **corporation**. In this legal form of business ownership, the business declares itself to be a separate entity and is governed by a **board of directors**.[3] Corporate ownership is in the form of stock that is sold to generate capital. Unlike the sole proprietorship, this form of business protects its owners from the liabilities of the corporation. However, corporations are taxed, making them seem less attractive than partnerships. Business owners may pay tax at the corporate level and again when they draw a salary or dividends. So why incorporate?

Let's look at some of the different types of corporations and some of the advantages and disadvantages of each.

There are many different types of corporations. Some are very attractive to small business owners and address issues concerning liabilities and taxation. Let's look at a few examples:

- **S-corporation**

    Formerly referred to as a sub-corporation, an S-corporation is a good option for small businesses. It allows profits and losses to pass through the corporation to the shareholders, where the shareholders claim them on their personal taxes.[4] This means that the S-corporation is not taxed; only its shareholders are. In many ways, this mimics a partnership. Each S-corporation is allowed up to one hundred shareholders.

- **C-Corporation**

    In a C-corporation, the corporation pays taxes on profits at the corporate rate. Salaries paid to employees and officers of the corporation are deductible to the corporation but taxable to the individuals. One of the disadvantages of a C-corporation is that profits are double taxed—once at the corporate rate and then again as income to the individual shareholders, officers, and employees. However, the costs of fringe benefits given to employees are deductible by the corporation. These deductions usually are not available to an S-corporation.

- **LLC (Limited Liability Corporation)**

    This form of corporation limits the personal liability of the members of the corporation for the debts and liabilities the corporation may incur.[5] Additionally, in an LLC, the profits pass through the corporation and are taxed as income to the individual, eliminating the double taxation found in a C-corporation. An LLC offers some of the advantages of a partnership and of a corporation. For this reason, it is sometimes referred to as a hybrid corporation.

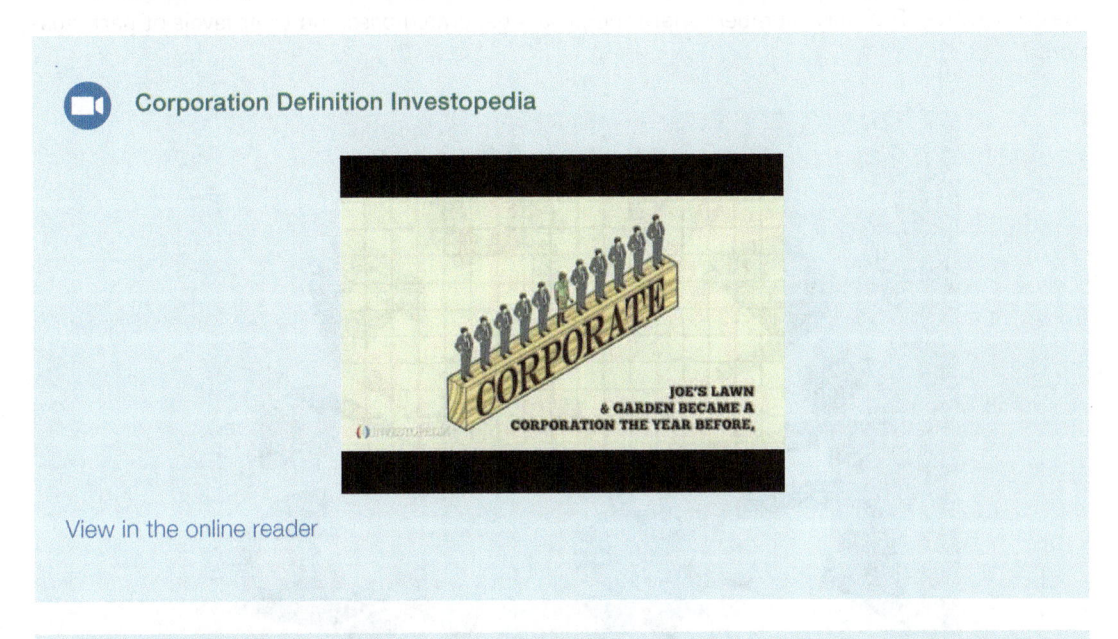

Corporation Definition Investopedia

View in the online reader

What Would You Do?

Remember our case study at the beginning of the chapter (refer to "Case Study—Golden State Surplus")? Joe and Dan decided on an S-corporation as the best form of business for their partnership. What do you think? Would you have recommended this form of business ownership for Golden State Surplus based on what you know about the scenario? What would you have done?

All corporations have some disadvantages. These include the following:[6]

- Corporations can be costly to start. While it is possible to go to legalzoom.com to form your corporation, it is advisable to seek the advice of an attorney, especially if there are partners involved.
- The state in which you set up your corporation can have a significant impact on how you do business, how you sell stock, and how you pay taxes. There are some states that are more advantageous for small business corporations. It is wise to investigate this carefully before filing articles of incorporation. For example, Delaware has no personal income tax for out-of-state residents and no corporate tax for businesses formed in Delaware that do business out of state.[7] In addition, Nevada has no personal income tax and does not have any corporate income tax or other corporate fees.
- There are several requirements that the corporation must meet to fulfill stockholder obligations. These include annual stockholder meetings and reports. A board of directors must be voted on and approved each year. There can be a considerable amount of work required to maintain a corporation in addition to the work involved in running the business.

Cooperatives

cooperative
A jointly owned business that produces goods or services.

The fourth form of business ownership is that of a **cooperative**.[8] In a cooperative, individuals join forces for mutual benefit. The Small Business Administration defines a cooperative as "a business or organization owned by and operated for the benefit of those using its services."[9] Based on the philosophy that there is power in numbers, cooperatives offer their members more opportunities to sell their products or to buy materials. Cooperatives are legal corporations and each member of the cooperative is an owner with a single vote. Although cooperative members vote for a board of directors who oversee the operation of the cooperative, they also vote to determine the direction of the cooperative. Typically, members share the profits generated based on their levels of participation.

Source: © Shutterstock, Inc.

Dairy Farmers of America is an example of a cooperative.[10] Member farmers sell their dairy products through the cooperative. The large member base allows Dairy Farmers of America to negotiate better prices for the products its members sell. Cooperative members also get better prices on equipment, insurance, and other goods needed to run their farms. This again is based on the power of numbers. A large member base means more leverage in negotiating prices.

Some advantages of cooperatives include, therefore, increased buying and selling power. Cooperatives also allow small business owners the opportunity to overcome barriers based on their size or location.[11] Perhaps the biggest advantage of a cooperative is that, because the income of the cooperative is paid to the owners, the cooperative itself incurs no federal or state income tax.

Additional advantages of cooperatives include the ability to obtain funding through government sponsored grant programs, the fact that members can join or leave the cooperative at will, and a democratic, organized structure.[12] One disadvantage of cooperatives is that obtaining investor money can be a challenge. This may be because cooperatives typically have lower individual involvement. Also, because of the democratic nature of cooperative voting, securing financing decisions can be more difficult.

FIGURE 2.1 Forms of Business Ownership and Their Pros and Cons

Sole Proprietorship

Pros
- One person responsible and accountable
- Easy to make decisions and come to consensus

Cons
- Personally responsible for all debts incurred by the business

Partnership

Pros
- More than one individual to share the business responsibilities
- Increased talent

Cons
- Challenges coming to consensus
- Each partner is personally responsible for all debts incurred by the business

Corporation

Pros
- Forms an entity separate from the individual(s)
- Eliminates personal liability

Cons
- May incur "double" taxation, depending on the type of corporation formed

Cooperative

Pros
- Many members earn profits and share losses based on their contributions
- Increased buying power/improved earnings on products sold
- Democratic leadership

Cons
- Often difficult to come to consensus when there are many owners
- Lack of owner involvement in the operations of the cooperative

Sources: Laura Portolese et al., images from © Shutterstock, Inc.

> **Choosing the Entity that Meets Your Needs**
>
> View in the online reader

In the next section, we will look at businesses that *sell* products or services and businesses that *produce* products or services. What you sell or make may have an impact on the business ownership model you choose.

Key Takeaways

- There are four main types of business ownership models: sole proprietorship, partnership, corporation, and cooperative.
- Each ownership model has distinct advantages and disadvantages in terms of both personal liability and tax implications.

Interactive Activities

1. In a group, identify three different business opportunities and discuss the pros and cons of each business ownership model. Decide which ownership model the group would recommend for each business and why.
2. Consider a small business that you know or one that you might approach. Discuss the business ownership model they have chosen for the business and why they selected that model.
3. When thinking about the previous business, evaluate whether the ownership model is appropriate for the business. What model do you think would be better suited for this business?

2.2 Service Businesses vs. Product Businesses

Learning Objectives

1. Identify the difference between a service-based business and a product-based business.
2. Describe some businesses with both characteristics.

Now that we understand some of the various forms of business ownership, let's explore the differences between businesses that focus on selling *products* or tangible goods to customers and those businesses that focus on selling *services* to customers. It's important to understand the distinction between these business types, because the customer model will determine the business structure.

Do You Sell a Product, Service, or Both?

Source: © Shutterstock, Inc.

As one might expect, **product-based businesses** are those businesses that sell physical products.[13] These businesses might include clothing stores, grocery stores, furniture stores, electronic stores, and business product stores. On the other hand, **service-based businesses** do not sell physical products, but instead sell services. These businesses might include real estate agencies, graphic artists, landscape designers, and other professional services (such as tax preparation, accountants and attorneys, and social media consultants). Often these businesses incur lower startup costs because there is no inventory and no large amounts of retail or manufacturing space are required.[14] There is a third type of business, a *combination business*, in which both products and services are offered.

product-based businesses

Businesses that rely on the sales of goods.

service-based businesses

Businesses that provide services rather than producing tangible products, although they may purchase products for resale.

Leveraging: An Example of a Combination Business

A heating and air conditioning service is an example of a combination business. The focus of the business may be servicing and repairing heating and air conditioning (HVAC) units, cleaning ducts, and replacing filters. However, parts may be sold as needed during the repair of these units. It is necessary to maintain an inventory stock of these items. Some HVAC repair businesses may sell entire replacement units, should a heater or air conditioner fail completely. Can you think of other businesses that offer both services and products?

These types of combination businesses are very common. Other examples of businesses that provide both products and services include landscapers, pool builders, auto repair shops, and most labor contractors (such as plumbers, electricians, and painters).

Are You a Product-Producing or Service-Producing Business?

product-producing

Businesses that make tangible goods for sale during their business operations.

service-producing

Businesses that resell tangible goods, provide a service, or both.

tangible goods

Physical products.

Your business may be a **product-producing** business or a **service-producing** business.[15] Product-producing businesses make things (**tangible goods**). They may be manufacturing, construction, or agricultural businesses. One easy way to think of product-producing businesses is that they will make the products other businesses sell.

Service-producing businesses do not produce tangible goods. They may, however, be retailers who purchase goods for sale from product-producing businesses. One example of a service-producing business is a wholesaler, who sells products to other businesses for resale or for use in the buyer's production of other goods. Other examples of service-producing businesses include those located in the professional service category, including attorneys, doctors, agents/agencies, recreation, and food services.

In the next section, we will examine franchise ownership as an alternative to starting your own small business.

Key Takeaways

- Product-based businesses focus on the sale of products. Service-based businesses focus on the sale of services. There are some businesses that might sell both products and services.
- Product-producing business make products. Service-producing businesses sell services, resell products, or both.

Interactive Activity

1. In small groups, brainstorm examples of service-based businesses, product-based businesses, and businesses that are both service- and product-based. Discuss the best ownership model for each business.

2.3 Franchising

Learning Objectives

1. Distinguish a franchise from other forms of business ownership.
2. Discuss the pros and cons of franchise ownership.

In the previous sections, we have looked at models of business ownership as well as both product and service business types. In this next section, we will examine one popular form of business ownership called the **franchise**.

franchise
A legal agreement, often a license that allows a franchisee to operate a business representing the franchisor.

Different Ways to Obtain a Business

Before we discuss franchises and franchise ownership, let's take a look at different options for starting a business. The first is to start the business from scratch. This may be the most common, as it allows the individual to begin the business based on their vision. This option may also involve the greatest risk of loss. However, with solid research (as we will discuss in Chapter 3), a good business plan, and some capital funding, many small business owners realize their dreams despite the unknowns involved. By following the principles put forth in this text, you can mitigate many of these risks.

The next way in which to start a business is to buy an existing business (or inherit an existing business from a family member). One of the advantages of buying an existing business is that you are buying a known entity. By requesting business documentation in advance, you can see the profit and liabilities of the business before making the purchase. Knowing past performance can help you develop a plan for the future operation of the business.

One disadvantage can include assuming the liabilities of the existing business. During the purchase of a business, sellers are required to disclose to potential buyers all debts or pending lawsuits. While full disclosure is expected, the reality of the company's liabilities may amount to more than expected, especially during the ownership transition period. Another disadvantage is not knowing how existing customers will react to the change of ownership. Customers of many small businesses are loyal to the owners rather than the business itself. They may be worried about how the change will impact their experience with the business.

Finally, there is the option of purchasing a franchise. A franchise is a business in which you purchase the rights to sell goods or services from a **franchisor** (the parent company), who owns the rights to those goods or services.[16] The franchisor has developed the goods or services, created a brand, and marketed the brand nationwide. Once established, the franchisor will sell licenses to individuals, known as **franchisees** (individuals who purchase a franchise business). These licenses allow the franchisee to sell the goods or services. According to Entrepreneur.com, the top ten franchise opportunities for 2017 included 7-Eleven, McDonalds, Dunkin', The UPS Store, Jimmy John's Gourmet Sandwiches, Dairy Queen, Ace Hardware, Wingstop Restaurants, Sport Clips, and RE/MAX.[17]

franchisor
A person or company who grants the license to the franchisee to operate a business representing the franchise.

franchisee
An individual (or group of individuals) who purchases a franchise and enters into an agreement with a franchisor.

Advantages of Franchise Ownership

There are many advantages of franchise ownership. During the process of startup, the franchisor typically assists the franchisee with location selection, development, training, and other services needed to secure a successful business launch. Because franchisors have worked with many new business owners, they have extensive experience in startups and a proven track record of success. With national advertising and marketing, a franchise already has name recognition, making it easier to ensure that the business will be profitable early on. It is often easier to attract customers that are already familiar with the goods or services offered by the business. Franchises, however, can be expensive to purchase. Many cost between $100,000 to $1 million. This makes some of the top brands out of reach to the individual seeking to start a small business.

The Origins of the Franchise

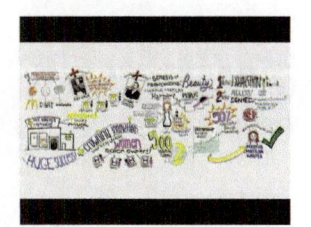

View in the online reader

FIGURE 2.2 Advantages and Disadvantages of Franchise Ownership

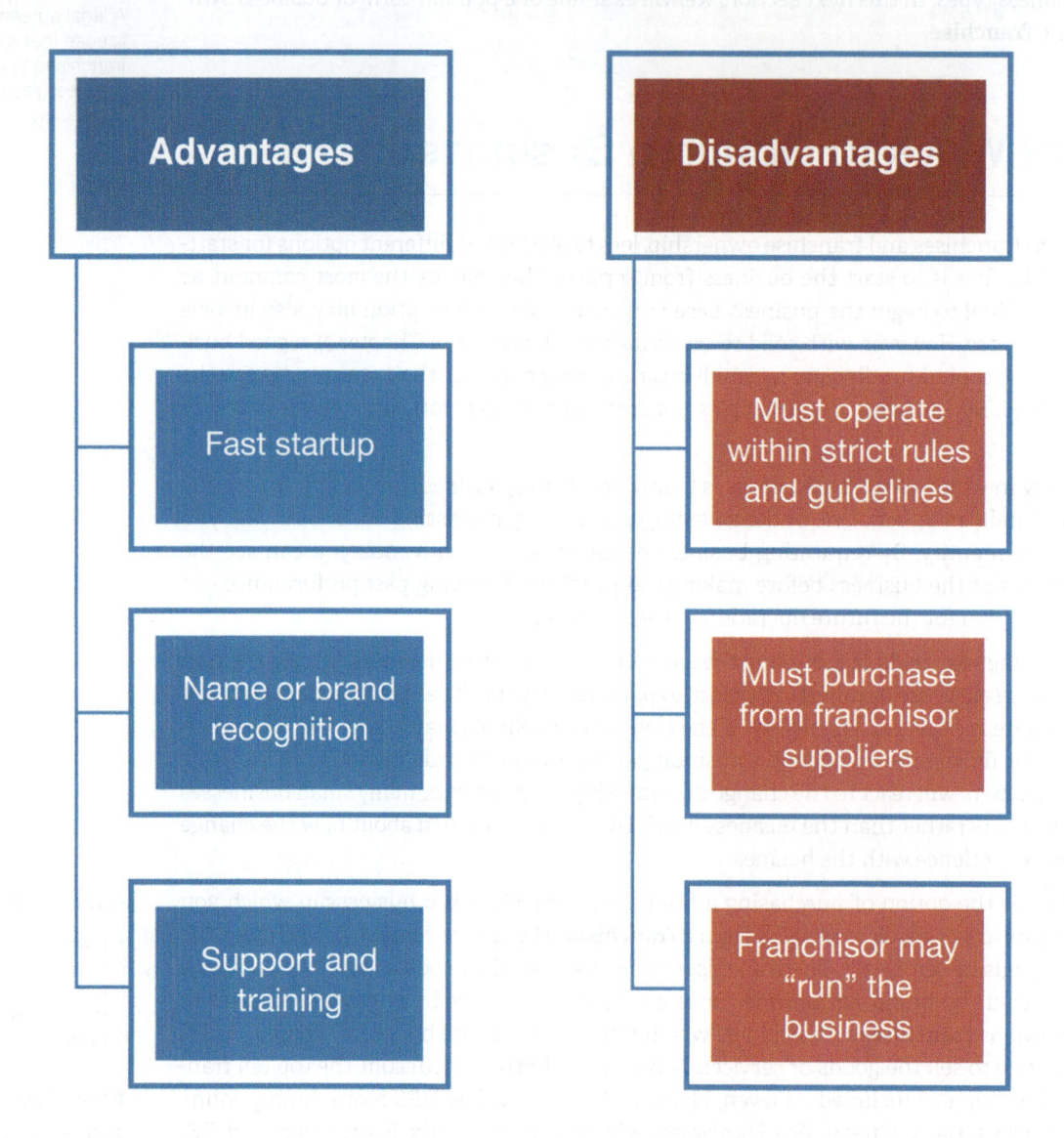

Advantages
- Fast startup
- Name or brand recognition
- Support and training

Disadvantages
- Must operate within strict rules and guidelines
- Must purchase from franchisor suppliers
- Franchisor may "run" the business

Source: Laura Portolese et al.

The Importance of Protecting the Brand

brand recognition
How well customers identify with or recognize a product or service.

The most important thing to a franchisor is to protect the brand. This is equally important to the franchisee. **Brand recognition** is essential to ensure a sustainable product or service, while national advertising promotes name recognition. A franchise lives or dies based on how customers perceive the brand. A big part of maintaining brand recognition is by maintaining consistency among franchise stores.

> **Leveraging: McDonald's and Brand Recognition**
>
> Consider the popular fast-food restaurant McDonald's. There are more than 3,000 owner/operators (franchise owners) in the United States.[18] When you walk into a McDonald's, regardless of where the store is located, you can expect a familiar look and feel to the store, including a standard color scheme, logos, and menus. Crew members typically wear familiar uniforms, all with logos and identification.
>
> Although McDonald's serves many different food items, they are especially famous for one item, the Big Mac. Imagine walking into a McDonald's store, ordering a Big Mac, and receiving something less than the "two all-beef patties, special sauce, lettuce, cheese, pickles, onions on a sesame seed bun."[19] Not only would this be disappointing, it would lead to brand confusion among customers. Uncertain if they would receive the Big Mac they are accustom to ordering, customers might not remain loyal to the brand. This could be devastating to the brand overall.
>
> In order to maintain the consistency of the Big Mac product from store to store, all franchise store owners must purchase products from the same vendors and prepare the food items following the standard, agreed-on processes. This includes not only the raw materials that go into the making of a Big Mac, but also the packaging and delivery of these food items. Think of bags, cups, and other non-food items that one receives with an order. Everything has the familiar McDonald's logos. This standardization of buildings, signage, raw materials, finished goods, and even the uniforms worn by employees are requirements imposed by the franchisor on the franchisee. This maintains product consistency and customer loyalty. It establishes consistency in the customer experience regardless of which store that customer visits.
>
> This example is consistent across all franchises. Protecting the brand is essential to protecting the investments of the franchisees.

Risks of Owning a Franchise

Owning a franchise is not without risk. Bad publicity at the national level can affect sales and even reputation of local businesses. Take, for example, the Jack in the Box crisis of 1993, when an outbreak of E. coli almost destroyed the entire fast food chain.[20] A combination of tainted meat from the distributor and improper cooking temperatures led to over 1,000 cases of E. coli. More than 170 people were hospitalized and four children died across Washington, California, Idaho, and Nevada.[21] The company faced decreased sales of over 15 percent nationally and over 30 percent in the Pacific Northwest (where the majority of illnesses and deaths occurred).[22]

Additional risks of franchises include the location of the business. While initially the location may seem appropriate, bad traffic patterns or increases in rents may prove that the location was not the best choice. Finally, the franchisor will dictate how you run your business. These restrictions on how you must operate may prove challenging or even bothersome.

In the next section, we will examine self-employment in terms of small business ownership.

Key Takeaways

- Purchasing a franchise allows the buyer the right to market and sell the products or services under the name of the franchise.
- Brand recognition is important to any business but may be even more important to a franchise.

> ### Interactive Activity
>
> 1. Identify a franchise you might be interested in purchasing. Investigate the requirements of purchase and what exactly you will get for your investment. Write a two-page report that discusses your choice for franchise and why you made the choice. Discuss your findings.

2.4 Self-Employment vs. Entrepreneurship

> ### Learning Objective
>
> 1. Differentiate between self-employment and an entrepreneurial endeavor.

One form of small business ownership that we have not addressed is that of the self-employed worker. In this section, we will examine how self-employed individuals differ from other small business owners in general and from entrepreneurs specifically.

What Does It Mean to be Self-Employed?

independent contractor

A person, business, or corporation that provides services to others and is not directly employed by those receiving the services.

Internal Revenue Service (IRS)

A government agency responsible for collecting taxes from individuals, businesses, and corporations on behalf of the United States Government.

Individuals who are self-employed work for themselves.[23] While that may seem redundant, there are some important considerations. You may be an **independent contractor** or own your own business. The form of business may be sole proprietorship, partnership, or limited liability corporation. For tax purposes, it is important to distinguish what types of self-employment the **Internal Revenue Service (IRS)** recognizes as legitimate activities. If you are self-employed, you will receive a 1099-MISC form from each company for which you do work (refer to Figure 2.3). As an employee for a company, by contrast, you receive a W-2 for your work at the end of each year.

Some of the advantages of being self-employed include being your own boss. Often, you have control over your work location (which may be your home), your hours, and even your clients. Many expenses that you incur while self-employed are tax deductible. These include insurance costs, healthcare, your office space (even if this space is your home office), business equipment, and even your car (when used for business purposes).

There are, however, some disadvantages to self-employment. As a self-employed worker, you are responsible for your own insurance. You must pay all of your own taxes including income tax, self-employment tax, social security, and Medicare without any assistance from your employer.[24] You do not earn paid time off, including holidays, sick leave, or vacation. A major illness may disrupt your work and cause a loss of income that may not be supplemented by other sources. The ability to pick and choose clients comes with a well-established business reputation. Occasionally, you might need to take work from clients you don't like in order to stay afloat. Self-employed individuals often work long hours, too—including nights, weekends, and holidays.

FIGURE 2.3 1099-Miscellaneous Income Form

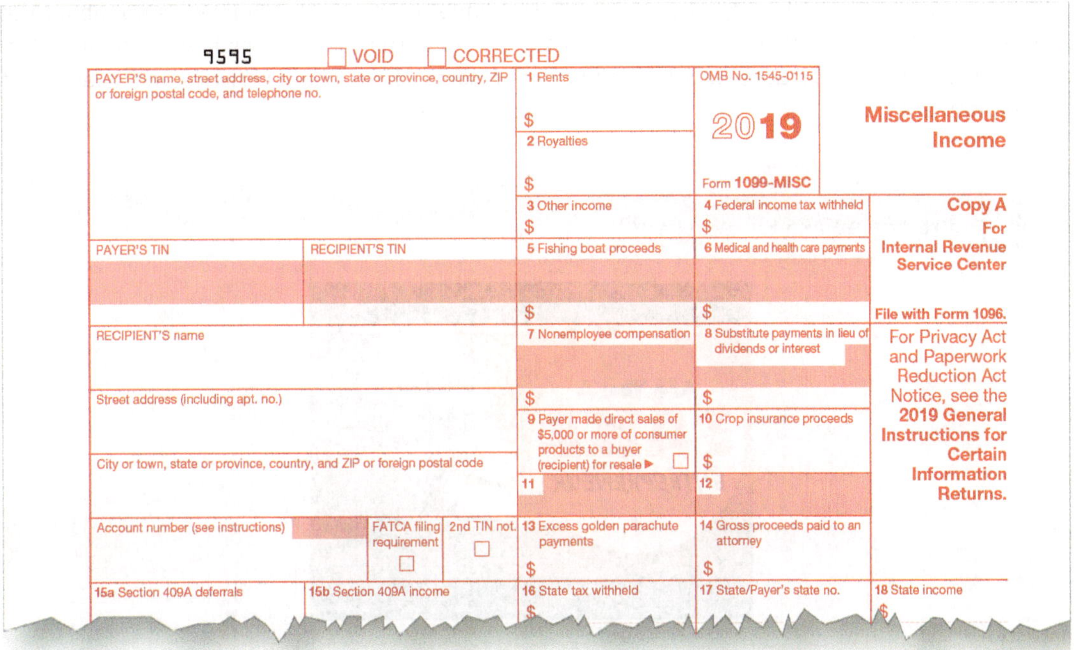
9595 VOID CORRECTED

PAYER'S name, street address, city or town, state or province, country, ZIP or foreign postal code, and telephone no.

1 Rents $

2 Royalties $

OMB No. 1545-0115

2019

Form 1099-MISC

Miscellaneous Income

3 Other income $

4 Federal income tax withheld $

Copy A For Internal Revenue Service Center

PAYER'S TIN

RECIPIENT'S TIN

5 Fishing boat proceeds $

6 Medical and health care payments $

File with Form 1096.

RECIPIENT'S name

7 Nonemployee compensation $

8 Substitute payments in lieu of dividends or interest $

For Privacy Act and Paperwork Reduction Act Notice, see the 2019 General Instructions for Certain Information Returns.

Street address (including apt. no.)

9 Payer made direct sales of $5,000 or more of consumer products to a buyer (recipient) for resale ▶

10 Crop insurance proceeds $

City or town, state or province, country, and ZIP or foreign postal code

11

12

Account number (see instructions)

FATCA filing requirement

2nd TIN not.

13 Excess golden parachute payments $

14 Gross proceeds paid to an attorney $

15a Section 409A deferrals

15b Section 409A income

16 State tax withheld $

17 State/Payer's state no.

18 State income $

Source: U.S. Department of the Treasury. Internal Revenue Service. (2018). *Miscellaneous Income*. Retrieved from https://www.irs.gov/pub/irs-pdf/f1099msc.pdf

Is Someone Who Is Self-Employed an Entrepreneur?

Is it safe to say that someone who is self-employed and owns their own business is an entrepreneur? Well, that depends. They might be. It's all about the type of business and the mindset of the individual. Let's put a few scenarios to the test.

Assume that you quit your corporate job to freelance and become an independent contractor. You are doing the same type of work that you did for your employer. However, now you are paid directly by those who contract your services. You are able to provide an excellent level of service while paying special attention to detail, which has earned you a strong reputation in the industry and has garnered you several clients. Because you do not require the same overhead as your previous employer, you are able to charge less for your service. You have incorporated your contracting business as an LLC. Are you an entrepreneur?

The answer is probably no, but let's ask a few questions. For example, is your work with clients new or innovative? Are you developing something new? If you answer no, if you are simply performing the same tasks for your clients that you did when you were working for your previous employer, then you would not be an entrepreneur.

Consider another scenario. This time, you have an idea for a new product. The product is outside your current employer's product line and they have no interest in pursuing any level of innovation in this area. You decide that this opportunity is too good to pass up. After some research, you find there is nothing like it in the industry and there appears to be a strong market for your product idea. You decide to quit your job to pursue this product. You form a partnership with an engineer you know who can design the prototype and help bring the product to market. Are you an entrepreneur?

Most likely, the answer is yes. While self-employed, you are developing an innovative, new product while working through the challenges this endeavor holds. Remember, it's not about the form of the business, but what you *do* with the business that determines if you are an entrepreneur. In the next section, we will further define some of the characteristics and qualities of entrepreneurs.

Are You a Fake Entrepreneur?

View in the online reader

Key Takeaways

- Self-employment is a form of business ownership in which individuals work for themselves. Requirements to claim self-employment include how you are paid by your clients.
- Individuals who are self-employed often are not considered entrepreneurs.

Interactive Activity

1. Think about an idea you have for a business. Based on the criteria that distinguishes a small business owner from an entrepreneur, decide which example best fits your idea. Justify your response.

2.5 The Characteristics and Mindset of an Entrepreneur

Learning Objectives

1. Describe the characteristics unique to an entrepreneur.

2. Differentiate between a small business owner and an entrepreneur.
3. Identify some of the common myths of entrepreneurs.

Just as there are different types of businesses and business models, there are characteristics that differentiate small business owners from entrepreneurs. In this section, we will explore the unique and sometimes subtle differences between being a small business owner and being an entrepreneur.

The Small Business Owner vs. the Entrepreneur

Throughout the first two chapters, we have been referring to small businesses, small business owners, and entrepreneurs as if these terms are interchangeable. In some basic ways, they are. It's not enough, however, to say that a small business owner is an entrepreneur. An entrepreneur is most certainly a business owner. However, there is a lot of debate over what it means to be a small business owner versus what it means to be an entrepreneur. When considering the differences, one striking difference is *attitude*. According to Bruce Bachenheimer, entrepreneurship encompasses much more than starting a new business venture. "At its core, it is a mindset—a way of thinking and acting."[25] Entrepreneurs seek to solve problems in new and innovative ways.

FIGURE 2.4 Differences Between a Small Business Owner and an Entrepreneur

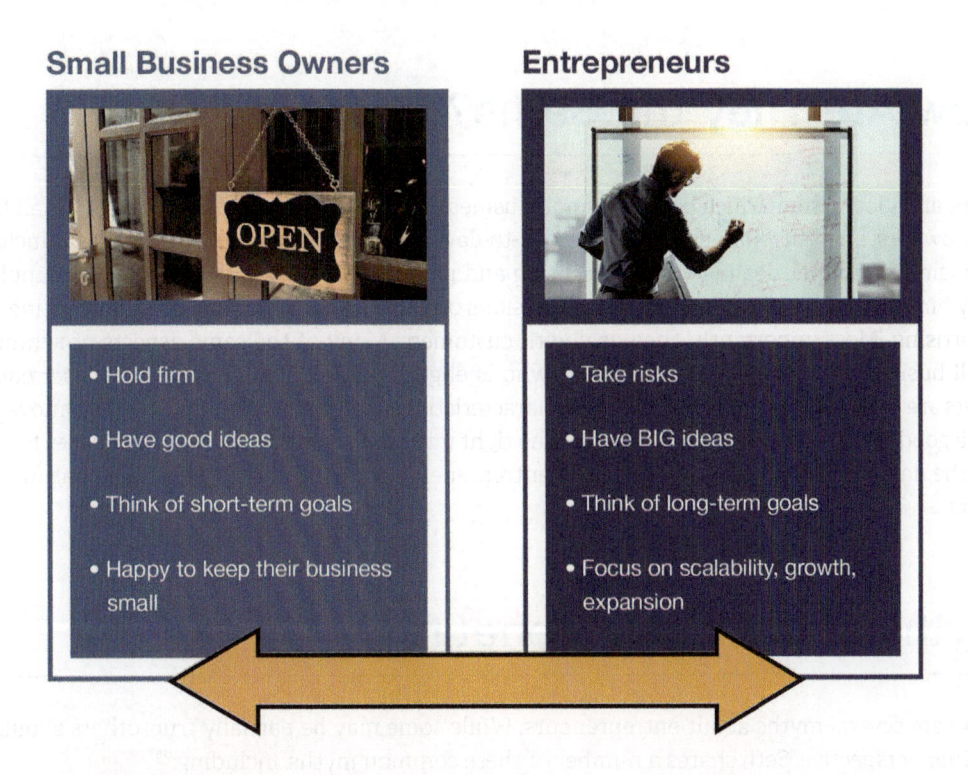

Small Business Owners
- Hold firm
- Have good ideas
- Think of short-term goals
- Happy to keep their business small

Entrepreneurs
- Take risks
- Have BIG ideas
- Think of long-term goals
- Focus on scalability, growth, expansion

Sources: Laura Portolese et al., images from © Shutterstock, Inc. Information retrieved from https://www.entrepreneur.com/article/233919.

There are several ways small business owners are different from entrepreneurs. Some characteristics we associate with entrepreneurs suggest these individuals will start a business with limited resources, are willing to take high-risks for high-rewards, and have ideas that are new and innovative. Entrepreneurs often seek to create value. For example, an entrepreneur might be interested in starting a business that offers a new product or service, something that has not been seen or offered before. On the other hand, a small business owner might consider opening an Italian restaurant in a town where the cuisine is not offered, or purchasing a franchise opportunity such as a UPS Store in a town that could benefit from such a service. The former is attempting something that has never been tried before, while the latter is seeking a business opportunity where there is considerable information, experience, and support services on which to draw. Entrepreneurs often seek to make a difference in a significant way.

The Surprising Habits of Original Thinkers | Adam Grant

View in the online reader

How Are They the Same?

There are a lot of similarities between small business owners and entrepreneurs. Both small business owners and entrepreneurs run the day-to-day operations of the business, which includes managing personnel, dealing with accounting and payroll, and managing vendors and suppliers. They hire and fire employees. They make decisions on business location, financing, marketing, and advertising. Most importantly, they deal with customers. Many of the same aspects of running a small business apply to the entrepreneur who is engaging in a startup. However, these requirements are often in direct conflict with the characteristics entrepreneurs have that spur innovation. It is a good idea for an entrepreneur to find the right mix of business partners or employees to manage the day-to-day operations. This allows entrepreneurs to spend their time implementing their vision.

Myths about Entrepreneurs

There are several myths about entrepreneurs. While some may be partially true, others should be put into perspective. Seth shares a number of these common myths, including:[26]

FIGURE 2.5 **Myths about Entrepreneurs**

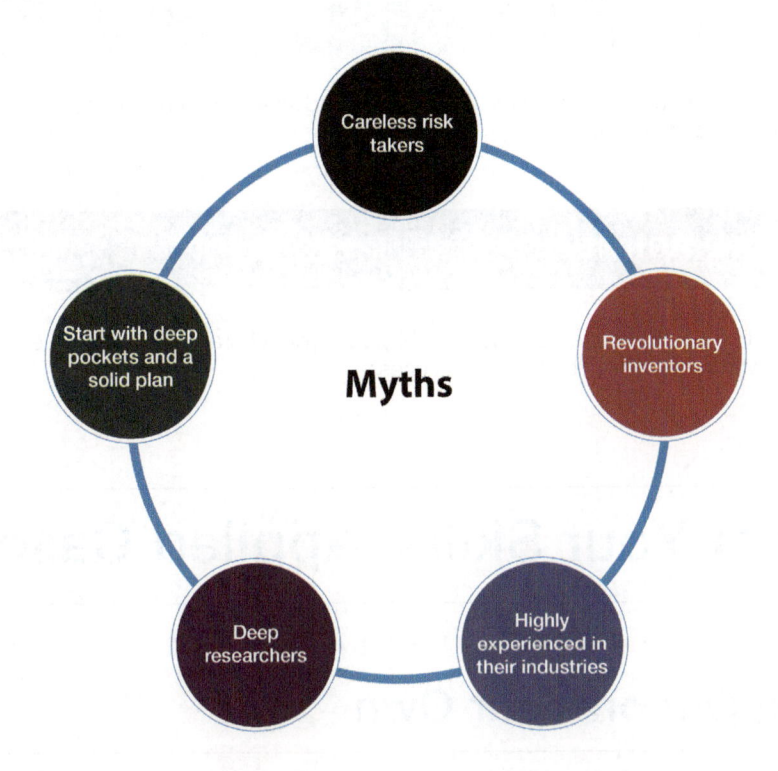

- Careless risk takers
- Revolutionary inventors
- Highly experienced in their industries
- Deep researchers
- Start with deep pockets and a solid plan

Source: Laura Portolese et al.

- Entrepreneurs take risks without plans. While this is partially true, most entrepreneurs realize that they are dealing with many unknowns using limited resources. During the COVID-19 crisis, some entrepreneurs were unprepared for a full close of their businesses. To handle unexpected crises, it's best to think through alternatives and be prepared.
- Entrepreneurs start businesses with revolutionary ideas. While some breakthroughs may be true, often entrepreneurs figure out ways of making something better through the improvement of an existing product or service.
- Entrepreneurs have extensive experience in their industry or area of expertise. Here we see that many entrepreneurs are young and inexperienced, but have an idea that is fueled by their passion.
- Entrepreneurs research before starting their business venture. While entrepreneurs generally don't do extensive research, they do seek **situational awareness**.
- Entrepreneurs start with a solid business plan and startup money. All too often, entrepreneurs do not have enough money to develop a working prototype of the concepts, let alone have enough to start a business from scratch. Furthermore, few have a business plan that could help them raise the needed funds.

While there are distinct differences between entrepreneurs and small business owners, both are important to society. As entrepreneurs bring forward new products and services, small business owners form the backbone of business.[27] As discussed in Chapter 1, our economy needs a strong small business presence. Small business owners provide jobs to the community while also providing needed goods and services.

situational awareness

The ability to perceive the environment around you and how it impacts a given situation. This means you must understand a variety of components and how they work together.

> ### Key Takeaway
>
> - Entrepreneurs tend to be risk takers, have big ideas, seek long-term goals, and seek scalability, growth, and expansion.

> ### Interactive Activity
>
> 1. In small discussion groups, identify several personality characteristics of an entrepreneur. Discuss why each is important to their success.

2.6 Test Your Skills: Applied Case

Striking Out on Your Own

Source: © Shutterstock, Inc.

Jorge decided to leave his job as an insurance agent and start his own, independently run insurance brokerage business. Although Jorge had the knowledge, experience, and education needed to start an insurance brokerage, he needed start-up money. Jorge's brother offered some "seed money" to help launch the venture. Jorge promised to pay him back but wasn't sure if that was enough. He didn't want to potentially damage his relationship with his brother if he had problems meeting his brother's expectations for repayment. Jorge wondered if drawing up a legal document might be appropriate. Then Jorge thought that maybe involving his brother formally in the business might be a good alternative.

1. What would be the best form of business for this situation?
2. Should Jorge form a business partnership? Why or why not?
3. What role might Jorge's brother take in the business?
4. How would Jorge assure that his brother's investment would be paid back if his brother was part of the business?

Endnotes

1. Sole Proprietorship. (n.d.). Entrepreneur Small Business Encyclopedia. Retrieved from: https://www.entrepreneur.com/encyclopedia/sole-proprietorship
2. Partnership. (n.d.). Entrepreneur Small Business Encyclopedia. Retrieved from: https://www.entrepreneur.com/encyclopedia/partnership
3. Corporation. (n.d.). Entrepreneur Small Business Encyclopedia. Retrieved from: https://www.entrepreneur.com/encyclopedia/corporation
4. S Corporation or C Corporation – Corporation Topics. (n.d.). LegalZoom. Retrieved from: https://www.legalzoom.com/knowledge/corporation/topic/choosing-the-best-type-of-corporation-s-corporation-or-c-corporation
5. Limited Liability Company (LLC). (n.d.). Investopedia. Retrieved from: http://www.investopedia.com/terms/l/llc.asp?lgl=myfinance-layout
6. S Corporation or C Corporation – Corporation Topics. (n.d.). LegalZoom. Retrieved from: https://www.legalzoom.com/knowledge/corporation/topic/choosing-the-best-type-of-corporation-s-corporation-or-c-corporation
7. Selecting the Best State to Incorporate a Business. (n.d.). BizFilings. Retrieved from: https://www.bizfilings.com/toolkit/research-topics/incorporating-your-business/best-state-to-incorporate
8. International Co-operative Alliance. (n.d.). What is a co-operative? Retrieved from: http://ica.coop/en/what-co-operative
9. The U.S. Small Business Administration. (n.d.). Cooperative. Retrieved from: https://www.sba.gov/starting-business/choose-your-business-structure/cooperative
10. Dairy Farmers of America. (n.d.). Join DFA. Retrieved from: http://www.dfamilk.com/membership/join-dfa
11. Fox, L. K. (1992). Business ownership. Retrieved from: http://www.cals.uidaho.edu/edcomm/pdf/CIS/CIS0939.pdf
12. The U.S. Small Business Administration. (n.d.). Cooperative. Retrieved from: https://www.sba.gov/starting-business/choose-your-business-structure/cooperative
13. Brandenberg, D. (n.d.). What Are the Differences Between Product-based Businesses and Service-based Businesses? Retrieved from: http://smallbusiness.chron.com/differences-between-productbased-businesses-servicebased-businesses-23372.html
14. Saba, C. (2015, June 28). Service vs Product. Retrieved from: https://medium.com/the-happy-startup-school/service-vs-product-2ef0636506fc
15. *Exploring business*. (2016). Minneapolis, MN: University of Minnesota Libraries of Publishing.
16. *Exploring business*. (2016). Minneapolis, MN: University of Minnesota Libraries of Publishing.
17. Entrepreneur. (2017). 2017 Top Franchises Ranking. Retrieved from: https://www.entrepreneur.com/franchise500
18. McDonald's. (n.d.). McDonald's U.S. Franchising. Retrieved from: http://corporate.mcdonalds.com/mcd/franchising/us_franchising.html
19. McDonald's. (n.d.). Big Mac®: 100% Beef Burger with Special Sauce. Retrieved from: https://www.mcdonalds.com/us/en-us/product/big-mac.html
20. New York Times. (1993, February 6). COMPANY NEWS - Jack in the Box's Worst Nightmare. Retrieved from: http://www.nytimes.com/1993/02/06/business/company-news-jack-in-the-box-s-worst-nightmare.html
21. MarlerClark. (1993). Jack in the Box E. coli Outbreak Lawsuits - Western States. Retrieved from: http://www.marlerclark.com/case_news/view/jack-in-the-box-e-coli-outbreak-western-states
22. Jack in The Box parent loses $29.3 million. (1993, May 13). Retrieved from: https://www.upi.com/Archives/1993/05/13/Jack-In-The-Box-parent-loses-293-million/9125737265600/
23. Murray, J. (2017, March 13). What Does it Mean to Be Self-employed? Retrieved from: https://www.thebalance.com/what-does-it-mean-to-be-self-employed-398471
24. Self-Employed. (n.d.). Investopedia. Retrieved from: http://www.investopedia.com/terms/s/self-employed.asp
25. Fernandes, P. (2018, February 19). Entrepreneurship Defined: What It Means to Be an Entrepreneur. Retrieved from: https://www.businessnewsdaily.com/7275-entrepreneurship-defined.html
26. Seth, S. (n.d.). Entrepreneur vs. Small Business Owner, Defined. Retrieved from: http://www.investopedia.com/articles/investing/092514/entrepreneur-vs-small-business-owner-defined.asp
27. *Frequently Asked Questions About Small Business*. (2016). Retrieved from: https://www.sba.gov/sites/default/files/advocacy/SB-FAQ-2016_WEB.pdf

CHAPTER 3
How Do I Determine a Good Idea and Opportunity?

Case Study—Firefighter and Handyman: Analyzing Opportunity

How does a firefighting paramedic become an entrepreneur? Kyle Tate decided to open a business because he saw a need in the market based on his own experiences.

Kyle graduated in 2002 with his Bachelor of Science in paramedicine. He became a paramedic in South Everett, Washington, where he still works full time in addition to running his business. Prior to taking the firefighter paramedic position, Kyle had extensive experience in real estate and property management. Because of this experience, he developed an interest in performing handyman work and maintenance around the town of Ellensburg, Washington. Ellensburg is a college town. Central Washington University is located there, which means the rental market is plentiful.

Source: Used with permission from Kyle Tate.

When working at his property management business, Kyle identified a major need in the market for a service that could help landlords with all things rental. Examples of his work include lawn care services, painting, and any upkeep and maintenance jobs needed to keep rentals in good shape for the next renter. Although similar services existed in Ellensburg, it was common for contractors to avoid smaller jobs needed by landlords (such as painting a small apartment). Kyle found a way to meet the market's needs. In the process, he created a thriving business.

Uncertainty was the name of the game at first; Kyle didn't know if the business would work. One thing he did know was that he had the customer service background necessary to be responsive to and approachable by customers. This allowed him to build trusting relationships. Perhaps equally important, he also had the drive to do it.

There were challenges along the way. Kyle explains that some of these had to do with the human resource aspect of the business (refer to Chapter 7)—that is, managing his crew effectively. This included management scheduling, timing, and managing resources. The other challenges, which Kyle has learned how to handle well over time, had to do with pricing his product (refer to Chapter 4) and bidding jobs at a fair price while still accounting for expenses. Learning all of the aspects of business can be challenging. This is why there are advantages to starting off small, as Kyle did.

Kyle and his wife, Mandi, started off small in 2012. They didn't invest a lot of money in equipment until their business grew. They avoided incurring debt as much as possible, paying cash for their equipment up front.

Between working full time as a paramedic and firefighter and running his business, Kyle spends one hundred hours per week working, but tries to manage his time well between the two. This includes allowing for family time, including coaching his son's baseball team. "You need a happy medium of family and work balance," he says.

Kyle Tate offers this advice: "Research what you are getting into and research the competition." That will be the focus of this chapter: to analyze opportunities while analyzing your skills to see if you can develop your business idea and determine the resources needed.

Opportunity entrepreneurship is defined as taking an action to introduce new products, services, or ways of organizing.[1] In order for it to be successful, there must be an economic need, as well as a personal interest. What does this mean to you as a future entrepreneur? It means that when you begin to generate ideas for your new business, your personal qualities should match the venture as we discussed in Chapter 2. You'll want to be sure the idea has potential in the market, too. As we explore generating ideas, we will discuss the driving forces behind finding opportunities, how you can generate ideas for a new business venture, how to assess those ideas, how to create an opportunity assessment plan, and finally, how to plan for product and service development.

> **opportunity entrepreneurship**
> The combining of individual qualities and favorable economic and social conditions to create a new product or service in a new or existing market.

3.1 The Timmons Framework

Learning Objective

1. Explain how the Timmons Framework relates to determining a possible entrepreneurship opportunity.

FIGURE 3.1 **The Timmons Framework of the Entrepreneurial Process**

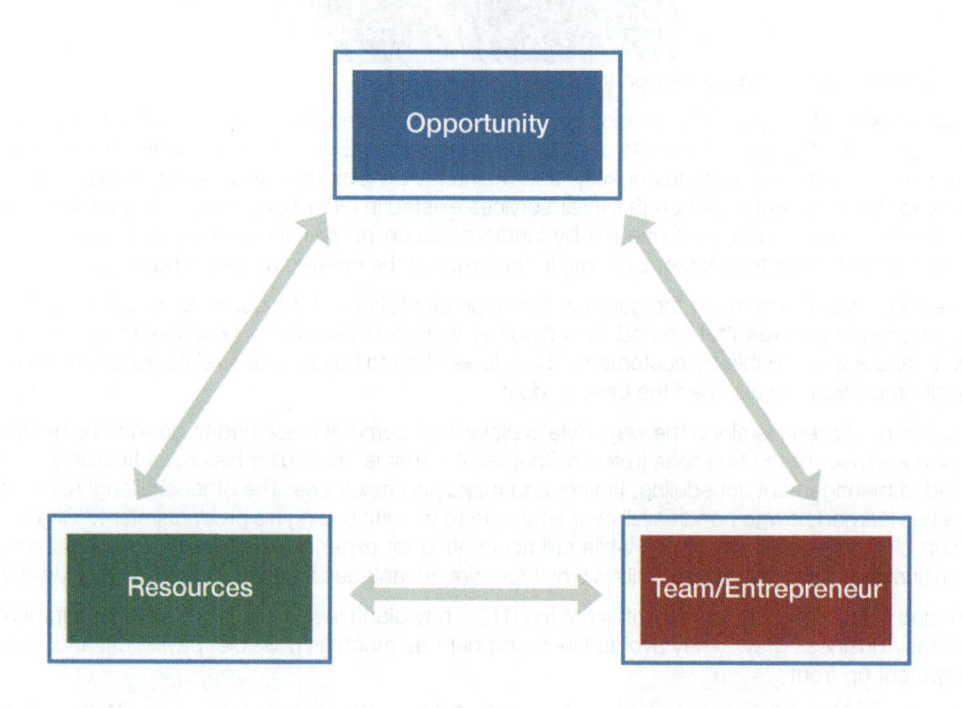

Source: Laura Portolese et al.

Chapter 3 How Do I Determine a Good Idea and Opportunity?

According to the **Timmons Framework of the entrepreneurial process**, there are three critical factors that speak to the success of a business venture.[2] These three factors are: opportunity, team/entrepreneur, and resources. The Timmons Framework states that opportunity must come first, but all three are necessary for a successful venture.

> **Timmons Framework of the entrepreneurial process**
>
> Three critical factors which speak to the success of a business venture. The three factors include opportunity, team/entrepreneur, and resources, but opportunity must come first.

Opportunity

First, the "opportunity" in the Timmons Framework addresses the business opportunity itself. Contrary to popular belief, a business does not start with the business plan, with resources, or with business strategy. It starts with fully determining whether the opportunity makes sense. This consists of several factors.

Market demand is a strong consideration in determining whether an opportunity makes sense. Market demand is defined as the sum of the individual demand for a product from buyers in a market. Questions to consider when determining market demand may include:[3]

- Does the product or service meet a new need?
- If the product or service doesn't meet a new need, can it satisfy an existing need at a lower cost?
- What is the economic value of the product or service?
- What is the market size?
- What is the market growth potential in the future?
- Is the customer easily defined?
- Can you, as the entrepreneur, effectively reach the customer?
- What competitive advantages can be created?
- What are the barriers to entry?

> **market demand**
>
> The sum of the individual demand for a product from buyers in a market.

When entrepreneurs ask these questions, they can better gauge whether an opportunity is worth pursuing. Besides addressing the opportunity, an entrepreneur should determine what resources are needed and how they will be managed. That is the focus of the next section.

Resources

The second aspect of the Timmons Framework is "resources." Resources comprise three main components: people, financial resources, and tools necessary to complete the task. These resources must not only be acquired, but effectively managed. Spending resources wisely and efficiently helps make a venture successful. For example, if you were to open a BBQ restaurant, you might need financial resources to buy the raw materials, but you also need to purchase ovens, grills, dishes, and other "things" necessary to bring your venture to fruition. Without the proper resources—and management of those resources—a business venture isn't likely to succeed. The final component, the "team" in the Timmons Framework, will be addressed next.

Team

The third aspect of the Timmons Framework is the team and/or the entrepreneur. First, the entrepreneur must have the qualities described in Chapter 2. The team the entrepreneur hires must have similar characteristics, but should also have a good balance of skills to make the business successful. For example, some of the qualities the team might need to have include:

- Leadership abilities
- Effective communication
- Adaptiveness
- Creativity
- Motivation
- Tolerance to risk and uncertainty

Consider the importance of a team in a restaurant business, for example. If you were to open a restaurant, you might want to hire a team consisting of an experienced restaurant manager and experienced head chef, as well as other team members (such as an accountant experienced in this type of business). You would also want people who work well together as a team and who can solve problems creatively. Without a strong team possessing the required skills, the business may not be successful.

So how are these three aspects of the Timmons Framework important to the new entrepreneur? According to Timmons, you must first start with the opportunity. Often, many entrepreneurs begin with themselves or the team and consider what they would *like* to do, rather than assessing a good opportunity first.[4]

Consider Shane, for example. Shane really enjoys cooking BBQ. His friends have told him his pulled pork, smoked beans, and ribs are the best they've ever had. Based on this feedback, Shane decides to open a BBQ restaurant in his town. Shane runs into trouble, however, when he discovers the market for BBQ in his town is too small. He closes his restaurant after eight months. In this scenario, if Shane had followed the Timmons Framework, he would have determined a good opportunity *first*, then made sure that opportunity matched with the skills and abilities of the team as he managed resources effectively.

Fifty Entrepreneurs Share Priceless Advice

As you listen to this video, note how much of entrepreneurship success depends on identifying the right opportunity.

View in the online reader

Keep in mind the main points of the Timmons Framework as you generate ideas for your business.[5]

- The venture should focus on creating value.
- The venture should be driven by opportunity.

- The venture should be driven by a lead entrepreneur or a lead team.
- Success depends on the fit and balance between the opportunity, the team, and the available resources.

Key Takeaway

- According to the Timmons model, the three critical factors of a business venture include: opportunity, resources, and the entrepreneur or team.

Interactive Activity

1. Using the Timmons model, address the differences between opportunity, team/entrepreneur, and resources. Which do you think is the most important and why?

3.2 Generating a Good Idea

Learning Objective

1. Discuss methods for idea generation.

As we discussed in the last section, identifying the right opportunity is the first step in the entrepreneurial process. You may be wondering, "How do I even begin to think about possible ideas for a business?" This process is called **idea generation** and can be used in many different settings for many different purposes. Idea generation is defined, generally, as the process of creating, developing, and communicating ideas that are abstract, concrete, or visual. There are many ways to practice idea generation. These will be the focus of this section.

Characteristics of a Good Idea Generation Process

idea generation

The process of creating, developing, and communicating ideas that are abstract, concrete, or visual.

People often assume that good ideas just "happen." You may hear someone say, "I'm just not very creative." In entrepreneurship, we want to avoid this type of thinking. Generating new ideas is a *systemic* process—but sometimes, new ideas occur by accident, based on economic situations and other factors. Consider the COVID-19 pandemic. Many businesses, around 4.4 million,[6] were started as people were laid off from their jobs and/or quarantined. Many of these new businesses revolved around physical products, such as handmade crafts and clothing, while others revolved around the introduction of new software apps.[7]

Consider 3M scientist Spencer Silver. In trying to invent a very strong adhesive, he instead invented a light material that was easy to pull off of surfaces. He spent five years meeting with colleagues at 3M, trying to find a way to use this product. Then a colleague became frustrated with bookmarks that fell out of hymnals during choir practice at church. The two decided to create a product called "press and peel," now known as Post-it® Notes.[8]

Successful idea generation processes—no matter which method you use—have some many similar characteristics.[9] These characteristics include the following:

Challenge assumptions.
For every situation, we have a key set of assumptions. For example, I want to purchase a new car but I don't have a down payment saved, so I may just give up because I haven't challenged my assumptions. The fact is, I may be able to think of creative ways to solve the issue. For example, I could borrow money from a relative for a down payment. I could research no-money-down options at certain dealerships. I could stop buying coffee every morning, brewing coffee instead to save that money—which could amount to $150 per month, enough for a down payment in six months. In other words, if we assume we *can't* do something, we likely prevent ourselves from thinking creatively.
Shift your perspective.
We often get caught up in our own thoughts and perceived limitations. For this reason, it can be helpful to talk to someone else, or brainstorm ideas with another person. Ask questions like, "What frustrates you about X?" Also, try playing the role of another person when generating ideas. If you are not a homeowner, for example, play the role of one. What problems do you think homeowners have? Choose whatever role applies. What problems do, say, golfers have? By getting into the mindset of someone else, we can think of ideas outside of ourselves.
No idea is a bad idea.
Often, when we are brainstorming, we reject ideas as soon as we come up with them, saying, "That will never work." Avoid judging your ideas when brainstorming. Just come up with ideas first. You can always sort through them later.
Brainstorm and generate as many ideas as possible.
When we generate ideas, we are looking for *quantity*. Generating as many ideas as possible will give you a greater selection through which to sort later. Thus, the goal is to generate as many ideas as possible during the first phase of the process.

Passion vs. Hobby vs. Real Business Idea

Sometimes a passion or a hobby can turn into a great business venture. There are thousands of articles making statements such as, "Find your passion and make a living," or "Passion in your work drives success!" While these things can be true, at least in part, passion is not the only thing necessary to start and run a successful venture. In fact, for some people, turning their passion into their work can make them lose interest in what they love.

Consider the green thumb who starts a lawn care business based on a passion for plants and landscaping. Day after day, for eight to ten hours, seven days a week, this person is doing what they thought they loved. The work soon becomes repetitive and perhaps frustrating, especially when tending to the other aspects of the business (dealing with customers, managing employees, etc.). Thus, while the business was born out of passion, it has become simply work over time.

Passion is the energy that allows the entrepreneur to keep doing tasks that may be unpleasant.[10] While it can be an important component to starting a business, there are many other important elements as well.

Hobbies may not be the best business idea, for that matter. For example, let's assume Trish loves to skateboard. To buy skateboarding supplies, she must either drive forty-five minutes to get to the nearest retailer, or order online. She decides to open a skate shop in her hometown, catering to the skateboarding and roller derby community. However, her hobby doesn't have much footing in the market. Her town is small and there aren't many opportunities for skating. In this case, trying to turn a hobby into a business won't work. This is why it is so important to determine the opportunity within the market first.

When considering turning a hobby into a business, the Internal Revenue Service (IRS) actually has rules revolving around what constitutes a "real" business versus a hobby. These stipulations are:[11]

- Does the time and effort put into the activity indicate an intention to make a profit?
- Does the taxpayer depend on income from the activity?
- If there are losses, are they due to circumstances beyond the taxpayer's control, or did they occur in the startup phase of the business?
- Has the taxpayer changed methods of operation to improve profitability?
- Does the taxpayer or his/her advisors have the knowledge needed to carry on the activity as a successful business?
- Has the taxpayer made a profit in similar activities in the past?
- Does the activity make a profit in some years?
- Can the taxpayer expect to make a profit in the future from the appreciation of assets used in the activity?

Your hobby or passion, therefore, might be a good starting point in the idea generation process. As with any other idea, however, you must make sure your idea is also an opportunity within the market. In the next section, we will discuss a variety of methods to generate ideas.

Terri Trespicio: Stop Searching For Your Passion

View in the online reader

Idea Generation Methods

Now that we have discussed the importance of identifying an opportunity, and discussed some of the aspects of generating a good idea, let's talk specifically about some processes for generating ideas.

mix and match method

A brainstorming method in which two things are combined that don't normally go together. This may produce a new idea for a product or service.

solve it method

Encourages you to tune into the world around you and question everything. This brainstorming method requires you to listen to those around you and attempt to solve complaints and common problems.

what if you could method

A brainstorming method that challenges the entrepreneur to think about things that can't be done currently, but that would be a benefit if possible.

One possible method for brainstorming business ideas is the **mix and match method**. In this method,[12] you'll put two things together that don't normally go together to think of a new product or service. For example, what about combining dog washing and car washing in the same business? This is what Auto Mutt dog and car wash in Kalispell, Montana, created. Dogs and cars are two things that don't normally go together, a thriving business resulted when the two were combined.

In the **solve it method**, tune into the world around you and question everything.[13] This method requires you to listen to those around you and attempt to solve complaints and common problems. For example, the "purse hook" or "handbag hanger" was created to discourage theft of purses left on the floor. The hook fits inside the purse and can easily attach to a table or restroom stall. This also prevents the purse from becoming soiled. This practical product solves a problem and was likely created using the solve it method.

Another method for brainstorming is the **what if you could method**.[14] This method challenges the entrepreneur to think about things that currently can't be done, but would be a benefit if possible. For example, what if you could listen to music while floating in the river (a question that produced waterproof wireless speakers). What if you could drink water while hiking hands-free (a query that resulted in the CamelBak®)? This method challenges the entrepreneur to think creatively about things that have not yet been created or developed in the marketplace.

Source: © Shutterstock, Inc.

passion

A feeling toward something that motivates and inspires you.

hobby

Something a person enjoys doing and chooses to do in their leisure.

In the last section, we discussed **passion** and **hobbies** as possible ideas for new businesses. These can indeed be used to generate ideas.[15] Consider Zagat, founded by Nina and Tim Zagat. They talked with friends at a dinner party about unreliable restaurant reviews. This prompted them to create a newsletter to send to friends, asking them to rate various restaurants. This hobby turned into a business sold to Google for $151 million.[16] Google has since sold it to The Infatuation for an undisclosed amount. This is a great example of how hobbies, passions, and interests can create entrepreneurial ideas.

You can also consider the **out with the old, in with the new method**. This brainstorming method looks at common products and attempts to change the products to make them better. For example, screen doors are pretty common, but Carol Lynch received a patent in 1992 for magnetic, removable screen doors.[17] Screen doors were common products at the time, but she was able to improve them to the point that hers became a multi-million-dollar business.

The **SCAMPER method** encourages the entrepreneur to consider a new or existing product and use action verbs to determine how a new product could be useful. The entrepreneur may also consider how an existing product could be changed. SCAMPER is an acronym for the following:[18]

- **S:** Substitute
- **C:** Combine
- **A:** Adapt
- **M:** Modify
- **P:** Put to another use
- **E:** Eliminate
- **R:** Reverse

The entrepreneur might use this method to consider what type of product could be substituted for another, or how products could be combined to make a superior product. The SCAMPER method asks how you can adapt a product, modify it, or put an existing product to a different use. It also encourages you to eliminate some aspect of a product that might be burdensome, while asking how you can reverse a product's use.

To use a **mind mapping method**, the entrepreneur will write a phrase or word (such as a problem to be solved) in the middle of the page.[19] The entrepreneur then writes down anything that comes to mind around that particular phrase before trying to make connections to solve a problem.

These are just a few of the ways you can use idea generation techniques to produce a new idea. There are many other methods. Choose one that gets you out of your comfort zone and thinking creatively. Once you've brainstormed ideas for a new business or product, you must evaluate your ideas. This is what we will discuss in the next section.

> **out with the old, in with the new method**
> A brainstorming method that looks at common products and attempts to change the products to make them better.
>
> **SCAMPER method**
> A brainstorming method that encourages the entrepreneur to consider a new or existing product, then use action verbs to determine how it could be changed or used in a new way.

Source: © Shutterstock, Inc.

> **mind mapping method**
> A graphical technique for making connections between ideas.

■ Ideas Are Everywhere!

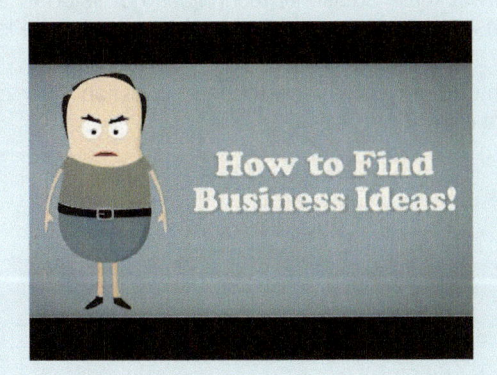

How to Find Business Ideas!

View in the online reader

Think Idea Generation

These videos address some of the ways you can find new business ideas.

View in the online reader

Key Takeaways

- In order to conduct an effective idea generation process, you should challenge your assumptions, shift your perspective, realize that no idea is a bad idea at this stage, and brainstorm to generate as many ideas as possible.
- You must understand the difference between a passion, a hobby, and a real business idea, as well as how these factor into the idea generation process.
- There are literally hundreds of idea generation methods, all of which can be used to come up with many new business ideas.

Interactive Activities

1. As we've noted in this section, there are hundreds of possible brainstorming techniques. Please research at least three additional techniques not listed in this chapter. Discuss at least three advantages and three disadvantages of each method. Please provide links to the resources.
2. Choose one of the methods you've researched in question 1, or one from the book, and brainstorm ideas for a new business.

3.3 Evaluating the Idea: Opportunity Assessment Plans

Learning Objective

1. Assess new business ideas.

Now that you have done the work to come up with potential business ideas, it is time to evaluate the merit of your ideas so you can move forward with the next steps in the development of your business. Before we focus on how to evaluate each of your ideas, it is important to understand where this step fits in the **ideation** process.

ideation
The formation of ideas or concepts.

The Stages of Successful Ideation

Ideation refers to the formation of ideas or concepts. There are three steps:
- Generate Ideas
- Evaluate Ideas
- Implement Ideas

From an entrepreneurial perspective, this is the brainstorming process we discussed in Section 2 of this chapter. Brainstorming, the first step, is the part of the process in which ideas are generated. Evaluating, the second step, is the part of the process in which you determine whether an idea should be implemented. The last phase in the ideation process refers to the actual implementation of the idea. This is the business plan and its execution.

FIGURE 3.2 The Ideation Process

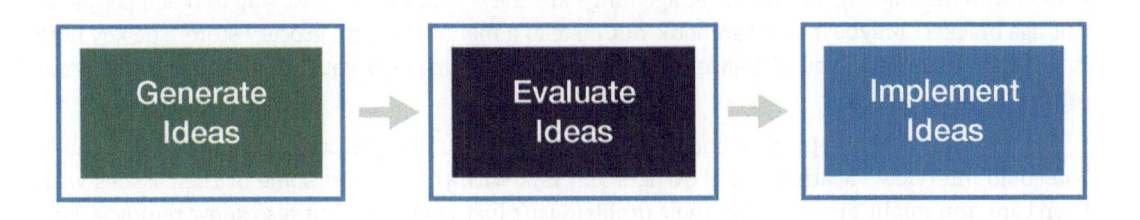

Generate Ideas → Evaluate Ideas → Implement Ideas

Source: Laura Portolese et al.

Opportunity Assessment Plans

opportunity assessment plan

Not a business plan, but examines several aspects of an idea you should consider before you choose the business for which you'll create and develop a plan. It helps you determine if your ideas are viable.

One way most entrepreneurs evaluate their ideas is through the use of an **opportunity assessment plan**. An opportunity assessment plan is not a business plan. Instead, it examines several aspects of an idea you should consider before you choose the business for which you'll create and develop a plan. Some of the research done for an opportunity assessment plan can also be used in your business plan, should you decide to go with this idea. The assessment plan gives you an opportunity to ask the "hard questions" related to future success and viability of your business idea. An opportunity assessment plan consists of the following components:[20]

1. What is the idea?
2. What problem will this product or service solve?
3. What is the target market? Who will our main customers be?
4. What is the market size?
5. How will we market to customers?
6. Who are our competitors?
7. What makes this product or service better than the competition?
8. Do the team and I have the skills and abilities needed to implement this business? If I don't have the skills, will I be able to hire people who do?

Through your idea generation process, you have determined several possible ideas. Now it is time to write your opportunity assessment plan for each of them. The first two components of your plan are to name your idea and to discuss what problem this product or service will solve. For example, if one of your ideas is, say, a landscaping business, you might state:

Idea:	A landscaping business specializing in basic yard maintenance.
Problem:	Because many people rent their homes as nightly rentals in my tourist town, many people do not have time to take care of their nightly rentals.

Now that you have named both the idea and the problem you hope to solve with your business idea, you will want to research the market size and the actual target market. You might search nightly rental websites such as Airbnb, VRBO (Vacation Rental By Owner), and Homeaway rentals in your area to help determine the market size. In addition, you should consider the "profile" of the person who has nightly rentals. What age range are they? What is the best way to reach people in this age bracket? Maybe it isn't Facebook, but instead a flier at the local grocery store. The key here is to begin thinking as you visualize your customer. Visualize how you can tell them about your service.

In addition to this type of online research, you may want to perform some primary research. You could interview vacation rental owners and talk with them about some of their issues with lawn care. You might discover that their problem isn't just lawn care, but also snow removal. This gives good, specific insights into the problem you are trying to solve. It can assist you in refining your idea, making your business plan easier to write.

Next, you will want to research the competition. Who are the competing lawn care services in your town? Do they cater to your specific market, or do they focus more on landscape design? Determining this may take a simple Google search. Consider asking friends and neighbors about lawn care services of which they are aware. Once you have identified the competitors, you may want to look at online reviews, such as on Yelp, to discover the strengths and weaknesses of each competitor (understanding, of course, that online reviews can be biased). Consider what you will do to differentiate your business from the competition.

Finally, you'll want to consider your own knowledge, skills, and abilities. Do you know what it takes to keep a lawn looking nice? Do you know how to trim around the edges for a clean look? Do you know enough about weeds versus plants to be able to perform basic weeding? Obviously, having the skills and abilities is an important part of the process. If you don't currently have the skills, can you learn and develop them? Can you hire personnel who have these skills?

Let's assume you have gone through this opportunity assessment process only to discover there are only one hundred rentals in your area. Of these one hundred, you estimate half of them perform their own lawn care. This leaves a pretty small market of only fifty rentals. You further determine that vacation rental owners are not willing to pay more than $20 per week to take care of the rentals. When you calculate this, you realize the market size and potential profit really aren't enough to make this a viable business. Perhaps, you decide, this isn't the best market to enter.

At this time, you can tweak your idea or review the other ideas you have. You might tweak the lawn care idea by adding a snow removal option as well. Perhaps you expand your market to all homeowners, rather than just rentals. As you refine your idea, you'll want to engage in a new opportunity assessment plan for each permutation.

The Components of an Opportunity Assessment Plan

View in the online reader

A **SWOT analysis** is another useful tool during this process. This is a detailed list of business strengths, weaknesses, opportunities, and threats. Outlining these details allows you to see a clearer picture of your potential business. It will help you better understand what pitfalls might exist when implementing your business idea. Chapter 4 explains SWOT analysis in more detail.

Another common assessment tool is a **PESTLE analysis**, which is also addressed in Chapter 9. A PESTLE analysis allows you to see potential threats to your business from a political, economic, social, technological, ethical, and environmental perspective.

In our next section, we assume you've gone through the opportunity assessment plan process and have chosen the most promising option for your new business. The next section discusses the planning process for a product or service.

> **Leveraging: Primary and Secondary Research**
>
> In order to write and consider an effective opportunity assessment, we must do research—not merely take our "best guesses" at such elements as market size.

SWOT analysis

A process used to determine an organization's strengths, weaknesses, opportunities, and threats.

PESTLE analysis

A process used to determine how political, economic, social, technological, legal, and environmental factors might affect an organization.

secondary research

Involves the summary of existing research from government publications and websites.

primary research

Any type of research you go out and collect yourself.

There is a lot of good research already out there that we can term **secondary research**. Secondary research involves the summary of existing research from government publications and websites. This type of research might include census bureau data, which can help you determine such things as demographic information for specific areas. When we discussed Airbnb, VRBO (Vacation Rental By Owner), Homeaway, and Yelp in our opportunity assessment, we were employing these as secondary sources.

Primary research is any type of research you go out and collect yourself. This could be interviews, focus groups, surveys, and so forth. In the landscaping business example, talking to current vacation rental owners is an example of primary research.

In order to make good decisions, we want a mix of primary and secondary research. Be careful, though. When gathering primary research, it is possible to ask "leading" questions to try to obtain the answers we want. Avoid this. The more accurate and objective your data, the better your overall plan will be.

Leverage your resources. Here are two articles that describe how to research for an opportunity assessment plan:

https://www.entrepreneur.com/article/217345

https://www.entrepreneur.com/article/241080

What other resources could you use to research your opportunity assessment plan?

Key Takeaways

- Ideation refers to the formation of concepts or ideas and consists of three steps: generate ideas, evaluate ideas, and implement ideas.
- The ideation process allows entrepreneurs to decide if the good idea is worth pursuing.
- SWOT Analysis and PESTLE analysis are common tools for determining if an idea is a good one.

Interactive Activity

1. Choose three ideas you'd like to develop further. Perform an opportunity assessment plan for each of the three ideas, including a SWOT analysis and a PESTLE analysis. Please provide links to all research performed for this activity.

3.4 Nailing Down the Idea: Planning for Product or Service Development

Learning Objective

1. Address considerations for the planning process of a product or service.

Now that you have brainstormed ideas, performed an opportunity assessment on each idea, and chosen your best idea, it is time to get into the details of your product or service. This phase will help you hone your idea and prepare you to begin writing your business plan. We will discuss business plans in more detail in Chapter 4. In this section, we will discuss some of the main factors that will help you decide on which steps in the product planning and development process to focus. This will depend on your product or service type.

There are many ways to approach the product or service planning and development process. We will first address two elements directly related to the development of your product or service: product lifecycles and the type of innovation. Depending on the stage of your product or service, you may choose to approach the product development process and the business plan writing process in different ways.[21]

Product Lifecycle

FIGURE 3.3 The Product Lifecycle

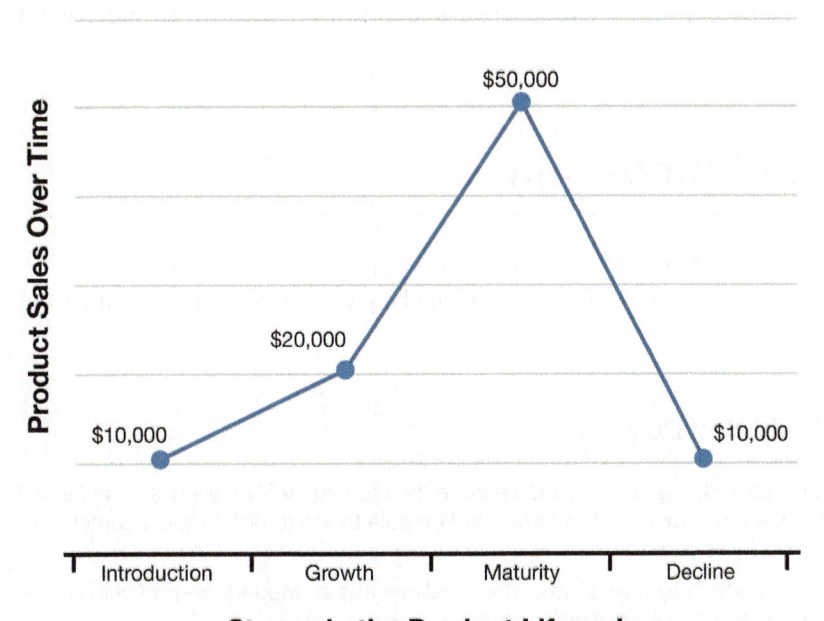

[Line graph titled "Stages in the Product Lifecycle" with y-axis "Product Sales Over Time" showing four stages: Introduction ($10,000), Growth ($20,000), Maturity ($50,000), Decline ($10,000).]

Source: Laura Portolese et al.

The first stage in the product lifecycle is **introduction**. In this phase, when a product or service is new, it can be very expensive. For example, the cost of research and development for a new product, and testing the product, could be expensive. The size of the market for a new product is likely to be small. In this phase, sales might be low and expenses might be high. If your new product or service is at this phase, you might want to consider the amount of funding you have—your ability to sustain the marketing of the product over the long term—before pursuing the idea.

The second phase of the product lifecycle is **growth**. This is when the product is known and desired. During this phase, a company can begin to recoup some of the costs it spent in the introduction phase. If your product idea is already in the growth stage, this can be a good time to enter the market, as other companies have already shouldered the costs of the introduction phase and customers are used to the idea of the "new product."

introduction

The first phase of the product lifecycle. This phase of a new product or service can be expensive, because costs are high while sales are low.

growth

The second phase of the product lifecycle, during which the product is known and desired.

maturity
The third phase of the product lifecycle, during which the product is well-established and there are many competitors. Developing a competitive advantage is important during this stage.

decline
The fourth stage of the product lifecycle. In this phase, sales drop rapidly.

Consider the iPod and MP3 players. Once iPods became popular, many other manufacturers jumped on the opportunity to sell portable music devices. Customers now demanded the product. Prior to iPods, customers didn't even know the product existed.

The third phase of the product lifecycle is **maturity**. In this phase, the product is well established. As new competitors enter the market, developing a competitive advantage is important to the businessperson. This is also the phase during which an entrepreneur may consider how to improve or change the product in order to continue competing in the marketplace. Because the product is so common and there are many competitors, making the product better or innovating new products is key to success.

In the final phase, the **decline** phase, sales drop rapidly. The entrepreneur must turn to new ideas or to innovations of the previous idea in order to stay in business. Some products may remain in previous phases for many years. For example, consider products like ceiling fans. These have changed little over the years, but continue to sell.

Always consider the lifecycle phase of your product. Make marketing decisions based on that phase. If your product is already in the decline phase, but your idea is to make improvements to the existing product, it could bring the product out of decline and back into the introduction phase. We discuss the stages and types of innovation in the next section. Innovating a product will likely drive the company's marketing efforts, as well as the planning necessary to open and maintain a successful business.

Types of Innovation

In addition to product lifecycles, it is important to discuss the two different types of innovation. Understanding these two types of innovation will help you better position your product or service in the marketplace.

> ### What Would You Do?
>
> Confidence in your idea (assuming you've done the research we've discussed so far in this chapter) is one of the most important ways you will be able to sell to potential consumers once you've written your business plan.
>
> How will you handle "naysayers" who don't believe it is a good idea—particularly when you've done the research and believe it *will* work?

incremental innovation
A type of innovation that includes a series of small improvement or upgrades to existing products.

radical innovation
Sometimes called disruptive or discontinuous innovation. A radically innovative product makes a significant impact on the market. Often it is brand new and has never before been offered.

The first type of innovation is **incremental innovation**. This type of innovation includes a series of small improvement or upgrades made to existing products. Consider the smartphone market, for example. Although smartphones existed when the iPhone came along, features such as a larger screen and ease of use helped smartphones to become mainstream.[22] As a result, you cannot discount the significant differences to the market made through small changes in the product.

A **radical innovation**, sometimes called a *disruptive* or *discontinuous* innovation, is a product that makes a significant impact on the market. Often, it is brand new, something that has never before been offered. It may be similar to previous products, but represents a complete change in the way the product is viewed by the consumer. For example, plastic bottles are getting a facelift which includes directly embossed branding, removing the need for a sleeve,[23] which helps the environment and also the bottom line.

So, which type of innovation is your product or service? Are you going to change something existing, making an incremental innovation? Or do you have a brand new, never before seen, radical innovation? Understanding the type of innovation better prepares you for the development process, which is the focus of our next section.

Product Planning and Development Process

You've gone through the process of generating ideas for your business and then evaluating those ideas. You understand the product lifecycle and where your idea fits. You also understand the different types of innovation to determine where your product fits. This prepares you for the final phase in the idea process (before you begin your business plan in Chapter 4). This is the product (or service) planning and development process.

FIGURE 3.4 **The Product Development Process**

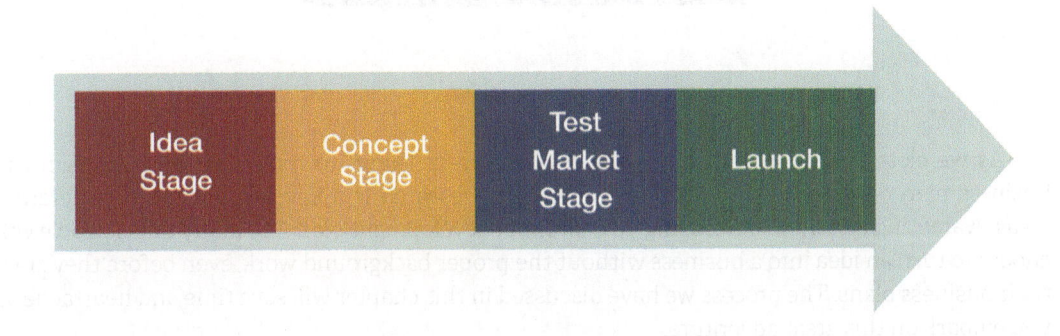

Idea Stage → Concept Stage → Test Market Stage → Launch

Source: Laura Portolese et al.

The first stage in the product planning and development process is the *idea* stage. That is the stage in which you generate ideas for your business and evaluate them for validity. We have already covered that at this point in the chapter.

The second stage in the process is the *concept* stage. The goal of this stage is to develop further your product or service idea. In this phase, you will want to consider and be able to answer a number of questions. These questions include:

- The features of your product or service
- The benefits of your product or service
- The price of your product or service
- How your product or service compares with the competition (a deeper analysis than prepared during idea generation)
- The strengths and weaknesses of your product or service (and how you will overcome the weaknesses while marketing the strengths)
- What special patents or other legal forms might be necessary to start the business (more on this in Chapter 6)

The third stage is the *test market* stage. This is the stage during which you have a physical product or service that is fully developed and you are ready to test the reactions of potential customers. For example, if your idea is to develop a new app that tracks all textbook rentals, this is the stage during which potential customers would beta test the app to make sure it is ready to market.

In the final stage of the product or service development process, you will write the business plan and launch your business.

> **The Product Development Process**
>
> View in the online reader

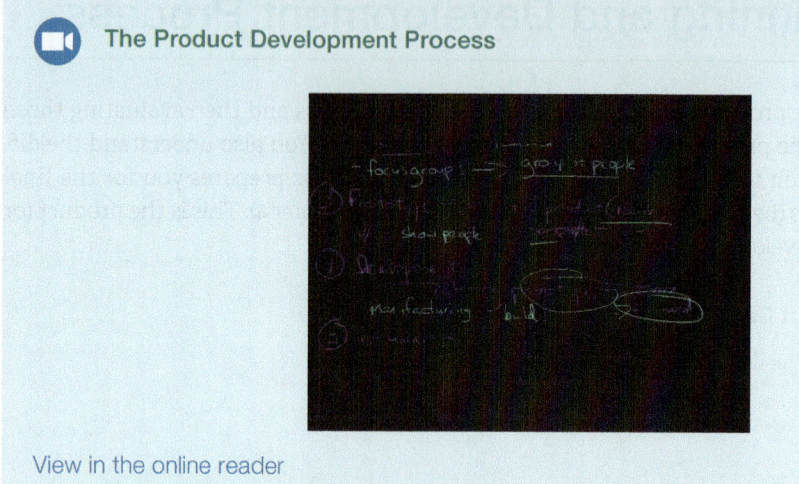

As we close this chapter, there are a few important things to remember as you begin the business plan development part of this book. First, research is a key component to generating ideas, evaluating ideas, and developing your product development plan. Too many times people will choose to turn an idea into a business without the proper background work, even before they start their business plans. The process we have discussed in this chapter will save time and heartache as you embark on this great adventure.

Key Takeaways

- The opportunity assessment plan allows the entrepreneur to dig into the ideas generated in the first step of the process to determine which have the most merit.
- Entrepreneurs must understand at what point in the product lifecycle their product or service will enter the market. The phases include introduction, growth, maturity, and decline.
- There are two types of innovations: incremental and radical. Incremental means to "tweak" an existing service or product to make it better, while radical innovation changes the market entirely (often representing a brand new, never-before-seen product).
- The product planning and development process allows entrepreneurs to fully develop their ideas before moving to the next phase, the writing of the business plan.

Interactive Activities

1. In small groups, brainstorm examples of radical innovations and incremental innovations. Be prepared to discuss.
2. In small groups, brainstorm examples of at least three products in each of the lifecycle phases.
3. Choose the most viable product or service idea from question three. Now address each phase of the product or service planning process related to your product.

3.5 Test Your Skills: Applied Case

Maria's Cakes and the Product Development Process

Maria Gonzalez has been working as a night stocker at a local retail store. However, she is finding the hours don't work well as her children are growing and need to be driven to after school sports and activities. Maria wants to come up with a new idea for a business, but isn't sure where to start. After several months of trying to come up with an idea, she was just approached by a few acquaintances who saw the beautiful specialty cakes she made for her children's birthday parties on social media. These cakes are special though—because one of her children is diabetic, she has developed a formula to make delicious and beautiful cakes especially meant for people who are diabetic. The cakes use avocado oil instead of butter, nut flours, and she uses home made applesauce to cut the sugar in her recipes.

Source: © Shutterstock, Inc.

They've asked her to make cakes for them, and are offering to pay top dollar for her work. This gave Maria an idea: could she earn enough to support her family making diabetic specific cakes for others? As Maria ponders this idea, she wants to consider the product development process to determine if this is a viable idea. Answer the questions that follow, below, to help her decide.

1. What phase in the product lifecycle would Maria's cakes fall into and why?
2. Perform an analysis of the product development process, with a focus on the second phase, "concept." Leveraging research, answer each of the questions as described in the concept phase.
3. Prepare some examples of how Maria might test her concept.
4. Would you consider her cakes innovative? Why or why not? What type of innovation do you think they most closely match with, and why?

Endnotes

1. Wood, M.S. (2021, 25 March). Entrepreneurial Opportunity: Bedrock in entrepreneurship research. Retrieved from: https://oxfordre.com/business/view/10.1093/acrefore/9780190224851.001.0001/acrefore-9780190224851-e-312
2. Timmons, J. A., Muzyka, D. F., Stevenson, H. H., & Bygrave, W. D. (1987). Opportunity recognition: The core of entrepreneurship. *Frontiers of entrepreneurship research*, 7(2), 109-123.
3. Timmons, J.A. & Spinelli S. (n.d.). The Timmons model of the entrepreneurship process. Retrieved from: http://www.innovationventures.sg/Entrepreneurship-resources/timmons-model-of-the-entrepreneurial-process
4. Timmons, J. A., Muzyka, D. F., Stevenson, H. H., & Bygrave, W. D. (1987). Opportunity recognition: The core of entrepreneurship. Frontiers of entrepreneurship research, 7(2), 109-123.
5. Timmons, J.A. & Spinelli S. (n.d.). The Timmons model of the entrepreneurship process. Retrieved from: http://www.innovationventures.sg/Entrepreneurship-resources/timmons-model-of-the-entrepreneurial-process
6. Grossfield, B. (2021, June 29) Entrepreneurs started businesses in record numbers during the pandemic. Retrieved from: https://www.salesforce.com/blog/small-business-pandemic-entrepreneurs
7. Grossfield, B. (2021, June 29) Entrepreneurs started businesses in record numbers during the pandemic. Retrieved from: https://www.salesforce.com/blog/small-business-pandemic-entrepreneurs
8. Post-it Brand (n.d.) History timeline: Post-it notes. Retrieved from: https://www.post-it.com/3M/en_US/post-it/contact-us/about-us/
9. Mind Tools (n.d.) Generating new ideas. Retrieved from: https://www.mindtools.com/pages/article/newCT_88.html
10. de Mol, E.M, Cardon, M & Khapova S. (2020, February 20) When entrepreneurial passion backfires. Retrieved from: https://hbr.org/2020/02/when-entrepreneurial-passion-backfires
11. Internal Revenue Service. (2020, August 25). Earning side income: Is is a hobby or business? Retrieved from: https://www.irs.gov/newsroom/earning-side-income-is-it-a-hobby-or-a-business
12. Edison Nation. (2020, September 24) Back to basics: Idea Generation. Retrieved from: https://blog.edisonnation.com/2020/09/back-to-the-basics/
13. Edison Nation. (2020, September 24) Back to basics: Idea Generation. Retrieved from: https://blog.edisonnation.com/2020/09/back-to-the-basics/
14. Edison Nation. (2020, September 24) Back to basics: Idea Generation. Retrieved from: https://blog.edisonnation.com/2020/09/back-to-the-basics/
15. Lewis, M. (2020, June 29) 21 hobbies you can turn into a business. Retrieved from: https://www.moneytalksnews.com/slideshows/25-hobbies-you-can-turn-into-a-business/
16. Rosenblatt, B. (2018, March 6) Google sells Zagat to the Infatuation, freeing it to become relevant again. Retrieved from: https://www.forbes.com/sites/billrosenblatt/2018/03/06/google-sells-zagat-to-the-infatuation-freeing-it-to-become-great-again/?sh=4e65bb7c4428
17. Bug off Screens (n.d.) About us. Retrieved from: http://www.bugoffscreen.com/about-us.html
18. Cleverism (n.d.) The 18 best idea generation techniques. Retrieved from: https://www.cleverism.com/18-best-idea-generation-technique
19. Cleverism (n.d.) The 18 best idea generation techniques. Retrieved from: https://www.cleverism.com/18-best-idea-generation-technique
20. Peltier, J. (2018, August 25). How to conduct a product opportunity assessment. Retrieved from: https://medium.com/@johnpeltier/how-to-conduct-a-product-opportunity-assessment-e48671e09f5a
21. Sraders, A. (2021, October 29) What is the product life cycle? Stages and examples. Retrieved from: https://www.thestreet.com/markets/commodities/product-life-cycle-14882534
22. Kishore, S. (n.d.) The power of incremental innovation. Wired Magazine. Retrieved from: https://www.wired.com/insights/2013/11/the-power-of-incremental-innovation/
23. Packaging Europe. (2021, December 15) Outlook for 2022:trends and disruptive innovations. Retrieved from: https://packagingeurope.com/outlook-for-2022-trends-and-disruptive-innovations/

PART 2
Entrepreneurship Planning

Source: © Shutterstock, Inc.

CHAPTER 4
How Do I Write a Marketing Plan?

> **Case Study—Jake Boomer: Passionate about His Business!**
>
> Source: Used with permission from Jake Boomer.
>
> When Jake Boomer graduated with an engineering degree from the University of Idaho in 2000, he had no idea that twelve years later he would be the owner of the first direct-to-consumer fishing rod company in the United States.
>
> Alpha Angler was born out of—and is sustained by—passion and a changing industry. Jake, an avid semi-professional bass fisherman, already had a job when he started Alpha Angler. He was a full-time IT executive at a well-known outdoor products company.
>
> Because of his experience in the industry, Jake recognized a shift in the way retail is done in the United States—the direct to consumer market. Consumers, he felt, were paying high prices, yet products in the fishing pole market lacked innovation.
>
> Jake decided to do something any engineer would do: He built his own fishing rod.
>
> At a variety of tournaments, people would ask where he got his equipment, and from that, the idea for Alpha Angler began. Starting out small, Jake built poles in his garage while working his full-time job. When demand grew, Jake left his full-time executive position to focus on Alpha Angler. That was in December of 2016.
>
> One of the first things Jake did was hire a general manager whom he put in charge of operations. This way, Jake could focus on what he liked—talking with customers about fishing and about his products.
>
> This newer model, direct to consumer sales, eliminated sales channels and mark-up. This met Jake's goal for the product and the price: an innovative product, at a reasonable price. Because of the lower mark-up rate, Jake's prices were lower than what retailers could charge. This model allowed Jake to communicate directly with the customer on needs and wants, getting immediate product feedback.

> Jake identified his target market as one of the first goals. Realizing he could not market to every angler, he focused specifically on the bass market—adult males who tend to fish in freshwater. This market has disposable income to spend on leisure activities, such as fishing, and likely spends time hunting as well. Jake's market is not people who might purchase fishing gear at big-box discount stores, but fishermen who prefer to buy high-quality equipment that will last.
>
> Alpha Angler focuses its marketing dollars and time on social media for promotion. It specifically uses social media to which the target market pays attention. This includes:
>
> - Facebook
> - Instagram (@alphaanglerfishing)
> - YouTube
>
> "I spend thirty to forty hours per week on marketing," Jake says. "This is the advantage of having hired a general manager. This allows me to connect with my customer. Some people just don't want to purchase a high-end product until they talk with someone. This also allows me to be positioned as an expert and create a trust-building relationship."
>
> Born out of passion, Jake was able to turn his fishing expertise into a growing business. He knows there will be challenges. Running a business is "still scary," he says, but with many "lines in the water" and his focus on marketing, he is sure to succeed.

As you've probably guessed, the focus of this chapter will be on how to market your business and how to write a marketing plan. Let's start now!

4.1 Market Research Methods

Learning Objective

1. Discuss the different types of market research and their uses.

marketing plan
A part of the business plan, normally spans one year, and addresses the target market and promotional strategies.

This chapter will address the first step in writing your business plan: the **marketing plan**. The marketing plan normally covers one year's time and should be reviewed on a monthly basis once you start your business. The marketing plan normally will address the following areas of your business:

- Situation analysis
- Marketing goals and objectives
- Target market
- Product pricing
- Marketing budget
- Promotional strategies

All of these areas combined will show readers of your marketing plan that you have a strong understanding of your market, giving them (and you!) confidence in your marketing efforts.

market research
The process of gathering, analyzing, and interpreting information about a market, product, service, or competitor.

The first step to writing your market plan is to perform **market research**. Market research is defined as the process of gathering, analyzing, and interpreting information about a market, product, service, or competitor.[1] Although you did perform some research in Chapter 3, in this step you will analyze your customers and the market in much more detail. It will become part of your overall marketing strategy.

Why perform market research? Often, entrepreneurs will not perform research because they "just know" the product or service will sell well, or because they do not want to hear negative feedback on their idea.[2] As you've likely guessed, this is all the more reason to perform market research. It allows you to fully understand at what price you will be able to sell the product or service. It also informs any changes to your existing idea that you may want to make before you go to market with it. Additionally, market research can help you determine if there is a need for the product or service within the market in the first place.

"A lot of companies skim over the important background information because they're so interested in getting their product to market," says Donna Barson, president and owner of Barson Marketing, Inc., a marketing, advertising, and public relations consulting firm. "But the companies that do the best are the ones that do their homework."[3] Market research can also help guide you in determining your audience and market, help you understand your customers better, and can even allow you to assess your competition.[4]

Before we discuss the specifics of market research, let's talk about the two types of market research in the next section.

Secondary Research

Secondary market research is defined as research that is already compiled and organized for you. This might include government publications, case studies performed by industry associations, and research compiled by other companies in the same industry. The main advantage to using of this type of data is cost savings. It is very expensive to compile such information yourself, so utilizing secondary research can save time and money. The data is usually extensive and can provide a good start for any primary research you will need to develop.

secondary market research
Research that is already compiled and organized for you.

A disadvantage of secondary research is potential accuracy of the data. Before using secondary data, making sure it is reliable. Some "published" data, such as that on Wikipedia, can be written by and added to by anyone, which means it may be flawed (and could even be wholly fabricated). Other information may be biased, skewed, or otherwise built on unreliable sources. Try to avoid sources like Wikis, blogs, or other questionable outlets when performing market research.

There are three main types of secondary data: public sources, commercial sources, and educational institutions.[5] Public sources might include the following:

- **State and metropolitan data book**

    This contains statistics covering a variety of areas. It is compiled by the U.S. Census Bureau.

- **The Statistical Abstract of the United States**

    This provides information about social conditions in the United States.

- **U.S. Industry and Trade Outlook**

    This provides information about specific industries. It can be a good way to identify industry trends.

- **The U.S. Census Bureau**

    This provides information on demographics in the United States.

These public sources are usually free and can provide plentiful data on industry trends, population information, and other useful information.

Commercial sources might include research and trade associations specific to your industry. Two useful tools for investigating the commercial resources related to your industry include:

- The Encyclopedia of Associations (published by Gale Group)
- The Encyclopedia of Business Information Sources (published by Gale Group)

Educational institutions can provide a rich variety of data. To find scholarly articles related to your industry, you can try to the following:

- **Google Scholar**

    This is a search engine within a search engine and can help you find scholarly information (published by professors in colleges or universities) about a particular industry.

- **Reference USA**

    This source requires only a library card. It allows you to research thousands of articles for your business plan.

- **Your school database**

    Most university libraries provide databases with thousands of publications, searchable online. Check out your college or university library to learn how to access this.

In this chapter, we will address the types of information you might want to look for and include in your marketing plan. First, though, let's look at primary research.

Primary Research

> **primary market research**
>
> Research that comes directly from the source. It is information you gather yourself from potential customers through interviews, surveys, and focus groups.

Primary market research is research that comes directly from the source. It is information you gather yourself from potential customers through interviews, surveys, and focus groups. The main advantage of primary research is that you get data specific to your business. There are several types of primary research you can perform for your marketing plan. They include:

- **Personal interviews**

    This can be done via email, phone, or in person. This involves asking a series of questions related directly to the research questions you pose when developing your research plan (refer to Section 1).

- **Focus groups**

    This would involve gathering a group of individuals who can provide feedback on your product or service idea, designs, pricing, or other marketing components. For example, if you are considering opening a barber shop, you might want to gather people from the community and ask questions regarding pricing, location, and hours.

- **Surveys**

    These can be traditional pen and paper surveys, or you can create a survey using online tools such as SurveyMonkey®. Electronic surveys can be emailed to participants or even posted to social media sites like Twitter and Facebook.

- **Personal observation**

    This might include watching someone and recording their reactions when using your product.

- **Tracking**

    Let's assume you want to open a physical, brick-and-mortar location. You might want to stand outside the proposed location over several weeks on different days to count the walk-by traffic, then include this data in your marketing plan.

Now that we have discussed the two types of research, let's discuss how we can combine the data we've gathered and apply it to the marketing plan.

Market Research Steps

It is time to follow the research process steps to begin your research before you start work on your marketing plan. The steps to market research include:

FIGURE 4.1 **The Steps in Market Research**

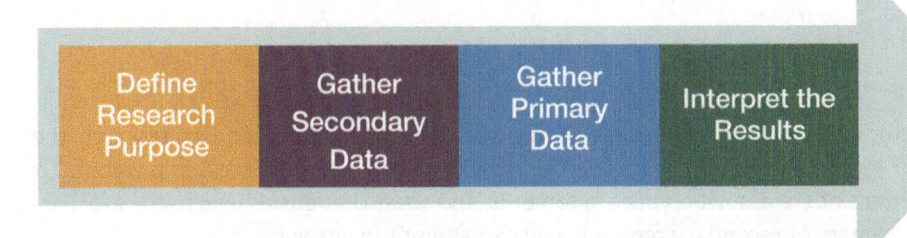

[Define Research Purpose → Gather Secondary Data → Gather Primary Data → Interpret the Results]

Source: Laura Portolese et al.

1. **Define the research purpose**

    This is where you define the goal. What type of information do you need for your marketing plan? Are you trying to determine the best price at which to sell your product, or do you want to narrow down your target market? It's crucial to have goals for your market research.

2. **Gather secondary data**

    To save time and money, see to what extent you can address your research purpose and goals by using secondary sources.

3. **Gather primary data**

    Determine the gap in information between what you are able to find in secondary research and what you need to know for your marketing plan. Determine how you will gather the primary research (e.g., personal interviews, surveys). Gather the data.

4. **Interpret the results**

    This involves **synthesis** of the data, which combines your secondary and primary research to produce the answers to your market research queries. This can be the most challenging part of the process. Done correctly, it will help you create a well-researched marketing plan.

synthesis
The combination of ideas to form an idea or a system.

> **The Difference between Primary and Secondary Market Research Sources**
>
> View in the online reader

No matter which path you choose to perform both primary and secondary research, there are a number of questions you may want to pose to help you define your research purpose. This will help you better understand who your customer is, and what that customer's needs are. For example, in your primary or secondary research, you can attempt to answer:[6]

- Who will be the likely customer for your service or product?
- What societal trends are affecting people's lives? Can you help solve problems relating to these trends?
- Where, when, and how will consumers use your product or service?
- What image do people have of the product or service?
- What is the right price to charge?
- Who are your competitors?
- What types of promotional activities could be used that will engage your audience?
- What improvements could be made to existing products or services that might entice customers to buy from you?
- What are the best methods of communication to let customers know about your product or service?

Now that you have done the research, it is time to begin writing your marketing plan. We will start this discussion in the next section.

Key Takeaways

- Prior to starting the marketing plan, market research is necessary.
- Primary research is research you do yourself, such as through surveys and personal observation, while secondary research is research someone has done for you that you must find. There are advantages and disadvantages to each type of research.
- The steps in the market research process include: Define the problem you are trying to solve, perform secondary research, perform primary research, and interpret results.

Interactive Activities

1. Using at least three secondary sources, look up market segmentation information for your chosen target market. Write two pages on why this market will need your product.
2. Create a primary research study for your target market, such as a focus group or survey. Discuss the questions you will use and how you will distribute volunteers for the activity.

4.2 Target Markets

Learning Objective

1. Explain the important factors related to segmenting your target market.

A **target market** is a particular group of customers at whom a product or service is aimed. For example, a hairstylist might focus on a target market of women, while a barber might focus on a target market of men. The importance of a target market is in the idea that no business can satisfy all market needs. We must therefore have a clear picture of where to focus our marketing efforts.

Market segmentation refers to subdividing your target market into smaller groups to better understand how the product can meet a customer's needs. Early research in this area suggests that, due to real or perceived differences in products and services, it is necessary to make different appeals to different customers in order to support a company's marketing efforts.[7] As you begin to segment your target market, you'll want to consider the following characteristics of a market segment:

- **Durable**

    The market characteristics do not change quickly. They are stable enough to identify over a long period of time. If a segment's preferences change often, this would not be considered a durable market segment.

- **Measurable**

    It is easy to define the market and therefore measure sales within the specific market segment.

- **Accessible**

    You must be able to reach the market, both in the ability to deliver a physical product and in your ability to reach the market through a variety of marketing channels. For example, a segment might not be accessible if you are unable to get the product into their hands. A hairstylist, for example, might not select a market segment of customers living two hours away, because it is unlikely that segment would drive the two hours to obtain a haircut. An accessible segment would be individuals who live closer to where the hairstylist works.

- **Different**

    Each segment should have distinct characteristics, such as age or lifestyle differences. This makes the market easier to access via marketing strategies.

- **Substantial**

    The market must be large enough to be profitable. Those within the market must be able to afford your product or service. If you are an outdoor equipment retailer, for example, you

---

target market
A particular group of customers at whom a product or service is aimed.

market segmentation
Subdividing your target market into smaller groups to better understand how your product can meet their needs.

How to Use Market Segmentation: Developing a Target Market
How to use market segmentation in your marketing plan.

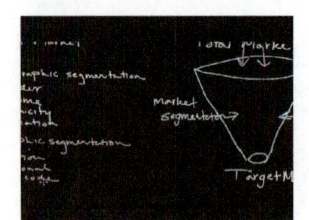

View in the online reader

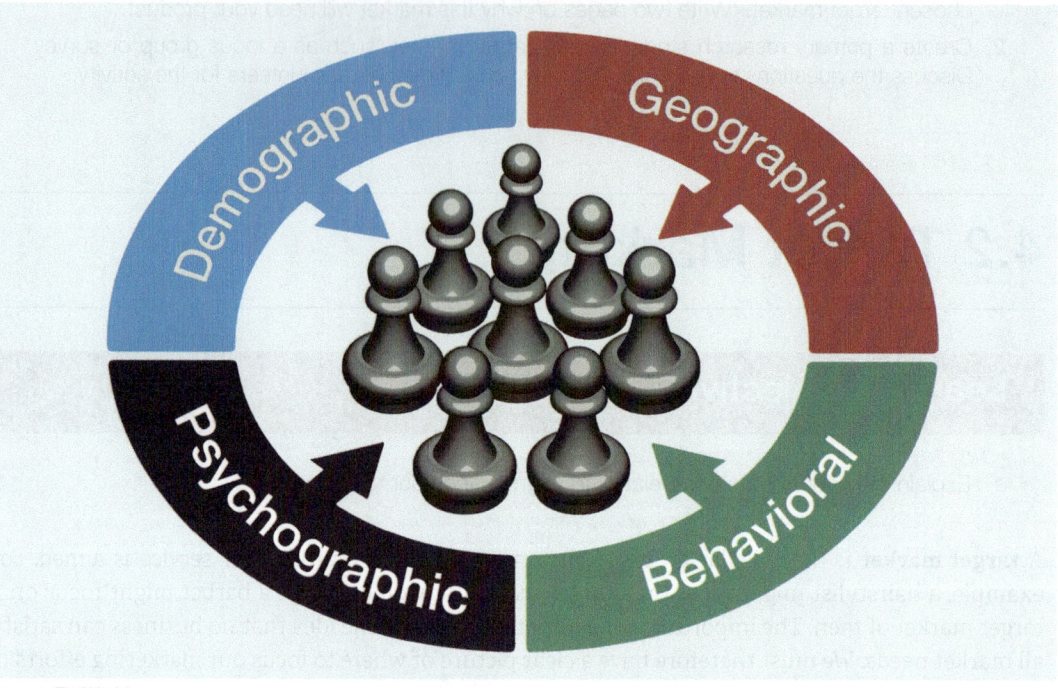

wouldn't want a market that is too specific, such as "women between the ages of 18-24, who enjoy kayaking the Wenatchee River." This segment would be far too small to be profitable.

There are several ways to define the target and segment a market. We will look at each of these.

Source: FlatWorld

Demographics

demographics
A statistical view of a population.

disposable income
The money left after one pays taxes.

discretionary income
The household income left after taxes and expenses for necessary items are subtracted.

Demographics are an important first step to determine the profile of the customer to whom you intend to market your products.[8] **Demographics** are defined as a statistical view of a population. Demographics might include:

- **Age**

    Age can be an important measure to define your target market because age often dictates what people buy. For example, 47 percent of people in the baby boomer age range rely on Cyber Monday for holiday shopping.[9] Having this information will make it easier to understand how to segment your market. Overall, understanding buying habits and needs based on age can help you more narrowly define your market. People in the same age range tend to buy similar products and services.

- **Marital status/Family status**

    Marital status and whether people have children greatly affects how they spend their money. Singles in their twenties, for example, might spend more on eating out, while singles or couples with children might spend more on groceries and childcare. Understanding family status can help narrow down who will be financially able and willing to buy your product.

- **Income levels**

    Disposable income refers to the money left after one pays taxes. For example, if a family earns $75,000 as a household, and the tax rate is 25 percent, the family's disposable income would be $56,250. Compare this to **discretionary income**, which is what the family has left to spend after paying necessary expenses. These expenses include the cost of rent or a mortgage, food, and other essentials. In this example, say the disposable income is $56,250, but yearly rent, groceries, and living expenses total $30,000. The amount left over, $26,250, would be the household's *discretionary* income. This is important, because discretionary income is the amount a household may spend (potentially) on the goods or services you sell.

- **Education levels**

    Education levels often determine how much and the types of expenditures a household makes. They are a good predictor of spending patterns. For example, in households with a master's or doctoral degree, yearly spending on eating out is $5,182, while a high school graduate spends $2,016.[10] Understanding these spending patterns is a key component to understanding your demographics.

- **Leisure activities**

    Understanding how your customers like to spend their time can be a good clue into what types or products or services you might offer to them—and how you market to them. For example, if you start a retail business that rents outdoor equipment, such as skis and snowshoes, one of your market segments might be people who ski casually four times per year.

Market segmentation often involves demographic factors.

Source: © Shutterstock, Inc.

There are many resources you can use to determine your ideal target market. One of these is the United States Census Bureau. This website allows you to look up demographic data for your county. Another useful website is the Bureau of Labor Statistics, which has significant amounts of information on consumer spending patterns.

Let's discuss how you might tie together this demographic information. Assume your business idea is to open a gym. Valuable information to know might include:

- How many people work out on a regular basis?
- What age range tends to spend the most on gym memberships?

- Do married individuals spend more on gym memberships than single people? If not, how many single people vs. married people live in my county?
- What is the average income of those who frequent gyms? How much discretionary income do they have to spend on a membership?

This valuable information is important because it helps you narrow down the type of customer who has the need and the resources to purchase your product or service.

Geographic Segmentation

Geographic segmentation refers to the division of a market based on physical location. If you open a neighborhood bar and grill in a specific neighborhood in, say, Seattle, Washington, you might consider using geographic segmentation. This means you will determine the radius of potential customers based on the location of your business. An entrepreneur might be tempted to classify everyone in Seattle as part of the geographic segmentation, which isn't realistic. Most people, for example, will not drive through traffic for forty-five minutes to reach a specific restaurant or bar unless there is something remarkable about it. Based on this, a viable geographic segment might be people who live within a five-mile radius. Or, for example, if you own a handyman service, you might only service areas within thirty miles. The advantage to this type of segmentation is that it provides a clear picture of where your customers live.

Price Segmentation

Segmenting the market based on price may be a good choice if you have more than one product offering. For example, let's assume you design and create handbags and sell them on Etsy. After understanding demographic information, you might want to offer two different types of bags at two different prices. Perhaps you offer a more expensive handbag option with more detailing, double stitching, and leather at $95. You also offer a less expensive option that consists of faux leather with less detailing for $45. This would be an example of price segmentation. You are trying to capture two different markets with the two different product offerings.

Psychographic or Lifestyle Segmentation

In this type of segmentation, you determine the attitudes, values, behaviors, emotions, perceptions, and/or the interests of your customers. For example, if you decide to start a travel business, it is likely your target market's psychographics will be people who enjoy travel. But you can further narrow down this market by utilizing other market segmentation methods discussed. For example, you may decide you will focus on adventure travel for the 35–55 age group, based on demographic factors. Then, you target the 56–75 age group, which prefers a more moderate type of travel such as cruises as opposed to adventure travel. These are two distinct markets, which you will want to approach differently with your marketing strategy. These two distinct markets are based on not only demographic segmentation (age) but also lifestyle segmentation.

Behavioral Segmentation

Behavioral market segmentation refers to the division of the market by observable behaviors when customers are making a purchase decision. This concept, created in the mid-1970s, is still an important market segmentation concept used today.[11] Examples of behavioral segmentation include:

- **Benefits sought**

    Benefits sought refers to the advantage customers expect to receive by using one product over another. If you visit any drugstore's body products section, there are products for oily skin, normal skin, and combination skin. If you search for toothpaste, you find toothpaste geared toward whitening or fighting cavities. Understanding the benefits sought allows you to create promotions that speak to customers based on benefits they wish to receive from using a product.

- **Usage rate**

    Usage rate refers to how often people use a particular product or service. Usually, they can be divided into light, medium, or heavy usage. Consider the importance of this type of segmentation to the fast-food industry. If you were to open a pizza delivery service in your town, it would be important to know how many potential customers eat fast-food on a regular basis—that is, light, medium, or heavy usage. You'd also want to know what fast food items they purchase and how often that fast food is pizza. If you live in a college town, for example, pizza deliveries are likely higher than average. As a business owner in that town, it would be important to note how much business slows during summer when college students go home. Having this information better prepares you to market your business.

- **Brand loyalty status**

    Brand loyalty status segmentation refers to how loyal customers are to a particular product. Do you purchase coffee at the same coffee stand daily or weekly? This is a good example of brand loyalty. If you do purchase coffee, you likely buy at the same place most of the time. This is why many coffee stands offer loyalty punch-cards or similar promotions to develop brand-loyal customers. If, by contrast, your service is one in which customers are focused on getting the lowest price, you would instead compete based on this segmentation rather than on brand loyalty.

- **User status**

    The user status segmentation method means you will divide customers based on whether they could be future users of your product or service, regular users, non-users, or ex-users. This way, you can better tailor marketing plans to meet the needs of each segment.

Now that we have addressed segmentation methods, we will discuss some considerations regarding the way your customers might purchase products.

Buyer Behavior

Entire books have been written on buyer behavior, so this next section will provide only a very basic understanding of buyer behavior. We will also discuss how to relate this to entrepreneurship generally and to your marketing plan specifically. The buyer decision-making process is outlined in Figure 4.2. Every time a customer purchases a product or service, that customer will go through each of these steps.

---

benefits sought
A type of market segmentation referring to the advantage customers expect to receive by using one product over another.

usage rate
A type of market segmentation referring to how often people use a particular product or service. Usually, they can be divided into light, medium, or heavy usage.

brand loyalty status
A type of market segmentation that refers to how loyal customers are to a particular product.

user status
This segmentation method means you will divide customers based on whether they could be future users of your product or service, regular users, non-users, or ex-users.

FIGURE 4.2 The Buyer Decision-Making Process

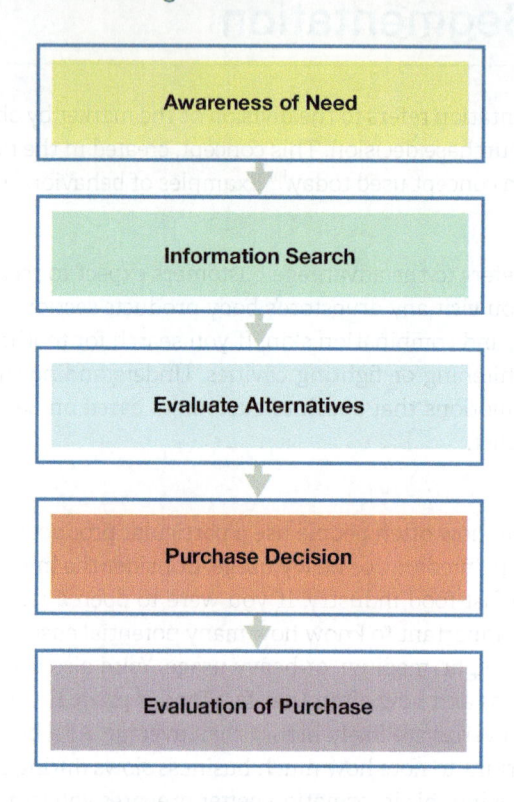

```
Awareness of Need
      ↓
Information Search
      ↓
Evaluate Alternatives
      ↓
Purchase Decision
      ↓
Evaluation of Purchase
```

Source: Laura Portolese et. al

In the first step, *awareness of need*, customers will realize they have a need for a product. Let's say it is summer and your house does not have air conditioning. If it is too hot to relax, you might decide you need a solution.

The second step is *information search*. Suppose you decide to purchase something to cool down the house. You will research your options. For example, you might consider installing central air conditioning, buying fans, or buying window air conditioning units.

In the third step, you *evaluate alternatives*. For example, you might have contractors bid on installing central air conditioning. You might also visit websites to research the cost of window units and to compare fan options. In this phase, you are examining and comparing all the alternatives.

Suppose you decide central air conditioning is too expensive and fans will just blow hot air around, so you decide on a window unit. This is the fourth phase, the *purchase decision*. You will now look for more specific information based on square footage and cost. You might also compare prices around town to determine the best value for your money. Finally, you make a purchase decision based on the specifications you've determined.

Once you buy your new window unit(s), you will feel some way about your purchase. You may be satisfied or dissatisfied. You may even write reviews noting the advantages and disadvantages of the unit. This is the final step, *evaluation of purchase*.

As an entrepreneur, understanding the phases customers go through can help you create a better marketing plan. At each stage of the buying process, you can implement a variety of marketing methods to meet the needs of your market. We will discuss these marketing methods in the next section.

Key Takeaways

- A target market is a particular group of customers at whom a product or service is aimed.
- Market segmentation involves subdividing your target market into smaller groups to better understand how the product can meet that specific group's needs.
- You can segment a market in many ways; some of the ways include psychographic, behavioral, geographic, and demographic.
- The decision-making process is important to understand in marketing, because depending how customers make buying decisions, you may want to market to them differently.

Interactive Activity

1. Do geographic research in your county using census information found here. What are the demographics of your area in terms of age ranges and marital status? Based on this information, what types of products or services might be successful in this area?

4.3 The Marketing Mix

Learning Objective

1. Implement the marketing mix into a new business.

The **marketing mix** is a tool used to help companies determine the best way to market products and services to their chosen market segment. It has been used as a basis for understanding marketing since the early 1960s.[12] There are many different types of processes to discuss the choices made. Probably the most popular is the **4Ps method**, which addresses four major components of the decision to be made: product, price, place, and promotion. This section will address each major area of the marketing mix and considerations for each.

marketing mix
A tool used to help companies determine the best way to market products and services to their chosen market segment.

4Ps method
A way to look at the marketing mix. It consists of product, price, place, and promotion.

Source: © Shutterstock, Inc.

Product (or Service)

total product concept

Both the tangible and intangible aspects of your product or service.

Ultimately, your product or service, the first P, is your business idea or concept. However, to fully explain it in your marketing plan, it should be explained in terms of the **total product concept**. The total product concept includes both the tangible and intangible aspects of your product or service. This marketing concept was first introduced in the 1980s.[13] It suggests that customers do not merely purchase a product or service. Rather, there are tangible and intangible aspects of the product that affect purchase decisions. These aspects might include:

- Size
- Shape
- The variety of colors it will come in
- Performance characteristics
- Pricing
- Branding
- Warranties
- Customer service provided before and after sale

For example, if you recently earned your cosmetology degree and decide to rent a station from a popular salon, you might address your personal skills as a colorist or stylist (performance characteristics), how you will price your products (pricing), any warranties (what happens if the customer isn't happy with a haircut or a color), scheduling and availability (customer service), and so on. When you think of a product or service, you don't want to think of it as "just a haircut" because a haircut or color is a lot more than just the specific task. It is focused on all aspects of your customers' experiences, from the moment they walk into the salon to their ability to style the haircut themselves once they are home.

As you address the product in your marketing plan, think of everything the customer will encounter, not just the product or core service itself. Discuss this in detail.

Price

Setting the price for your product might be one of the most difficult decisions, because you want to price it high enough to cover expenses and earn a profit. At the same time, you want to price it low enough to gain the interest and purchase decision of customers. There are several pricing strategies which could be used, some of them in combination:

cost-plus pricing

A process wherein you determine the cost to produce the product or service, then add a mark-up either in percentage or dollar amount.

- **Cost-plus pricing**

    Determine the cost to produce the product or service, then add a mark-up either in percentage or dollar amount. For example, assume you are a hair stylist performing a partial hair color on a client, which normally takes about two hours. You might determine the cost for you to rent the space for two hours, the cost of the actual products used, the mark-up necessary for you to earn $25 per hour. It might look like this:

    Space rental: $20

    Product cost: $10

    Labor: $50

    In total, you should charge at least $80 for the partial color when using a cost-plus pricing methodology.

- **Penetration strategy**

    With this strategy, you will charge a lower cost up front so you can gain new customers, then likely raise the price over time. With this strategy in our hair stylist example, you might be willing to earn only $15 an hour so you can gain new clients. The total cost for the color would be $60. Suppose you advertise this "special price" on social media sites and Groupon. This can be an effective way to gain new customers, but be warned: You may only gain temporary customers who are very sensitive to price. If you are trying to establish your product or service as a prestige product—one that commands a higher price—you should consider how the strategy of lower prices might influence the perception of your service or product.

- **Bundle pricing**

    Bundle pricing offers a discount to customers for purchasing more than one product or service. For example, at the hair salon, pricing for a haircut might be $40, and a color $80, for a total of $120. Using bundle pricing, the entrepreneur might charge $110 for the bundled service to encourage customers to buy both. Obviously, when implementing this option, you will want to make sure you are still earning a profit.

- **Psychological pricing**

    This encourages customers to respond to pricing based on emotional factors. Have you ever wondered why so many prices end in 9? For example, $39 or $19.99? This is called *charm pricing*, and it is proven to work. Customers will be more likely to purchase if a product ends in 9 or if the product has a sale price that shows the original price.[14] When you consider pricing your product, charging $19 instead of $20 could be a good strategy.

The key points for pricing remain true no matter what strategy or combination of strategies you choose. First, you must be able to make a profit. Second, you do not want to underprice, or have your product or service perceived as "cheap," but you also don't want to overprice to the point that your target market can't afford your product.[15] This is where primary research comes in. Ask potential customers what they'd be willing to pay for a product or service like yours to gain information to help you set prices.

Next, we will address the third P in the marketing mix, place.

> **What Would You Do?**
>
> What would you do if you determined your product or service was more costly to produce than the price for which it could be sold? What are some ways you could make changes to your plan or product to handle this situation?

penetration strategy
A pricing strategy in which you charge a lower cost up front so you can gain business, then likely raise the price over time.

bundle pricing
A pricing strategy that offers a discount to customers for purchasing more than one product or service.

psychological pricing
A pricing technique used to encourage customers to respond based on emotional factors.

Place

Place addresses where you will sell your product and how you will get the product into consumers' hands. For example, are you planning on starting an Etsy business selling your custom designed shirts for roller derby players? If so, your "place" is online. Perhaps you have an idea for a brand new product. This part of the marketing mix would address how you will physically distribute the product to customers. Will you do it through retail stores? If so, which ones? How will you sell the product to the retail stores?

Suppose you have chosen to open a brick-and-mortar business with a physical location, such as a restaurant. When you address this area of the marketing mix, you will want to address the specific location and the reasons for selecting it. In your primary research, for example, you could find that a specific location receives X amount of walk-by traffic daily. This is where you would address your reasoning for choosing that site.

Promotion

The final P, promotion, addresses how you will let your target market know your product is available for sale. Advertising, public relations and events, personal selling (one-on-one selling), direct marketing (emails and text messages) and sales promotions (special offers such as buy one get one free) are all options you can utilize in your promotions. During the COVID-19 pandemic, internet sales reached all new highs,[16] which most definitely speaks to the need for a viable promotion plan, especially in the area of social media. Most small businesses will use some mix of social media because it is more cost effective than more traditional forms of marketing and advertising.

Source: rvlsoft/Shutterstock.com

The key to promotion is to ensure the following:

- Understand your target market.
- Know what message will resonate with your audience.
- Stay consistent with your message in all marketing efforts.
- Don't discount word of mouth as an effective marketing tool.

Let's go back to our hair stylist example. How might the hair stylist develop a promotional plan? Here are some examples:

- YouTube channel informing customers of new hair trends
- Website with contact information
- Mobile application for scheduling appointments
- Facebook page sharing before and after pictures
- Twitter account to promote sales promotions specials
- Advertising on social media sites, or options such as Groupon®
- Promotional discounts if clients book an appointment before leaving their current appointment

Now that we have discussed the marketing mix, it is time to begin putting your marketing plan together. That will be the focus of the next section.

Leveraging: Using Videos in Your Business Venture

In a world that bombards you with advertising on social media websites, it takes some creativity and an understanding of your audience to get attention.

There are several types of videos you can use to build brand awareness:

- Explainer videos explain your product or service simply and demonstrate why your product or service is superior to its competitors.
- Tutorial videos explain how to use your product or service.
- About Us videos introduce viewers to your office and staff, and provide testimonials for your product or service.
- Demo videos show your product or service in action.
- Social videos bring awareness to your brand as well as your product and service.

> **How Much Does Laser Tattoo Removal Cost?**
>
> This video by Miami-based Body Details explains the advantages of laser tattoo removal.
>
> View in the online reader
>
> The Body Details video shown above (refer to "How Much Does Laser Tattoo Removal Cost?") combines characteristics from all five kinds of videos to effectively promote the Body Details brand. Using these strategies will help establish your business as an expert resource in a given area and can generate customer interest.[17] If you own a restaurant, why not take video of tonight's special and post it to social media sites to help remind customers of how much they like coming to your restaurant? The videos you create may generate new customers but may also remind past customers of your business. Both of these activities will generate revenue.

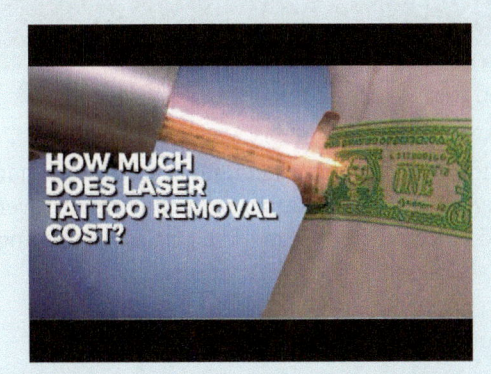

Key Takeaways

- Market segmentation, or understanding your market, is key to knowing how to best serve your customer. There are several types of market segmentation techniques that can be used.
- The 4Ps of marketing include product, price, place, and promotion. Identifying aspects of each of these in your marketing plan will help make the plan clear and concise.

Interactive Activities

1. Brainstorm ways to market your small business idea. Create at least three ideas from each area of the promotional mix: advertising, sales promotion, personal selling, direct marketing, and public relations and events.
2. Generate a list of possible goals for your marketing plan in terms of sales and the types of promotion you wish to implement. Discuss how each goal is a SMART goal.
3. Research prices of products or services that are similar to the product or service you hope to bring to market. Discuss the other pricing methods in detail. Form your own cost-plus analysis pricing formula. Will you be able to earn a profit with this pricing model? If not, what can you change to earn a higher profit?

4.4 Writing the Marketing Plan

Learning Objective

1. Write a marketing plan with all major components included.

Now that you have done the research and understand the basics of marketing your business, it is time to write the marketing plan. The marketing plan consists of several components, including situation analysis, goals and objectives, target market, pricing, marketing budget, and promotional strategies. These will all be addressed in the next sections.

FIGURE 4.3 Components of the Marketing Plan

- Situation Analysis
- Goal and Objectives
- Target Market
- Pricing and Place
- Promotional Strategies
- Budget

Source: Laura Portolese et al.

Situation Analysis

The first step to writing your marketing plan is to write a situation analysis. The situation analysis accomplishes the following:[18]

- It describes your product or service.
- It discusses the benefits of your product or service.
- It describes your main competitors, including their strengths and weaknesses.

- It determines your total product offer. What are the benefits customers will seek and what will you provide?
- It includes a SWOT analysis (refer to Chapter 9). A SWOT analysis is a detailed list of business strengths, business weaknesses, opportunities, and threats. Outlining these details allows you to see a clearer marketing picture. It also helps you better understand what you might be able to do from a marketing perspective to combat any threats while exploiting market opportunities.

FIGURE 4.4 Sample SWOT Analysis

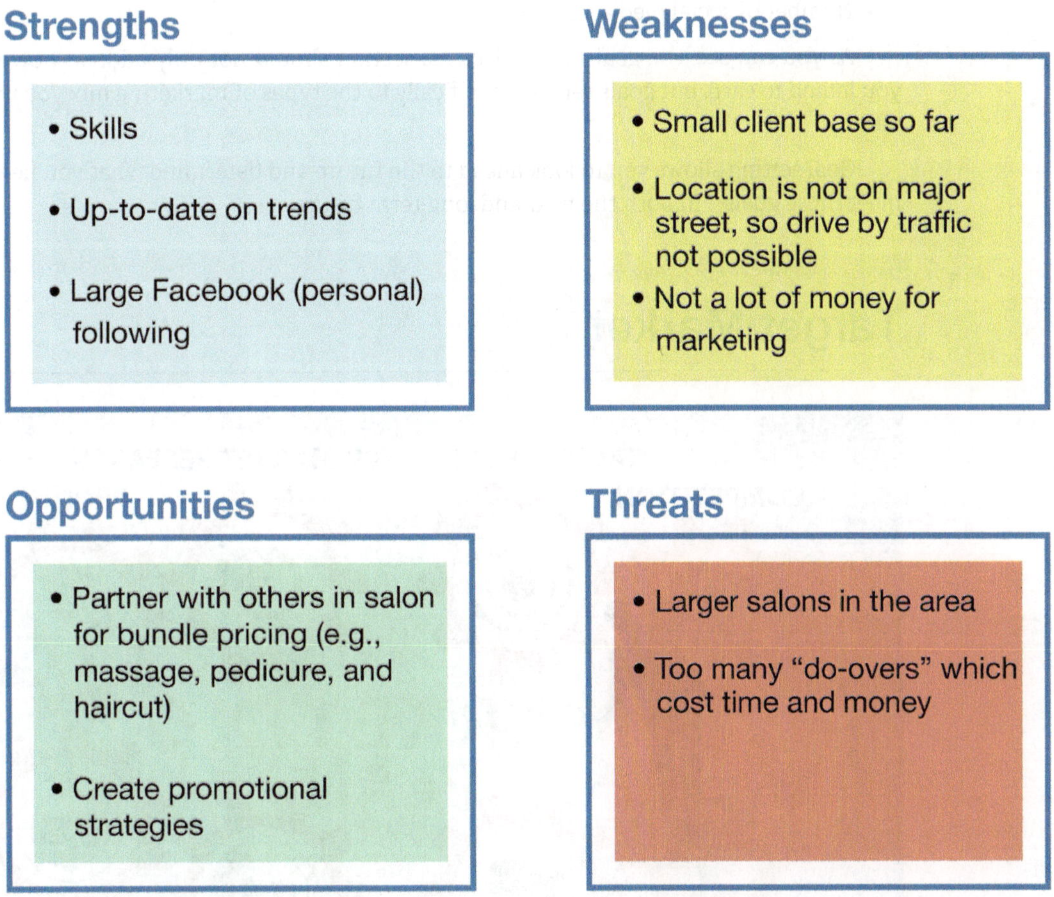

Strengths
- Skills
- Up-to-date on trends
- Large Facebook (personal) following

Weaknesses
- Small client base so far
- Location is not on major street, so drive by traffic not possible
- Not a lot of money for marketing

Opportunities
- Partner with others in salon for bundle pricing (e.g., massage, pedicure, and haircut)
- Create promotional strategies

Threats
- Larger salons in the area
- Too many "do-overs" which cost time and money

Source: Laura Portolese et al.

For an example of a situation analysis for a coffee shop, refer to this website.

Goals and Objectives

In this section, we will discuss establishing the goals and objectives of your marketing plan. What do you hope to accomplish with your marketing plan? The goals and objectives should be SMART goals: specific, measurable, attainable, realistic, and time-bound (attached to a time frame to achieve them). An example of a SMART goal might be to obtain ten new clients per month. As you can see, this goal is specific, it can be measured (did I get the new clients?) and time-bound (we hope to achieve this goal every month).

When formulating goals and objectives, consider numerical expectations for sales, such as, "Earn $2,500 per month after taxes and expenses." Other goals and objectives to include in your marketing plan might include:

- Sales dollars
- Number of units sold
- Increase customer awareness of your product or service
- Increase mix of products or services
- Return on investment on marketing expenditures
- Number of social media posts

As you can see, the goals and objectives section should not only address how much revenue you intend to earn, but goals related specifically to the types of marketing mix you intend to implement.

Goal setting allows you to look ahead to the future and determine what you need to do *now* to meet those goals—in both the near and long-term future.

Target Market

Source: © Shutterstock, Inc.

We have already discussed target markets, the importance of knowing your market, and the need to segment your market so you can better develop products that meet your customers' needs. We have also discussed creating promotional plans that will reach your target audience. In this section of the marketing plan, you will want to discuss demographics, your specific market segmentation, and all of the information you learned in your primary and secondary research. The reader should have a very clear picture of exactly the type of customer to whom you will market your product or service.

Pricing and Place

In this section, you want to address the location of your business, such as "I will sell online via Etsy and eBay." In other words, you will provide a complete rationale for why you chose a specific location (physical or online) for your business. Use some of the research we discussed in Section 1 to support your choice of location.

In this section, you will also want to discuss how you plan on setting prices. What strategy will you use to set prices? If you are using a cost-plus strategy, include how you determined your calculations for pricing. Discuss both the specific strategy chosen as well as why you picked it.

Promotional Strategies

Using the data you gathered about your target market, discuss each and every promotional strategy you intend to use. Include the time frame in which you plan to use each strategy. For example, you could say, "I will post an article on hair trends to Facebook weekly." This type of very specific promotional strategy—with a timeline attached—will assist you in planning your time and efforts accordingly. This section of the marketing plan should be a complete list of every effort you would like to implement over the first year of your business.

Budget

The last section of your marketing plan will address the marketing budget. How much do you intend to spend for marketing? List each of the promotional strategies discussed in the last section and attach an expected cost to them. While we tend to think of budgets in financial costs, consider also the *time* cost. For example, how many hours a week do you plan on spending to record videos? This time should be included as part of your budget. It can serve as a reference as to how much time you should set aside monthly or weekly for these types of promotional efforts. Also, should you choose to hire a professional marketing agency, this helps you quantify the potential cost.

As we've discussed, outlining your marketing plan in terms of goals and objectives will help you get on the right track to market your product. A marketing plan should be updated monthly and adjusted as needed. Think of the marketing plan as a moving target that will change as you learn more about your customers—and as you learn more about what is working as part of your marketing strategy.

Key Takeaway

- The major components of a marketing plan include situation analysis, goals and objectives, target market, discussion of place and price, promotional strategies, and budget.

Interactive Activity

Perform a SWOT analysis on your business, or a business of your choice. After you perform the analysis, consider how you might turn weaknesses into opportunities and discuss.

4.5 Test Your Skills: Applied Case

LaPorchea's Dog Walking and Promotion

Source: © Shutterstock, Inc.

LaPorchea Jones has always had a passion for animals, especially dogs. A few months ago, she decided to move from full time to part time at her accounting job. She was every enthusiastic when she decided to go to part-time, because she was sure she would make lots of money with her new dog-walking business. LaPorchea posted an ad on a dog walking app in order to gain clients for her new business, and didn't hear from any potential clients for several days. Finally, she gained two clients, but is concerned that this isn't enough to justify moving to part time in her position. She just thought there would be higher demand.

Upon further investigation, she's noticed there are over forty other dog walkers in her area of town alone. With high competition, and nothing to differentiate her services, she is having a hard time, and wondering if her company would let her go back to full time. However, she isn't ready to give up yet. She thinks she might need to dig into marketing a bit more in order to gain the clients she needs. Can you help her determine how to segment her market and leverage promotion to grow her new business?

1. What steps should LaPorchea have taken prior to making the decision to start a dog walking business?
2. Consider the market and the major competition. Discuss at least three ways she might consider differentiating her product from her competitors.
3. What market research might she need to perform in order to gain more clients? How would she go about doing this?
4. What are some options she should consider leveraging for promotion and what makes these the best options for this type of business?

Endnotes

1. Small Business Encyclopedia (n.d.) Entrepreneur magazine. Retrieved from: https://www.entrepreneur.com/encyclopedia/market-research
2. Entrepreneur Staff (n.d.) Conducting market research. Entrepreneur magazine. Retrieved from: https://www.entrepreneur.com/article/217388
3. Entrepreneur Staff (n.d.) Conducting market research. Entrepreneur magazine. Retrieved from: https://www.entrepreneur.com/article/217388
4. Kuhn, G. (2021, June 3) What are the benefits of market research? Retrieved from: https://www.driveresearch.com/market-research-company-blog/what-are-the-benefits-of-market-research-company-in-ny/
5. Entrepreneur Staff (n.d.). Secondary market research. Retrieved from: https://www.entrepreneur.com/encyclopedia/secondary-market-research
6. Brown, R. (n.d) Top 20 questions research can help you answer. Retrieved from: https://www.marketingdonut.co.uk/market-research/questionnaires-surveys-and-focus-groups/top-20-questions-that-research-could-help-you-answer
7. Smith, W. R. (1956). Product differentiation and market segmentation as alternative marketing strategies. Journal of marketing, 21(1), 3-8.
8. Small business encyclopedia, (n.d.) Entrepreneur Magazine. Retrieved from: https://www.entrepreneur.com/encyclopedia/demographics
9. Law, L. (2021, February 8). Baby boomer spending habits in 2021. Retrieved from: https://www.lexingtonlaw.com/blog/credit-cards/baby-boomer-spending-habits.html
10. Desjardins, J. (2019, June 10) How Americans make and spend their money by education level. Retrieved from: https://www.visualcapitalist.com/how-americans-make-and-spend-their-money-by-education-level/
11. Plummer, J. T. (1974). The concept and application of life style segmentation. The Journal of Marketing, 33-37.
12. Grönroos, C. (1994). From marketing mix to relationship marketing: towards a paradigm shift in marketing. Management Decision 32(2), 4-20.
13. Levitt, T. (1986). Marketing Imagination: New. Simon and Schuster.
14. Anderson, E.T & Simester, D.I. (2003, March). The effects of $9 price endings on retail sales. Quantitative Marketing and Economics, 1(1), pp 93-110; Poundstone, W. (2011). Priceless: the myth of fair value. New York, NY: Hill and Wang.
15. Wasserman, E. (n.d.). How to price your products. INC Magazine. Retrieved from: https://www.inc.com/guides/price-your-products.html
16. Moorman, C. & Shkil, B. (2021, May 12). How COVID-19 changed marketing. Retrieved from: https://www.cmswire.com/digital-marketing/how-covid-19-changed-marketing/
17. The European Business Review. (2020, November 24) How can small businesses leverage video marketing to grow. Retrieved from: https://www.europeanbusinessreview.com/how-can-small-businesses-leverage-video-marketing-to-grow/
18. Lorette, K. (2019, February 12). A situation analysis of a strategic marketing plan. Retrieved from: https://smallbusiness.chron.com/situational-analysis-strategic-marketing-plan-1474.html

CHAPTER 5
How Do I Perform Financial Analysis?

Case Study—Event Dynamics/Africa Dynamics

Source: Used with permission from Sandra Collier.

Sandra Collier owns a travel (Africa Dynamics) and event management (Event Dynamics) business that serves two very distinct types of clients. She is originally from South Africa and focuses one part of her business on specialty travel to Africa. The second focus of her business is working with clients to manage large-scale events that focus on various global challenges, such as clean water. The common threads in both businesses are sustainability and conservation.

Sandra freely admits that finance and accounting are not her strong suit. She had to face the fact that an accountant stole money from her by forging her name on checks. She will be the first to acknowledge that turning a blind eye to the financials is not a good thing, and while she had a hard time trusting accounting professionals after that experience, she has learned how to focus on important financial figures. For example, she examines every tour and event by requiring a margin analysis before closing out that project.

Source: Used with permission from Sandra Collier.

Sandra's business model is one in which the clients front cash for travel and events. For example, customers who travel to Africa might pay a percentage of the total costs of the trip as non-refundable deposits. These deposits are used to start booking elements of the customer's trip. When Sandra is managing an event anywhere in the world, her company is responsible for taking in registrant fees. These fees are used to pay expenses for the event. The fact that she has worked for a decade with her major client, The Bill and Melinda Gates Foundation, is testament to how well Sandra manages the budget and finances of these events.

Furthermore, Sandra has built exclusive relationships with her suppliers and clients (refer to Chapter 6). For example, she has the highest conversion rate for Wilderness Safaris—a partner she works with for South African tours and adventures. On the event side of her business, the partnership she has with The Bill and Melinda Gates Foundation is built on the financial trust she has built with them in managing the money flowing through their annual global challenges summit. These partnerships (found in Chapter 11) are the cornerstone of her success.

Source: © Shutterstock, Inc.

Ultimately, Sandra's advice for entrepreneurs is to be willing to take risks, but you must know your market and your clients. She has demonstrated that, by focusing on the relationships among suppliers, customers, and employees, you can face all of the challenges that may come your way while enjoying great success in your business.

Taking care of the finances and accounting of your small business is a crucial element of success in the marketplace. As a small business owner, you do not necessarily have to know how to make journal entries or prepare your own financial statements, but you *do* need to know what you are looking at. You must know how much money your business needs to function and how your cash flow works for your business. In other words, you need to know enough financial information, among other important elements of your business, to make appropriate decisions for the success of that business. In this chapter, we will examine funding sources and how you can estimate your needed funding. We will also look at how to read financial statements and conduct a Break-Even Analysis. Finally, we will look at how to begin writing the financial plan for your business.

5.1 Funding Source Options

Learning Objectives

1. Assess your credit worthiness.
2. Identify a funding source for your small business.

What Is Your Personal Credit Score?

Before you find and assess funding sources, you must assess your own credit. Do you pay your bills on time? Have you ever defaulted on a loan? Do you know your **credit score**?[1] While finding a funding source could be easy, getting someone to loan money to *you* might be difficult if the funding source sees you as a credit risk. Knowing your personal credit score will better prepare you for asking for financing for your business.

How does a bank or other funding source assess your ability to pay a loan? One key piece of data will be your credit score—and the credit scores of the people you may be working with on your entrepreneurial idea. Your credit score comprises data compiled on your financial history. These data points include (in order of importance and weighting in the calculation):

- **Payment History**

    Do you pay your loans and credit cards on time?

- **Amounts Owed**

    How much do you owe on loans and credit cards?

- **Length of Credit History**

    How long have your accounts been open?

- **New Credit**

    Do you have a lot of new credit?

- **Types of Credit**

    What is the breakdown of credit (how much is credit cards, loans, type of loans [e.g., car versus home])?

credit score

A three-digit rating number that gives lenders a way to asses an individual's ability to repay a loan. The credit score ranges from 300 (not good) to 850 (exceptional).

- Payment History 35%
- Amounts Owed 30%
- Length of Credit History 15%
- New Credit 10%
- Types of Credit 10%

Source: © Shutterstock, Inc.

> **credit-reporting agencies**
> Include Experian, Equifax, and Transunion.

There are three **credit-reporting agencies**: Experian, Equifax, and TransUnion. Each credit report may have a different score. One great, free resource you can use is Credit Scorecard® sponsored by Discover Card. You do not need a Discover card to sign up for this service. Credit Scorecard® uses Experian to report your credit score, giving you a glimpse into your credit worthiness.

Another way to look at your credit score for free is with Credit Karma®. The company offers a smartphone app. This website pulls your credit information from Equifax and TransUnion, so you will see both credit scores. Using Credit Karma® and Credit Scorecard® together will give you a full picture of how a bank or other funding source assesses your credit.

Finally, there is AnnualCreditReport.com. By federal law, you can request each of the reporting agencies' credit reports once a year for free. The drawback to this website is that you can only request a free credit report once a year from each agency. Your credit score can change a lot during a year, which means this is not a great way to monitor your credit.

Next, you will learn about some funding sources for starting a business, or for when you need cash for any reason.

What Are Funding Sources?

> **funding**
> The money necessary to start a business or provide money for a business project.
>
> **crowdfunding**
> Funding a project or a business venture by raising money from the public.
>
> **Small Business Administration (SBA)**
> An arm of the U.S. government that assists small businesses with financial, training, and mentoring resources.

As you consider all of the elements that it takes to start a small business, one important aspect is **funding** for your startup. Funding for initial startup costs represents the money you will need to run the business before you have sales. The Small Business Administration (SBA) has templates and links that can help you determine the amount of cash (funding) you may need for your idea.[2] Depending on your needs for cash (funds), you will consider some or all of the following:

- Can you use funds from your current job/savings and start part-time in building your business? Some businesses can be started without quitting your current job. You have likely heard many times about companies that have been started in a garage, or in the evenings after the day job ended. In these cases, extra discretionary income,[3] the money left over *after* your taxes and living expenses have been paid, can be used to fund your small business idea. Besides, until your small business takes root, quitting your job may be premature. Yes, you may be working long hours (as noted in Chapter 1), but this extra work can give you the incentive to get your business up and running so this overlap does not persist. This approach also gives you the ability to run a trial of your idea, on a limited basis, to see how the market reacts to your product and/or service.

- Have you considered **crowdfunding** sources?[4] Crowdfunding is a way of obtaining money from a large number of people. If you Google "crowdfunding," you will find various websites set up to allow you to solicit money from the public. One of the more popular websites for crowdfunding is GoFundMe. If you look for startup funding there, regardless of the amount of money you seek, provide excellent detail regarding your business plan. Offering incentives to backers can help. For example, you can offer different rewards for different levels of funding.

- Have you beaten the bushes in your social network? You never know who you know—or who *they* know—who might be willing to invest. You can ask your connections for potential customers, but you could also be connected to funding sources. Perhaps there is someone in your network who knows a good banker who has funded businesses like yours. Perhaps someone in your network knows a company whose management would be willing to invest in a small business like yours. Every person you meet and with whom you connect could hold the key to helping you secure funding. Always be prepared with an "elevator speech" about your business idea. When asked, be ready to explain how funding could help you while benefiting the investor.

- Have you considered how your customers could reverse the cash flow cycle? In many businesses, cash must be spent before it is received from sales. There are, however, some business models that get cash up front from customers before providing the service or product. For example, if you buy an airline ticket, the airline is getting the cash before you actually fly. If you can build a business that obtains cash up front from customers, your customers can front the money for your operations.

- Have you considered using your 401k? There are various companies that allow you to borrow against your 401k. An example of this type of loan can be found here at Guidant Financial's website. Guidant Financial has quite a bit of information on their website about the different options for financing a small business, with comparison charts that outline fees and penalties while comparing different financing sources.
- Have you talked with someone at the Small Business Administration? The (**Small Business Administration (SBA)** does not actually loan money to small businesses. Instead, it provides loan guidelines and loan guarantees to other organizations that loan money to small businesses.
- Have you considered family and friends? Businesses have been started out of inheritance funds or trust funds. If a friend or family member invests in your business, however, make sure you have a legal document spelling out the rights and responsibilities of those involved—including how the money will be repaid.

It is worthwhile to explore the SBA website and the section called the Service Corps of Retired Executives (**SCORE**). There you can find a mentor who, perhaps, has started a business similar to yours. The SCORE website has a great tool that will help you identify an acceptable mentor who may even live in your area.

Next, we will discuss how to estimate your funding. Other sources of funding are covered in Chapter 8.

SCORE

The Service Corps of Retired Executives, a mentoring service linked to the Small Business Administration.

Key Takeaways

- Before seeking funding sources, understand what your credit score is so that you know you are an attractive customer to a lender.
- Your credit score is easily accessed for free.
- There are many funding sources for a startup, so be clear on the money you need and why. Once you know that, you can find the best funding sources.

Interactive Activities

1. Go to any of the crowdfunding sources. Look for other entrepreneurs who are seeking funding for a business idea that is similar to yours. Provide the links to the projects and develop an assessment of what they have done well in their request for funding. What could they have done better in their pitch to the public?
2. Sign up for free credit score reporting. Assess your credit score and identify at least three strategies through which you could improve your score.

5.2 How Do I Estimate Needed Funding?

Learning Objectives

1. Identify where you can research financial information.
2. Identify necessary fixed assets versus monthly expenses.
3. Differentiate operating expenses from cost of goods sold (COGS).
4. Identify fixed costs versus variable expenses.
5. Understand your cash cycle.

In order to determine the funding you will need to start a business, you will have to understand, financially, how the business works. This means that you must understand your expected sales, the cost of those sales, and other expenses that will occur in your business. One great way to understand these costs is to assess how businesses like yours operate. You could potentially take up a part-time job in a business similar to what you want to start. You could also talk to the SCORE executives at the SBA. Also, refer to Chapter 3 to research ideas and your competition.

We will explore financial statements next to give you a conceptual framework for the financial side of planning a business.[5]

Source: © Shutterstock, Inc.

Not every business will need enormous amounts of money to start. Understanding how cash moves through your proposed business will be essential to planning out your **startup costs**.[6] Startup costs are the costs of conducting business *before* you make your first sale. These costs can include deposits, legal fees, and first and last month's rent on facilities.

Financial needs also can occur after you have started your business. Perhaps you do not generate enough cash to buy a new piece of equipment or to fund other large expenditures. Once you determine your cash needs, you will need a funding source. Funding sources are outlined in Chapter 8.

Next, we will discuss how to find financial information about companies in your selected industry. Doing this important legwork and researching the financial landscape of your industry is crucial to understanding how the business will work—and how best to fund it.

> **startup costs**
> The costs of conducting business before you make your first sale.

Where Can You Research Financial Information?

Financial information on companies can be found from multiple sources. You can find financial information on company websites and through financial analysis sites on the internet. If you are interested in starting a business of any kind, you will already have an idea of the businesses that exist in the market. The important thing is to find out if a particular company is publicly traded.

For example, maybe you want to start a consulting company that helps organizations with information technology, leadership, and organizational behavior. Perhaps you want to model your new business venture after a company like Accenture. First, you will search the internet to determine if Accenture is publicly traded and what its stock symbol is. Then you can find financial information about the company.

Source: © Shutterstock, Inc.

In order to find other companies in the industry that Accenture belongs to, visit Yahoo! Finance and look up the Accenture's stock symbol. The website includes companies that "people also watch." There will be various stock symbols there. You will find that Accenture is often compared to Cognizant Technology Solutions Corporation, Computer Sciences Corporation, and Automatic Data Processing, Inc.

You can also use the search string, "What is the NAICS code for Accenture." You will find that Accenture has a **North American Industry Classification System (NAICS) code** of 541611 and a **Standard Industrial Classification (SIC) code** of 8742. The NAICS code is a code used for gathering statistical information about similar companies in an industry. The SIC code is similar, but it is the older coding structure that was used to group businesses. The NAICS code is a more recent coding system, but some government agencies still use the SIC Code. With these codes you can search for companies that are included in that classification.

By gathering this information, you can start analyzing publicly traded companies. This will give you an idea of how the business operates financially. Even though you will not start out as large as some of these firms, the information you collect will give you a good idea of how the cash flows through the business and how revenue is generated.

> **North American Industry Classification System (NAICS) code**
> A code used for gathering statistical information about similar companies in an industry.
>
> **Standard Industrial Classification (SIC) code**
> A code similar to the NAICS. It is an older coding structure used to group businesses. Some government agencies still use the SIC code despite the prevalence of the more recent NAICS code.

Balance Sheet

A financial statement that shows an entrepreneur all of the assets, liabilities, and equity of the business.

Securities and Exchange Commission (SEC)

An arm of the United States Federal Government that enforces federal laws regarding securities traded on stock exchanges.

10-K report

Financial reports are submitted to the Securities and Exchange Commission (SEC). The report contains a great deal of information about how a company operates.

asset

An item of value to the business—cash, Accounts Receivable, inventory, or buildings and equipment.

fixed asset

An item purchased for a business that has a long-term life expectancy of more than a year and which costs more than $5,000.

Find the following data for each company: (1) the annual profit and loss statements, (2) the annual **Balance Sheets**, and (3) the 10-K filed annually to the **Securities and Exchange Commission (SEC)**. The SEC enforces federal laws regarding securities traded on stock exchanges. The 10-K is a description of the financial picture of a company. You can learn much about a company by reading its **10-K report** and the financial data presented in the company's financial statements. (The 10-K report is submitted to the SEC and explains the business in relation to the financial statements.)

Next, we will discuss fixed assets, monthly expenses, and where to find this data on the company's financial statements.

How Do I Identify Fixed Assets and Monthly Expenses?

Any business that requires expensive equipment or other high-cost items to operate will often need a larger up-front investment. For example, if you wanted to start a food truck business you would have to consider how you would actually pay for the food truck, which can amount to a great deal of money in startup costs. You may want to consider getting a loan for this **asset** (something you purchase that has an ongoing value to the business). From a finance perspective, you would consider this food truck to be a **fixed asset**,[7] which is an item that you buy that has a life expectancy of more than one year and a cost of more than $5,000. Instead of paying, say, $150,000 upfront for the food truck, you might be able to secure a loan for twenty years at 6 percent interest. You would have a monthly payment on the food truck for $1,074.650.

FIGURE 5.1 Elements of the Loan Payment

20 years

6% interest

$150,000

= $1,074,650

Source: Laura Portolese et al.

The payment would then be considered a **monthly expense**, an expense that occurs on a regular payment schedule. It could be easier to raise twelve months of food truck payments for your startup costs (for a total of $12,895.80 for the first year, or $1,074.65 times twelve), rather than the full $150,000. Take heart, though. Not every business requires a large upfront investment of money. You do, however, need to know of any initial startup costs to be covered.

A word of caution: Your startup costs are not all fixed assets. You can pay for buildings, equipment, and land over a long period of time. By contrast, salaries, rent, and other monthly expenses must be paid at the time those expenses are incurred. In other words, if you want to make a salary of $250,000 in your business, you will have to pay that in the year incurred, according to whatever pay schedule your company uses for payroll. You cannot take that $250,000 and expense it over twenty years because it is not a fixed asset. Next, you will learn how to identify operating expenses versus cost of goods sold (COGS).

You will find fixed assets on the Balance Sheet. As you study your company and industry financial information, you will look for the section called "Assets." After the "Current Assets" will be listed the long-term assets. You will likely *not* find a line item called "Fixed Assets." Instead, you may see a line item called "Property, Plant, and Equipment" (refer to Figure 5.2).

> **monthly expense**
> An expense that occurs on a regular payment schedule.

FIGURE 5.2 Fixed Assets on the Accenture (ACN) Balance Sheet

Balance Sheet All numbers in thousands

Period Ending	8/31/2020	8/31/2021	8/31/2022
Current Assets			
Cash and Cash Equivalents	4,905,609	4,360,766	4,921,305
Short-term Investments	2,875	2,448	2,602
Net Receivables	6,222,399	5,725,424	6,395,154
Inventory	-	-	-
Other Current Assets	845,339	611,436	585,381
Total Current Assets	11,976,222	10,700,074	11,904,442
Long-term Investments	198,633	45,027	66,783
Property, Plant, and Equipment	956,542	801,884	793,444

Source: Laura Portolese et al.

It is important to review the 10-K for the company to see how they describe the equipment they purchase, when they purchase it, etc. Your experience with a company similar to the one you wish to start is vital here. A 10-K report does not contain all of the information you might need to know. Rather, it gives you a general sense of how they invest in equipment, buildings, and land. Next, you will turn to finding the monthly expenses. The monthly expenses are on the profit and loss (P&L) statement (or Income Statement). You are looking for a section called "Operating Expenses" (refer to Figure 5.3).

FIGURE 5.3 **Monthly Expenses on the Accenture (ACN) P&L**

Income Statement All numbers in thousands

Revenue	8/31/2020	8/31/2021	8/31/2022
Total Revenue	34,797,661	32,914,424	31,874,678
Cost of Revenue	24,520,234	23,105,185	22,190,212
Gross Profit	10,277,427	9,809,239	9,684,466
Operating Expenses			
Research Development	-	-	-
Selling, General, and Administrative	5,466,982	5,373,370	5,401,969

Source: Laura Portolese et al.

The monthly expenses that it takes to run a business are included in a line item called "Selling General and Administrative" expenses. There are *many* different kinds of expenses here. Search through the 10-K for explanations of what is included in this line item on the Income Statement. It may include salaries, rents, utilities expenses, legal expenses, and other items.

You are basically looking for as much detail as you can find in what companies disclose in their 10-K documents to validate your own thinking concerning the expenses of the business. More importantly, you are looking for trends over time. You want to make sure you understand the business model from a *financial modeling* point of view.

Next, you will learn about the difference between operating expenses and the cost of goods sold.

How Do I Differentiate Operating Expenses from the Cost of Goods Sold?

cost of goods sold (COGS)
Costs, for a business, that are directly associated with producing a product or service.

There are business costs that are directly associated with producing a product or service. These are called **cost of goods sold (COGS)**.[8] For example, if you run a food truck business that makes sandwiches (product), the bread used for the sandwiches would be the cost of producing the sandwiches. If you run an information technology consulting business, any of the consultants you place on-site with a customer will be a cost (salaries) of providing that service. Cost of goods sold in service businesses largely involve the cost of employing the people who execute those services.

To find cost of goods sold, examine the Income Statement. Look at the very top and the second line item will be the Cost of Goods Sold (this may also be called "Cost of Revenue"). Refer to Figure 5.4.

FIGURE 5.4 COGS on the Accenture (ACN) P&L

Income Statement   All numbers in thousands

Revenue	8/31/2020	8/31/2021	8/31/2022
Total Revenue	34,797,661	32,914,424	31,874,678
Cost of Revenue	24,520,234	23,105,185	22,190,212
Gross Profit	10,277,427	9,809,239	9,684,466
Operating Expenses			
Research Development	-	-	-
Selling, General, and Administrative	5,466,982	5,373,370	5,401,969

Source: Laura Portolese et al.

Again, you want to review these numbers in conjunction with reviewing the 10-K of the company. You will get some good information about the cost of goods sold. You are looking for *when* a company recognizes revenue. Different products and services can have very different revenue streams. It's important to recognize those revenues and corresponding expenses.

There are also costs of running the business that occurs regardless of the production of goods or services. For example, there may be marketing costs, legal fees, and even accountant fees to keep the books. These costs are called **operating expenses**.[9] In the previous section, you were shown where the operating expenses are on the Income Statement. Ask yourself: Why would the monthly expenses and operating expenses be in the same spot? It all comes down to timing differences and the purpose of the cost.

For example, costs of production are recognized at the time a product is sold. Regular operating expenses, on the other hand, have to occur in the period the cost occurred. This is why they are separated into different line items on the financial statements.

Next, you will learn about the difference between fixed and variable costs in a business.

operating expenses
The costs of running the business that occur regardless of the production of goods or services.

How Do I Identify the Fixed Costs of My Business vs. the Variable Expenses?

fixed costs

Costs that occur regardless of how much or how little a business produces. An example would be the business owner's salary.

variable costs

Costs that go up or down as production increases or decreases. An example would be the raw materials used in production.

Fixed costs are *not* tied to how much you produce in products or services.[10] For example, you will pay rent, or pay off a loan, regardless of how many products or services you sell. **Variable costs** are costs that *are* associated with producing your product or service.[11] These costs can include raw materials, the cost of labor, and the costs of production machinery.

It matters a great deal how many fixed costs your business has. These costs must be minimized wherever and whenever possible. Why? Because these expenses must be paid even if you have no production and make no sales. Consider the COVID-19 crisis and the fact that many small business had to shut down. Because of this, variable costs were lower because business owners didn't need to order supplies or pay employees. However, fixed costs, such as the cost of rent or a loan, were still present.

Next, you will learn how to determine your cash conversion cycle.

How Do I Determine My Cash Cycle?

In finance, you must know two fundamental things:
- How do I use cash in my business?
- How long does it take me to generate cash in my business?

Cash is generated in two ways:
- Converting inventory into sales.
- Converting those sales to cash.

Businesses can sink a lot of money into inventory. This means inventory must be sold as quickly as possible. At the same time, once you make a sale, you want that sale to turn into cash as quickly as possible. Inventory turnover is calculated by taking the cost of goods sold number from the Income Statement and dividing by the average inventory from the Balance Sheet. (Understand, however, that this calculation is for any business that actually carries inventory. Service businesses may not have inventory.) Here is the formula:

$$\text{Cost of Goods Sold} / ((\text{Inventory Period One} + \text{Inventory Period Two}) / 2)$$

Refer to "How to Calculate Inventory Turnover" to understand how to calculate inventory turnover. This is how you measure how quickly you turn inventory into sales:

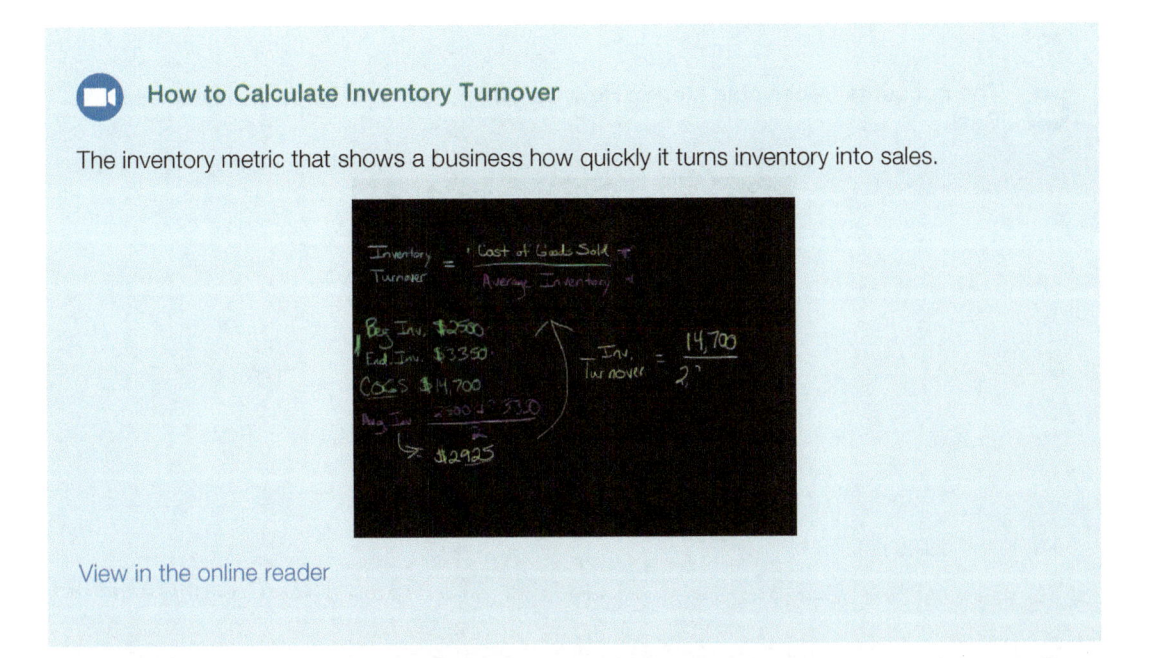

How to Calculate Inventory Turnover

The inventory metric that shows a business how quickly it turns inventory into sales.

View in the online reader

Once you know the inventory turnover rate, then you can also determine the number of days it takes to convert your inventory into cash. This is what is called the **Days Sales in Inventory** metric.[12] The formula is as follows:

365 days in a year / Inventory Turnover Rate

In addition to the inventory turnover, once you make a sale, you may or may not be paid in cash upfront. If your business is one in which you invoice your customers, you will also want to measure how quickly you turn receivables into cash. Any time you make a sale on an invoice, the transaction should automatically create an entry to **Accounts Receivable**.[13] Accounts receivable is an account that temporarily holds the dollar value of money owed to you. You want to make sure this money converts into cash as quickly as possible.

Receivables turnover can be calculated for any business. The calculation uses Revenue from the Income Statement divided by the average accounts receivable from the Balance Sheet. Here is the formula:

Revenue / ((Accounts Receivable Period One + Accounts Receivable Period Two) / 2)

Days Sales in Inventory

The number of days it takes to convert your inventory into cash.

Accounts Receivable

The amount of money on your Balance Sheet that represents how much your customers owe you for products and services the customers have purchased.

Refer to " The Accounts Receivable Metric: How Quickly a Business Turns Receivables into Cash" to see how this is calculated:

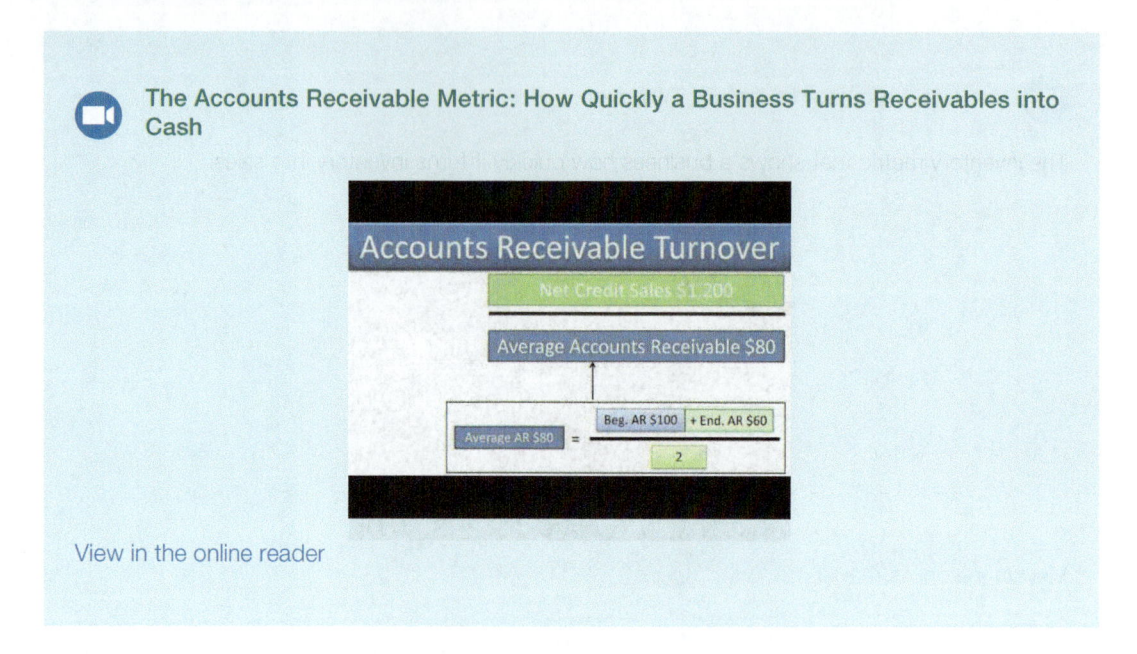

> **The Accounts Receivable Metric: How Quickly a Business Turns Receivables into Cash**
>
> Accounts Receivable Turnover
> Net Credit Sales $1,200
> Average Accounts Receivable $80
> Average AR $80 = (Beg. AR $100 + End. AR $60) / 2
>
> View in the online reader

Days Sales Outstanding (DSO)
A metric used to tell you how many days it takes for your company to turn receivables into cash.

terms
Granted by vendors/suppliers for credit (e.g., you must pay invoices within thirty days).

Accounts Payable
The amount on the Balance Sheet that represents how much you owe to your suppliers.

Days Payable Outstanding (DPO)
Determines how many times in a year you use cash to pay suppliers.

Once you know your accounts receivable turnover rate, you can turn that number into the number of days it takes for your company to turn receivables into cash. This is what is known as the **Days Sales Outstanding (DSO)** metric.[14] The formula for this metric is as follows:

$$365 \text{ days in a year} / \text{Accounts Receivable Turnover Rate}$$

Finally, one of the most significant uses of your cash will be the money that you pay your vendors. As a business owner, you will want to pay attention to the **terms** granted to you by your suppliers. If a vendor gives you thirty days to pay an invoice, accounting software will keep track of the amounts you owe and cut checks on the appropriate day of the month.

Payables Turnover can be calculated for any business (although service businesses can present some challenges). The calculation uses cost of goods sold from the income statement divided by the average **Accounts Payable** from the Balance Sheet. Accounts payable is the amount of money that is owed to your suppliers. Here is the formula for payables turnover:

$$\text{Cost of Goods Sold} / ((\text{Accounts Payable Period One} + \text{Accounts Payable Period Two}) / 2)$$

Once you have the accounts payable turnover calculated, you will then know how many times in a year that you are using your cash to pay suppliers. Now, you can take the accounts payable turnover number and determine how many days on average you are using that cash. This is known as the **Days Payable Outstanding (DPO)** metric.[15] This measure is calculated as follows:

$$365 \text{ Days in a Year} / \text{Accounts Payable Turnover Rate}$$

Refer to "The Accounts Payable Metric: How Quickly A Business Uses Money in Paying Suppliers" to see how this information can be assessed for your business:

> **The Accounts Payable Metric: How Quickly A Business Uses Money in Paying Suppliers**
>
> Liked This Video And Want More?
>
> View in the online reader

> **What Would You Do?**
>
> Your potential business partner thinks it is a great idea if the new business venture simply adopts a policy of paying vendors late—up to a week after the vendor terms. Your partner thinks that very few vendors will complain.
> 1. What ethical problems does this create?
> 2. Who would be harmed and who would benefit from instituting such a practice?
> 3. Would you adopt this practice? What choices do you have in addressing the idea?

Ultimately, your **cash conversion cycle** can then be calculated. The cash conversion cycle measures how well you generate and use cash in your business. Understanding your cash conversion cycle is important because you want to make sure you are getting money *into* the business before you are paying money *out* of the business. The calculation for cash conversion cycle is:

$$\text{Inventory Turnover (DSI)} + \text{Accounts Receivable Turnover (DSO)} - \text{Accounts Payable Turnover (DPO)}$$

cash conversion cycle

A calculation that helps you to see how quickly you turn inventory into sales, how quickly you turn receivables into cash, and how effectively you manage the money you owe your suppliers. This is a critical concept for business owners.

Consider "Applying the Cash Conversion Cycle", which examines the cash conversion cycle of Amazon:

Applying the Cash Conversion Cycle

View in the online reader

Next, you will learn about how to read financial statements.

Key Takeaways

- Understand how you will set up your business for a solid cash flow. The more you pay attention to how cash is generated and used in your business, the more successful you can be.
- Pay attention to your accounts receivable, inventory, and accounts payable. These accounts are critical in making sure your cash flow works for the business.

Interactive Activity

1. Find an accountant that works with small businesses. Talk to them about how to assess a profit and loss statement for the variable versus fixed costs and perform an analysis of a company you would like to start.

5.3 How Do I Read Financial Statements?

Learning Objectives

1. Read and interpret an Income Statement.
2. Read and interpret a Balance Sheet.

3. Read and interpret a cash flow statement.
4. Hold people accountable.

As you work through this section, find a company similar to the one you are creating. Visit its website. For example, if you are thinking of opening a coffee shop, visit Starbucks' website and locate its financial statements. Search for an "About Us" link and/or an "Investor Relations" link. Here you will likely find PDF downloads of the financial statements, including the 10-K.

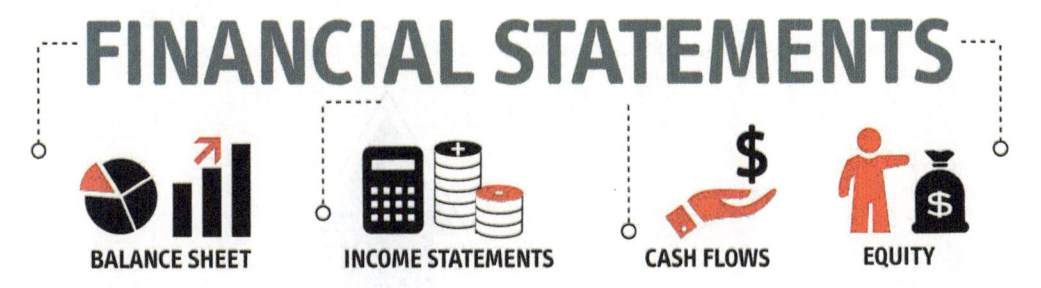

FINANCIAL STATEMENTS

BALANCE SHEET · INCOME STATEMENTS · CASH FLOWS · EQUITY

Source: © Shutterstock, Inc.

Income Statement

The **Income Statement** is an *estimate* of profit or loss.[16] Very often, you will hear accountants refer to the Income Statement as the profit and loss statement or the P&L. An estimate is made because it is usually expensive to identify exactly every cost that goes into producing a product or service. For example, can you identify exactly how many kilowatts of electricity one machine uses versus another? Companies often have to trade off the costs of "tracing" costs to products and may decide to estimate certain costs for each product. This section will examine the items on the Income Statement that often have the most activity: Revenue, Cost of Goods Sold, and Operating Expenses.

Income Statement
The estimate of the profit or loss of a company for a given period. The major sections of the financial statement to understand are Revenue, Cost of Goods Sold, and General, Selling, and Administrative accounts.

Revenue

The first line on the Income Statement is the value of the **revenue** (or sales) recorded for the company in a given period (example, a calendar month).[17] There are two important concepts to remember when it comes to revenue. One is *when* revenue is recognized in a business and the other is that revenue does not always mean you received cash. Let us explore these ideas just a bit more.

Revenue recognition is important because it affects your cash flow. Consider Starbucks and how it generates cash. One way the company generates cash is to sell products in a store. For example, when a person goes in and buys a coffee, Starbucks receives cash or a credit card payment. In a cash sale, at the time revenue was recognized, the company also received cash. In a credit card sale, it may take a few days for the transaction to be converted into cash.

revenue
The sales a company has transacted in a given period.

FIGURE 5.5 The Timing of Sales: Cash Sale

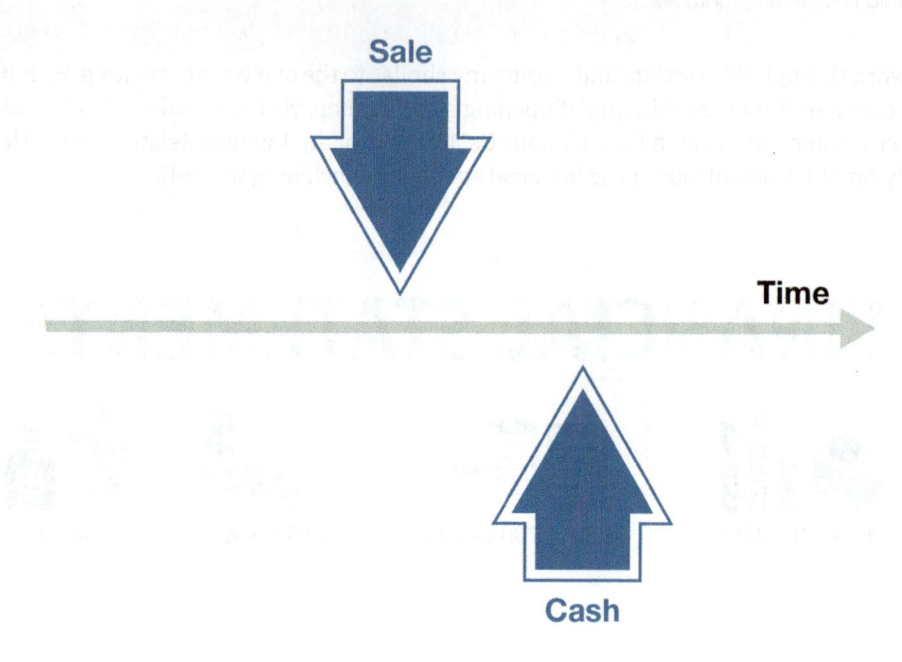

Source: Laura Portolese, et. al

Starbucks also sells bulk coffee to companies like Costco, Alaska Airlines, and HMS Host. These customers will be invoiced for the sale. The date of the invoice is when revenue is recognized, but cash may not come until thirty days later or more (depending on the terms given to the customer by Starbucks).

FIGURE 5.6 The Timing of Sales: Credit Terms

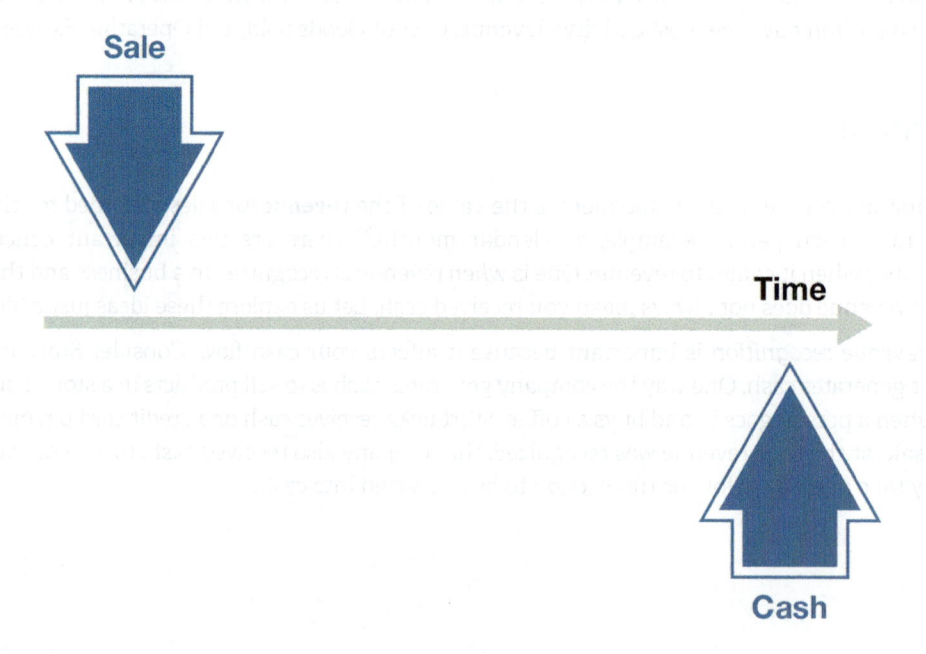

Source: Laura Portolese, et. al

In addition, in the age of gift cards, Starbucks receives cash *before* it actually makes sales. This means it is receiving cash before any revenue is recorded. According to one source, for the period

September 2014 through September 2015, Starbucks received $15 billion in cash through gift cards.[18] Many large companies use gift cards. Even if your company does not, you may include some sort of gift certificate program. The cash generated from these gift certificates would work the same way.

FIGURE 5.7 Cash Coming in Upfront Before a Sale

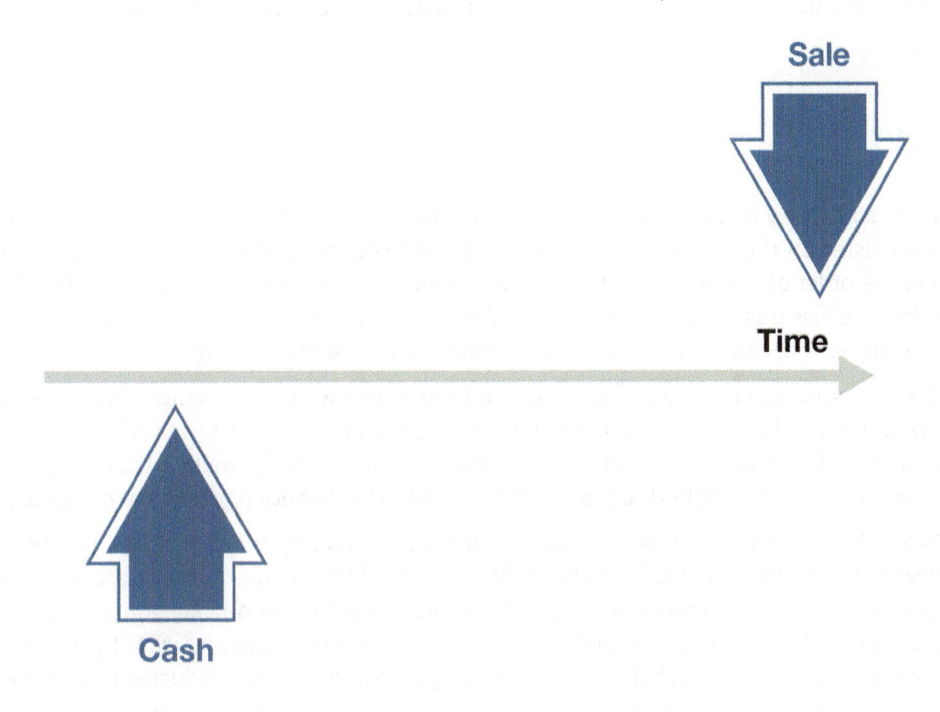

Source: Laura Portolese, et. al

Cost of Goods Sold

The next line on the Income Statement is Cost of Goods Sold.[19] This line represents the direct costs that it takes to produce the goods and services your business sells. If you are a manufacturer, this line will represent the money that it takes, directly or indirectly, to produce your product.

Companies that have production as part of their business will often have a separate building that houses the production and warehousing facilities. The costs of maintaining and running those buildings and machinery are the costs that are part of the "Cost of Goods Sold" line on the Income Statement. For a consulting or services company, the costs of running that job or project will be the costs of goods sold. In the case of a food truck, your business has a stock of ingredients in the truck, as well as utensils, paper napkins, etc., used to make the food you sell. All of those costs would be represented in your cost of goods sold.

Operating Expenses

Another section of the Income Statement represents the operating expenses. The largest account that is usually in this section is called **General Selling and Administrative Expenses**.[20] These expenses cover salaries of different groups that are not production-related. Various other expenses that have to do with running the business are also included. For a small business, it is vitally important to understand the breakdown of these costs so that they do not get out of hand.

Next, you will learn about the Balance Sheet.

General Selling and Administrative Expenses

The expenses that occur for a business that are not directly traced to the cost of a product/service.

Balance Sheet

While the Income Statement looks at one reporting period and provides an estimate of the profit and loss, the Balance Sheet is a different tool. It lists all of the company's assets, liabilities, and equity.[21]

Assets

cash conversion
The order of how long it takes for the account to be turned into cash.

There are some very common assets that most businesses will carry on the Balance Sheet. The assets are listed on the Balance Sheet in the order of **cash conversion**.[22] In other words, they are listed in the order of how long it takes for the account to be turned into cash. Therefore, "cash" is listed first because it is already in the "state" of cash (this can include "cash equivalents," which are often securities that can be turned into cash within a short period of time).

The next account on the list of assets would be Accounts Receivable, which represents the cash you are waiting to have paid to you from customers who have credit terms with your business. Depending on the terms you have given your customers, you could be waiting thirty days or longer to receive the cash. You will find Accounts Receivable on the Balance Sheet in the Assets section.

inventory
The value of the raw materials that are used to produce a product, or the product that your business is holding to resell.

Next, the Balance Sheet would list the amount of money your business has tied up in **inventory**.[23] If your business sells products through a production process or you are reselling products, you will carry an inventory. It is very important to know how quickly you are turning your inventory into sales so that cash is not being tied up in inventory unnecessarily. If you have inventory that is not moving, then that inventory is not generating sales or producing products for sale. This means your money is not working most efficiently to generate cash flow. Inventory is found on the Balance Sheet in the Assets section.

Finally, all of the cash, Accounts Receivable, and inventory you have on hand could be turned into cash in less than a year. However, you could hold assets that have a "life" that is longer than a year. For example, you could own a building, land, or machinery. These assets help you to generate revenue but do not turn into cash. The account you might see on the Balance Sheet for these assets would be "Fixed Assets" or "Property, Plant, and Equipment."

On the other hand, a service business likely won't carry inventory. A service business will have cash and potentially will have accounts receivable. As you research your company's industry, you will find out exactly what you would expect to see on these financial statements.

Liabilities

Liabilities represent everything the business owes to suppliers, lenders, employees, and—in some cases—customers. One of the larger liabilities that can be found in this section is accounts payable. When you buy services and products, a supplier will give you credit terms. After your company has received the invoice, this will be entered into your accounting software and the vendor will be paid on the date that the money is due to be transferred (either by check or by electronic funds transfer). Accounts payable is listed in the Liabilities section of the Balance Sheet.

notes payable
The balance of money owed to lenders and creditors on the Balance Sheet.

In addition, a business can borrow money. If you do borrow money, it is very likely you will see a **Notes Payable** on the Balance Sheet.[24] There could be a notes payable account in current liabilities and a notes payable in long-term liabilities, too. The reason for this is that the amount due in the current year is a current liability. Often, a note can represent the mortgage on a building, which would be paid for fifteen to thirty years. In other words, the liability can span a period of time longer than one year.

Further, you can have **Taxes Payable** and **Wages Payable**.[25] These amounts are those dollars that are associated with payroll. Most accounting software can run payroll ahead of when the checks need to be cut. The payments are held on the Balance Sheet until they are actually paid to the employees or to the taxing authorities. All of these different payables will be on the Balance Sheet; however, they may be combined. Thus, you have to be careful in reading the financial statements. This is where the 10-K helps a great deal, because if it is a PDF file, it will be searchable for terms.

Finally, if your business sells gift cards or gift certificates, you would have an account called **Unearned Revenue**.[26] This represents the amount of money you have received for revenue you have not actually earned yet. A gift card or certificate is a promise to provide a product or service to a customer at a later date. Until that product or service is actually transferred to the customer, the dollars have to sit in the unearned revenue account. Unearned revenue, if it exists for a company, will be in the Liabilities section of the Balance Sheet.

Equity

For a small business just starting out, the Equity section of the Balance Sheet will likely only represent the **Retained Earnings**.[27] This is the amount of profit or loss, over time, that your business has generated. Every Income Statement, when it is produced, creates a profit or a loss. Every period, these "earnings" (positive or negative) are moved to the Balance Sheet into the retained earnings account. In the end, retained earnings show how profitable your business has been over time.

Eventually, if your business grows to where you start to sell stock in your company (referred to as *incorporating*, which we will cover in Chapter 11), the retained earnings balance would be the only equity you would represent on the Balance Sheet. In addition, if your business grows to be that big, you will likely have a fourth financial statement prepared: the **Statement of Equity**.[28]

Next, we will revisit the opening case.

Revisit the Opening Case

In the opening case study (refer to "Case Study—Event Dynamics/Africa Dynamics"), you were introduced to a small business that specializes in two distinct services: high-end African travel and event planning. This company is an interesting study in the timing of revenue recognition.

On the Africa Dynamics travel side of the business, a customer will often pay an initial deposit for a trip to Africa. On a trip that costs $20,000, a customer may put down a $10,000 deposit. That deposit is *not* revenue yet. Until the person actually travels, this amount of money becomes an "Unearned Revenue," or a liability on the Balance Sheet. Now, for the business, this is money that can be used to start paying the expenses of the trip. Therefore, as the business collects money from the customer, and is paying for the hotels, guides, air travel, and other experiences, the company is using the clients' money to make those arrangements. As these arrangements are paid, the expenses are considered "prepaid" and will be sitting on the Balance Sheet as well.

Anything that the company pays for the client to travel is a "Prepaid Expense." Thus, all of the money being paid for the client, and the deposits given by the client to the company, are being held on the Balance Sheet. When the trip is completed, the company transfers all of the "Unearned Revenue" to "Revenue" and all of the "Prepaid Expenses" to the "Cost of Goods Sold" lines of the Income Statement. This process can take six months from the first time a client calls and books a trip. All of these trips have a markup of 10 percent to 30 percent and that markup is then recognized as gross profit.

In addition, the Event Dynamics event planning side of the business goes through a similar process. Many clients have Event Dynamics process all of the participant registrations for large

---

taxes payable
Taxes owed to various levels of government.

wages payable
An amount of money that must be paid to employees.

unearned revenue
The amount of money that represents products or services owed to customers.

retained earnings
The balance of the profit and loss that has been moved from the Income Statement to the Balance Sheet each period.

statement of equity
A financial statement that outlines all of the equity in your business. This includes retained earnings and any stocks that are offered by the company.

events. The company can use that money to hire vendors to assist with the event (like catering services). In addition, Event Dynamics receives the sponsorship money as well to pay for expenses of putting on the event. Finally, the company will bill these clients a management fee for the time spent planning and managing the event. All of this revenue and expense will be kept on the Balance Sheet, just as for the Africa travel business, until the conference or event is completed. At that time, the revenue and expenses will be recognized on the Income Statement.

This is why timing issues are so important to both revenue recognition and cash flow. Both sides of the case study business must have a healthy number of clients. Salaries and expenses occur every month, so cash flow must be steady enough to cover those expenses.

Next, you will learn about cash flow statements.

Cash Flow Statements

cash method of accounting
The method of accounting that records transactions only when cash has been exchanged.

accrual-based accounting
The method of accounting that records transactions even if cash has not been exchanged.

In a new company, financials are often based on a **cash method of accounting**.[29] What this means is that your checking account for your business is the driver behind building your financial statements. Therefore, any cash flow analysis would basically be "money coming in" and "money going out." This is easy enough to understand because it is how most of us conduct our personal financial accounting.

However, once you start to grow and need to have a more formal accounting structure, you may move to an **accrual-based accounting** procedure.[30] In this case, you will likely need a cash flow statement. When a cash flow statement is produced, it shows you how your business has "generated" cash and "used" cash through operating, financing, and investing activities.

Operating Activities

When you are looking at the operating section of the cash flow statement, Operating Activities represent the money that has been generated or used in the operations of the business.[31] Money can be generated or used through buying and selling inventory, creating and reducing Accounts Receivable, or creating and reducing accounts payable.

Financing Activities

Financing activities are when a company borrows money from a bank or from investors.[32] For example, as you grow, you may need the funds for a building and you may decide that you want to obtain the cash through offering a bond issue. You might also go to a bank and obtain a mortgage for the building. Any cash generated from these activities would be shown in this section of the statement.

Investing Activities

Finally, as you start to have more cash on your books, you may want to move some of the cash into investments.[33] Because a company can generate larger amounts of money, it can get much better rates of return on investments in securities than the average person can. Furthermore, if you have cash sitting around, you can invest in securities that earn a respectable interest rate until the time you need to convert those securities into cash.

Entrepreneurs must determine how much cash they will need on hand to pay bills and cover current costs. They may have more cash on hand than is required to cover these. Rather than having it sit and earn no interest, it can be invested in securities as a way of earning some return on the cash on hand.

Next, you will learn about accountability—and how to interact with your accountant.

Accountability

Even though you, personally, may not be creating your financial statements, you must always know your financial information. While your bookkeeper or accountant can help explain your financial information, you must insist that they help you to control that information. *As a business owner, you are personally responsible for your financial information.*

One of the best things you can do when hiring a bookkeeper and/or accountant is to ask how they plan to educate you on financial information. This can include sitting with you on a regular basis to go through the financial statements, making sure that you understand what each account represents, and giving you a solid appraisal of your financial picture.

In addition to this, your bookkeeper and/or accountant should help you to make sure that controls are in place for your books. For example, no adjustment to your financial statements should be done without you knowing what the adjustment is and why it is being made. Accountants can write journal entries to adjust balances and make corrections to accounts. Any time an accountant writes one of those entries, someone other than the accountant should see it and sign off on it. The documentation should be saved for an audit trail. One way you can insist this happens is to get a monthly report of all of the journal entries created (they should all be uniquely numbered). Review all of these with the bookkeeper/accountant.

There are many different controls that can be implemented. Having this conversation early and often with your bookkeeper/accountant is vital to the long-term viability of your company. There are many websites and other resources dedicated to financial controls, such as the one found here.

Familiarize yourself with financial controls. Charges of fraud are not merely a setback; they might be a problem your business cannot overcome. Here are some examples of fraud perpetrated on small businesses. Do not be one of those entrepreneurs who ignores financial responsibilities. Even if it is outside your comfort zone, make it a priority to understand, over time, how the finances of your company work.

Next, you will learn about the break-even analysis.

Key Takeaways

- Remember, an Income Statement is only an *estimate* of profit or loss.
- Be sure you hold your accountant/bookkeeper accountable. They should be advising you of how quickly you are turning inventory into sales, how quickly you are converting receivables into cash, and how quickly you are paying your suppliers.

Interactive Activity

1. Research the companies in your industry, where you will compete for business.
    a. Google publicly traded companies that exist in your selected industry.

b. Go to Yahoo! Finance's website and find the stock symbol for that publicly traded company.
c. Pull the financial information you can find on the Yahoo! Finance website.
d. Go to the company website and seek other financial information that may be in the "About Us" or "Investor" sections of the website. The SEC 10-K is the important document to download. If you have access to EGAR, you can obtain the 10-K from there as well.
e. Prepare your financial analysis of key line items on the Balance Sheet and Income Statement.
f. Examine the cash conversion cycle.
g. How does this analysis change your financial plans or funding requirements for your business?

5.4 How Do I Perform A Break-Even Analysis?

Learning Objective

1. Conduct a Break-Even Analysis.

Identify Your Fixed and Variable Costs and the Price of Your Product

Break-Even Analysis

A calculation that uses the price of your product/service, the fixed costs, and the variable costs to determine at what quantity you would have to produce/sell to meet those costs.

The break-even point is an essential calculation you must perform to validate your financial assumptions about your business.[34] For example, you may think that you can produce and sell 500 units of product a month. What if the break-even calculation tells you that you need to produce and sell more than that in order to break even? (Refer to Chapter 4 concerning how to set prices for your product/service.) The **Break-Even Analysis** tells us at what point our sales would equal our expenses. Any sale beyond that point adds to your profitable bottom line.

In a previous section of this chapter, we discussed fixed and variable costs. Consider Table 5.1 below.

TABLE 5.1 Sample of Costs

Category	Payment Basis	Cost
Rent	Monthly	$5,000.00
Wages	Monthly	$10,000.00
Benefits	Annually	$50,000.00
Insurance	Quarterly	$5,000.00
Raw materials	Per unit	$7.00

Category	Payment Basis	Cost
Packaging	Per unit	$3.00
Labor	Per unit	$15.00

Consider, also, that the sales price per unit is $50. What would be the break-even?

Fixed costs would be:

$$= \text{Rent } (\$5{,}000 \times 12) + \text{Wages } (\$10{,}000 \times 12)$$
$$+ \text{Benefits } (\$50{,}000) + \text{Insurance } (\$5{,}000 \times 4)$$
$$= \$60{,}000 + \$120{,}000 + \$50{,}000 + \$20{,}000$$
$$= \$250{,}000$$

Variable costs would be:

$$= \$7.00 + \$3.00 + \$15.00$$
$$= \$25.00 \text{ per unit}$$

Plug the Information into the Break-Even Formula

The formula for break-even calculation is:

$$\text{Break-Even Quantity} = \text{Fixed Costs} / (\text{Price} - \text{Variable Costs})$$

Using the information provided, the result is as follows:

$$\text{Break-Even Quantity} = \$250{,}000 / (\$50 - \$25)$$
$$= \$250{,}000 / \$25$$
$$= 10{,}000 \text{ units}$$

Remember that these 10,000 units would be an *annual* production figure. You should ask yourself if this is feasible. Can you produce 833 units per month *and* sell that many? This is why the break-even point is so important.

Finally, if you want to achieve a certain level of profit, you can use the break-even for this calculation as well. Your formula would look like this:

$$\text{Quantity} = \text{Fixed Costs} + \text{Desired Profit} / (\text{Price} - \text{Variable Costs})$$

Using the data from before, if you want to achieve a profit of $50,000, then you would need to produce and sell:

$$= \$250{,}000 + \$50{,}000 / (\$50 - \$25)$$
$$= \$300{,}000 / \$25$$
$$= 12{,}000 \text{ units}$$

Therefore, instead of producing and selling 833 units a month, you would have to produce and sell 1,000 units in order to achieve a $50,000 profit. With the information you have gathered about your business, you can now move on to how this information can be used to build the business financial plan.

A major consideration many companies had in the COVID-19 crisis is that when you have a drop in sales, fixed costs like rent on a commercial space can be a huge expense obstacle in staying afloat financially. The company profiled in the beginning case, Event Dynamics, was challenged in COVID-19 because a part of the business was travel related services. Revenue dropped significantly. The business was paying several thousand dollars a month for a small business space and the owner decided to go virtual until business picked up. This move definitely improved their break-even point with the drop in sales.

Next, we will be putting this together and discuss how to build your financial plan.

Key Takeaway

- A great way to check your operational and financial projections is to calculate your break-even quantity through a Break-Even Analysis.

Interactive Activity

1. Prepare a Break-Even Analysis for a company that you would like to start.

5.5 How Do I Write a Financial Plan?

Learning Objectives

1. Write a financial plan.
2. Evaluate a bookkeeper/accounting partner.

How to Write the Financial Plan

bookkeeper
An accounting professional who enters the day-to-day financial transactions of the business.

Writing a financial plan, by yourself, may not be the best course of action, especially if accounting and finance are not in your skill set. However, this does not mean that you should not engage with the process of planning your business finances. In this section we will assume that you will engage a **bookkeeper**/accountant to help with developing your budgets, financial statement projections, and Break-Even Analysis.

Before you start your business and look at funding options, talk with an accountant to help you with this section. The important contribution you will make to this process is to help your accountant understand your business model. You will need to give the accountant an idea of the products or services you sell, who your customers would be, and how the customers would pay you for your products and services.

An important piece of information will be how long you think you will have to operate without a sale. Some businesses are financed at the start with extra cash already on hand. If you have salaries to pay long before you make sales, you will need to estimate your startup costs. After that, your accountant will help you to flesh out the financial section of your business plan.[35]

This part of the business plan includes all of your projections for startup costs (if applicable), your financial assumptions, and your projected financial statements over several years. If you have done your homework on other sections of the business plan, you will have an excellent idea of your financial assumptions. For example, if you understand how your product differs and you have done your homework on the market demand (as discussed in Chapter 4), you should have a decent idea of how much you can sell over time. If you require machinery to produce your product, with the specifications of that product in hand, you should know how much product you can produce. If you sell services, you should know how many people you will need to fulfill the roles they play for your clients.

Expect to spend quite a bit of time with your bookkeeper/accountant to go through all of the information in the business plan and project out all of the financial requirements of the business. It will be time well spent.

Next, you will learn how to select and evaluate an accounting partner.

How to Evaluate Your Accounting Partner

Leveraging: Finding Accounting Resources

There are two accounting professionals you will have to consider hiring as part of your team (either as direct employees or as contractors). One professional is the bookkeeper, or the person who runs your accounting software, runs your payroll, pays your vendors, and processes other accounting transactions for your business.

The other accounting professional will be a Certified Public Accountant (CPA). This person will help you with taxes and other financial planning for the business.

Review this article as a resource.

Task: Using Google, develop a list of questions to assess the qualifications of a bookkeeper or accountant (CPA) for your business.

You may already have expertise in the financial aspects of the business you want to start. If that is the case, you may complete this section of your business proposal. However, you do not necessarily have to know how to put together budgets and financial statements. This is where an accountant makes a great partner for your business.

You must first understand the difference between a bookkeeper and an accountant. An accountant may be a **Certified Public Accountant (CPA)**. A CPA is a professional designation that gives an accountant the ability to give accounting advice in the United States. Even though a CPA can be expensive, you will definitely want a good one to handle your personal and business taxes. It is wise to use a CPA for overall strategic direction with the finances of your business.

The bookkeeper, on the other hand, will be the person who keeps your books. Think of this role as *transactional processing*. There are all kinds of transactions that occur in a business. These must be recorded in accounting software that produces financial statements. A good bookkeeper can do these for you and will be cheaper, by the hour, than a CPA.

Once you understand the difference between the two resources, you will then want to prepare questions for the hiring/contracting process. Here is a list of possible questions to ask a bookkeeper:

- Have you worked with a business like mine? If so, how?
- How do you communicate financial information that aids decision-making in the business?
- Explain your experience with _____ (fill in the blank) accounting software.
- What do you enjoy about being a bookkeeper?

Certified Public Accountant (CPA)

A professional who helps a business with financial strategy and who will often help the business and the business owners with taxes.

Beyond these questions, you may want to ask behavioral questions, such as asking them how they would handle a given scenario. Finally, you may want to consider asking the candidates technical accounting questions to see how they respond. For example, you could ask about year-end reporting that needs to be done for taxes.[36]

When hiring a CPA, you will ask similar behavioral questions and background questions, but there are certain questions that will be pertinent only to the CPA. For example:

- Have you worked with clients like me?
- How do you help a client save on taxes?
- How do you respond to clients? How long does it take you to return a phone call?
- How are your fees calculated?[37]

If, for any reason, you decide to forego using an accountant's expertise, you will have to consider whether you have the expertise to keep your books on your own. Given the financial and legal trouble in which you might find yourself, obtaining the help of a professional may be the better choice.

Key Takeaways

- Even if you do not have accounting and financial expertise, learn as much as you can so that you can check your bookkeeper/accountant.
- Finance is the life blood of your business!

Interactive Activities

1. In the United States, the Small Business Administration offers financial training. Search this website to find a course on accounting, funding, or other topics from this chapter. See how the SBA can help you as an entrepreneur.
2. One way to hire a bookkeeper is to talk to someone at the Small Business Administration or at a company like Accountemps. Accountemps is a division of Robert Half. The company has people whom they contract out to small businesses to help you with keeping your books. See if there is a local office near you at this website. Talk to them about what they can offer a small business.
3. SCORE has financial templates located here. Download one of the templates and assess the template for "concepts I know" versus "concepts I do not know." Develop a plan concerning how you will learn the items you do not know.

5.6 Test Your Skills: Applied Case

A Handyman Story

Ron has always been handy with tools doing small home improvement jobs and repairs. A few months ago, his condo associate knew he had these skills and asked him to bid on the maintenance contract for the condo development. He bid on it and won the contract.

Not too long after taking on the project, he started the business and hired a couple of extra hands to help him out as work ebbed and flowed. However, he was constantly being surprised by taxes and other costs that go into running a business. He was smart and hired a new bookkeeper that helped him to understand that the hourly rate you pay for payroll is not all of the costs that you have to be aware of in setting revenue rates to your customers.

As he worked with the new bookkeeper, he found out that the employer has to pay into Medicare and Social Security. This is an extra cost to the employer that the employee's wages do not cover. He also discovered that sales tax is not something he took into account when setting his prices to the client, nor did he account for it as an expense he had to pay to the state tax authorities. Plus he had business and occupancy (B&O) taxes that he did not account for in his presentation to the condo association.

Consider this data:

- He is charging the client $60 an hour.
- Ron, when he does pay himself, pays himself at $40 an hour.
- He is paying his assistants $25 per hour.
- B&O taxes are 4 percent of gross revenue.
- Sales Tax is 10 percent of gross revenue.
- Employer Medicare and Social Security Tax is 6.5 percent of gross wages.

1. How can you avoid the mistake Ron made in not knowing his costs?
2. What sources could help you identify these kinds of costs for your business?
3. How much money is Ron potentially losing with this client?
4. What can Ron do if the client is not willing to entertain a change in the hourly rate for services?

Endnotes

1. Bankrate.com (n.d.), What is a credit score? Retrieved from: http://www.bankrate.com/finance/credit-cards/what-is-a-credit-score.aspx
2. Small Business Administration (n.d.), Funding request. Retrieved from: https://www.sba.gov/starting-business/write-your-business-plan/funding-request
3. Rakoczy, C. (2021). What is discretionary income? Retrieved from: https://www.thebalance.com/what-is-discretionary-income-5116501
4. Johnson, S. (2021). What is crowdfunding? Retrieved from: https://www.businessnewsdaily.com/4134-what-is-crowdfunding.html
5. SBA (n.d.). Calculate your startup costs. Retrieved from: https://www.sba.gov/business-guide/plan-your-business/calculate-your-startup-costs
6. Berry, T. (n.d.). How to estimate realistic business startup costs - 2021 guide. Retrieved from: https://articles.bplans.com/estimating-realistic-start-up-costs/
7. CFI (n.d.). Fixed assets. Retrieved from: https://corporatefinanceinstitute.com/resources/knowledge/finance/fixed-assets/
8. Accounting Tools (2021). Cost of goods sold definition. Retrieved from: https://www.accountingtools.com/articles/2017/5/4/cost-of-goods-sold
9. CFI (n.d.). Operating expenses. Retrieved from: https://corporatefinanceinstitute.com/resources/knowledge/accounting/operating-expenses/
10. Accounting Tools (2021). Example of fixed costs. Retrieved from: https://www.accountingtools.com/articles/what-are-examples-of-fixed-costs.html
11. CFI (n.d.). Variable costs. Retrieved from: https://corporatefinanceinstitute.com/resources/knowledge/accounting/variable-costs/
12. CFI (n.d.). Days sales in inventory (DSI). Retrieved from: https://corporatefinanceinstitute.com/resources/knowledge/modeling/days-sales-in-inventory/
13. Accounting Tools. (2021). Accounts receivable definition. Retrieved from: https://www.accountingtools.com/articles/2017/5/7/accounts-receivable
14. CFI (n.d.). Dales sales outstanding (DSO). Retrieved from: https://corporatefinanceinstitute.com/resources/knowledge/accounting/days-sales-outstanding/
15. CFI (n.d.). Days payable outstanding. Retrieved from: https://corporatefinanceinstitute.com/resources/knowledge/accounting/days-payable-outstanding/
16. Stobierski, T. (2020). How to read and understand an income statement. Retrieved from: https://online.hbs.edu/blog/post/income-statement-analysis
17. Schneir, J. (2021). Revenue versus profit: what's the difference? Retrieved from: https://www.caminofinancial.com/revenue-vs-profit-whats-the-difference/
18. Wattles, J. (2015). Starbucks set a record gift card sales. CNN Money. Retrieved from: http://money.cnn.com/2015/12/22/news/companies/starbucks-christmas-gift-card/index.html
19. Accounting Tools. (2021). Cost of goods sold definition. Retrieved from: https://www.accountingtools.com/articles/2017/5/4/cost-of-goods-sold
20. CFI. (n.d.). SG&A. Retrieved from: https://corporatefinanceinstitute.com/resources/knowledge/accounting/what-is-sga/
21. CFI. (n.d.). Balance sheet. Retrieved from: https://corporatefinanceinstitute.com/resources/knowledge/accounting/balance-sheet/
22. Shpak, S. (2018). What is the correct order of assets on a balance sheet? Retrieved from: https://bizfluent.com/info-8346862-correct-order-assets-balance-sheet.html
23. Jenkins, A. (2020). What is inventory? Types, examples, and analysis. Retrieved from: https://www.netsuite.com/portal/resource/articles/inventory-management/inventory.shtml
24. Accounting Tools. (2021). Notes payable definition. Retrieved from: https://www.accountingtools.com/articles/what-are-notes-payable.html
25. Lumen Leanring. (n.d.). Payroll accounting entries. Retrieved from: https://courses.lumenlearning.com/finaccounting/chapter/entries-to-accrue-salaries-and-taxes-for-employees/
26. Accounting Tools. (2021). Unearned revenue definition. Retrieved from: https://www.accountingtools.com/articles/what-is-unearned-revenue.html
27. Accounting Tools. (2021). Retained earnings definition. Retrieved from: https://www.accountingtools.com/articles/what-are-retained-earnings.html
28. Accounting Tools. (2021). Statement of shareholders' equity definition. Retrieved from: https://www.accountingtools.com/articles/what-is-a-statement-of-shareholders-equity.html
29. Accounting Tools. (2021). Cash basis of accounting definition. Retrieved from: https://www.accountingtools.com/articles/what-is-the-cash-basis-of-accounting.html
30. Accounting Tools. (2021). Accrual basis of accounting definition. Retrieved from: https://www.accountingtools.com/articles/what-is-the-accrual-basis-of-accounting.html
31. Accounting Tools. (2021). Operating activities definition. Retrieved from: https://www.accountingtools.com/articles/what-are-operating-activities.html
32. Accounting Coach (n.d.). What are some examples of financing activities? Retrieved from: https://www.accountingcoach.com/blog/financing-activities-cash-flow-statement-2
33. CFI. (n.d.). Cash flow from investing activities. Retrieved from: https://corporatefinanceinstitute.com/resources/knowledge/accounting/cash-flow-from-investing-activities/
34. Ali, R. (n.d.). What is break-even analysis and how to calculate it for your business. Retrieved from: https://www.netsuite.com/portal/resource/articles/financial-management/break-even-analysis.shtml
35. Wasserman, E. (n.d.). How to write the financial section of a business plan. Retrieved from: https://www.inc.com/guides/business-plan-financial-section.html
36. Casarez, R.A. (n.d.). Top 13 questions to ask when hiring a CPA for your business. Retrieved from: https://www.proadvisorcpa.com/blog/top-13-questions-to-ask-when-hiring-a-cpa-for-your-business
37. Tyndall, G. (2018). How to interview bookkeepers for your business. Retrieved from: https://www.thebalancesmb.com/interview-questions-to-help-you-find-the-best-bookkeeper-14085

CHAPTER 6
How Do I Write an Operational Plan?

Case Study—Herbfarm

Carrie Van Dyck and Ron Zimmerman joined Bill and Lola Zimmerman's retirement hobby Herbfarm in Fall City, WA. Starting with a five-year budget, Ron and Carrie expanded various aspects of the business—a nursery, retail, mail order, manufacturing, educational experiences, and other events. At the center of this expanding offering was a true farm-to-table dining experience that was sold out months in advance. The philosophy of their dining experience is found in how the food is prepared. They believe that "no dish can be better than its ingredients" and that "the best ingredients are usually local."

Source: Used with permission from The Herbfarm.

In 1986, a fire broke out and destroyed the original restaurant, but did not destroy the Herbfarm spirit. The management of Herbfarm spent two years trying to work through the permitting process of the county to rebuild in Fall City, Washington. Eventually, to avoid bankruptcy, the plan to rebuild in Fall City was abandoned. Herbfarm moved to Woodinville, Washington, which was rapidly becoming a wine mecca in the Pacific Northwest.

The new location for the restaurant was built on a business plan. This time around, Ron and Carrie needed investors to re-open in Woodinville. The investors were rewarded with dining credits for the restaurant. There are several wineries near the restaurant, not to mention the foot traffic of the Willows Lodge Hotel and Spa. When patrons visit for the first time, they cannot help but talk about the nine-course meal experience to family and friends.

The Herbfarm focuses on local sourcing for ingredients and products for customers' dining experience. In the many years since the fire, The Herbfarm continues to garner accolades from around the world, including an award for #1 destination restaurant in the world from National Geographic Traveler. It is clear that local, fresh ingredients and a focus on the smallest details culminate in a unique dining experience. The Herbfarm shows how vision and attention to detail can create unmatched customer satisfaction.

> The Herbfarm has its own five-acre farm and serves nine-course meals that are matched with wine, beer, or herbal botanicals. Menu themes change every few weeks with the rhythm of the land and sea as seasons change. One of the exquisite dining experiences of The Herbfarm is the 100 Mile Dinner, in which all of the ingredients are sourced within one hundred miles of The Herbfarm. The 100-mile dining experience includes a local farm that is raising wheat for this dinner.

As we discussed in Chapter 5, understanding your operations cycle is crucial to understanding the cash flow of your business. Entrepreneurs have gone out of business through failing to understand their operating cycle and how that relates to their cash flow.[1] In this chapter, we will review important aspects of your operations plan, including location, facilities and equipment, employees and insurance, and how to manage your suppliers.

6.1 Location

Learning Objectives

1. Assess the best headquarters location for your business.
2. Assess the best location for a manufacturing operation.

How to Assess Your Needs for a Location

A good location helps customers access your products and services (see also Chapter 4). Entrepreneur.com gives you some elements to think about, including:[2]

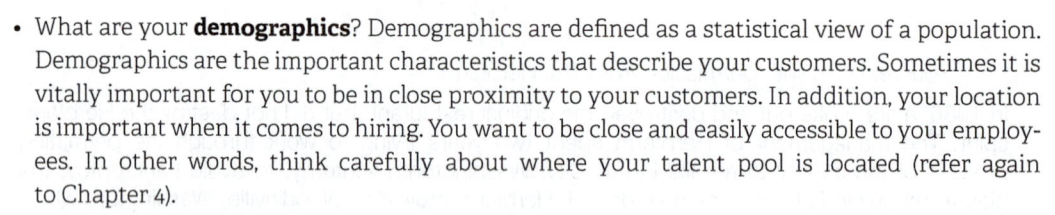

- What is your style? Are you laid back or formal? Do you need an actual brick and mortar store or will a kiosk suffice?
- What are your **demographics**? Demographics are defined as a statistical view of a population. Demographics are the important characteristics that describe your customers. Sometimes it is vitally important for you to be in close proximity to your customers. In addition, your location is important when it comes to hiring. You want to be close and easily accessible to your employees. In other words, think carefully about where your talent pool is located (refer again to Chapter 4).
- Do you require **foot traffic**? Foot traffic means that your ideal customers would be walking by your business. This is often of great importance to a retail business. If you have confidentiality concerns (e.g., a counseling office) for your customers, you may not want to be too visible.
- How easily can a customer access your business? One important thing to consider is to watch the location at different times of the day to see how people come and go. Is there any activity that would irritate customers (for example, the only way to get into an office building is trying to turn across traffic). If there is any kind of challenge in accessibility, you can lose customers fast. Furthermore, how easy will it be for suppliers to deliver product? That could also cause you problems that you want to avoid.
- Is there competition nearby? This can be a good thing or a bad thing. For example, if you are a small coffee shop, it might actually be a boost to your business to be close to a very busy Star-

Source: © Shutterstock, Inc.

demographics
A statistical view of a population.

foot traffic
Comprises potential customers who will be walking by and discovering your business.

bucks location. Coffee customers do not like to wait in long lines and you can obtain customers by acting as an alternative in a busy location.

Choosing a Location

View in the online reader

- What kinds of businesses would be around you? Assess the **clientele** (customers) that go to the businesses near your location. They may be ideal customers for your business. Secondly, if there are local services nearby that can make your employees' lives easier, you may have the perfect location.
- What image will the location convey? For some businesses, being in a town's historical district is vitally important. Others might be better served by locations near sporting venues, and so on.
- What legal ramifications are connected to this location? Be sure to check in with local authorities, including city hall, to find out what **local ordinances** could affect your business. Zoning laws, for example (regulations governing commercial versus residential property) may affect your business. You may also need certain permits for your business.
- Is the building ready for your business? Some older buildings, while they have a lot of old world charm, may not have the electrical capacity for businesses today. Depending on your technical needs, some older buildings may not work for your business without a significant amount of upgrade money. This should be considered part of your start-up costs (refer to Chapter 5).
- What other costs should you consider? For example, will you have to pay utilities? Are these included in your rent? Contact your utility providers to see the history of what the utilities cost. In some locations, you may have to consider how much it costs to park and whether you will pay for that for your employees.

Your location is a reflection of your business. Make it easy for your customers and suppliers to find you and make it easy for employees to come to work every day. The more you pay attention to these details, the more likely you are to set up your business for success. Working with a commercial real estate agent is recommended. Make sure the agent is well versed in local zoning laws, too.

Next, we will examine various considerations in selecting a manufacturing location.

clientele

The customers of a business.

local ordinances

The local laws, rules, and regulations that apply to businesses.

Source: Patrick Poendl/Shutterstock.com

Selecting a Manufacturing Location

manufacturing operations

The part of the business that produces product(s).

tax incentives

May be provided by local and state governments to reduce tax liabilities and encourage businesses to open in certain locations or make certain products.

If your business will have **manufacturing operations**, where you will be producing products, there are some additional considerations in choosing a location. The manufacturing location may or may not be a completely separate location. Your headquarters and manufacturing locations may be in separate states, for example. Some of the key components to consider in selecting a manufacturing location are:[3]

- What layout will you need? In manufacturing, it is important to consider the layout of the facility (Refer to this link to familiarize yourself with different layouts that you may want to consider.) Included in this assessment is the amount of warehouse space to house raw materials, packaging materials, machinery, and space to hold finished products. Consider, as well, the amount of money it takes to make a location work for you. These costs would need to be considered in your start-up costs (refer to Chapter 5).

- Who will you employ to work at the location? Often, manufacturing sites are located in rural areas because of the cheaper labor pool available. That can have some drawbacks, however. For example, does your production require highly technical skills? It may be hard to find the personnel you need in a very rural area. Considerations like these will influence where you locate your manufacturing facility.

- Can you take advantage of **tax incentives**? Local and state governments can save a business money on taxes by granting tax incentives. Find out from the local government if there are tax incentives associated with opening a location in the area. For example, you could be given tax credits to reduce your tax bill by setting up in a location that is in an underdeveloped area (or one subject to an urban renewal project).

Your initial location might be in your home or garage. As you grow, you may need a more visible site to enhance your credibility. Regardless of where you are located, make it easy for your clientele to find you and work with you.

Next, we will look at the facilities and equipment for your business.

▶ How to Choose a Location for a Restaurant

View in the online reader

Key Takeaways

- Spend an appropriate amount of time assessing the best location for your business.

- Operations are crucial to understanding the cash flow of your business.
- Understanding your customer will help you select a successful location.

Interactive Activity

1. Navigate to your local city hall's website. Find out which department handles city ordinances. Talk to someone there about your business—and which local ordinances may affect it.

6.2 Facilities and Equipment

Learning Objectives

1. Assess how much space is required for your location.
2. Assess equipment needs for your location through buying or leasing.

Depending on the business you build, you may operate out of your home, or you may need more space than a home office can provide. Even if you start at home, as your business grows, you may need to expand into a different location.

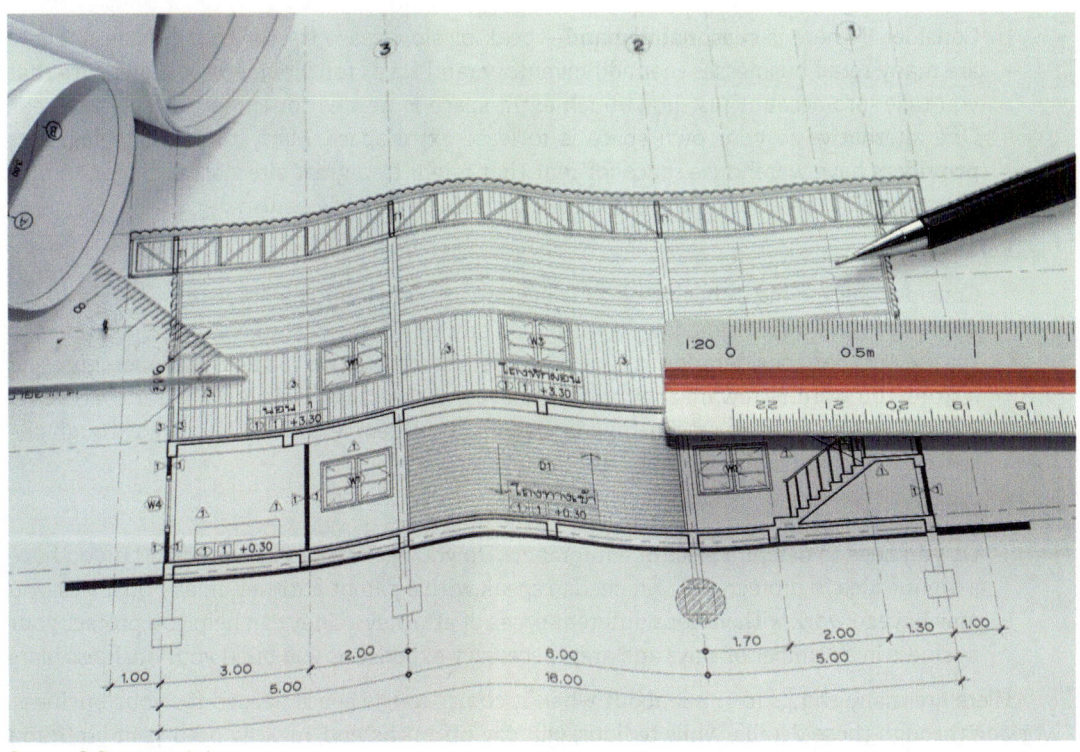

Source: © Shutterstock, Inc.

Space Requirements

There are several things to consider when estimating space required for your facilities. You must consider not only what you need *now*, but also how the space will handle the *future* growth of your business.[4]

- **Inventory considerations**

    Many businesses, even service businesses, may carry **inventory**. These are the products needed to maintain your equipment or the products used in producing whatever you sell. You will need to consider, at your current level of sales, how much inventory you have to carry in order to meet demand. How much space does that inventory occupy? For example, let's say that in a given month your demand for a product is 2,000 units. Those 2,000 units require 4,000 units of inventory. That is how much inventory you would need on hand, at a minimum. The dimensions of these products (the raw materials and the finished goods) will need to be calculated to determine if you have enough space. In addition, you want to make sure that you know how quickly your inventory moves (for inventory turnover calculations refer to Chapter 5). If your inventory moves well, you could have space left over for the future growth of your business. It then becomes important to have a solid projection of the growth of your business in order to assess how long you may (or may not) be able to remain in a particular location.

- **Materials movement considerations**

    If you have a warehousing and/or manufacturing facility, you will need to consider the movement of materials. You must have adequate capacity to receive product. Depending on the space required to handle trucks or railroad cars coming into the facility, there could be a "traffic jam" of materials and suppliers trying to get into your space.

- **Seasonal demand**

    Consider if there is **seasonal demand**— peak or slow seasons—for your business. There are many retail businesses that add inventory (and staff) for the holidays. Make sure that you take into account just how much extra space is needed for those times of the year. One alternative to your own space is to lease extra space. Many **third party logistics providers** have warehouse space for rent that might be a great alternative. To get an idea of how one of these services could help you, check out Penske Logistics.

- **Retail**

    Consider the buying behavior of your customers. How will customers enter your store? Are they bombarded immediately with "buy, buy, buy?" Are customers welcomed into the space? Another consideration is that customers tend to move to the right when entering a store. You want to reward that impulse; have eye-catching displays ready for that movement. You also want to establish wide aisles so that people can easily move through the space.[5] Here is a helpful website on retail layouts.

- **Patents**

    Do you need to patent a piece of equipment? Do you need to patent a product? If you have a unique idea to protect, you will need to speak with a patent attorney. In any business, you may have to work with various different types of attorneys. They can help you protect your business in a number of ways and are a necessary expense as you build your business plan.

There are many things to think about when it comes to the space needed for your business. Working through these details, while tedious, will pay off in the end, making both your staff and your customers happy.

---

inventory

The products you carry for maintaining equipment and the products you carry for production of your products (or for resale).

seasonal demand

Customer demand for product that varies at different times of the year, such as during the holiday season.

third party logistics providers

Companies that provide warehouse space for product inventory. They also provide shipping and fulfillment services.

Assessing Equipment Needs for Your Location Through Buying or Leasing

One of the things to consider with equipment and property is whether you will buy or lease.

Leases, depending on your situation, can be very attractive. For example, leases make it easier for you to keep up with advancing technology while also making your monthly expenses more predictable.[6] However, one of the downsides of leasing is that you may end up paying more over time for the leased equipment than you would if you simply bought it. An advantage of owning equipment is that you can factor in **depreciation**. This means you can **depreciate** the equipment over time as an expense that reduces your taxable income (refer to Chapter 5). At the same time, buying your own equipment requires having the financial resources to do so. It is therefore essential to plan out the equipment you'll need and make the necessary decisions about leasing versus buying.

> **depreciation**
> An expense to reduce taxable income as the value of a high-cost, long-term asset decreases with time.
>
> **depreciate**
> To reduce taxable income as the value of a high-cost, long-term asset decreases with time.

Leasing versus Buying Decisions

View in the online reader

Leveraging: Developing Your Own Checklist

Start developing your own checklist of things to consider when acquiring machinery and equipment for your business.

1. Make a list of the groups of machinery and equipment you may need (e.g., computers, production equipment, office equipment).
2. Research costs, methods of purchase leasing options, and other considerations pertinent to your business.
3. Prepare an analysis, based on your research, and determine whether to lease or buy.

Next, we will examine the personnel and insurance considerations for the operations plan.

> ### Key Takeaways
>
> - When considering a manufacturing location, examine the traffic flow and demand to determine if there will be enough space for people and machines to maneuver through the area.
> - Make sure you have a strategy for moving material through your facility.
> - Consider carefully whether you will purchase or lease equipment.

> ### Interactive Activities
>
> 1. Contact your local utilities. Find out what kind of cost information they can give you when you have selected a potential location.
> 2. Consider how you will build your company culture. What behaviors should your employees demonstrate? How will you enforce this culture?
> 3. Consider the costs of producing your product or service. How can you reduce those costs without sacrificing quality?

6.3 Employees and Insurance

> ### Learning Objectives
>
> 1. Differentiate personnel decisions for the operations plan.
> 2. Identify the necessary insurance for your business.
> 3. Identify your staffing needs for business operations.

Employees who are directly involved in your operations plan must be included in the operations section of your business plan. How you present the critical skills needed for a successful operation shows just how much you understand the product or service you will be providing. It also indicates how you will serve your target markets. A thorough description of the key operations personnel needed is important to selling your business idea.[7] In this section, we examine the important elements to consider when it comes to the people who fulfill your operations plan.

Personnel Decisions in the Operations Plan

sole proprietor
A business model in which there is only one owner of the business.

If you start out as a **sole proprietor**, you may not have any personnel requirements. However, as you grow your business, you may need to hire employees to help your business grow and thrive. There will be much more detail on Human Resources in Chapter 10. For now, there are a few things to consider when it comes to the operations plan.

First, some businesses require very special skills. For example, if you provide technology services, you will need to know exactly the kinds of technical skills you require in your employees. Consider also how your employees' skills will help you differentiate your product or service.[8]

Second, the **culture** (i.e., the customs and rituals that define your business) within your company is an important factor for attracting the right talent.[9] For example, showing employees that they are valued can be a big factor in hiring good people (for more on culture considerations, refer to Chapter 9).

Consider **employee turnover** (how often you lose and must replace employees). This is especially high in retail businesses—as much as 50 percent or more among part-time workers.[10] One way to mitigate this high turnover involves the perks and recognition employees receive.

More importantly, the employees who build your product and who interact with your customers have a huge impact on how your business is perceived and valued as a brand. This is why you want to pay attention to how you describe your employees' needs in your operations plan.

Finally, do not forget your suppliers and contracting partners.[11] These individuals are key. They are not directly hired employees, no, but you must have great relationships with them to succeed in business. Especially if you have a very seasonal business, or demand for your business is otherwise erratic, you may have a base number of employees whom you supplement with staffing services.

> **culture**
> Includes the rituals and habits that reveal the beliefs and values of an organization.
>
> **employee turnover**
> A metric that represents how often you have to rehire employees.

Insurance Considerations for Employees and Facilities

There are many types of insurance to cover just about anything. The best way to find the right insurance policies is to speak with insurance professionals about recommended coverage for your specific type of business. Here are a few things to consider when it comes to insurance for your property and equipment:[12]

- You will need insurance for vehicles and transporting. If you use trucking companies to move your product, for example, the trucking company will have its own insurance. Alternatively, you may have your own delivery fleet, which will need coverage. Consider also providing insurance for employees who drive those vehicles.
- **Product liability** is for any potential lawsuits that might arise from the use of your products. What you sell will determine how much coverage you will need. For example, selling clothes involves very different liability compared to products that use electricity. Product liability lawsuits are much more likely to arise from the latter, which could shock, burn, or electrocute people.
- Some businesses will need **malpractice insurance**, or what can be called *errors and omissions insurance*. This is very common if you are a doctor setting up a practice to see patients.
- Your property will need to be covered by **property insurance**. This type of insurance covers you for fires, vandalism, and other concerns involving the continuity of your business operations.
- Home-based businesses should consider extra insurance. Often, homeowner insurance policies that cover a home will not cover a business. Especially if you have clients coming to your home, you will want to have a **general liability policy** added to your homeowner's policy.
- Also consider safety precautions for employees. Often, this aspect of operations will be covered by OSHA (Occupational Safety and Health Administration). This aspect of operations can include how a company responds to outside forces like pandemic responses as experienced with COVID-19.

Now that we have gone through personnel and insurance concerns, we will look to include all of the information in this chapter within the actual operations plan.

> **product liability**
> Insurance that protects a business from lawsuits arising from use of its products.
>
> **malpractice insurance**
> Insurance that protects you if you carry out wrongful practices in your business.
>
> **property insurance**
> Insurance that helps the policy holder regain losses due to fire, theft, vandalism, and other issues affecting continuity of the business.
>
> **general liability policy**
> An insurance policy that protects home-based businesses.

Key Takeaways

- Insurance choices can mitigate risk in your business.
- Carefully build a corporate culture. If you fail to set a vision for your company's culture, one will be created without your influence.

Interactive Activity

1. Contact insurance agents. Ask them about product liability, general liability, and other insurance plans. Find out what information an insurance agent requires to give you a quote.

6.4 Suppliers, Supplier Management, and Cost Decisions

Learning Objective

1. Identify your supplier requirements for your business.

Supplier relationships are critical to any business. These relationships, like any personal relationships, begin and end with trust. Trust is built when both sides uphold their ends of the bargain.

Source: © Shutterstock, Inc.

Selecting Suppliers

Selecting suppliers for your business directly influences your success. This is true even for service-oriented businesses. Consider the following:

- In selecting suppliers, you want to know that they deliver on time. Ask your potential suppliers if you can obtain references or talk with current customers. Sometimes you will choose suppliers with whom you have worked before precisely because you know they are reliable.
- Consider how long suppliers have been in business.[13] Their long-term success lends credibility to your procedures and processes.
- Know what you need so you are clear on how to assess your suppliers.[14] For example, if delivery is most important to you, then that may be the most heavily weighted criterion for assessing potential suppliers. Other considerations are quality, cost, and the nature of how the potential supplier will partner with you for mutual success.
- Approach your relationship as a partnership. Make sure your suppliers are committed to your success and vice versa.[15] This approach can include strategies like sharing resources and information that can help each business be successful. For example, if you need maintenance supplies from a local hardware store, might they be willing to work with you to provide tools on a consignment basis (in which you are charged for product only when you pull it from inventory to be used)? This would be one way to manage your costs while guaranteeing the supplier a stream of purchases. Both parties benefit in this relationship.
- Consider any risks when it comes to supplier selection. For example, is there only one supplier for a product or service that you need? Make **contingency plans** so you have alternatives in place to mitigate risk when possible. Consider engaging a team of people to look at how the product or service is designed so that you are not relying on a single supplier. In other words, know the risks and have a plan to address them over time. In addition, be sure to include how you may manage extraordinary events, like the experience of the COVID-19 pandemic.
- In operations, there are plenty of quality approaches that you can use for assessing suppliers. These approaches can also be used in improving quality throughout your supply chain—from sourcing materials through to distribution to end customers. Some of these approaches are Kaizen, Total Quality Management, Lean Manufacturing, or Six Sigma. These approaches tend to focus on what quality means to the company and to customers and may not necessarily focus on cost.

The important concept here is to choose suppliers strategically. You will be working with these suppliers over the long term. Solid relationships can ensure your own longevity in business.

> **contingency plans**
> The alternatives you must identify to mitigate supplier risks.

What Would You Do?

Cheap raw materials and inexpensive services are a tempting way to cut costs. For example, you might select a trucking company that charges $1.00 per mile versus one that charges $1.75 per mile.

1. What other cost considerations should you consider?
2. How will you define quality, regardless of cost, for your business?
3. Develop your plan for addressing costs and quality for raw materials, equipment, and services that your business may purchase.

Supplier Management

When it comes to supplier management, you want to think beyond just buying products or services from a supplier. This relationship is not simply transactional; it is *strategic*.[16] When we discuss strategy, we are thinking much more broadly and deeply than just ordering and paying for products and services. Here are some strategic considerations:

- Consider making metrics part of your relationship agreement. For example, do you have specific product and service requirements? Many companies, when it comes to products, require certain specifications for qualities that can be measured: length, width, height, etc. If your specifications are critical to your process, you will have to spell them out in agreement with the supplier. Additionally, what are the consequences if these specifications are not met? Never underestimate the impact on your processes if specifications are not met. There are many costs associated with a shutdown or slowdown of production and with rework costs.
- Consequences can be both positive and negative. What reward system will you put in place for suppliers? For example, some companies may be willing to pay a little extra for a focus on quality and reliability. This incentivizes suppliers to meet their requirements.
- Share information as much as possible. For example, do not surprise your supplier with unexpected demand. You must prepare to meet demand, so give your supplier time to gear up for it, too. In fact, some companies share forecasted demand with their suppliers, which helps the supplier be ready when needed.
- Make sure that you review mutual performance periodically. You can use these meetings to share metrics, review what is working and what is not working, and make plans to address any deficiencies.

Your suppliers are an extension of your business. This partnership is an important component of your operations plan. Carefully consider these relationships when selecting suppliers and when evaluating their performance.

Managing Supplier Performance

View in the online reader

What Would You Do?

Imagine a pandemic similar to COVID-19 has occurred, and you currently have several thousand dollars worth of food on order from a supplier. You made this unusually large order because you've been preparing for a large event. Unfortunately, the event may get canceled if the pandemic continues to worsen.

Consider the following questions:

1. Would you cancel the food order or would you hope for the best?
2. Are there other options you might be able to implement should you keep the order and the event does get canceled? What are some of those options?

Cost Decisions

Finally, selecting suppliers demands that you look at the cost to produce your product or service. Let's consider some of these.

- **Direct materials:** These are the materials needed to produce a product.[17] For example, some of the direct costs of a coffee shop include the following:
  - The coffee
  - Different kinds of milk products and creamers
  - Different kinds of syrup
  - Different kinds of toppings
  - The cup and lid
- **Direct labor:** These are the costs associated with the personnel involved in the business. In our coffee shop example, there is typically a barista whose labor is part of the direct cost of making the drink.
- **Overhead:** These are the costs of running the facility. In our coffee shop example, this includes the rent for the building, facility supplies (such as for cleaning and maintenance), and other items.

You may not have a lot of influence over the costs of making your product. You can lower these by buying in quantity, sometimes, but the quality of your product should be your primary focus. Price your product accordingly. Direct labor can be expensive in some markets and certain labor laws can make labor more expensive.[18] Overhead will be directly related to how you finance equipment purchases and depreciate the equipment over time as well as how well you manage your indirect costs.[19]

Next, we will pull together all the aspects we've discussed into the actual operations section of the business plan.

direct materials
The materials needed to produce your product or service.

direct labor
The employee work involved in producing your product or service.

overhead
Costs for your product/service that are harder to trace directly to it.

Key Takeaways

- Decide what kind of relationship you will have with your suppliers. This relationship should benefit both parties.
- Understand thoroughly, in your operations plan, the costs to produce your product or service.

The Three Types of Manufacturing Costs

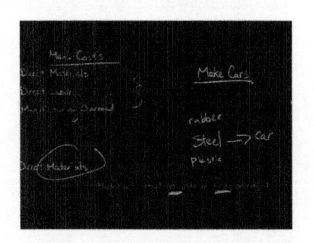

View in the online reader

Interactive Activities

1. Contact potential suppliers. Compare at least three companies providing a similar product or service. Analyze these suppliers. How might you choose from among them for your business?
2. Find a commercial real estate agent and talk to them. Have they helped businesses like yours to find suitable locations? The more you network, the more you will find great resources to support your efforts. Real estate agents can help you narrow down your location requirements. Develop a list of requirements for a location that are important for your business.
3. Contact a local attorney. Explore how that attorney can help you with various aspects of your business. For example, what types of hiring documents can they develop for your company? Can the attorney assist in lease or purchase agreements? If you need to protect an idea, you may also need to speak to a patent attorney.

6.5 Writing the Operational Plan

Learning Objective

1. Write an operational plan.

Now that you have examined various elements of the operations plan, you must tell the story in your business plan document. Your story should explain how your operations plan will best serve your clients, manage your costs, and drive your profitability.[20]

FIGURE 6.1 Finalizing the Operations Plan

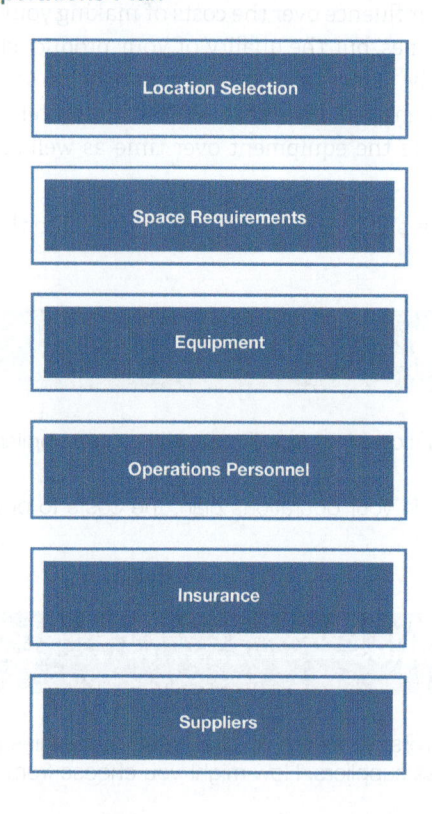

- Location Selection
- Space Requirements
- Equipment
- Operations Personnel
- Insurance
- Suppliers

Source: Laura Portolese et al.

Putting It All Together

Your plan should be more than a number of bulleted lists. A convincing plan tells a story. Because your production processes are the lifeblood of your company, you want to put your passion on display. The operations plan can sound very boring—it doesn't seem interesting to write about the equipment or facilities you will need, your inventory, your suppliers, etc.—but the more you connect this part of the plan to the vision of your business, the better it will sound. Examine the sections of this chapter and use them to build a solid operations description in your business plan.

For example, you can start by talking about the current state of the market or of your competition. Explain how your operations will create a well-informed consumer of your products/services, or how your plan will improve something that is currently happening in your market that represents a strategic opportunity. What drama exists in the market you want to enter? The story of your operations plan explains how you will overcome these challenges and provide a market solution for this issue. Writing this way will paint a picture in the reader's mind, explaining why you are the key to overcoming this challenge. You may, in fact, make some bulleted lists . . . but use them to summarize your story.[21]

Key Takeaway

- Your operational plan is the story of your company.

Interactive Activity

1. Prepare the draft operational plan for your company.

6.6 Test Your Skills: Applied Case

Jill's Manufacturing

Jill has a small manufacturing facility. She is under constant pressure to cut costs. Her small business manufactures a product that is used in the construction of buildings and homes. She distributes the product all along the east coast, and she specifically sells the product into the New York City market in Manhattan from her location in Virginia.

Jill's partner, Eden, wants to cut costs by utilizing a trucking company that has cheap rates. Jill has done her research and found that customers of the cheaper trucking company have had complaints about damage to property. Jill has also discovered that this trucking company has lost a few loads and completely destroyed some deliveries for customers in the last three years.

Source: © Shutterstock, Inc.

Consider the following:

1. Why is it so easy to focus on costs in decision-making?
2. Why is it challenging to look at all the costs of a decision?
3. How should Jill prepare for this conversation with her partner Eden?
4. How do you encourage all employees to balance long-term solutions with short-term results?

Endnotes

1. Murray, J. (2021). Cash flow - how it works to keep your business afloat. Retrieved from: https://www.thebalancesmb.com/cash-flow-how-it-works-to-keep-your-business-afloat-398180
2. Entreprenuer.com (2019). 10 things to consider when choosing a location for your business. Retrieved from: https://www.entrepreneur.com/slideshow/299849
3. Lovering, C. (n. d.). Seven key factors to a facility location. Retrieved from: http://smallbusiness.chron.com/seven-key-factors-facility-location-33442.html
4. Barry, F. C. (n. d.) Warehouse planning: how much space is needed in a distribution center. Retrieved from: https://www.fcbco.com/blog/warehouse-planning-space-in-distribution-center.
5. Fabregas, K. (2017). Planning your store layout: Step-by-step instructions. Retrieved from: http://fitsmallbusiness.com/planning-your-store-layout/.
6. Alexander, P. (n.d.). Should you lease or buy your tech equipment? Retrieved from: https://www.entrepreneur.com/article/80230
7. Fontinelle, A. (n. d.). Business plan: Your organizational and operating plan. Retrieved from: http://www.investopedia.com/university/business-plan/business-plan6.asp
8. Entrepreneur.com (2015). First steps: Writing the operations section of your business plan. Retrieved from: https://www.entrepreneur.com/article/241076
9. Reffkin, R. (2015). 3 must use tactics to differentiate your company from the competition. Retrieved from: https://www.entrepreneur.com/article/242063
10. The Retail Doctor (2015). 8 reasons why your retail employee turnover is so high. Retrieved from: https://www.retaildoc.com/blog/8-reasons-why-your-retail-employee-turnover-is-so-high
11. Entrepreneur.com (2015). First steps: Writing the operations section of your business plan. Retrieved from: https://www.entrepreneur.com/article/241076
12. Small Business Administration (n. d.) Types of business insurance. Retrieved from: https://www.sba.gov/managing-business/running-business/insurance/types-business-insurance.
13. The Business Professor. (n.d.) Business plan operations. Retrieved from: http://thebusinessprofessor.com/knowledge-base/business-plan-operations/
14. InfoPreneurs.com (n.d.). Supplier selection process. Retrieved from: http://www.infoentrepreneurs.org/en/guides/supplier-selection-process/
15. Stevens, C. (2020). How to choose the right supplier for your business. Retrieved from: https://www.business.org/finance/inventory-management/how-to-choose-the-right-supplier-for-your-business/
16. Webb, J. (2018). How to manage strategic suppliers. Retrieved from: https://www.forbes.com/sites/jwebb/2018/03/30/how-to-manage-strategic-suppliers/?sh=48db32147994
17. Accounting Tools. (2021). Direct materials definition. Retrieved from: https://www.accountingtools.com/articles/what-are-direct-materials.html#:
18. Accounting Tools. (2021). Direct labor definition. Retrieved from: https://www.accountingtools.com/articles/2017/5/6/direct-labor
19. CFI. (n.d.). Overheads. Retrieved from: https://corporatefinanceinstitute.com/resources/knowledge/accounting/overheads/; Accounting Tools. (2021). Indirect costs definition. Retrieved from: https://www.accountingtools.com/articles/what-are-indirect-costs.html
20. Haden, J. (n.d.). Inc.com. How to write a great business plan: operations. Retrieved from: https://www.inc.com/jeff-haden/how-to-write-a-great-business-plan-operations.html
21. Gilbert, M. (2017) Why you should rewrite your business plan every 90 days. Retrieved from: https://www.inc.com/mandy-gilbert/why-you-should-rewrite-your-business-plan-every-90-days.html

CHAPTER 7
How to Write a Management Plan

Case Study—Steve's Plumbing

Source: Used with permission from Steve's Plumbing.

Steve Egner went into the plumbing profession while in college in 1978. He moved to Washington in 1995; met and married his wife, Rachel, in 1988; and began running Steve's Plumbing out of their house (visit their website here). Starting the small business was a learning process. While he achieved success initially, Steve realized he would never be able to grow the business and achieve other financial goals unless he expanded out of his home.

In 2006, Steve and Rachel decided to turn Steve's Plumbing into a "real" business. Steve worked with a consultant to build a roadmap for success. Steve and Rachel have since grown the company from a thriving home-based business, earning a profit of approximately $200,000 a year, to a business that in 2017 earned an estimated $2.8 million.

The mission for Steve's Plumbing comes down to this: Everybody Wins. For Steve and Rachel, that is not just a slogan. They believe that employees win when they work at a company that offers them a future. They believe each client wins through having a reliable and trustworthy partner protecting that client's most valuable asset—the home. The company, in turn, wins by making a profit, which makes all the other "wins" possible. All of Steve and Rachel's business activities center on this philosophy.

This philosophy is obvious in how the couple trains and equips their technicians and customer service employees. For example, every technician in the field has a "warehouse on wheels." Each of the trucks carries about $40,000 worth of equipment, tools, and parts so that what needs to be done in the field can be done quickly and efficiently. In addition, the company has never outsourced its call center. Customer service employees who answer the phones are trained to be empathetic. Many customers who contact the business have experienced something catastrophic, such as through water damage, and may be in distress when they call. With every interaction, Steve and Rachel's employees focus on building a relationship with the client. Their goal is for each client to think only of Steve's Plumbing when a plumber is needed.

Steve and Rachel have given some thought to their exit strategy as they get older. Their children are currently in college and have worked in the business in various capacities. It is possible that one of the children may want to take on a bigger role in the business, but Steve and Rachel both know that a lot can change over time. They have established a living trust to protect the business in the event that something happens to either one of them before they have firmed up their exit strategy.

Source: © Shutterstock, Inc.

They're also aware that selling the business is an option, although they haven't determined the details. They could, for example, sell but remain involved as minority owners. They might even be retained by the business as consultants. Regardless, they take great pride in maintaining their books, customer files, and other business data. They know that the information *about* their business is as valuable as their store, their trucks, and their inventory.

Regardless of what the future holds, Steve and Rachel are very passionate about business ownership and the role entrepreneurs play in building a pathway to their own success. Steve recalls the one-cent piece designed by Benjamin Franklin. It stated, "MIND YOUR BUSINESS." Steve believes that starting your own business is about taking calculated risks. Minding your business carefully, he says, is the only way to achieve true financial independence.

A lot of small businesses start out in a home or garage. As the business grows, however, you may need to add staff and relocate. You may need someone to keep your books. You may need a team of managers. You'll almost certainly need team members who possess specialized skill sets, such as for legal advice. In this chapter, we will turn our attention to the management plan as a section of the business plan. The management plan takes into account your internal team, your strategic external partners, and the organizational structures of your business.

7.1 Building a Team

Learning Objectives

1. Assess your own skills for gaps.
2. Identify internal team members.
3. Identify external team members.
4. Assess leadership versus management skills.

Skill Assessment

Starting a business is quite a task. Initially, you may start your business as a single entrepreneur. Some businesses can actually stay that small, with one business owner, and do quite well. There are, however, some specialized knowledge areas of a business that may very well require you to hire an internal or external team member who has those skills. According to Patrick Hull, a contributor at Forbes, understanding your skills—and knowing which skills you lack—is the number one task when it comes to assessing your management plan.[1]

Source: © Shutterstock, Inc.

Assessing your skills should include the following:[2]

- **Technical skills**

    Do you have the technical skills to produce your product or service? This includes the technical skills necessary for production, the skills necessary to obtain the required raw materials, and the skills needed to identify the correct equipment.

- **Managerial skills**

    Do you have the management, marketing, sales, financial, legal, administrative, and problem-solving skills necessary for success?

- **Entrepreneurial skills**

    Do you have the presentation skills, the business plan skills, the environmental scanning, and the networking skills necessary to be successful?

- **Personal maturity skills**

    Do you have the self-reflection, accountability, emotional coping, and creative skills necessary to be successful?

Ultimately, in any area where you think your skills are lacking, you'll be faced with some choices. You can develop those skills in yourself or you can hire someone to handle those tasks. Another way to approach it is to **outsource** those skills by adding an external team member. Outsourcing just means that you will hire a professional to do that job rather than hiring an employee.

outsource
The hiring of external team members rather than hiring direct employees.

Assessing Your Skills

Start a journal that addresses the following items:

1. What technical skills do you have already? You would typically find these answers on your own resume.
2. What soft skills do you have already? For example, you may be a really good communicator, you may have good coping skills, or you may have great empathy.
3. Identify stories you like to tell about your skills. What do these stories tell you about your technical or soft skills that you may have missed?

4. Interview people you know. What skills do they see in you?
5. Make a list of the technical and soft skills needed for the business you intend to start. Compare that list to your skills inventory.
6. What gaps do you have? How would you shore up your own skills? Will you hire someone to fill that gap?

Assessing Your Business Skills

View in the online reader

Internal Team

There are many reasons you might hire staff. For one, you may need specialized help, especially when it comes to keeping books for your business. You may also need to add staff to expand your capacity, as you've reached the limit of what you can do on your own. Before you actually hire your first employee, there are some things to consider:[3]

- **How will you pay?**

    If you are hiring a person to be on staff, you will want to make sure that you have the money to pay for their salary or an hourly wage. You must also account for all of the taxes and other costs that are part of hiring an employee. For example, employers must pay taxes for Social Security and Medicare programs (as we will discuss in Chapter 10). Make sure that you have room in your budget for all of the costs associated with additional staff.

- **What will the employee do to help you?**

    You want to get the most benefit for the associated cost. For example, when you go into business for yourself, you may have no interest in keeping books. Thus, you may hire a bookkeeper so you can focus on marketing and selling your product. You may find yourself doing a lot of administrative work, when you instead should be focused on growing your business and adding new clients. Hiring administrative personnel would make sense in that situation. Every business and its needs are different. A travel business might hire someone to develop itineraries for clients, for example. Regardless of your approach to hiring, there must be a direct impact on your bottom line. If the new hire helps you increase your sales and expand your business, the added costs of hiring that employee may be worthwhile.

- **What skills do you need?**

    When you are considering hiring, especially in a small business, you don't merely want to hire someone with the right skills. You'll also want to assess how well that person operates within a small business environment. Small businesses often require people to wear many hats in order to accomplish tasks that are not necessarily in their job descriptions. The people you hire should be flexible and willing to learn and grow as the demands of the business evolve.

- **Where will you find good people?**

    You may have to get creative in finding people to help you. If it is a professional you need, such as a bookkeeper, there are professional staffing agencies that might be able to help. This is where you need to be smart in how you network. If you belong to local chambers of commerce, ask around. Ask other business owners—particularly if their businesses are similar to yours—where they have found good talent.

- **Do you need legal assistance?**

    Finding legal help can be daunting, but an employment or contracting agreement may be very helpful when hiring internal or external staff. Paying a law firm to help you draw up hiring documents can save you money in the long run. Hiring a law firm can be expensive, but it can save you a lot of headaches later on if you engage a lawyer to craft documents that you would use in hiring (refer to Chapter 8 and Chapter 9 for more assistance on legal considerations). You can find sample agreements here that can be modified for your purposes.

- **How will you describe the position(s)?**

    Job descriptions should define the necessary skills, basic educational requirements, and years of experience necessary for the position. Consider also including what your company culture represents.[4] Convey what it will feel like to work at your company. How you describe the working environment is critical in inspiring the right people to apply for your jobs.

External Team

Your direct employees are part of your internal team. You may also contract external team members. Some external team members to consider include the following:

- **Accountants**

    Before hiring an accountant, be sure to review Chapter 5. The most important thing to remember in hiring an accountant is this—*do not hand over your financial records with no accountability*. In other words, you *must* be involved in the finances of your business. You do not, however, have to handle the day-to-day transactions. Thus, you will want to have checks and balances in place to help you direct the activities of an accountant. Those checks and balances will also help you verify that the accountant is handling your finances appropriately.

---

board of directors

An external group of people who advise your company. In some legal forms of business, a board of directors is required.

board of advisors

An external group of people who advise your company. These are not required, but making use of such a board might be a great strategy to reach a certain market or demographic.

- **Lawyers and Legal Assistance**

    Small business frequently outsource legal assistance. Finding a good legal firm is important. This is another area in which your network may be able to provide suggestions and referrals. The Small Business Trends website is an excellent resource. The bottom line is this: You will need to engage legal assistance, so be prepared ahead of time to engage this resource early in your entrepreneurial journey.

- **Boards**

    Many different types of businesses have a **board of directors** or **board of advisors**. Depending on the business structure you choose (such as an S Corporation or C Corporation), this may even be a legal requirement. Any businesses can have an advisory board.[5]

If you contract with or employ external staff, consider developing a **non-disclosure document**. A non-disclosure document is a legal document that details what external contractors or service providers may not disclose about your business. For example, you may have unique or **proprietary** processes in in place. You also may not want people sharing information about your product or service platforms. You certainly don't want anyone sharing information about your profitability with outside parties.

Finally, it is important to think through *why* you may want to hire internal employees versus contracting with external vendors/service providers.[6] For example, it can cost more to hire a direct employee because of the added costs of benefits packages. However, hiring external contractors for long-term assignments might run afoul of state laws preventing this practice. You'll need to be aware of these regulations when making hiring decisions.

In the next section, we will discuss management versus leadership.

> **non-disclosure document**
>
> A legal document that details what external contractors or service providers may not disclose about your business.
>
> **proprietary**
>
> Private information which you would not want competitors to have access to. This includes specific information about your operations and products. It also includes sensitive financial information.

Management vs. Leadership

Management includes planning, organizing, leadership, and controlling.[7] Leadership focuses more on empowerment, inspiration, vision, and team-building strategies.[8] These two areas of business overlap slightly but use very different skill sets that businesses owners and employees can develop. While we can tend to use these terms interchangeably, it is important to understand the differences so that you will be able to assess your own development in these areas.

Typically, when you hire a new employee, they are hired often to complete tasks in the business. Thus, as a manager, you are planning the tasks they need to complete each day, you are organizing all the employees to work in concert with each other during the day, motivating the employees to do their best, and you are ensuring that these tasks are completed to your satisfaction. As those employees start getting promoted, or as you start to expand your business, you may have someone moving from a task oriented position to a more managerial position. Thus, you have to constantly think about how you develop each employee to learn how to do the planning, controlling, organizing, and leading activities.

As a business owner, you are in the position of setting the overall vision for the company. You are setting the tone of the business and setting the culture of the business. These different aspects of strategy require a focus on how relationships are built with each other and customers, how you will talk to customers, and how complaints are handled. These aspects will definitely have to be translated into actual behavior on a day-to-day basis.

As a person progresses from a front-line employee to a manager, to perhaps an executive in your organization, it is important to consider how you develop your employees through these levels. As a front-line employee, more of the focus may be on task accomplishment, management of their individual tasks, and some leadership skills required. As the person moves to management, more of the managerial skills will have to come into play, because the person may not know every function in-depth and thus will have to rely on the specific skills of the individuals they manage.

As a career progresses, very few finite tasks may be done and more reliance may fall in the harder defined leadership skill arena. This does not mean that leadership skills cannot be defined, it just means that a person has to be able to have a lot of tactics that they are aware of and can utilize, and be savvy enough to know what tactic has a higher likelihood of being successful in a certain situation.

Finally, during the pandemic of COVID-19, a lot of businesses had to work virtually. Doing this requires the ability to focus on tasks being completed and measuring work performance in potentially different ways. In the past, management of others largely meant being able to observe others. However, leading others when we manage or lead from afar means we may still be able to use certain managerial methods, but we may have to learn new methods. For example, leading at a distance may require more deliberate tactics of managing conversations.

In the next section, we will discuss organizational structures to consider in building your management team and staff.

Key Takeaways

- As an entrepreneur, you will need internal and/or external team members. Learn now how to identify your needs for these key roles.
- Assessing the gaps in your skills is a critical component to an effective management plan.
- Hiring an employee versus hiring outsourced help has different costs to the business.
- A good bookkeeper and good legal advice are often the top external resources you need for your business.
- Depending on your legal form of business, you may be required to have a board of directors.
- Having an advisory board may be a great idea for your business.

Interactive Activities

1. Make a list of the external team members you will need for your business. Make a list of the behavioral expectations that you would have of these professionals.
2. Identify a target market for your product or service. Identify how an advisory board could help you attract the individuals in that market as customers.
3. Based on number two, once you have identified how an advisory board could help you with a target market, identify the skills and background of individuals you would like to ask to be on the board.

7.2 Organizational Structures

Learning Objectives

1. Select the best organizational structure for your business.
2. Identify pros and cons of the different organizational approaches.

Selecting an Organizational Structure

How you set up your organizational structure impacts the efficiency of your business. As you read and work through this material, always consider how communication will work in your organization. What are your expectations for how your team will work together? Regardless of the structure you use, make sure your expectations for performance are clear. Organizational structures can cause communications problems if you do not address your expectations.

When you start hiring employees, you will want to consider how you organize your business. There are various ways to do this. Here are a few to consider:[9]

- **Functional:** A functional approach to organizing means that you will group people together by a function, or purpose, of your business. For example, all of the sales employees might report to your sales manager. You might have an accounting team, legal team, operations team, finance team, etc.

> **functional**
> An organizational design structure that organizes functions (such as accounting, sales, customer service, and production) into groups. Employees who serve in that function report to a manager of that function.

FIGURE 7.1 Functional Organizational Design

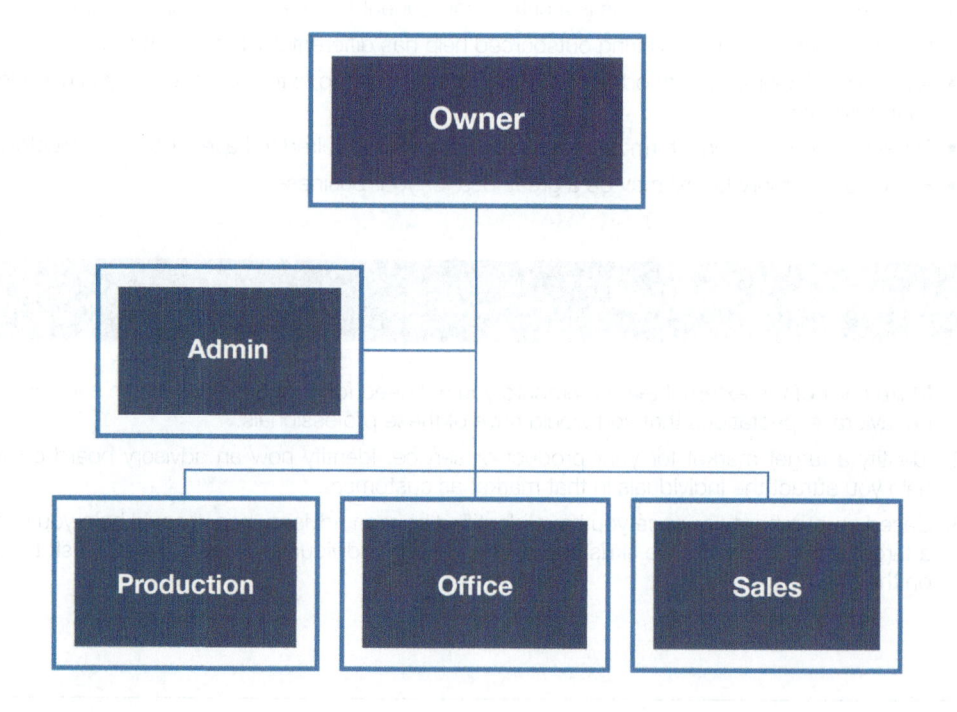

```
                    Owner
                      |
                    Admin
                      |
        ┌─────────────┼─────────────┐
    Production      Office        Sales
```

Source: Laura Portolese et al.

- **Divisional:** As you grow, you may need to consider geographic boundaries as a way to organize your staff. For example, if your business covers an entire state, it might make sense to organize into regions of the state. Geographic boundaries may make sense because of the specific requirements that apply to different areas of the state.

> **divisional**
> An organizational design structure that organizes by geography. Employees in each geographical area report to a division manager.

Chapter 7   How to Write a Management Plan   153

FIGURE 7.2 Divisional Organizational Design

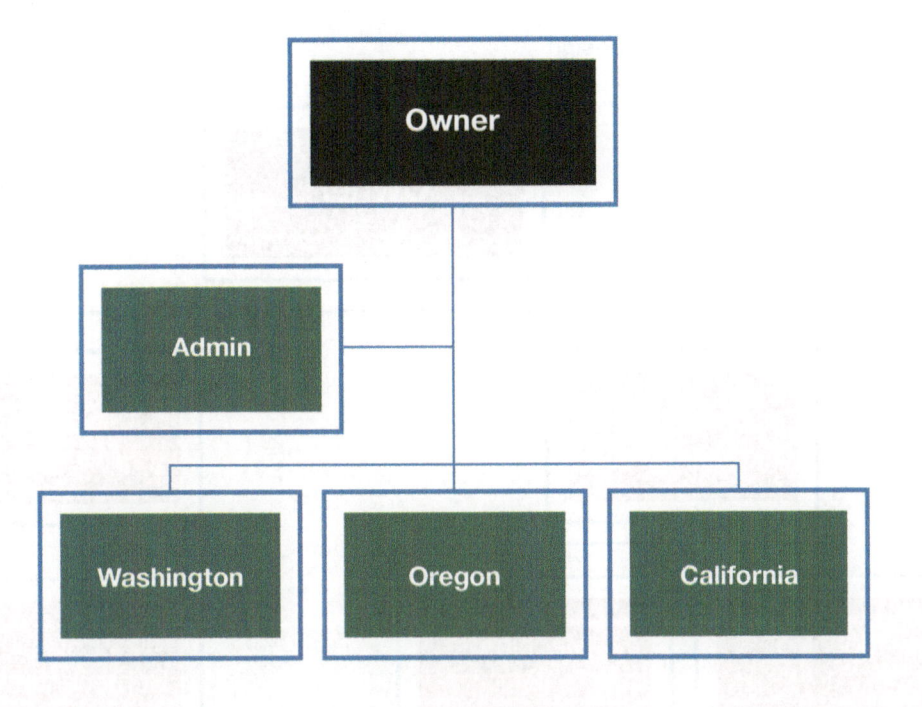

[Organizational chart: Owner at top, Admin below, with Washington, Oregon, and California as divisions.]

Source: Laura Portolese et al.

- **Matrix:** A matrix organization is a hybrid mix of the functional and divisional approaches to organizing your business. The manager of a consulting company, for example, might manage consultants in a geographic area, say the state of Illinois. Those consultants might work on different projects that may or may not be in that geographic area. Therefore, consultants would report to their geographic managers for performance reviews and also report to project managers responsible for the projects on which they are working.

> **matrix**
> An organizational structure that combines functional and divisional structures. This is common in consulting businesses.

FIGURE 7.3 Matrix Organizational Design

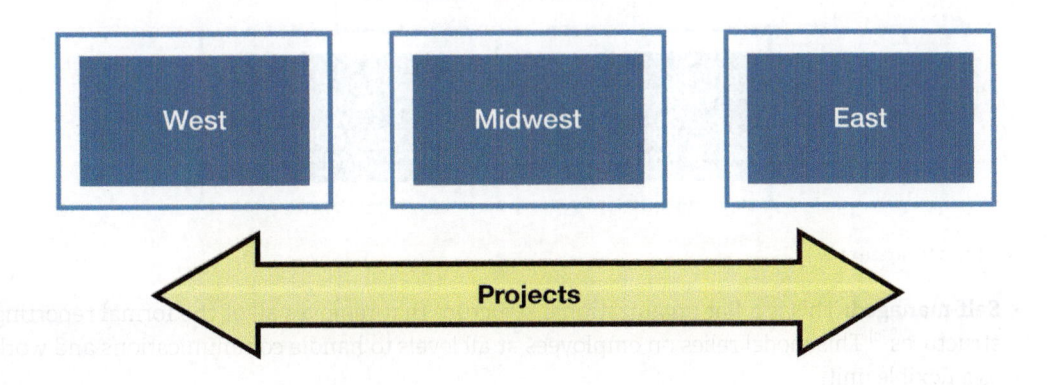

[Diagram: West, Midwest, East boxes with a double-headed arrow labeled "Projects" beneath them.]

Source: Laura Portolese et al.

flat

An organizational structure that attempts to remove layers of reporting relationships.

- **Flat:** Flat organizational structure attempts to reduce or eliminate the levels of reporting relationships.[10] This type of structure also encourages cross collaboration among the functions.

FIGURE 7.4 Flat Organizational Design

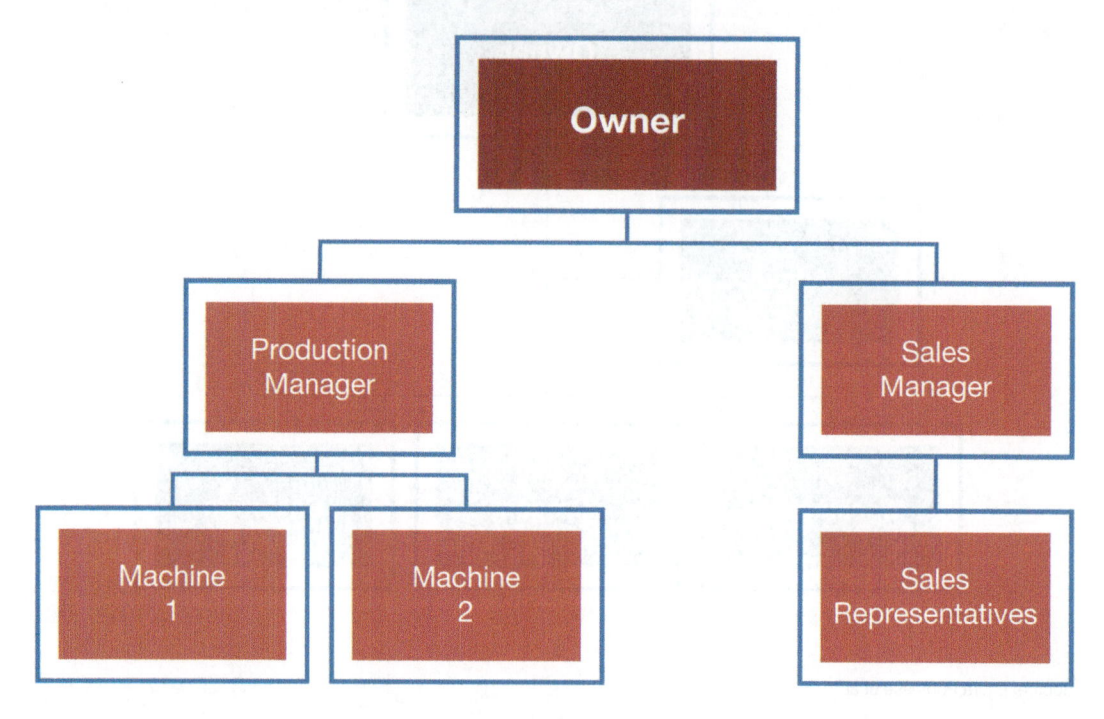

Source: Laura Portolese et al.

FIGURE 7.5 Another Example of Flat Organizational Design

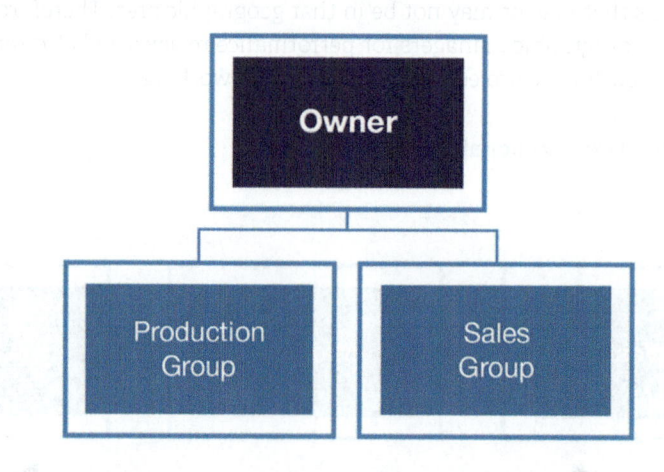

Source: Laura Portolese et al.

self-managed

An organizational structure that removes all formal reporting structures.

- **Self-managed:** This is a flat organizational structure that removes all of the formal reporting structures.[11] This model relies on employees at all levels to handle communications and work as a flexible unit.

FIGURE 7.6 **Self-Managed Organizational Design**

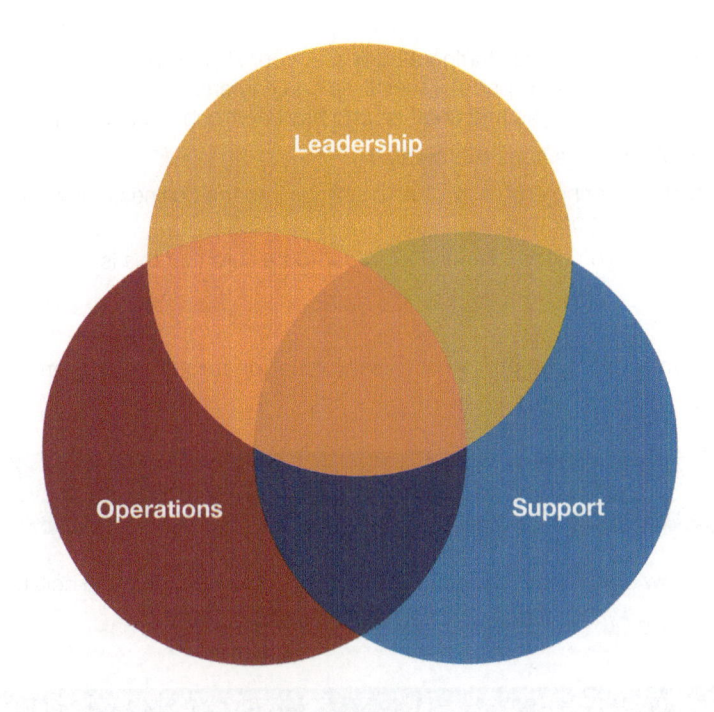

Source: Laura Portolese et al.

While any of these structures may be appropriate, there are certain things to consider when choosing your organizational structure model.

Choosing an Organizational Structure

When you are trying to decide which organizational structure to use, there are pros and cons to each model that may help you to determine the right approach.[12] One very important consideration is that of communication. This concerns how the organization communicates with its employees. In a truly hierarchical structure, communications can break down. It is like the game of "telephone" most of us have played as kids: As information trickles down from the top, it can become inaccurate as it moves through the organization. If you choose a hierarchical format such as a traditional model, consider carefully how you will communicate to maintain the integrity of your message throughout the organization.

Another important consideration is efficiency. You want to organize in a way that gains efficiencies in costs and/or expertise. For example, a company can have multiple manufacturing locations. If each manufacturing facility buys its own supplies, would it be smarter to buy supplies on a national basis to gain a reduction in costs?

Finally, you want to consider how the design impacts collaboration. In functional or geographical structures, collaboration issues may result from the **silo mentality**.[13] When a company is structured in a strict reporting hierarchy, the different groups may stop communicating with each other. This creates "silos" in which employees tend to communicate only within their respective reporting structures.

When you choose an organizational structure be sure to build a culture that promotes the type of behavior you want from your employees. In more formal structures, how you reward behavior becomes much more important.

silo mentality

A phenomenon that causes collaboration and communication to stop flowing within organizational structures.

> **What Would You Do?**
>
> Your siblings find out that you are starting a business. Your siblings have great skills, but some of them have had trouble in various parts of their lives and careers. For example, you have one sibling who has had financial trouble and another who has had trouble with alcohol and drug abuse.
>
> 1. What ethical problems does this create?
> 2. If you decided to bring any or all of your siblings into the business, how would you handle the performance expectations?
> 3. Who else would you need to consult in order to be sure that this is a good idea?

Next, we will consider how to pull all of this information into the management plan section of the business plan.

Key Takeaway

- Be aware of how organizational structures can limit communication and collaboration in your business.

Interactive Activity

1. Develop your first draft of your management plan.

7.3 Writing the Organization and Management Plan

Learning Objectives

1. Write the organization and management section of a business plan.
2. Describe your organizational structure.
3. Assess an initial succession plan.

Once you have determined the team you need in place and decided on an organizational structure, you are ready to write the organization and management plan.

Team Bios and Roles

Identify your owners and/or management team.[14] In this section, you would consider any combination of the following data:

- **For owners:** Identify each one's percentage of ownership, if they are **active** or **passive** owners, and what title they will carry. An active owner will be involved in the day-to-day decision making and in operations. A passive owner may be someone who invests in the business, but is not involved in the day-to-day decisions or operations.
- **For the management team:** Identify their roles/titles, educational backgrounds, previous experience, skills and expertise that can be leveraged in the business, and how the team complements one another.

If you have a board of directors/advisors, you would describe how the board will help your business. Include board members' bios as well as information on each one's expertise. Also add how the board members were selected, how they are involved in the business, and how they will offer guidance to your business specifically.

If you are engaging in a business venture through a partnership, be aware that while this can mitigate risk, it may also invite risk.[15] One of the documents you will need is a **partnership agreement**. This document spells out what is expected of the partners, how money is handled among the partners, and what happens if there is a dispute. These important discussions must occur before entering into a business agreement. You must be prepared for all outcomes, positive or negative.

Finally, identify any of the external partners you will use, including the Certified Public Accountant who handles your taxes, your legal team or advisors, and any other consultants you may use. Early on, you may not have a full-time financial officer, instead contracting with someone to handle those duties. It may be important for these external team members to have expertise in your industry. If this is the case, it is essential to highlight this fact.

> **active**
> An owner who is involved in the day-to-day operations and decisions of a business.
>
> **passive**
> An owner who is *not* involved in the day-to-day operations and decisions of a business.
>
> **partnership agreement**
> A document that spells out what will happen among partners regarding financial distributions. It also explains how disputes and other matters will be handled among partners.

Source: © Shutterstock, Inc.

Organizational Structure

In the organizational structure section of this plan, you will want to describe your organizational structure and show it graphically. Explain in detail why you chose this structure and give the reasons you think this structure will help your business be successful. In addition, describe how you safeguard against the common problems this structure might produce. How will you minimize the potential downsides? For example, if a structure tends to produce "silo" thinking, describe how you will prevent this through your culture and performance management process.

Succession Plan

> **succession plan**
> The plan that determines how to develop staff to take on leadership roles and how you will pass your business on when you choose to retire.

The final section will address your succession plans for your business. A **succession plan** determines how to develop staff to take on leadership roles and how you will pass your business on when you choose to retire. It is very important to think about your succession plan when you start your business. You must tweak that plan over time. If you don't, you might forget to do it, or you might wait until it is too late to drive the plan in the way it should work.[16] There are a few things to consider, which we will address in greater detail in Chapter 12:

- **Define your objective**

    For some, having a family member continue on with the business may not be the way you want to go. It is not a given that a business moves to a family member. Even if you do decide that your objective is to pass it on to a family member, you may still want the everyday management of the company to be in the hands of a professional management group. The objective is critical because your succession plan will look very different if you plan on handing over your business to a family member versus selling the business.

- **Define and communicate**

    You will want to define how family members are involved in decision-making. This may be driven by which legal form of business you choose (such as a partnership or a limited liability corporation). In addition, you may need to consider how you will communicate the plan and how to handle disputes concerning the plan or its execution.

- **Identify the succession**

    This means you will want to take the owners of the company and the key management players and identify who would be the likely successor for that role. This should include an assessment of skills. You must identify how you will fill in any gaps in skills or experience the successor might possess.

- **Consider how tax and legal implications will be addressed**

    This might include how you'll handle estate taxes or how ownership of the business will transfer from one person to another.

- **Identify transition details**

    Determine whether the business will be gifted or sold and how financing may work.

> ### Case Study—Maui Dreams Dive Company
>
> Rachel Domingo did not start out thinking that she would buy a business. She and her husband, Don, found themselves between jobs. They took on part-time jobs at a dive shop, Rachel in retail and Don in diving. Rachel saw that the dive shop was suffering from absentee ownership. The current owners had another dive shop on the island of Maui, where they spent more of their time. Rachel was business savvy enough to know that if an owner paid attention to some small details, the business could be very successful.
>
> As Rachel and Don considered buying the dive business, they wrote a business plan. This was a way of validating the feasibility of buying the business and making it a successful venture.

Of course, Maui is a wonderful travel location. Rachel observed that the business sees a roughly 50/50 split between local customers and tourist customers.

Maui Dreams honors and recognizes local and vacation customers through community events. These events typically include a dive, food, and prizes that are donated by local businesses. The event itself is a gift (for free) to all dive customers in the area.

In addition, Maui Dreams is a member of the local Chamber of Commerce and a member of a professional association, the Professional Association of Diving Instructors (PADI). These organizations are great ways to connect with potential customers. Maui Dreams is connected to the concierge desks at major hotels on Maui, too. The company also participates on smartphone apps that offer local experiences for Maui vacation travelers. The shop further advertises in and is mentioned by all kinds of publications on the island.

Rachel and Don created another company and purchased a boat that sails out of Maui Harbor. When their boat is booked at full capacity for boat dives, they also charter other boats. Once a year, they put together a dive that can occur anywhere in the world, taking guests—including themselves—on great diving adventures all around the world. This is a wonderful way to connect with guests while taking a vacation at the same time.

Eventually, the business will likely be sold to new business owners. Rachel and Don do have children, but their kids are not interested in the dive business. Their exit strategy will most likely involve having one of their employees take over the company. They might also sell to someone from outside the business. For now, though, they're having a lot of fun—and seeing the world.

A Look at Succession Planning

View in the online reader

Be aware of, and realistic about, any biases you might have in creating your business plan. You may want to have your plan reviewed by a neutral third party (such as a consultant). What kind of biases could you experience? For one, there is **confirmation bias**, which means we prefer information and opinions that confirm what we already believe—as well as people who agree with us.[17] You may have to become creative in handling and spotting your own biases. Devise performance measurements that, regardless of whom you are analyzing for a job or promotion, will prompt you to approach all candidates in the same way.

confirmation bias
People prefer information and opinions that confirm what they already believe.

Assessing Bias

Review the different kinds of biases someone can have when appraising others here.

Prepare a list of things that you can do to minimize bias errors in the workplace.

The key to the succession plan is that it may change over time. Most importantly, as you start your business, you should already be thinking about how you will develop the talent you have in your business. You do not want to leave this to fate. It is best to have a plan, even if that plan changes over time.

Leveraging: Assessing Your Exit Strategy

As you start a business, you should start to think about how you will exit. Will you close the business? Will you transition it to a child or other relative? Will you sell it to a non-relative?

Task: Using Google, develop a list of the pros and cons for different succession plan alternatives.

Toward which option do you lean? Why? How do you think your preference could change over time? How might changes in your life cause you to rethink your choices (e.g., marriage, divorce, birth of a child)?

Key Takeaways

- Make sure to create a culture or define performance measurements that can ensure teams are collaborating and communicating effectively.
- Start early in addressing your succession plan.
- Your objective in a succession plan is the key to writing the details.

Interactive Activities

1. Make a list of the skills that are needed for you to be successful in your proposed business. Do you have these skills? It would be a good idea to share your list with individuals who will be honest with you and offer their perspective as well. How will you shore up the skills gaps you find?
2. Culture in a company happens with or without your guidance. How will you ensure that your cultural behaviors support the success of your business through the organizational structure you choose?
3. Prepare a draft of your management plan. Share it with a couple of trusted advisors and receive their feedback.

7.4 Test Your Skills: Applied Case

Stella's Stellar Salesperson

Eric has been a stellar employee and Stella decides he is ready for his first managerial role. Stella developed a software package that combines project management and computer-aided design. She has had great success in building teams all around the Pacific Coast with three small offices—one in Seattle, one in Portland, and one in San Francisco. Eric has been a stellar salesperson, consistently building up clients that purchase a continuing subscription for the software and increasing sales consistently every year. One of his best skillsets is how he builds relationships with potential and ongoing clients.

Stella runs a pretty lean business with small teams. As a software business, Stella manages development teams out of India for the development of the software itself. She sells the software all over the world on a virtual basis, but also has sales teams that focus on sales to engineering firms all around the West Coast. Her sales teams are on the road at least 150 to 200 days a year.

One of her teams—the one in Portland—is having some issues. Their sales have fallen off and it sounds as if the office and relationships are souring a little bit. She is wondering how to move forward and how to promote Eric in the same plan.

1. If Stella wants to promote Eric to a sales management role, would he be ready for that role? Why, or why not?
2. What skills do you think would make Eric successful in a new leadership role? (Hint: you can use skills that appear apparent in the case, but beyond that, what makes a manager successful?)
3. What other roles could it be possible for Eric to perform in the company that Stella may not be thinking about yet?
4. If Eric were promoted out of his peer group, to manage his peers, what special challenges may that present to him? How could Stella help him prepare for the challenges?

Endnotes

1. Bryant, A. (n.d.). How to build a successful team. Retrieved from: https://www.nytimes.com/guides/business/manage-a-successful-team
2. Hill, B. (n.d.). How to assess the skill level of your managerial team. Retrieved from: https://smallbusiness.chron.com/assess-skill-level-managerial-team-79303.html
3. Laurence, B. K. (n.d.). Hiring your first employee: 13 things you must do. Retrieved from: https://www.nolo.com/legal-encyclopedia/hiring-first-employee-13-things-29463.html
4. Tekir, A. (2020). Culture Matters: How great startups will thrive in 2020. Retrieved from: https://www.forbes.com/sites/ellevate/2020/02/11/culture-matters-how-great-startups-will-thrive-in-2020/?sh=1173290d7c76
5. Entreprenuer.com (n.d.). Advisory boards. Retrieved from: https://www.entrepreneur.com/encyclopedia/advisory-boards
6. Insureon Blog. (n.d.). Employee vs. contractor: How to make the right choice. Retrieved from: https://www.insureon.com/blog/employee-vs-contractor-save-money-by-choosing-right
7. Management Study. (n.d.). What is management? Retrieved from: https://www.managementstudyhq.com/what-is-management.html
8. MindTools. (n.d.). What is leadership? Retrieved from: https://www.mindtools.com/pages/article/newLDR_41.html
9. Writing, A. (n.d.). Different types of organizational structure. Retrieved from: http://smallbusiness.chron.com/different-types-organizational-structure-723.html
10. Meehan, C. L. (n.d.). Flat vs hierarchical organizational structure. Retrieved from: https://smallbusiness.chron.com/flat-vs-hierarchical-organizational-structure-724.html
11. MacDonald, L. (2019). What is a self-managed team? Retrieved from: https://smallbusiness.chron.com/selfmanaged-team-18236.html
12. Maglof, M., (N.D.). Advantages & disadvantages of the structure of an organization. Retrieved from: http://smallbusiness.chron.com/advantages-disadvantages-structure-organization-2767.html
13. AGH (n.d.). Six reasons your strategic plan isn't working. Retrieved from: https://aghlc.com/resources/articles/2016/6-reasons-your-strategic-plan-isnt-working-160824.aspx
14. Duermyer, R. (2016). Business Plan: Organization and management section. Retrieved from: https://www.thebalance.com/business-plan-organization-and-management-section-1794228
15. Murray, J. (2017). Why your partnership needs a written agreement. Retrieved from: https://www.thebalance.com/why-your-partnership-needs-a-written-agreement-398401
16. SHRM (n.d.). Engaging in succession planning. Retrieved from: https://www.shrm.org/resourcesandtools/tools-and-samples/toolkits/pages/engaginginsuccessionplanning.aspx
17. Silverstein, M. (2021). 8 examples of unconscious bias in hiring. Retrieved from: https://blog.criteriacorp.com/8-examples-of-unconscious-bias-in-hiring/

CHAPTER 8
How to Put Together a Business Plan

Case Study—Coffee Café

Fred and Caroline lived in a small resort community. During the summer, visitors came to the area to enjoy boating and fishing on the lake as well as hiking, camping, and playing golf. During the winter months, only a few thousand residents remained in town. The community had only a few fast-food chain restaurants, a couple of grocery stores, and a hardware store. All other food-related offerings were mom-and-pop-style places that struggled to stay open without the support of the community and tourists. The locals liked it that way, but visitors to the area frequently commented negatively about the lack of diversity in food options.

Fred and Caroline had always wanted to open some type of business. There were few employment opportunities in their area; to find real work required at least an hour drive in either direction. Rather than pursue something out of town, they decided to investigate some underserved opportunities within the community. After some time, they determined that as there was no coffee shop in the area, that might be a good opportunity. They had a small savings they could invest and were able to find a fairly nice location to rent near the interstate off-ramps leading into town. They knew the location would not only provide a good first impression to visitors, but could also provide locals a quick stop for coffee on their way to work. Thus, the Coffee Café was born.

Source: © Shutterstock, Inc.

With no real business plan, Fred and Caroline decided to start with both hot and cold coffee beverages typically found in coffee houses (along with various hot and cold teas). They decided to include pastries and doughnuts, both from a local shop as well as some they made themselves. They let demand dictate what they sold with the idea that they would have to be adaptable. They did not plan much for an advertising budget but instead relied on word of mouth and location for locals and for visitors.

Business was good for the first three years. They had a steady stream of regular customers. They attributed this to the fact that their prices were fair and they had weekly specials that were fun and interesting. But when a Starbucks moved into the local grocery chain store, Fred and Caroline noticed their share or customers dropped off dramatically and they knew they need to act fast.

> They decided to add simple breakfast and lunch offerings to the menu; they would not be a full-scale restaurant but could include egg sandwiches and frittata-style dishes as part of their menu for breakfast, and deli sandwiches, chips, and salads for lunch. They wished to keep the café as a counter-style service with dishes brought to the table. Expanding their offerings to include food would provide some differentiation between the Coffee Café and Starbucks. Problem was, they didn't have enough money to expand in such a way to fully realize their goals. They needed a business loan, which would require a business plan.

In this chapter, we will look at different types of business plans and provide suggestions for when they are used. In addition, we will look at various finance and funding opportunities. Finally, we will focus on how to put together your plan for presenting to funding sources.

8.1 Formal vs. Informal Business Plans: When You Need Each

Learning Objective

1. Determine in which situations an informal or formal business plan is needed.

You may have heard the old expression *"When you fail to plan, you plan to fail."* In principle, this saying can be applied to your small business. While you may not always need a formal business plan, you should consider *having* a plan—even if it is informal.

🎥 **Three Reasons Why You Need a Business Plan**

[Video: Explains — 3 reasons you need a business plan]

View in the online reader

As you can see from " Three Reasons Why You Need a Business Plan ", a business plan is a path your business can take to move forward. When you take the time to identify and document where you want your business to go, you can review the plan often, make appropriate course corrections, and keep your business on course to achieve your goals. But do you need a formal business plan? Will an informal plan suit your needs?

Let's first look at the differences between a formal and an informal business plan.

FIGURE 8.1 Formal vs. Informal Business Plans

Formal Business Plan 
- Lengthy written document
- Used to obtain funds from lending institutions
- Used to provide direction

Informal Business Plan 
- Less formal, may or may not be written
- May be used to obtain funds from less formal sources such as friends or family
- Used to provide direction

Sources: Laura Portolese et al., images from © Shutterstock, Inc.

A **formal business plan** is a written plan which may contain several different documents. There are many reasons for preparing a formal business plan. Some of these reasons include:

- Defining the direction and purpose of the business.
- Attracting financing.
- Attracting team members and business partners.
- Managing the business.

One purpose for preparing a formal business plan is to obtain **funding** from an outside source. The plan is presented to banks or other lending institutions.[1] A formal business plan typically contains a great deal of detail about your business and will take a good deal of time and effort to prepare. Lenders will want to know that you have carefully and fully reviewed things such as your potential customers, your competition, your marketing strategy, and how you will differentiate yourself from your competitors (to name a few). With a formal plan, you will need to dig deep in your evaluation, because basic, surface-level responses will be insufficient to obtain funding. As a result, formal business plans can take a lot of time to prepare.

On the other hand, an **informal business plan** is more of a roadmap intended to provide a direction for the business.[2] Although an informal plan should be written, it is not as rigorous and may even be handwritten if the situation warrants. The plan must be easily followed, however. This plan will be used frequently to make sure the business is still on course.

Let's say you have a really good idea of where you want your business to go and you do not need any additional outside funding. Do you still need a business plan? Statistics from the Small Business Administration suggest that as many as 90 percent of all new small business fail within the first two years.[3] There is a lot at stake. Even if you don't need outside funding for your business venture, you may be risking more than you are willing to lose. It's a good idea to prepare some form

formal business plan
A written document that details the goals of the business and how the goals will be achieved. Typically it is a lengthy document used to obtain funding for the business.

funding
Money to start, grow, or run a business.

informal business plan
A plan that defines the goals and direction of the business. It is not used to obtain business funding.

of a plan. Furthermore, the Small Business Administration suggests that a good business plan can help you run your business from startup, through maintenance, through growth.[4]

The remainder of this chapter will focus on preparing a formal business plan. Before we cover that, let's first take one last look at some components of an informal business plan. "Informal Business Plan" provides some simple techniques for creating a brief, informal business plan.

Informal Business Plan

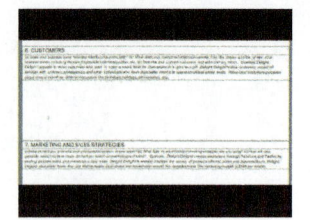

View in the online reader

Key Takeaway

- Business plans can be formal or informal. The type of plan you have depends on the purpose. Formal business plans are needed to help obtain funding. Informal business plans help provide direction to the business.

Interactive Activity

1. Think about a business you know. Prepare an elevator speech that would describe the business, identify an opportunity for expansion, and discuss possible opportunities for investors in this expansion.

8.2 The Components of a Business Plan: From the Executive Summary through the Appendix

Learning Objectives

1. Identify the components of a formal business plan.
2. Identify the appropriate detailed information to include in each section of a formal business plan.

In the previous section, we looked at the differences between a formal and informal business plan and discussed when you would want to use each. While an informal plan is just that—an informal map providing direction and guidance for your business—a formal business plan is intended to serve a much greater purpose. It is used to obtain needed funding to start or grow your business. In this section, we will look at the different components that make up this important business document.

Source: © Shutterstock, Inc.

> **Leveraging: Using Business Plan Templates and Samples**
>
> Not sure what to write? Why not take a look at any one of a number of free example business plans from Bplans.com? They have numerous examples of completed business plans for many different types of businesses. These include restaurants, cafés, bakeries, medical and health care, retail (both storefront and online), and other service-based businesses.

Business Plan Organization

Just as with all business documents, your business plan should be well organized, professionally formatted, consistent in appearance, and free of spelling and grammatical errors. There are a number of templates available to help you. We will discuss these in greater detail later in this chapter. Your business plan should have a title page, table of contents, and properly defined sections throughout. You may need to include tables, charts, or graphs for visual representation of some data. Finally, you may need to include other images or media embedded within your document as appropriate.

For example, you may want to include photos of the location where you plan to open your business or images of the product you intend to build. However, if word processing is not your strongest talent, you may want to seek professional help with writing and formatting. While appearance may not be everything, a document that is difficult to read due to formatting errors may not even be reviewed by those who will make financial decisions. Appearance matters!

Business Plan Sections

As mentioned earlier, there are a number of different formats for business plan templates. Most will contain some or all of the same information. Be sure that you use the appropriate format required by the funding source. For example, when applying for an SBA loan, there is a specific format to follow. Other lending institutions might have different paperwork requirements. The good news is that much of the information you will need to complete your business plan can be pulled from your work in preparing a marketing plan (refer to Chapter 4), a financial plan (refer to Chapter 5), an operational plan (refer to Chapter 6), and a management plan (refer to Chapter 7).

Let's look at a few common sections needed for a formal business plan as defined by the SBA:[5]

1. **Title Page and Table of Contents**

    Be sure that your title page includes the proposed name of your business as well as your name and contact information. Don't forget to include the date the plan was prepared.

2. **Executive Summary**

    Briefly summarize some basic information regarding your business, such as its mission statement, the purpose (in a sentence or two), the products or services offered, some basic information about the ownership structure of the business, and its location. The purpose of an executive summary is to give the reader an overview of the main components of the document to come. Your executive summary should address each section of the document with just a few sentences that hit the key elements.

3. **Company Description**

    Provide a detailed description of your business, including the problems that your business solves for its customers. Discuss how your business provides a competitive advantage over

fiscally responsible
Being reliable, dependable, and accountable in how you manage money and financial transactions.

other, similar businesses. (Don't forget that you worked through some of this information when you developed a marketing plan.)

4. **Market Analysis**

   Here you will need to demonstrate that you have a thorough understanding of your market segment. Again, the marketing plan you prepared in Chapter 4 will come in handy. You can use information from target market sections here. You will want to show your research on your competition as well as trends within your market sector. Investors will want to know that you have done extensive research into what is necessary for your business to succeed in your market. For example, if you are interested in opening an automotive repair shop in a small town where there are already two other auto shops, it's important to explain why your shop is needed. Maybe there has been a recent increase in population in the area. Maybe you plan to offer mobile repair in customers' homes or on the road. You will want to demonstrate that you understand your competition, the need for your business, and how you will stand out from the crowd.

5. **Organization and Management**

   Here you will want to identify how your company will be structured and who will run the business. Consider using information from Chapter 2, Chapter 6, and Chapter 7 when putting together this section. You will want to include an organizational chart as well as the qualifications and experience of each person who will be involved in the management of the business. For example, if your business is established and you are looking for additional funding to expand, you will have a good organizational chart with detailed management roles and responsibilities. By contrast, a newly formed business may only have one or two people in the start-up. It's fine to state that up front and provide a simple image of the organizational structure.

6. **Service or Product**

   Describe exactly what you will sell, produce, or offer as a service to your customers. What is your product lifecycle? Describe any intellectual property, patents, copyrights, or trademarks that influence and inform your product or service.

7. **Marketing and Sales**

   In a previous section, you evaluated your target market. Here, you will identify specifically how you intend to sell to this target. What advertising will you do? Where? How often? How do you intend to attract and keep customers? Here is where you will be able to use information from Chapter 4 related to promotional strategies. For example, maybe you intend to use advertising through Facebook or Google, or direct email campaigns using Constant Contact. It's important to be specific about how you intend to gain your customers.

8. **Funding Request**

   Here is where you ask for the funding you need to start or grow your business. Be specific about how much you will need, for how long, and for what purpose. Be very specific about how you will spend the money requested. For example, define how much will be used for salaries, new equipment, and rent.

9. **Financial Projections**

    Here is where a good financial analysis comes in handy. Remember the work you did in Chapter 5? You must demonstrate that you understand how much money you need to make in order to achieve your profit goals. This will help demonstrate stability and a focus on financial success. Lenders want to know that you're **fiscally responsible**. You may be asked to provide copies of financial statements, such as profit and loss statements, cash flow statements, or income statements for a business that is established. For new businesses, you will be presenting a financial forecast with projections of income and expenses. Here, charts and graphs can tell a compelling story.

10. **Appendix**

    Provide any supporting documentation that does not appear in the body of your business plan in the appendix. This may include résumés, credit histories, letters of reference, licenses or permits, and other legal documents (such as articles of incorporation).

What Would You Do?

Suppose you were planning on opening a small coffee house in your community. There is no coffee house presently. Everyone you've spoken to thinks it's a great idea. You have performed a preliminary survey of the community and you know that there is a strong percentage of residents that say they would support your shop. However, those surveyed suggested that adding baked goods, in addition to coffee, would really help sell the shop. Your problem is that you know nothing about baked items. Fresh is best; you think perhaps you could find a good supplier for bakery items that would fit the need. You remain a little concerned. Will this supplier meet the expectation of your clientele? You are set to pitch your business plan to a lender to secure a loan for the business. Right now, the business consists of you. There is no management team. How can you convince the lenders that you know what you are doing? What specific experience do you have that you feel can help convince them that you are a good risk?

In the next section, we will identify various sources for business funding as well as where a small business owner can get help in preparing a formal business plan.

Key Takeaways

- A formal business plan has several key components. Business plans should be written to support the business based on the needs of the lender or investor.
- Specialized software can be used to prepare business plans. Some software allows for collaboration with business partners and integrates with small business accounting software.

Interactive Activity

1. Visit this website and choose a sample business plan that is most like a business you might want to start. As you read the plan, identify at least three things that you would include in your own business plan.

8.3 Resources to Help You Prepare Your Plan and Obtain Funding

Learning Objectives

1. Identify various resources to assist in preparing your small business plan.
2. Identify multiple sources for obtaining loans or grants for small business startup or expansion.

In the previous sections, we looked at both formal and informal business plans and identified the typical components of a formal plan. In this section, we will look at resources available to assist small business owners in preparing a business plan to obtain funding. Let's first examine a variety of funding sources.

Source: © Shutterstock, Inc.

Loans vs. Grants vs. Investors

If your business needs money to get started, your first instinct might be to apply for a small business loan. As you would expect, a **loan** is money that is given to you, the small business owner, with the expectation that the money will be paid back—usually with some fee (**interest**) for the use of the money. Loans are usually for a given period of time and require regular payments be made on both the **principal** and interest.

Grants, on the other hand, are money given for the business with no expectation of repayment. There is tough competition for grants, making them difficult to obtain. Finally, it may be possible to encourage investors, or **venture capitalists**, to invest money in your business with the goal of making money in return. Have you seen the popular show Shark Tank, in which five millionaires sit on stage and review the prospective business ideas of contestants who are hoping to land a "shark" to invest in their businesses? There are several venture capital firms who invest in a wide variety of projects, often demanding a share of your business in return. Let's look at options for obtaining a small business loan, grant, or investor.

Sources for Obtaining Loans

Chapter 5 identified several sources for obtaining money to fund your small business. Some of these sources included your personal savings or 401K, family, crowd-source funding, your personal social network, or even your potential customers. In this section, we will look at another way: obtaining a small business loan.

The best place to start when looking for a small business loan is to check the many resources available on the Small Business Administration website.[6] Although the SBA does not give loans directly, they do help facilitate obtaining a loan from one of their loan partners. The SBA defines the guidelines used by approved lenders. When you have a small business loan approved from the SBA, the loan will be guaranteed by the SBA. This makes your business loan much more attractive to lenders. The SBA offers many types of loans, including the following:[7]

- 7(a) general small business loans are the most common SBA loan. There are several requirements that must be met in order to qualify for this type of funding. Some requirements involve where the business receives its income, where the business operates, and certain ownership factors.
- Microloans provide small, short-term loans. Loan amounts can range up to $50,000.
- Disaster loans include low interest rate loans. These help a business recover from any declared natural disaster. The money can be used to replace equipment or real estate, personal property, inventory, and other business assets.
- Real estate and equipment loans help provide money to purchase **fixed assets**.

---

loan

A sum or money that is borrowed with the expectation that the money will be paid back with interest.

interest

The fee applied to a loan for borrowing money and is typically defined as a percentage.

principal

Either the initial amount of the money borrowed or the amount remaining to be repaid.

grant

A sum of money given by the government or another organization. Typically, there is no expectation of repayment.

venture capitalists

A person or group that invests money in businesses, either through startup or expansion. Typically, the investor provides the funding in exchange for an equity position in the business.

fixed assets

Items purchased for the business that are intended for long-term use and will not be converted quickly into cash.

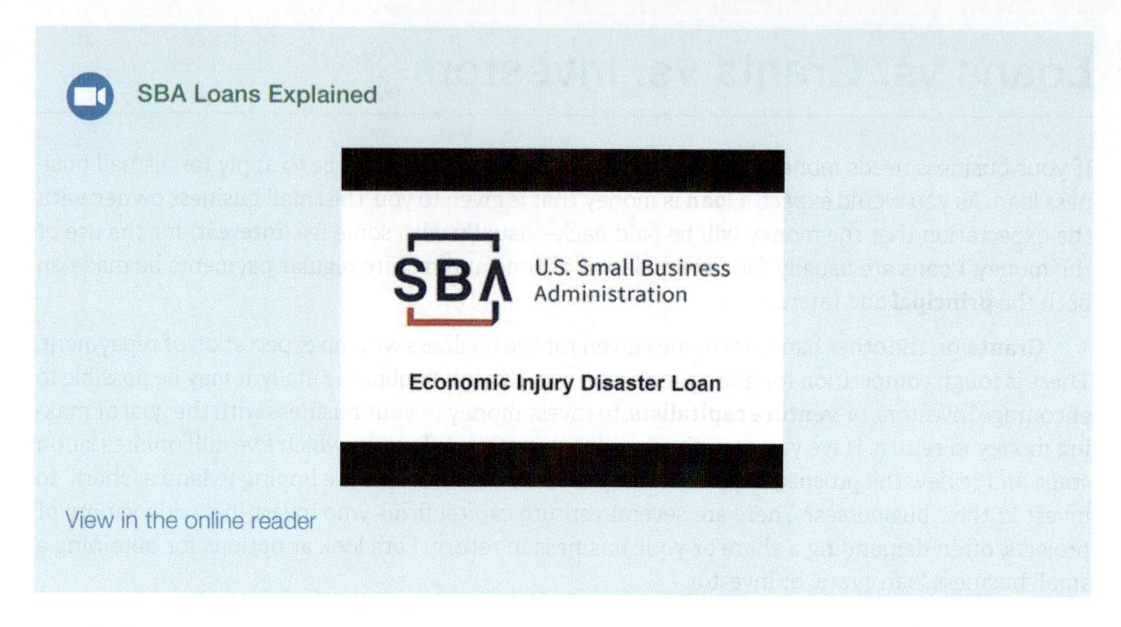

> **SBA Loans Explained**
>
> U.S. Small Business Administration
>
> Economic Injury Disaster Loan
>
> View in the online reader

The best part about applying for an SBA loan is that there is a significant amount of assistance available on the SBA website in the form of videos, templates, and step-by-step instructions. There is a complete learning center that offers many different online courses to help the small business owner. Finally, the USA Financing Tool helps small business owners find other sources of government funding.

In addition to startup and operating capital loans, there are other loans for more specific purposes. Some of these loans include:

- short-term loans, which are typically paid back within one year;
- lines of credit, an amount of money extended to the borrower for use as the borrower sees fit;
- invoice financing, which is borrowing money against the money that is owed to the business by customers (accounts receivable); and
- merchant cash advance, a lump sum payment for a percentage of future credit sales.

There are numerous companies available to help with all forms of small business loans. Of course, there is always your bank. Establishing a good relationship with the bank where you run your business account can be very beneficial should you need to apply for a business loan. However, there are other options.

Fundera is one such company that helps small business owners connect with lenders and secure funding. By applying online with Fundera, you can see a variety of lending options available, including loan terms. This allows you to pick the one that best suits your needs. Another source for finding different loan options is NerdWallet, which provides a list of many different lenders that handle online applications.

Sources for Obtaining Grants

Another way in which a small business owner can obtain much needed cash is by obtaining a grant. Remember, grants are funds given to businesses that do not need to be paid back. Grants are much more difficult to get, but if you know where to look, they are a viable funding option.

Grants are given for a variety of reasons. For example, if your small business is involved in research, you may be able to apply for one of several grants related to your research. The Small Business Innovative Research program offers grants for businesses involved in federal research and development activities that show potential for **commercialization**. A number of government agencies participate in this program. These include the Department of Agriculture, the Department of Commerce, the Department of Defense, and the Department of Energy, to name a few. Refer to the Small Business Innovation Research website for complete details. There are also grants available through the U.S. government which you can search for here.

Often, there are grants available for specific groups such as women, minoritized people, and veterans. For example, Teddy Nykiel offers a variety of sources for grants for women looking for funding for their businesses (found here).[8] Other minoritized groups might find helpful this article by Steve Nicastro which outlines available grant resources for people who are minoritized.[9]

Writing a winning grant proposal is the key to winning one. As mentioned previously, grants are competitive. It's important that you write a grant proposal that meets all requirements and tells a compelling story. Grant writing is a challenging skill—but one that can be learned. There are several sources for learning how to write a successful grant, as well as various professional grant writers who can assist you for a fee. Carolyn Brown suggests that you should be prepared to do plenty of legwork in preparation for your grant proposal.[10] This generally entails research, research, research. Be prepared to do whatever the request for proposal states. Also, make sure the goals for your business are specific and measurable.

commercialization
Introducing a product or service to the general market and making the product or service available for purchase.

Sources for Obtaining Investors

There may be times when a loan is not appropriate or a grant is unobtainable. In those cases you may wish to consider taking on an investor who may want to become a partner in the business. Not all investors want a "piece of the action." Some just want a quick return on their money with a sound exit strategy that allows them to invest and profit. Before we go too far talking about venture capitalists, let's stop and take another look at a type of investor who should not be overlooked: family and friends.

Family and friends may be a great source for obtaining funding for your small business. They may share your enthusiasm and be equally excited as you begin your journey. However, borrowing money from family and friends should not be taken lightly. Approach it in a professional manner. It's a good idea to put down the terms of the loan, including the amount and repayment plan, in writing.[11]

Just as a bank or investor will want to know how you intend to spend the money you receive, your family or friend investor will probably want to know how you intend to spend the money. It's a good idea to capture this information in your business plan. If there is an expectation that the investor will be included in the decisions of the business, this should be documented (and the extent of involvement should be specified). If there is some form of **collateral** or security in place for the loan, this should be documented too.

Finally, there are some important tax considerations that further suggest the importance of putting the agreement in writing. The IRS allows gifts of up to $14,000 annually to be given without expectation of repayment and without tax payments incurred by the donor.[12] If the amount of money loaned by a family or friend exceeds this amount, it's necessary to clarify that the money is a loan and not a gift to avoid any additional taxes the donor may incur.

collateral
Some form of asset that is used to secure a loan. Should the borrower fail to make loan payments, the collateral may be seized.

angel investors

Private investors, typically affluent individuals, who provide investment money for a share of ownership in the business startup.

If family and friends are not options, you may wish to pursue other investors, including **angel investors** and venture capitalists. An angel investor is an individual who wishes to invest in your business early for a share of ownership in the company. Venture capitalists, on the other hand, are typically groups of investors who form a partnership to create a venture capital fund.[13] A fund manager will then find business opportunities in which the fund can invest.

Both angel investors and venture capitalists will choose to invest different amounts of money and will perform different levels of due diligence. For example, the average angel investor will keep the investment of any personal money to under $100,000 and may agree to the deal after some informal conversations and a little background investigation. By contrast, venture fund managers must answer to a larger number of investors and must demonstrate proper responsibility for the money they lend. As a result, venture firms will do much more thorough background investigations before investing any money.

equity

The value of ownership in the business. This is often stated as a percentage or, in the case of stock, in shares of the business.

Caron Beesley suggests that investors and lenders look for different things.[14] For example, investors are often interested in entrepreneurial efforts. They are willing to take greater risks for higher returns on their investments. Investors are interested in holding some **equity** position in your company, such as being a member of your board or participating in some form of business governance. Finally, although an exit strategy is important to most investors (when they will realize their rewards for their investment), most investors are willing to stay engaged with the business longer than most lenders.

A great place to start looking for venture capital firms, if this is the route you have chosen to take, is the National Venture Capital Association (NCVA). The NCVA is the voice for the venture capital industry and comprises hundreds of member organizations. These organizations work to help fund innovative business projects.

Some other helpful resources include the following documents:

- **Voting rights agreement:** used to define the rights and responsibilities of the member/owner/partners.
- **Stock purchase agreement:** used to define the terms with which one will purchase stock in the business, as well as rights and responsibilities that result from the purchase.
- **Right of first refusal:** documents the right of an individual to purchase the business before the business is offered for sale to anyone else. The individual then has the option to purchase or refuse the opportunity.
- **Indemnification agreement:** used to define the responsibilities of each party involved in a contract should there be loss or injury as a result of executing the contract.

How to Write a Winning Business Plan

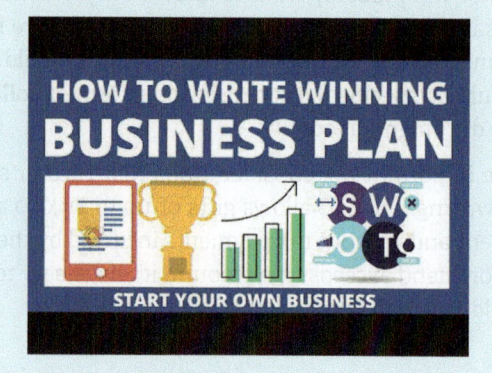

View in the online reader

How the Small Business Administration Can Help

By now you probably have come to realize that the Small Business Administration is a great resource for all things related to your small business. What you might not know is that the SBA offers a variety of training courses through their Learning Center, found here. These courses are typically short in duration, free of cost, and include video training together with written material. Furthermore, you may be able to gain some personal assistance by visiting a local SBA district or regional office. These offices may offer personal counseling, training, and business development specialists who can help you start or grow your business.

Additional Resources

Aside from the Small Business Administration, there are a number of resources available to help you, the small business owner, develop a winning business plan. Some of these resources are free; others may involve a fee for service. Some may provide consulting services face-to-face, over the phone, or online. Additionally, there is software that can help you prepare various plans, such as a marketing or business plan.

Palo Alto Software offers software to help you develop a professional business plan. The company offers a wide variety of free resources to help you get your business plan moving in the right direction.

FIGURE 8.2 Free Resources Offered by Bplans.com

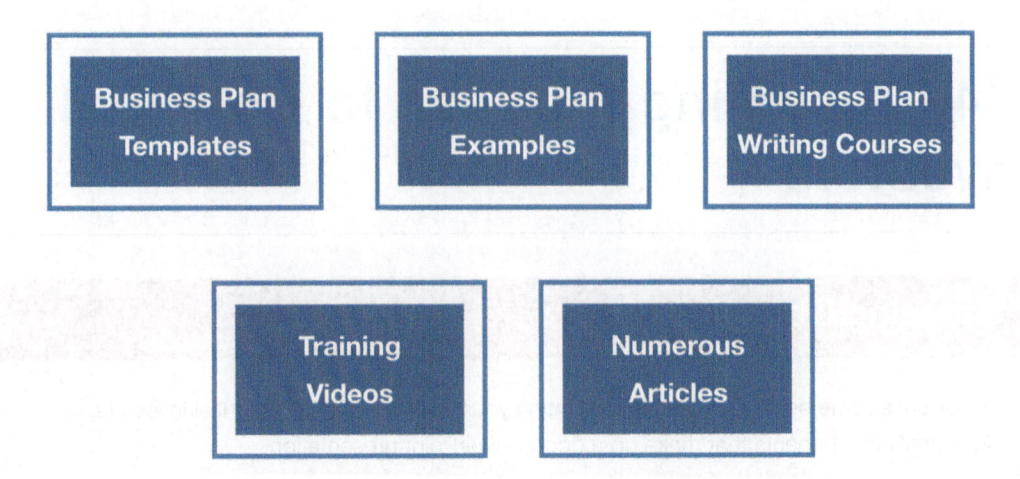

- Business Plan Templates
- Business Plan Examples
- Business Plan Writing Courses
- Training Videos
- Numerous Articles

Sources: Laura Portolese et al., data from http://www.bplans.com/

LivePlan is an online software available from Palo Alto Software that can help you develop a business plan. Because the software resides online, collaboration with business partners is easy. The software provides instructions and videos to walk you through the steps necessary to create a business plan. Once the plan is finished, LivePlan will help track your progress. Finally, LivePlan can integrate with some common small business accounting platforms such as QuickBooks.

In the next section, we will look at the skills needed to prepare and present your business plan to loan officers or investors.

> ### Key Takeaways
>
> - There are several sources of funding for your small business, including loans, grants, and investors.
> - Small business loans must be paid back over a specific period of time. The Small Business Administration does not give loans directly, but will help small businesses obtain loans through their partners (and by securing the loans).
> - Grants are money that is not required to be paid back. They are given for specific purposes, such as for research and development.
> - Investors are individuals or firms willing to invest money in your business for a portion of the business equity.
> - Some loans may require collateral to secure the repayment of the loan. Some investors may ask for a share of the business ownership.

> ### Interactive Activities
>
> 1. Visit the Small Business Administration's website and complete this course on preparing a business plan. Use the information to consider preparing a business plan for your own business start-up.
> 2. Using the work you have completed in previous chapters for a marketing plan (refer to Chapter 4), a financial plan (Chapter 5), an operational plan (Chapter 6), and a management plan (Chapter 7), prepare a business plan for the business you want to start (identified in Chapter 3).

8.4 Presenting the Plan to Potential Investors

> ### Learning Objectives
>
> 1. Discuss some best practices for presenting your business plan to potential investors.
> 2. Identify components that make up a good PowerPoint presentation.

In the previous section, we looked at multiple sources for securing funds, either in the form of loans, grants, or investors, as well as some resources for helping you prepare your business plan. We discussed at length the different sources for funding your business because the way in which you develop your business plan and prepare your presentation are influenced by the type of funding you seek. In this section, we will look at some presentation skills that will help you present your business plan in the best possible manner.

Preparing for the Business Presentation

There are numerous courses that can help you learn presentation skills. There are special interest groups such as Toastmasters that can help you become comfortable in preparing and delivering presentations to both small and large audiences. While you might feel uncomfortable speaking to groups, there are some great tips for helping get past your initial stage fright. Preparation is key. When you think about it, who knows your business better than you? The better prepared you are with your presentation and your business plan, the more comfortable you will be when presenting your ideas. Let's look at two different types of presentations you should prepare.

The first presentation you will want to prepare is an **elevator speech**. An elevator pitch or speech is a quick, sixty-second discussion intended to describe your business idea to anyone who might be interested. Your presentation need not be given in an elevator; it could occur anywhere you encounter a potential investor. The emphasis here is on time. Your presentation should be very short, to the point, and concise in the description of your intentions and needs.

Source: © Shutterstock, Inc.

elevator speech
A brief pitch for an idea, project, or business. The goal is to keep the speech short, about sixty seconds—the typical length of an elevator ride.

For example, imagine that you have the attention of a potential investor for just a few short minutes as the two of you ride an elevator together. Now is your chance! What will you say that will compel this person to want to know more about your opportunity? If you are seeking funding, whether through a loan or through investors, you should have a well-defined elevator speech prepared and ready for delivery.

How to Give the Perfect Elevator Pitch

View in the online reader

After preparing a good elevator speech, make sure you have a well-defined presentation prepared. Depending on the audience or purpose, this might be a short presentation or could be a longer one. One big difference between an elevator speech and a short or long presentation is that in the latter, you will be expected to have slides, handouts, and other supporting material. You must not only prepare what you want to say, but the visuals and documentation that will accompany your presentation.

For a short presentation, think about what you want to say in ten to twelve minutes. Noah Parsons offers some advice on the specific information you will want to include in a short presentation.[15] If your goal is to keep the presentation to ten to twelve minutes, you should spend about one minute each on the following topics. Be sure to allow time for questions at the end:

- Present your value and vision proposition, which should provide a concise statement about the value that your business will offer its customers.
- Describe the problem to be solved. Remember, your business should not only provide value, but should fulfill a real need in the community.
- Define your target market, define the size of the market, and paint a picture of your ideal customer.
- Provide a description of your business that clearly demonstrates how your business solves the customer's problem.
- Describe how you will charge your customers or how you will generate income from the business.
- Validate your solution. Have you started your business and have some demonstrated success to discuss? Here you want to provide evidence that shows your solution is solving a real problem and making money.
- Discuss your marketing or sales strategy. Describe how you will promote your business and gain customers.
- Discuss the team of people who are helping or will help you achieve your business goals.
- Discuss *realistic* sales forecasts and projections. Present data that demonstrates financial analysis three years in the future.
- Demonstrate that you know your competition and how your business is different. What will make your business stand out from the rest?
- Discuss how the money obtained from the loan/grant/investment will be used. Be sure to discuss the amount you are looking for and exactly how that money will be spent in the business.

A longer presentation may need to dive deeper into these points. To further clarify your business plan, here are some additional suggestions:[16]

- Be sure to tailor your presentation to the appropriate audience. If you are presenting to lenders or investors, be sure that your presentation highlights the information that each is looking for about your business.
- Investors are typically looking to the future. Be sure your presentation focuses on growth and breakthroughs.
- Investors want to know when they will make money, how much money they will make, and when they can expect to receive their full return on investment.
- Lenders are typically concerned with risk. Be sure to present clear financial data explaining why your business is worth the risk. Avoid vague possibilities and focus on concrete information.
- As part of a risk assessment, the lender will want to know that your management team is able to execute the vision and repay the loan as agreed. This means they want to know how expenses will be controlled and how business owners will share the risk.
- Both lenders and investors want to know that you are reliable. Use facts and figures to support your assertions. Be clear and concise. Prove that you have done your research. Stay focused on your business and be realistic.

Preparing a PowerPoint Presentation of Your Business Plan

As we discussed already, you will need to know how to prepare and deliver different presentations depending on the audience. This means understanding how to put together a presentation using PowerPoint or similar software. PowerPoint is a Microsoft product that is part of the Office suite of tools. It helps you prepare a presentation by creating slides on which you will include your information. If you are not familiar with Microsoft PowerPoint, here is a link to a series of YouTube videos from Simon Sez IT that can help you get started.

Once you are comfortable using PowerPoint, you will want to choose an attractive template. This template should allow you to feature your business and its information in the way you feel perfectly represents both. There are many free PowerPoint templates available for download, including many additional templates from Microsoft. If your business has a logo, you will be able to insert your logo into the template for a more professional look. You will want to use a template that works well with your logo.

There are a few important things to remember about creating slides. Because the focus of your PowerPoint slides are **bullet points**, it's important to capture what you want to say in the slide in short, concise bullets. Do not write sentences on your slides. When you present, do not read directly from your slides. Provide a more detailed discussion of the information presented in each bulleted point. Remember, your slides are just visuals. You will speak during the presentation and, at that time, you will expand on the information you provided on the slides. Remember, too, that your slides should be short and concise. Don't swamp the viewer in dizzying arrays of numbers or walls of text. Include charts and graphs as appropriate.

> **bullet points**
> A list of items preceded with symbols.

How do you know if you have enough information? How do you know if you have too little or too much? Entrepreneur suggests that you use the 10-20-30 rule.[17] To apply this rule, you should make sure your presentation is *around* ten slides that take no more than *about* twenty minutes to deliver, and which use a font size of *around* thirty points. This means that when you rehearse your presentation, you should spend a few minutes or less discussing each slide. And yes, you should rehearse! The key to any good presentation is being comfortable with the information you are presenting. Knowing what you are going to say takes practice. Rehearsing will help you gain confidence.

Some final tips about your presentation include the following:[18]

- Keep your slides and your verbal presentation free of jargon. Use words that everyone understands or, if you must use domain-specific terminology, be sure to define those terms.
- Again, don't read from your slides word for word.
- Pace yourself. Breathe. Do not be in too much of a hurry. If you feel yourself rushing through the slides during rehearsal, think about how you can simplify your presentation.
- Don't overload slides with too much information. Remember to let your passion speak for your business. Less is often more.

Reviewing Contracts, Agreements, and other Loan Documents

In Chapter 9, we will discuss situations in which you might want to hire an attorney to help with legal matters related to your business. Consider using an attorney to review any contracts, agreements, loan documents, or other documents related to obtaining funds or inviting investors into your business. We have talked a lot about various types of lending and investment arrangements that can help provide financing for your business. With each one of these comes certain legal documents. Mistakes at this level could cost you more than you realize. Before entering into any legal arrangement, it's a good idea to get professional legal advice.

An attorney is very useful, but if you want to learn more on your own, the website FindLaw can be very helpful. This site provides a great deal of help for a variety of business issues including starting a business, employment law, incorporation, finances, intellectual property, and business operations. FindLaw's resources on Business Contracts and Forms (found here) could be especially useful in learning how to read some of the contracts you may be asked to sign.

Remember that there are attorneys who specialize in different forms of law, such as when entering into rental agreements for commercial property. Make sure your attorney specializes in commercial real estate law when dealing in these matters.

Key Takeaways

- You must be able to present your business plan in a variety of ways. While written plans may be essential for obtaining funding, it's important that you have prepared a concise elevator speech, short presentation, and long business plan presentation for potential investors.
- Good presentation skills can help sell your business to potential lenders or investors.
- It may not be necessary to consult an attorney for all business start-ups. Whenever entering into a legal, binding contract, however, consulting an attorney is a good idea. Attorneys specialize in different areas of the law. Be sure you contact an attorney appropriate for your needs.

Interactive Activity

1. Following the 10-20-30 rule, prepare a presentation for your business plan. For bonus points, record narration for each slide of your presentation. Visit this website if you are unsure how to record narration on PowerPoint slides.

8.5 Test Your Skills: Applied Case

Ahmed's Gasoline Additive

Ahmed has invented a gasoline additive that boosts gas mileage in most vehicles by as much as 35 percent. Ahmed has applied for a patent for his invention and is now looking at ways of manufacturing the additive and getting it into the hands of the consumers. He has considered several sources for the manufacturing of his product and settled on one company that he feels can meet his quality and price goals. However, he wants to handle the marketing and distribution through a business he wants to start. However, Ahmed needs money.

1. Identify the three best sources for obtaining capital for Ahmed and his invention. Justify why each is good for his needs.
2. For each capital source you identify, consider the challenges involved in obtaining the funds.
3. Prepare an elevator speech for Ahmed that demonstrates his business concept.

Source: © Shutterstock, Inc.

Endnotes

1. Duermyer, R. (2016, November 26). Creating a Business Plan (Basics and Types). Retrieved from: https://www.thebalance.com/business-plans-the-basics-of-creating-a-business-plan-1794264
2. Duermyer, R. (2016, November 26). Creating a Business Plan (Basics and Types). Retrieved from: https://www.thebalance.com/business-plans-the-basics-of-creating-a-business-plan-1794264
3. Duermyer, R. (2016, November 26). Creating a Business Plan (Basics and Types). Retrieved from: https://www.thebalance.com/business-plans-the-basics-of-creating-a-business-plan-1794264
4. The Small Business Administration. (n.d.). Write your business plan. Retrieved from: https://www.sba.gov/business-guide/plan/write-your-business-plan-template
5. The Small Business Administration. (n.d.). Write your business plan. Retrieved from: https://www.sba.gov/business-guide/plan/write-your-business-plan-template
6. The U. S. Small Business Administration: SBA.gov. (n.d.). Loans & Grants | The U.S. Small Business Administration. Retrieved from: https://www.sba.gov/loans-grants
7. The U. S. Small Business Administration: SBA.gov. (n.d.). Loans & Grants | The U.S. Small Business Administration. Retrieved from: https://www.sba.gov/loans-grants
8. Nykiel, T. (2015, November 19). Small-Business Grants for Women: 10 Go-To Spots. Retrieved from: https://www.nerdwallet.com/blog/small-business/small-business-grants-for-women/
9. Nicastro, S. (2016, January 8). Small-Business Grants for Minorities: 9 Opportunities - NerdWallet. Retrieved from: https://www.nerdwallet.com/blog/small-business/small-business-grants-minorities/
10. Brown, C. (2010, July 12). How to Write a Winning Grant Proposal. Retrieved from: https://www.inc.com/guides/2010/07/how-to-write-a-grant-proposal.html
11. Entrepreneur. (n.d.). How to Keep Family and Friends Loans Strictly Business. Retrieved from: https://www.entrepreneur.com/article/24380
12. Internal Revenue Service. (n.d.). Frequently Asked Questions on Gift Taxes. Retrieved from: https://www.irs.gov/businesses/small-businesses-self-employed/frequently-asked-questions-on-gift-taxes
13. How do Angel Investors differ from Venture Capitalists? (2014, January 12). Retrieved from: http://www.rockiesventureclub.org/colorado-capital-conference/how-do-angel-investors-differ-from-venture-capitalists/
14. Beesley, C. (2016, April 27). How to Find the Right Private Investor for Your Small Business | The U.S. Small Business Administration. Retrieved from: https://www.sba.gov/blogs/how-find-right-private-investor-your-small-business-0
15. Parsons, N. (n.d.). The 11 Slides You Need to Have in Your Pitch Deck. Retrieved from: http://articles.bplans.com/what-to-include-in-your-pitch-deck/
16. Business Development Bank of Canada. (n.d.). How to present your business plan effectively. Retrieved from: https://www.bdc.ca/en/articles-tools/start-buy-business/start-business/pages/presenting-business-plan.aspx
17. Entrepreneur. (2015, February 10). 10 Tips for Creating a Winning Business Plan in PowerPoint. Retrieved from: https://www.entrepreneur.com/article/241537
18. Entrepreneur. (2015, February 10). 10 Tips for Creating a Winning Business Plan in PowerPoint. Retrieved from: https://www.entrepreneur.com/article/241537

PART 3
Entrepreneurship Execution

Source: © Shutterstock, Inc.

CHAPTER 9
How Do I Manage Change?

Case Study—Golden State Surplus, Revisited

Source: Used with permission from Golden State Surplus.

In Chapter 2, we introduced you to Golden State Surplus, an outdoor gear outfitter in Lake Isabella, California. The company specializes in a variety of goods for both residents of and visitors to the Kern River Valley. In this case study, we will revisit how changing social and technological factors are affecting this business.

When asked about the biggest challenges facing Golden State Surplus, owner Joe Ciriello specified three areas of concern. First, he says, Golden State Surplus does not offer online sales or engage in e-commerce. This is one area in which Joe feels the company could attract more national attention while improving local sales. A fully functioning website with online sales would help customers understand the various types of merchandise available in the store and through the website. Joe would like to work on developing the website himself, but has not found the time in his busy day.

Second, Joe worries that the changing preferences of younger buyers are preventing them from visiting his store. Joe feels that younger buyers are only interested in name brands and, although his store is one of the largest Wrangler dealers in the Kern County area, this isn't enough to encourage the younger demographic of buyers to come into the store.

Finally, the larger name brands preferred by some buyers are brands that are reluctant to sell to small retailers. These manufacturers prefer to sell to larger chain stores that have greater name recognition. Such "mega marketers," as Joe describes them, have greater buying power and flexibility over smaller retailers. Many name brands have high initial purchase requirements. This essentially locks out smaller retailers, driving customers interested in trendy merchandise to larger stores.

Each of these external factors—technological, social, and economic—influence how Golden State Surplus can sustain its business while providing for future growth. How a business adapts to change can have a strong influence on its success. In this chapter, we will look at managing change within your business, including change from both internal and external forces.

9.1 Understanding Factors that Impact the Business

Learning Objectives

1. Discuss the importance of understanding how internal and external forces influence your small business.
2. Discuss the value of a SWOT analysis and how it can help a business.

external influences

Influences on the business that come from outside the company and which are outside the business owner's control.

internal influences

Influences on the business that come from within, over which the business owner has at least some control.

Change—whether in your personal life or your business—is inevitable. Change can come from **external influences** (from outside of the business) or **internal influences** (from within your business). How well you prepare, adapt, and adjust to these changes will determine how well your business will weather the storms . . . and exploit the opportunities. In this section, we will look at a variety of factors that can influence your business. We will also learn how a SWOT analysis can help identify both positive and negative influences.

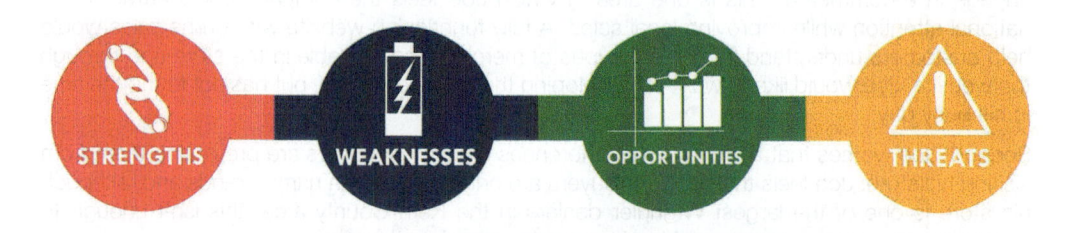

STRENGTHS · WEAKNESSES · OPPORTUNITIES · THREATS

SWOT ANALYSIS

Source: © Shutterstock, Inc.

SWOT Analysis

Influences on your business are all around. Some are good; some are bad. They can come from many different places and are often out of your control. How you react to these influences can determine your success.

For example, many states are changing the **minimum wage** that business owners are required to pay employees. While there are many studies concerning the business impact of such increases, it is a fact that small business owners must plan for these changes.[1] For example, in Seattle in 2015, a wage ordinance required all businesses to raise the minimum they pay employees by fifty cents per hour each year until 2021 (when the minimum wage throughout the city will be $15 per hour).[2] This forced Seattle's affected businesses to determine how best to adapt to this change. Being prepared in advance and ready to make the change are key skills for the small business owner.

Performing a **SWOT analysis** (strengths, weaknesses, opportunities, and threats) is one way a small business owner might begin to examine the factors that influence a business. The SWOT analysis was discussed in Chapter 4 as a way of examining marketing influences. Here, we will examine how SWOT can be used as a way of looking at both internal and external influences. For example, examining the strengths and weaknesses of the business is one way to uncover internal influences. Examining opportunities and threats, by contrast, is one way of looking at external influences.

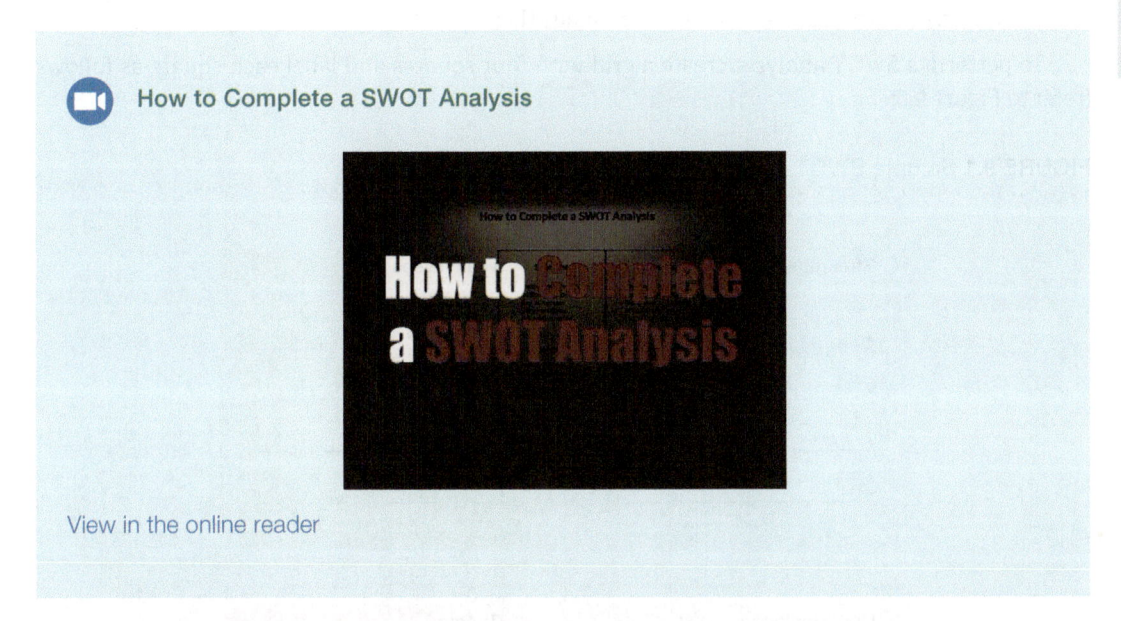

> **minimum wage**
> The lowest hourly wage an employer can pay a worker. This wage is mandated by law and involves certain exceptions.
>
> **SWOT analysis**
> A procedure for analyzing your company's strengths, weaknesses, opportunities, and threats. We often see a SWOT analysis performed for businesses, but this process can be implemented for a variety of situations.

How to Complete a SWOT Analysis

View in the online reader

A SWOT analysis can be broad in focus or specific to a given purpose (such as creating a marketing plan). The key to a good SWOT analysis is to be sure that you determine the objective of the analysis before beginning the task.[3] When managing change, we must examine the factors that might *force* us to make changes.

We perform a SWOT analysis so that we can take appropriate actions to exploit our strengths, shore up our weaknesses, invest in our opportunities, and mitigate our threats. What exactly does that mean? Strengths and weaknesses are considered internal factors because often the company has some control over them. Informed business owners know what they are good at and what they could do better. They have plans in place to manage both strengths and weaknesses. Opportunities and threats, on the other hand, are considered external factors. These are factors over which the business has little or no control. Unprepared business owners may operate in a **reactive** manner (after the fact), rather than a **proactive** manner (prior to the occurrence).

> **reactive**
> Actions in response to situations. This refers to responding after something has happened.
>
> **proactive**
> Preparing to act based on planning ahead of time.

Let's now break down a SWOT analysis:

- **Strengths** refer to what the business is good at; what it does well. For example, maybe your business excels in customer service, and you know this because of the many positive reviews your company has received on social media. You may wish to exploit this strength by mentioning this in your advertising and marketing efforts. A business may have many strengths.
- **Weaknesses** refer to what a business could do better. For example, while your business may offer excellent customer service, it may be slow to ship products. This causes customers to make several inquiries as to when they can expect their orders. One way in which your busi-

ness could improve is through a process improvement analysis, which would uncover shipping problems so you can make necessary improvements. As with strengths, a business may have many weaknesses.

- **Opportunities** refer to things that may positively influence your business. For example, suppose your best-selling product was just featured in a major national magazine, exposing the product to a larger market. This opportunity may drive more customers to your website. To take advantage of this opportunity, your advertising may feature "as seen in" statements, drawing attention to the fact that you sell the same product that was featured in the national magazine. A business may experience many opportunities, each with different potential benefits.

- **Threats** refer to the actions or events that may negatively affect your business. For example, you find out that your shipping carrier is raising rates significantly. While it may be possible to pass on the increased shipping costs to your customers, a thorough analysis of the threat may reveal that switching carriers for a better rate might be the preferable solution. Businesses must watch for threats be proactive to manage them.

To perform a SWOT analysis, create a grid with four squares and label each square as follows (refer to Figure 9.1):

FIGURE 9.1 Sample SWOT Analysis Grid

Strengths	Weaknesses
• _____ • _____ • _____ • _____	• _____ • _____ • _____ • _____
Opportunities	**Threats**
• _____ • _____ • _____ • _____	• _____ • _____ • _____ • _____

Source: Laura Portolese et al.

What Would You Do? Increasing Minimum Wage

Let's say you have a small musical instrument repair shop in Seattle. Due to Seattle's minimum wage ordinance, you have had to increase the minimum wage you pay your two part-time workers to $13.50 per hour.[4] More increases are on the way over the next several years. While business is good, it's not great. The recession of 2007 hit your business hard. Although your business weathered the storm, you had to cut staff and run the business by yourself just to stay open. Now that the economy has improved, you have added back a few part-time workers. You're not sure you can keep them both on at the increased wage. What would you do? Would you reduce your employees' work hours? Can you (or will you) reduce the hours your store is open? Will you simply go back to running the business by yourself?

Brainstorm with your management team your strengths, weaknesses, opportunities, and threats. In the appropriate box, list each example you and your team define. Make the boxes bigger as needed. Add as many lines as necessary. When completing your analysis, it's important to be realistic.

When looking at each part of the SWOT analysis, consider the following:[5]

- **Strengths:** What advantages does your business have over similar business? What do you do better? What advantages do you offer your customers?
- **Weaknesses:** What could you do better? What should you avoid? What causes you to lose sales? Here it is critical to look at your business like a customer might. What weaknesses do you see?
- **Opportunities:** What technology or trends in the industry align well with your business? What opportunities can you take advantage of right now? What about changes in government policy, social patterns, demographics, of other lifestyle changes that would create opportunities for your business?
- **Threats:** What obstacles are preventing your business from operating at full throttle? What are some government regulations or other legal impositions that must be addressed? Just as social patterns, demographics, and lifestyle changes can be opportunities, they may also present threats (depending on your business).

A SWOT analysis is a good first start for uncovering both external and internal factors that impact your business. In the next section, we'll look at these factors in more detail.

Key Takeaways

- There are several internal and external factors that can affect how your business may need to change and evolve over time.
- A SWOT analysis is one tool that can be used to identify both internal and external influences on your business.

Interactive Activities

1. Pick a local small business with which you have developed a relationship. Interview the business owner and perform a SWOT analysis. Be sure to identify at least two strengths, weaknesses, opportunities, and threats.
2. Based on the SWOT analysis you just performed, prepare a one-page report of your findings. Make at least one recommendation or observation regarding each area of the SWOT analysis.

9.2 External Factors

Learning Objectives

1. Describe the PESTLE model for identifying external factors that influence a business.
2. Explain the importance of identifying and preparing a plan to manage external influences.

As we examined in the previous section, a SWOT analysis can help uncover both external and internal factors that may affect your small business. In this section, we will focus on external factors in more detail. We will also introduce another technique for further refining your analysis.

There are many external factors that influence a business. While they are beyond the control of the business owner, they must nonetheless be evaluated and considered. When considering external factors, it is good to be proactive rather than reactive.

PESTLE analysis

A model used to analyze external threats to a business.

There are many different models a business owner might use to evaluate these external factors. One model, the **PESTLE analysis**, is a common way of looking at the most significant factors. PESTLE is an acronym that stands for political, economic, social, technological, legal, and ethical/environmental.[6] You may see this model referenced many different ways. For example, PESTLE stands for political, economic, social, technological, environmental, and legal. When presented as PEST, the acronym stands for political, economic (which combines legal), social (which combines environmental), and technological. Regardless of the model or expression you use, the evaluation and results should remain consistent. Let's examine PESTLE more carefully by looking at each external factor in turn.

FIGURE 9.2 PESTLE Model

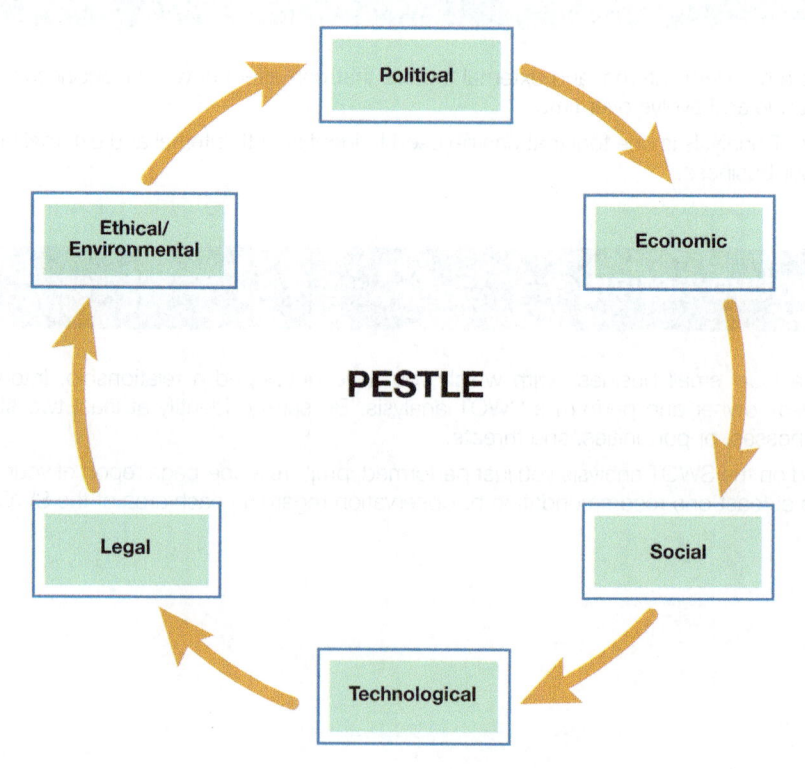

Source: Laura Portolese et al.

Political

Political factors are those factors that are imposed by government laws, regulations, and policies. For example, the Affordable Care Act was implemented in 2010 and required that all Americans have some form of health insurance.[7] By 2015, employers with fifty or more full-time employees were required to provide some form of health care or pay an employer's share of cost to the Internal Revenue Service (as addressed in Chapter 10). While the law did not necessarily affect smaller businesses, it was necessary for even small businesses to monitor it and implement its provisions where applicable. Similarly, the COVID-19 crisis left many small businesses constrained by government laws in regard to if, when, and how they will able to open. Planning for these types of constraints ahead of time can play an important role in helping you to deal with planned and unplanned changes and requirements.

> **political factors**
>
> The P in PESTLE refers to influences that the government may have on your business. These factors can include government influences on the economy, trade tariffs, and tax policies.

FIGURE 9.3 PESTLE Political Considerations

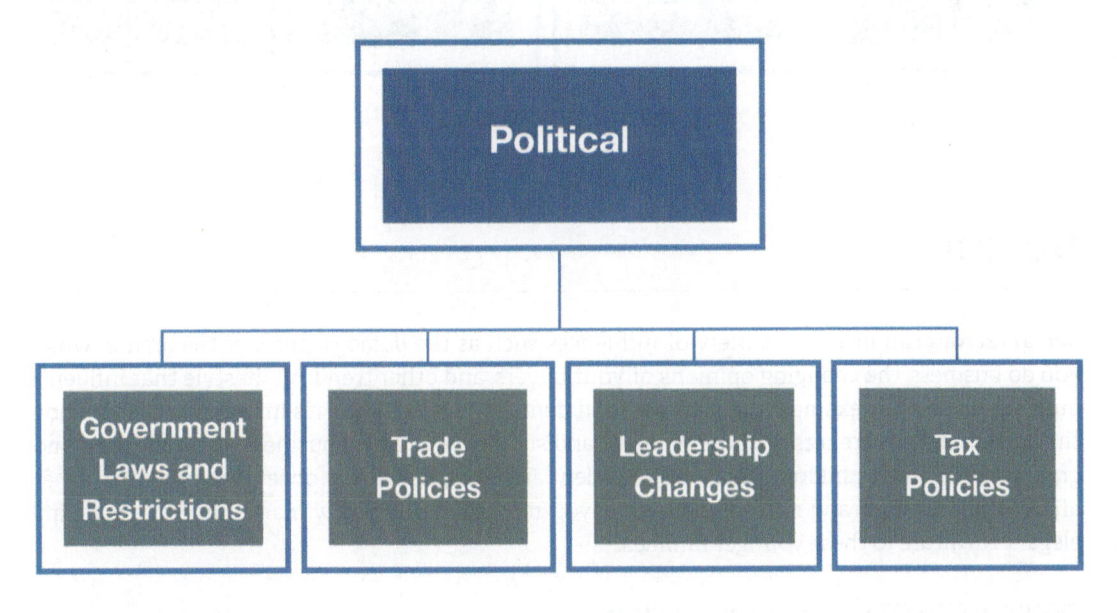

```
                    ┌───────────┐
                    │ Political │
                    └─────┬─────┘
        ┌────────────┬────┴─────┬────────────┐
┌───────────────┐ ┌────────┐ ┌───────────┐ ┌──────────┐
│ Government    │ │ Trade  │ │Leadership │ │  Tax     │
│ Laws and      │ │Policies│ │ Changes   │ │ Policies │
│ Restrictions  │ │        │ │           │ │          │
└───────────────┘ └────────┘ └───────────┘ └──────────┘
```

Source: Laura Portolese et al.

Economic

Economic factors are any factors that might affect how you use money in your business. These can include things like **inflation**, interest rates, and foreign exchange rates. For example, let's say your business needs to purchase a new piece of equipment for manufacturing. Inflation has been on the rise and interest rates are up. This means that it will cost more to borrow the money needed to purchase the equipment.

> **economic factors**
>
> The E in PESTLE refers to influences that the economy may have on your business.
>
> **inflation**
>
> An increase in prices of consumer goods, which in turn reduces purchasing power.

FIGURE 9.4 PESTLE Economic Considerations

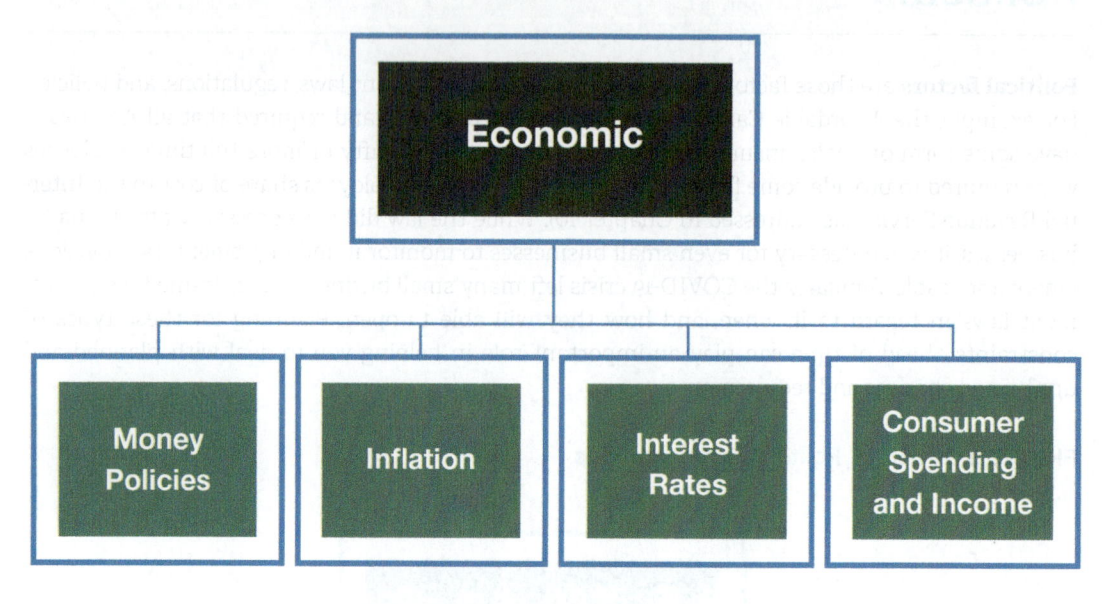

```
                        Economic
    ┌──────────┬──────────┴──────────┬──────────┐
   Money      Inflation          Interest     Consumer
  Policies                         Rates      Spending
                                             and Income
```

Source: Laura Portolese et al.

Social

social factors

The S in PESTLE refers to influences that community or societal pressures may have on your business.

Social factors can include a variety of influences such as the demographics of the area in which you do business, the changing opinions of your buyers, and other trends in lifestyle that influence buyer decisions. For example, as neighborhood demographics change, it's important to know how this affects the preferences of those who live and shop where you do business. If a younger demographic with small children becomes prevalent in a neighborhood once predominated by an affluent middle-aged and retiree population, you might have difficulty marketing your high-end, elegant furniture to these younger families.

FIGURE 9.5 PESTLE Social Considerations

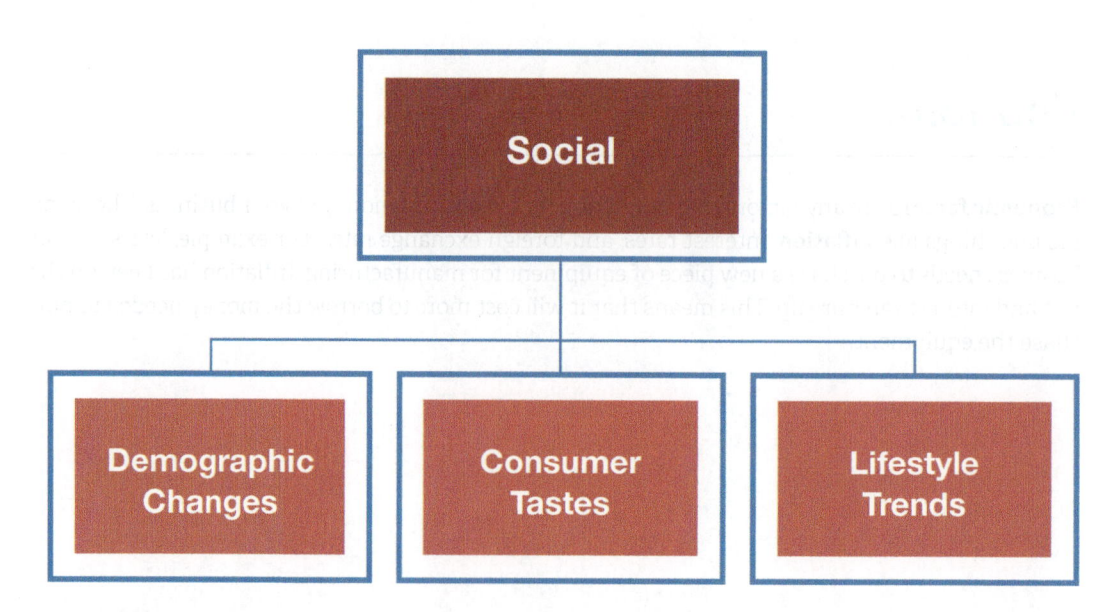

```
                    Social
    ┌───────────────┼───────────────┐
 Demographic     Consumer         Lifestyle
  Changes        Tastes            Trends
```

Source: Laura Portolese et al.

Technological

When we think of **technological factors** that can affect a business, one such trend is the proliferation of mobile applications. With the drop in price of cellular data services and the continuing improvements made to mobile devices, highly sophisticated mobile apps are popping up everywhere. While mobile technology may no longer be considered a "**disruptive technology**," there are many other types of disruptive technologies that may be significant factors in your business. For example, improvements in automation can mean that businesses can react quicker to customer needs. Consider technology that allows a business to accept credit card payments via smartphone. If you are a small business owner selling crafts at a farmer's market, having such a technology allows you to attract customers who might otherwise have expected you to be a cash-only business.

technological factors
The T in PESTLE refers to the way in which technology and its advances may influence your business.

disruptive technology
Any innovation that dramatically changes the way we think and do something.

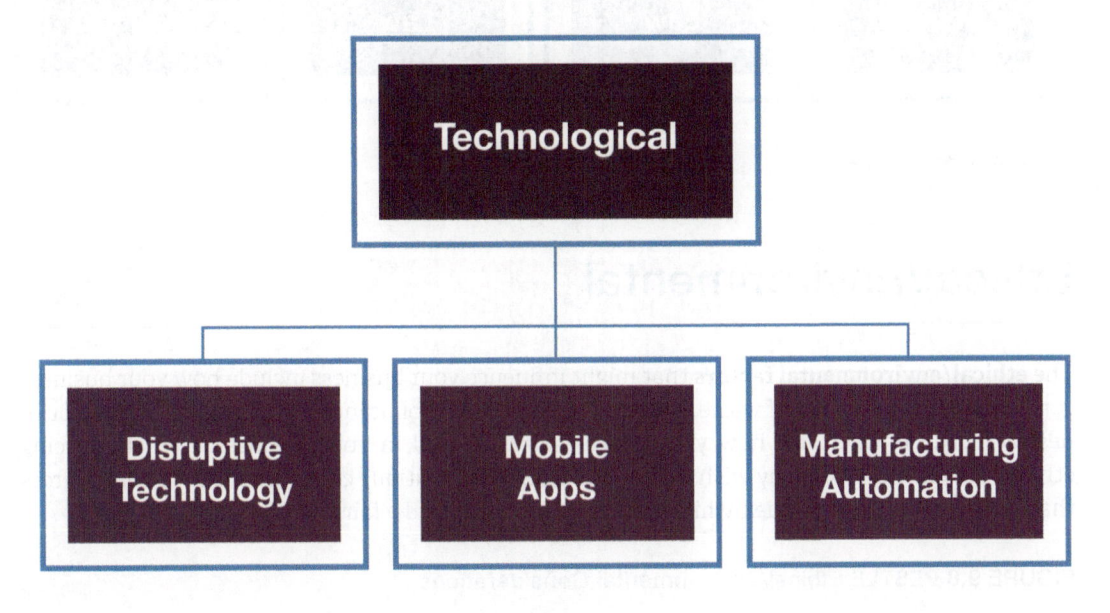

FIGURE 9.6 PESTLE Technological Considerations

Technological
- Disruptive Technology
- Mobile Apps
- Manufacturing Automation

Source: Laura Portolese et al.

Legal

Legal factors that can affect business include laws and regulations affecting companies. These laws and regulations can involve employment, issues of potential discrimination, copyrights and patents, consumer protection, import/export, intellectual property, and many other areas of business. For example, if you have a small craft business that sells handmade items mass-produced using mechanized embroidery machines, it is critical to know that you are not breaking any copyright or intellectual property laws regarding the images embroidered. Further, if you purchase the rights to an image, it is important to understand whether that license allows you to resell for profit items bearing the design. Additionally, the COVID-19 crisis levied several legal implications on business. Some of these included requiring customers to wear masks, employees to be vaccinated, and allowing employees the appropriate amount of time away from work when testing positive. The COVID-19 crisis proved that legal factors can appear unexpectedly.

legal factors
The L in PESTLE refers to the influence of laws at the local, state, and national levels that may affect your business.

FIGURE 9.7 PESTLE Legal Considerations

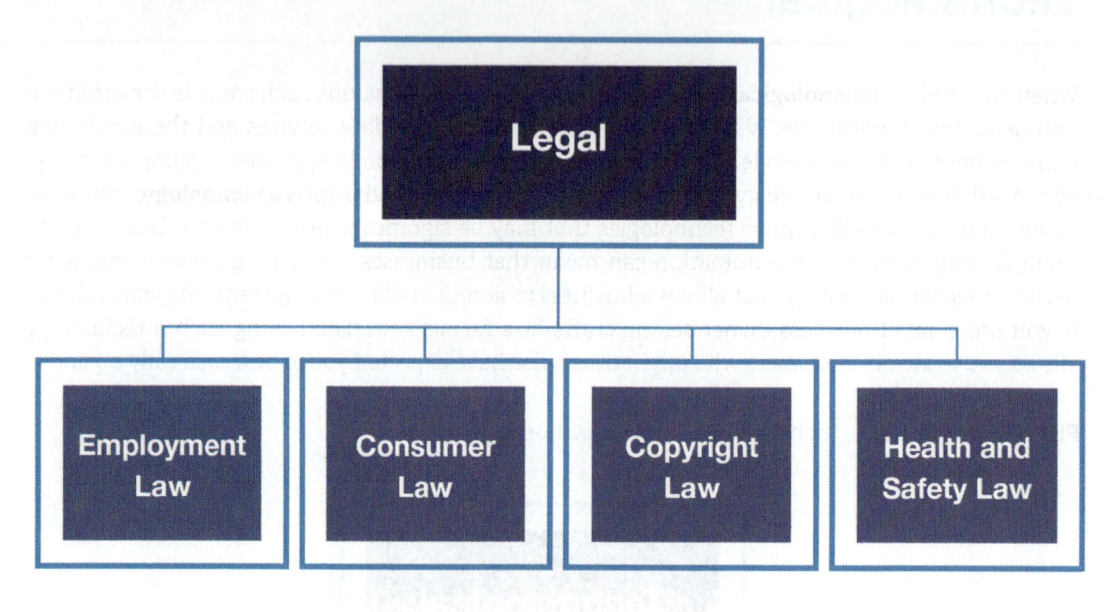

```
                    Legal
        ┌─────────┬─────────┬─────────┐
   Employment  Consumer  Copyright  Health and
      Law        Law       Law      Safety Law
```

Source: Laura Portolese et al.

Ethical/Environmental

ethical/environmental factors

The E in PESTLE refers to the way laws and restrictions regarding the environment may affect your business.

The **ethical/environmental factors** that might influence your business include how your business consumes energy, disposes of waste, and produces potential pollutants as a byproduct of your business activity. Consider also how you source materials used in your business. Is that sourcing ethical? For example, you may wish to buy coffee for your boutique coffee house from only sources that focus on *fair trade* policies, which ensure growers are paid a fair wage for their products.

FIGURE 9.8 PESTLE Ethical/Environmental Considerations

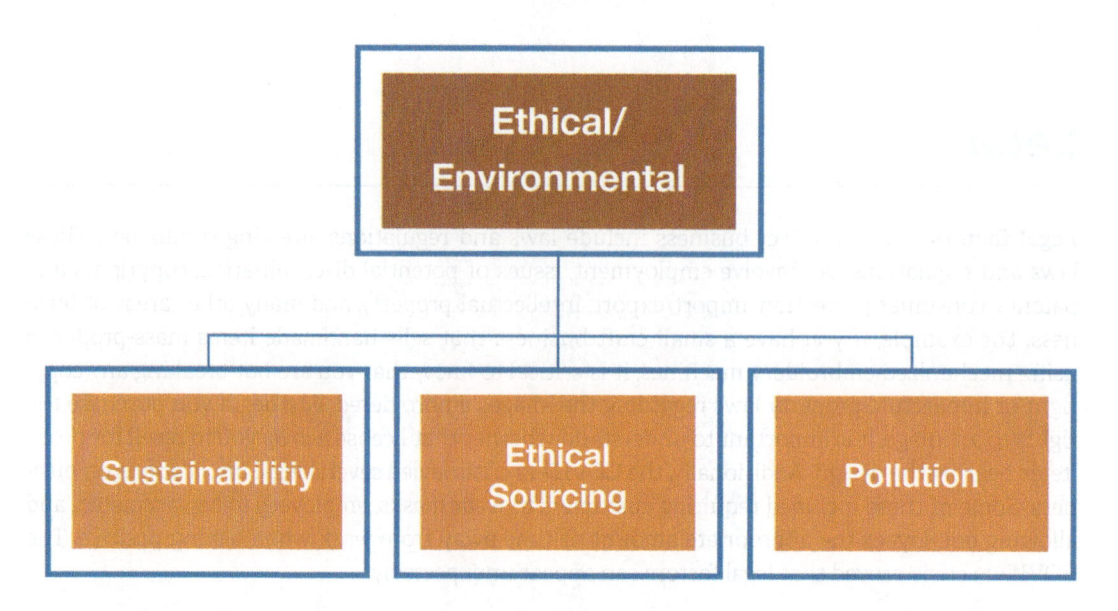

```
              Ethical/
           Environmental
        ┌────────┬────────┐
   Sustainabilitiy  Ethical   Pollution
                   Sourcing
```

Source: Laura Portolese et al.

One way to complete a PESTLE analysis is by documenting your findings using a matrix or template (like the one from PESTLEAnalysis.com in Figure 9.9). Templates are a great way to help get you started and make sure you capture all factors.

FIGURE 9.9 PESTLE Analysis Template Example

Source: Figure adapted from DecEasyT/Wordpress, https://akapps.wordpress.com/2011/08/30/pestel-analysis-template/

PESTLE Analysis

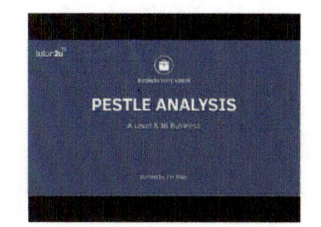

View in the online reader

> ### Leveraging: Taking Action
>
> Once you complete a SWOT and PESTLE analysis, you must act on the information these contain. First, carefully evaluate each item on your list. Think about how you might categorize similar threats. Rank each threat in order of priority and impact on your business. Think about those threats that need immediate attention and those that are of lower priority. Look for ways in which taking action might address multiple threats simultaneously.

Using SWOT and PESTLE for Strategic Planning

Both SWOT and PESTLE analyses can be used to help prepare a **strategic plan** for your business. A strategic plan is used to guide and direct the business to keep it on course.[8] A strategic plan starts by identifying the mission, vision, and purpose for your organization. These are referred to as the *core values* for your business. It's important not to skip this step, no matter how difficult this may be to articulate. This is because everything you do within your business should be driven by your vision and purpose for the business. Without a clear vision, it's difficult to determine the proper direction.

strategic plan
A plan that defines the direction of the organization and provides a means for achieving those goals.

The next part of your strategic plan should include your strategy for achieving your mission. To do this, you must understand thoroughly your strengths, weaknesses, opportunities, and threats. Performing a SWOT analysis and further defining these findings with a PESTLE analysis can help uncover roadblocks to success while identifying avenues to pursue.

Finally, your strategic plan should include your top priorities for completion. It's important to set a time frame. This can be as short as one year or as long as five years. Defining your top priorities helps further direct the course of the business. Priorities can focus on leveraging strengths or firming up weaknesses. Priorities might also involve developing a plan that addresses a change in employment law affecting your labor force within the year. Whatever priorities you set, they should support the core values of your mission. Following these analytical processes will help ensure that.

In the next section, we will look at internal factors that can affect your business.

Key Takeaways

- Strengths and weaknesses are considered internal influences, while opportunities and threats are considered external influences.
- Internal influences often are things you can control, while external influences are things that are outside of your control.
- The PESTLE model (political, economic, social, technological, legal, and ethical/environmental) can be used to identify external factors that may influence your business.

Interactive Activities

1. Interview a business owner and perform a PESTLE analysis. Be sure to identify at least two external threats in each category of the analysis.
2. Based on your PESTLE analysis, prepare a two-page paper that reports your findings. Identify the most important external influences. Choose one influence and make a recommendation for managing this impact.

9.3 Internal Factors

Learning Objectives

1. Describe how the company culture influences employee morale and productivity.
2. Develop effective strategies for identifying and managing stakeholders.
3. Recognize effective strategies for managing vendors and suppliers.

A small business may encounter many different issues which can affect its success. As we have learned in previous sections, awareness is the key to properly managing these issues. Awareness comes from spending the time to do a thorough analysis and participating in an honest evaluation and assessment of the business. While one might think that external factors are the most difficult to define and mitigate, it is really the internal factors that can pose the biggest challenges to a business. This may be because it can be difficult for a business owner to identify or admit their own weaknesses. This is where an *honest* assessment is important. It is normal to experience strong emotions when it comes to your business. After all, this is *your* business; you built it. Objective assessment is critical to developing the right plans for moving your business forward.

Source: © Shutterstock, Inc.

This section will focus on three internal factors: employees and your company **culture**, managing **stakeholders**, and managing **vendors** and suppliers.

Employees and Company Culture

Every business relies on their employees to succeed. Small businesses are no exception. This is especially apparent when a small business relies on one or two employees who open the business, run the front desk, and are the forward face of the business to the customer. Having a happy workforce is critical to any small business. Creating a happy workplace starts with hiring the right employees. (Chapter 10 focuses on the topic of human resources in more detail.) Let's look at a few things to consider when hiring the right person for the job. The right people, in other words, help create the right culture for your small business.

Hiring people who share your vision and passion will go a long way toward creating the business culture you seek. Mike Laven has some suggestions for finding people who fit perfectly into your small business:[9]

1. Make sure that the prospective employee is dedicated to doing the simple stuff right. Sometimes getting the boring details right are what separates good businesses from great businesses.
2. Hire someone who will help you create the culture you want. Do they share your passion for exceptional customer service? If so, you might have the right person.
3. What have they learned from their previous jobs? Knowing what the prospect has learned helps establish that they are *still* willing to learn.

Creating your business culture is an area of small business often overlooked by their owners. Why? Business owners tend to think a good business culture will create itself through good management and leadership. Essany offers a few tips to help business owners focus on creating a positive business culture:[10]

1. When hiring, be sure to consider the employee's attitude as well as that employee's ability to do the job. While job competency is important, a good attitude can go a long way.

culture

The norms, beliefs, and behaviors that are exhibited by employees and management in a business.

stakeholder

Any person or group impacted by or having an interest in your business.

vendor

A businesses that provides you with goods or services needed in your own business.

2. Be sure to include your employees when discussing and making decisions. Inclusion can go a long way toward helping employees feel they are a valued part of the organization.
3. Be sure your employees know that it's okay to have fun on the job (to a point).
4. Always prepare your staff to replace you. Train good people to excel.
5. When you lead by example, your employees will understand better your own expectations.
6. Share your goals for the company and help your employees to understand how they fit into achieving those goals.

Stakeholder Management

Stakeholders are any individuals or groups having an interest in your business. These can be your employees, investors, partners, customers, suppliers, the community where your business resides, or the city or state in which you do business. Each stakeholder has a unique investment in your businesses success.[11] Thoroughly understanding your stakeholders and their interests in your company can help you manage stakeholder expectations.

For example, your customers may expect your business to be open specific hours each day. Your investors expect that you will manage judiciously the money they have brought to the table. Your partners may expect targeted advertising or marketing campaigns that reach the right customers.

The first step in stakeholder management is to identify carefully all stakeholders and their interests in your business. This is important. Identifying stakeholders now can prevent you from being blindsided later by entities you did not consider. Here it is important to be specific, rather than general. For example, you may be an online retailer who sells digitized sewing patterns for plus-sized women. As you sell online and your products are delivered electronically, you may be tempted to say that "the world" is a stakeholder simply because of the far-reaching potential of the World Wide Web. It would be more accurate to suggest, however, that your stakeholders are plus-sized women who sew their own clothes and who want to print their own patterns. This is very specific and eliminates many demographics of people who would otherwise have no interest in what you sell online.

As you identify your stakeholders ask yourself: Who will be affected, positively or negatively, by your business? We want to believe that our business efforts will yield positive results for the community we plan to serve, but it's also important to consider negative impacts. Additionally, as you look at stakeholders, determine if they are internal (those who participate in your business in some meaningful way), or external (those whose opinions and viewpoints are important to your business).[12] It's a great idea to list stakeholders, identify their interests, and determine whether they are internal or external to your business.

Once you have identified all of your stakeholders, it's important to identify your *key* stakeholders. Key stakeholders have the most impact and influence on the success of your business. Knowing your key stakeholders helps you focus your time, attention, and energy. Kenny suggests that it's critical not only to identify your stakeholders, but to rate them in order of importance so that you focus on building relationships that matter to your business.[13] When rating stakeholders, Kenny suggests asking the following questions:

1. Does the stakeholder have a direct impact on your businesses performance?
2. Do you have a clear understanding of what you want from that stakeholder?
3. Is the relationship dynamic? Will it grow?
4. Can you exist without the stakeholder or can the stakeholder be easily replaced?
5. Is this stakeholder part of another group of stakeholders already identified?

Finally, Kenny suggests that when you are thinking about how you group your stakeholders, think about how your stakeholders will rate *you*. Group stakeholders with the same or similar criteria for evaluating your business in the same group. This will help you further identify areas in which you need to focus attention—areas that will impact the greatest number of stakeholders.

For example, suppose you own a large nursery and garden supply business. You sell to home gardeners, professional landscapers, and public institutions and businesses. No job is too small or too large for your business. You decide to create three different groups of stakeholders to identify your customers: home gardeners, professional landscapers, and large contractors. However, in doing so, you see overlaps in their needs from your business.

The first overlap is in quality. Each group wants quality, healthy, disease-free plants, shrubs, and trees. Additionally, both home gardeners and professional landscapers want a wide selection of plants that are regionally appropriate and guaranteed to grow. Contractors and professional landscapers, on the other hand, are interested in a long warranty period in case of problems with the plants once installed. Additionally, contractors and home gardeners are concerned about drought-tolerant plants. A Venn diagram like the one pictured in Figure 9.10 can help you visualize these overlaps in interests.

FIGURE 9.10 Venn Diagram of Overlapping Stakeholder Interests

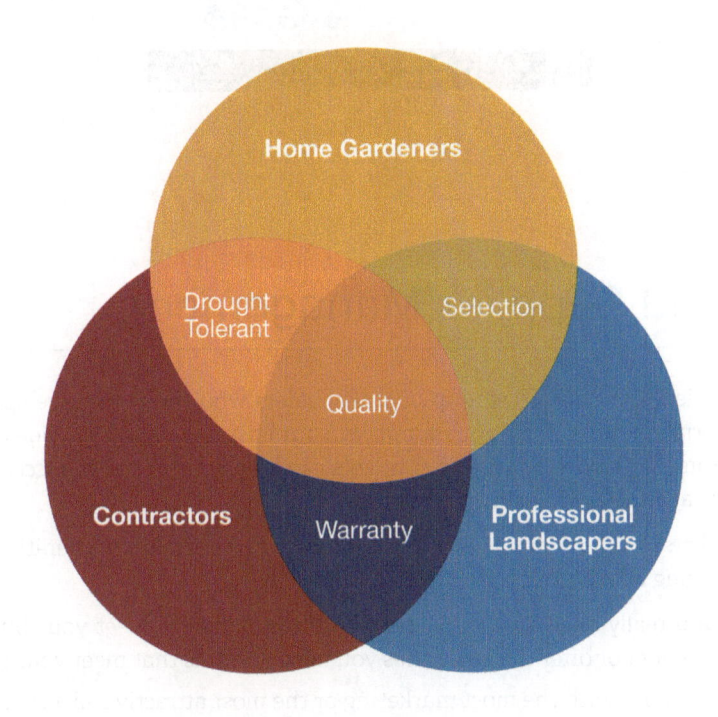

Source: Laura Portolese et al.

After you have identified your stakeholders, identified their interests in your business, determined the key stakeholders, and rated their importance to your business, it's necessary to develop a strategy for managing the expectations of those most important stakeholders. Remember that when managing stakeholders, we are **managing relationships**. Part of managing relationships is understanding what our stakeholders want from us and knowing what we are able to provide in kind. Don't forget that in order to manage a relationship, you must be monitoring that relationship. This means you are paying special attention to conversations, feedback, and other cues.

managing relationships

An effort to maintain and improve on relationships with vendors, clients, customers, and others who have direct influence over your businesses success.

power
Stakeholders who have some form of power over your bussiness' success.

interest
Stakeholders who have a specific interest in your business.

One tool that can help identify stakeholder **power** and **interest** in your business is Mendelow's Matrix, a grid on which you map stakeholders based on their levels of power and interest. " Mendelow's Matrix Model " demonstrates how to complete a power-interest grid for managing stakeholders. Completing a power-interest grid can help you identify best practices for managing each group of stakeholders. As always, focus your limited time on the areas with the greatest impact.

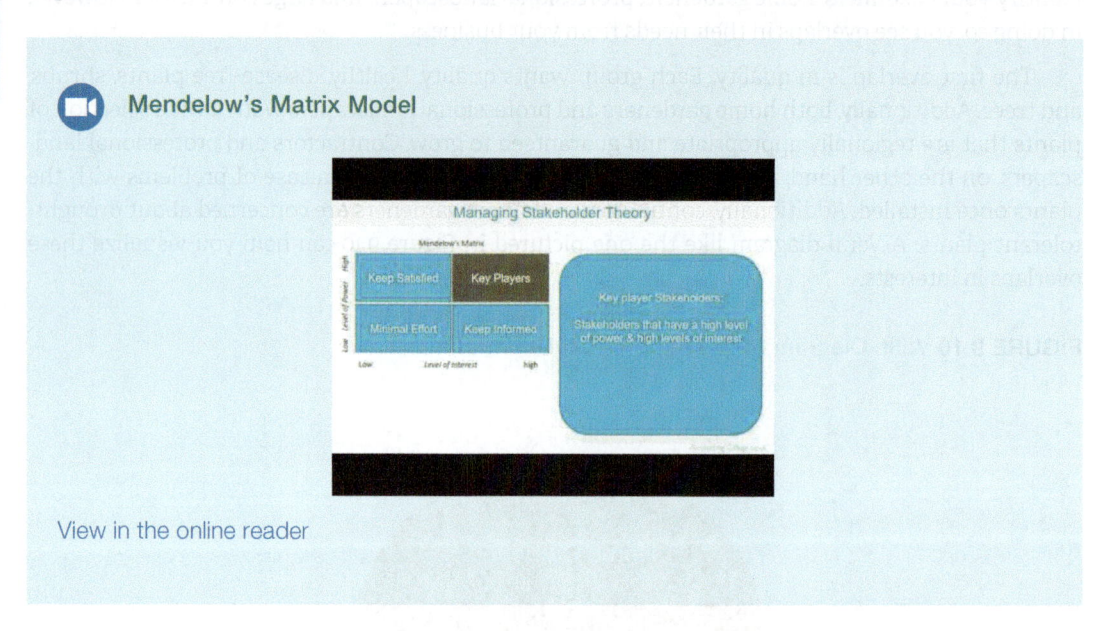

Mendelow's Matrix Model

View in the online reader

Vendor and Supplier Management

Vendors and suppliers are a specific group of stakeholders who should receive special attention. Without raw materials or goods from your suppliers, your business cannot provide products or services to your customers. Good vendors and suppliers can help your business succeed. Bad vendors and suppliers can cause delays in deliveries to customers.

Onspring, makers of vendor management software, suggests a few considerations for choosing vendors and managing relationships:[14]

- Know what you really need and find vendors who will scale to meet your business requirements. Does the vendor offer the quantities you need in terms that meet your budget?
- Don't pick the vendor with the most marketing or the most attractive advertisement. Pick the best option for your business needs.
- Make sure that your vendors support what they sell. Be sure that their support meets your needs and the needs of your customers.
- Ultimately, you are responsible for the products you sell. Be sure that your vendor has appropriate processes in place to ensure quality in its deliveries to you. Good quality assurance and risk management are very important.
- Verify your vendor's reputation on social media. Does your vendor have multiple complaints?
- Whenever possible, support local vendors. Just as you would want your customers to shop local, think local when choosing vendors. Sometimes just the convenience of being local can tip the scales in favor of one vendor over another.

Finally, just as with stakeholders; vendor management is about **relationship management**. As a small business owner, you cannot be expected to know every nuance of every aspect of your business. That's why relationships are critical to your success. It's important to choose wisely, communicate consistently, and plan for contingencies.[15] Developing relationships with vendors you trust can go a long way toward ensuring that you are well supported, especially in those areas of the business that might be challenging.

In the next section, we will look at a few additional areas to consider when managing change.

> **relationship management**
> An effort to maintain and improve on relationships with vendors, clients, customers, and others who have direct influence over your bussiness' success.

Key Takeaways

- Some additional internal influences that should be considered include your employees and your business culture, your stakeholders, and your vendors or suppliers.
- Choosing employees who share your vision and passion can go a long way to creating a positive business culture.
- Both stakeholder management and vendor management are about building and sustaining good business relationships.

Interactive Activity

1. Complete this test online to determine your leadership skills. Prepare a one page paper of your findings that includes an action plan for improving at least one skill identified in the results.

9.4 Additional Considerations for Managing Change

Learning Objectives

1. Recognize when to hire an attorney and describe some of the advantages.
2. Identify ways in which a small business owner can manage time effectively.
3. Distinguish between small business management and small business leadership skills.

In the previous sections, we addressed ways in which small business owners can identify and deal with changes that might affect their businesses. These include both external and internal sources. In the next section, we will look at a few other areas business owners should consider.

Should You Hire an Attorney?

There are plenty of "self-help" websites on the internet offering legal advice for small business owners. For example, LegalZoom.com offers several services for businesses. These include everything from formation, operations, **intellectual property** issues, **patent** issues, **trademark** and **copyright** matters, and even how to file for a **federal tax ID**. In addition, the site offers agents who can engage in live chats to help answer questions. If you read the information provided and struggle in understanding the terminology, or you just aren't comfortable with what you are reading, you might want to hire an attorney. There are also plenty of times when it's a good idea to hire a *specialized* attorney. Some attorneys specialize in patent law or tax law, for example.

Suzanne Kearns suggests six instances in which you'll want to hire an attorney. These include the following:[16]

1. When determining your business ownership structure. An attorney can help you decide on the best strategy for your needs.
2. When encountering employee issues. Small business owners do not always know employment law. An attorney can advise you on the proper way to manage a difficult situation.
3. When negotiating contracts. Here an attorney can help you avoid any pitfalls and make sure that you are aware of all aspects of the contract.
4. When a government entity files a complaint against your business. Whether your business is under investigation or a lawsuit has been brought, an attorney can help you understand and respond appropriately.
5. When environmental issues impact your business. There are a myriad of issues that could affect your business, such as waste disposal, hazardous materials, or other land-environment related issues. An attorney can help you make sure you stay on the right side of the law.
6. When you sell a business (addressed in Chapter 12) or when you buy a business. While purchasing a business may seem like a simple transaction, an attorney can help develop purchase agreements, make sure everything is as expected (performing due diligence), and transfer any licenses or other permits needed to make sure your business is operational on day one.

Time Management

There are only twenty-four hours in every day. While you cannot control how much time is available to you, you *can* control how your spend your time. As a small business owner, you may find yourself pulled in many directions at the same time. Often, you may feel as if you have no control over those demands.

One great suggestion for small business owners comes from Stephen Covey, who said in *The Seven Habits of Highly Effective People*, "Put first things first."[17] What does this mean? It means learning to focus your attention on those things that really matter. How do you identify these big things? Here is where the strategic plan comes in handy. Remember that in a strategic plan, you identify your company's core values, including the vision, mission, and purpose of your organization. You also identify your strengths, weaknesses, opportunities, and threats. You further define a strategy for achieving your mission and set priorities to achieve that mission. What you focus your attention on should serve to meet those goals and objectives, therefore, as defined in your strategic plan.

While that may sound simple, it frequently isn't. Small business owners, especially those with few or no employees, may find that they are inundated with competing priorities that all require their time and attention. The Small Business Administration has some suggestions for small business owners to help stay focused and on task.[18] These include the following:

---

intellectual property
The rights that individuals have to their own ideas and the resulting efforts and profits from those ideas.

patent
A legal, exclusive right to sell or market an invention by the inventor.

trademark
A legally registered symbol, word, or words that represent an entity.

copyright
A legal, exclusive right to artistic work such as writing, film, or music. These rights include the ability to print, publish, distribute, and sell such works.

federal tax ID
An identifying number issued by the Internal Revenue Service and used for tax purposes. For individuals, this is that person's social security number (SSN). For businesses, this is a nine-digit number that may be referred to as a taxpayer identification number (TIN) or employer identification number (EIN).

- Be sure you have your goals clearly defined and in writing. Goals should be SMART (specific, measurable, attainable, relevant, and time-bound).
- Prepare a detailed list of tasks. Here, break down your goals into tasks.
- Prioritize those tasks. Be sure to list the most important tasks first.
- Identify and list all ongoing operations tasks that are required to keep the business functioning. These are tasks that must be completed as part of normal business operations, such as ordering inventory, or processing payroll.
- Build flexibility into your schedule. Leave room in your schedule for the unexpected.

Carefully setting priorities can help ensure that you are working on the big things first. If you are unclear on how to set priorities, the SBA suggests four methods:

1. **Pareto Analysis**

    The Pareto principle suggests that 20 percent of your effort will produce 80 percent of your expected results. Use this technique to help you determine what tasks will yield the most results toward your goals.

2. **ABC Method**

    Use the letters A, B, and C to identify tasks that are most important (A), moderately important (B), and least important (C). Then, within each category of tasks, further clarify tasks to complete by adding a number. For example, the most important tasks of your day may be listed as A1, A2, A3, while the moderate tasks may be listed as B1, and B2. Finally, the least most important tasks would be listed as C1, C2, and C3.

3. **Eisenhower Method**

    This method was developed by President Eisenhower. Using it, you take all tasks—including business operational needs—and identify these tasks by placing them in one of four quadrants: *urgent and important*, *important but not urgent*, *urgent but not important*, and *not important or urgent*. Focus your time and attention on tasks that are both important and urgent first.

4. **POSEC Method**

    This method includes prioritizing tasks (arranging tasks in order), organizing tasks (structuring your most basic tasks), streamlining tasks (simplifying bothersome tasks), economizing tasks (working on some of those tasks you want to do but which fall lower on the list of priorities), and contributing tasks (when you complete a task and are able to give back).

Finally, when considering ways to manage your time, the National Federation of Independent Business suggests you do the following:[19]

- Develop a smart schedule, which includes understanding your priorities.
- Use the right tools, whether these are online to-do lists/calendars or paper planners.
- Be sure to plan for breaks by leaving white space in your schedule.
- Delegate. Trust the people you hired and delegate tasks appropriately.
- Avoid burnout by taking time to relax.

Leadership and Interpersonal Skills

manager
Someone who is responsible for controlling a specific part of the business.

leader
Someone who uses influence and persuasion to achieve results.

Management vs. Leadership

View in the online reader

soft skills
Skills that enable one to interact effectively with others.

Businesses need both managers and leaders to be successful. In a small business, the owner often fills both roles. What, then, do we mean by a manager as compared to a leader? A **manager** can be defined as the individual who is responsible for controlling and administrating the day-to-day activities of the business as well as setting priorities and goals. We often think of managers as those with power and authority over others. A **leader** is an individual who is able to influence others to see and implement their vision. Leaders do not influence with power, but through *social influence*.

While not all managers are leaders, in a small business, the business owner usually needs both sets of skills. Some of the most important interpersonal skills needed by both managers and leaders are **soft skills**. These skills include communication, listening, and attitude.[20] There are many others.

FIGURE 9.11 Communication Feedback Loop

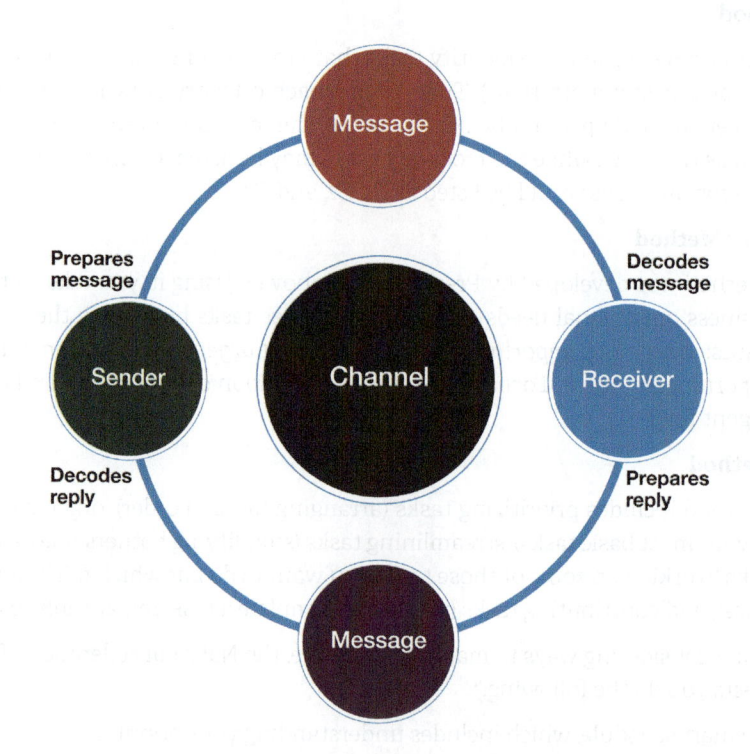

Source: Laura Portolese et al.

Effective communicators can communicate information with empathy, both verbally and in writing. Because they are empathetic, they can handle conflict and solve difficult problems. They communicate in a manner that is diplomatic and tolerant. One way to make sure you are communicating effectively is to employ effective listening skills. *Really* listening involves much more than just appearing to pay attention. Forbes magazine suggests there are ten steps to effective listening:[21]

1. Face the speaker. Maintain eye contact. Do not appear distracted. Avoid looking at screens or around the room.
2. Give your attention, but stay relaxed. Don't make the speaker feel uncomfortable.
3. Listen with an open mind. Do not assume you know what the sender is attempting to convey until you hear the entire message.
4. Try to create a mental image of the words.

5. Do not interrupt the speaker. Do not attempt to provide solutions before hearing the entire message.
6. When asking for additional information, wait until the speaker pauses.
7. Only ask questions that help you understand. Stay on topic and do not let the conversation stray.
8. Use empathy to try to feel what the speaker is saying.
9. Give feedback throughout. This demonstrates interest and understanding.
10. Look for non-verbal cues. Much of communication is through non-verbal body language.

Finally, there is a long-standing debate on whether leaders are born or made. To complicate the matter, there are numerous courses—short-term, long-term, and full college-level classes—on the topic of leadership. While some people are indeed born leaders, one can also develop good leadership skills.[22] Erika Andersen suggests that one of the first things a would-be leader needs to do is become self-aware. Being self-aware means that you understand your strengths and weaknesses, you know what you care about most, and you know and how you affect others. Self-awareness also involves understanding your moral compass and how your actions align with your moral intentions. In other words, you know how you "show-up" in your life and the lives of others.

Andersen offers some advice for those who wish to become more self-aware:[23]

- Report your experiences as through the eyes of someone witnessing the experience. When we are emotional about something, it's hard to view the situation objectively. When we try to view our actions as neutrally as possible, we can begin to reflect on how our actions affect others.
- Ask for feedback and be willing to hear honest comments.
- Listen. As we have discussed previously, listening with empathy and for understanding is a powerful way to see from someone else's perspective.

Crisis Situations and Planning Before Change Occurs

There are some situations that can be difficult to plan for. COVID-19 is one such example. The pandemic caused many entrepreneurs to close their doors entirely, or be creative in the way they offered services. For example, a restaurant may only be able to provide take-out during the crisis, which required the entrepreneurs to change, and change quickly. The amount of staff needed probably changed, the amount of food to order from the supplier changed, and new menus and marketing materials may have needed to be printed to work within the constraints of the crisis. From a staffing perspective, the COVID-19 pandemic, for example, required many entrepreneurs to furlough workers, and created the need to quickly change the way they staff their businesses. **Furlough** refers to the temporary layoff of a worker, in which the worker will likely go back to work after the crisis. Sometimes furloughs are not temporary layoffs, but instead result in requiring the employee to work fewer hours.[24] The entrepreneur had to determine if, how, and when the employees would be furloughed.

A **crisis communication plan** is designed to provide steps and guidance to support employees, suppliers, and customers should an emergency occur. Uncertainty can create undue stress for the entrepreneur, and by having a crisis communication plan, the entrepreneur knows exactly the steps to take should a crisis occur. Surprisingly, a survey performed by the Institute for Public Relations found that 44 percent of respondents did not address an infectious disease outbreak in their crisis communication plans. In fact, 10 percent of respondents did not have a crisis communication plan at all,[25] whether it be a natural disaster, workplace shooting, or a pandemic like COVID-19.

There are many considerations when developing a crisis communication plan. Some ways to develop this type of communication plan include:[26]

furlough
The temporary layoff of a worker in which the worker will likely go back to work after the crisis in question passes.

crisis communication plan
Designed to provide steps and guidance to support employees, suppliers, and customers should an emergency occur.

- **Determine the audiences that needs communication about the crisis.** For example, do you need to communicate with customers, employees, the news media, the community, investors, and other stakeholders? Making a list of the people or groups that need to be communicated with can ensure no one group is missed. In addition, gathering this contact information and putting it in one place can make the communication happen more quickly with each stakeholder group.
- **Pre-write messages.** Obviously, every situation may not be able to be addressed, but pre-writing messages to each audience for a variety of crisis situations can be helpful when, as an entrepreneur, you called to make quick decisions with quick communications.[27]
- **Communicate policies.** Be prepared to communicate any new policies or rules in place due to the crisis, especially to your employees. For example, perhaps you are reducing hours or closing all together. Communicate this information respectfully and in a straightforward manner so that employees are not left guessing the status of their position at your company.
- **Confirm trusted information sources.** Determine where you will obtain your facts about the crisis situation. For example, there is an immense amount of information about COVID-19 from a variety of sources. Choosing reliable sources for information, such as the Center for Disease Control (CDC) is key to making sure you have accurate information to communicate to your employees.

Key Takeaway

- Additional factors that can affect your business include hiring an attorney, your ability to manage your time, and your leadership skills.

Interactive Activity

1. For one week, track how you spend your time. Be sure to track every activity. Use a chart to capture each hour of the day and each day of the week. Write a one-page paper analyzing how you spent your time and make one suggestion for improving your overall time management.

9.5 Test Your Skills: Applied Case

The Millers Supply Chain Problems

Source: © Shutterstock, Inc.

    The Millers have owned a business that they started based on a technology enhancement they developed several years ago. They own the patent on the item. In order to help bring the item to market, they decided to do their own manufacturing while obtaining several parts from sources outside of the country. Unfortunately, when COVID-19 hit, their supply chain began to have problems. As suppliers all over the world were struggling to meet demands, the Millers knew they needed to find other reliable sources or consider building the parts themselves. This would require an investment in equipment that might be difficult to obtain and cause additional uncertainty in an already challenging market. What should the Millers do?

1. Complete the SWOT Analysis grid for this problem. Make a recommendation based on your findings.
2. Identify at least two internal and two external factors that could influence their decision.

Endnotes

1. Council of Smaller Enterprises. (n.d.). Small Business Impact: Raising Minimum Wage. Retrieved from: http://www.cose.org/Advocacy/Resource Library/Additional Public Policy Issues/Small Business Impact.aspx
2. Mendoza, J. (2017, July 27). Seattle's $15 minimum wage debate catches small businesses in the middle. Retrieved from: https://www.csmonitor.com/USA/Society/2017/0727/Seattle-s-15-minimum-wage-debate-catches-small-businesses-in-the-middle
3. Smartdraw. (n.d.). SWOT Analysis. Retrieved from: https://www.smartdraw.com/swot-analysis/
4. Mendoza, J. (2017, July 27). Seattle's $15 minimum wage debate catches small businesses in the middle. Retrieved from: https://www.csmonitor.com/USA/Society/2017/0727/Seattle-s-15-minimum-wage-debate-catches-small-businesses-in-the-middle
5. SWOT Analysis (Strengths, Weaknesses Opportunities, Threats). (n.d.). Retrieved from: https://www.mindtools.com/pages/article/newTMC_05.html
6. PESTLE Analysis. (n.d.). What is PESTLE Analysis? A Tool for Business Analysis. Retrieved from: http://pestleanalysis.com/what-is-pestle-analysis/
7. Internal Revenue Service. (2017, April 20). Questions and Answers on Employer Shared Responsibility Provisions Under the Affordable Care Act. Retrieved from: https://www.irs.gov/affordable-care-act/employers/questions-and-answers-on-employer-shared-responsibility-provisions-under-the-affordable-care-act
8. Mask, C. (2013, August 9). Invest in Your Success: Strategic Planning for Small Business. Retrieved from: https://smallbiztrends.com/2013/08/strategic-planning-small-business.html
9. Essany, M. (n.d.). 6 Ways to Build a Great Corporate Culture for Your Small Business. Retrieved from: https://quickbooks.intuit.com/r/employees/6-ways-to-build-a-great-corporate-culture-for-your-small-business/
10. Essany, M. (n.d.). 6 Ways to Build a Great Corporate Culture for Your Small Business. Retrieved from: https://quickbooks.intuit.com/r/employees/6-ways-to-build-a-great-corporate-culture-for-your-small-business/
11. Health Knowledge. (n.d.). Identifying and managing internal and external stakeholder interests. Retrieved from: https://www.healthknowledge.org.uk/public-health-textbook/organisation-management/5b-understanding-ofs/managing-internal-external-stakeholders
12. Health Knowledge. (n.d.). Identifying and managing internal and external stakeholder interests. Retrieved from: https://www.healthknowledge.org.uk/public-health-textbook/organisation-management/5b-understanding-ofs/managing-internal-external-stakeholders
13. Kenny, G. (2014, March 6). Five Questions to Identify Key Stakeholders. Retrieved from: https://hbr.org/2014/03/five-questions-to-identify-key-stakeholders
14. Onspring. (n.d.). 7 Vendor Management Tips for Startups. Retrieved from: https://www.onspring.com/blog/7-vendor-management-tips-for-startups/
15. Sullivan, M. (n.d.). 10 Tips for Managing Vendor Relationships. Retrieved from: https://quickbooks.intuit.com/r/products-and-manufacturing/10-tips-to-effectively-manage-vendors-and-suppliers/
16. Kearns, S. (n.d.). 6 Reasons to Consult an Attorney for Your Small Business. Retrieved from: https://quickbooks.intuit.com/r/hr-laws-and-regulation/6-reasons-to-consult-an-attorney-for-your-small-business/
17. FranklinCovey. (n.d.). Habit 3: Put First Things First. Retrieved from: https://www.stephencovey.com/7habits/7habits-habit3.php
18. The U. S. Small Business Administration. (n.d.). Time Management for Small Businesses. Retrieved from: https://www.sba.gov/sites/default/files/files/PARTICIPANT_GUIDE_TIME_MANAGEMENT.pdf
19. National Federation of Independent Business. (2014, July 1). Time Management Skills for Small Business Owners. Retrieved from: http://www.nfib.com/content/playbook/technology/5-time-management-tips-for-small-business-owners-mybiz-ja2014-65985/
20. Investopedia. (2015, March 4). How do interpersonal skills influence a business culture? Retrieved from: http://www.investopedia.com/ask/answers/030415/how-do-interpersonal-skills-influence-business-culture.asp
21. Forbes. (2012, November 9). 10 Steps To Effective Listening. Retrieved from: https://www.forbes.com/sites/womensmedia/2012/11/09/10-steps-to-effective-listening/#281ee49d3891
22. Andersen, E. (2012, November 21). Are Leaders Born Or Made? Retrieved from: https://www.forbes.com/sites/erikaandersen/2012/11/21/are-leaders-born-or-made/#36f1e07b48d5
23. Andersen, E. (2012, November 21). Are Leaders Born Or Made? Retrieved from: https://www.forbes.com/sites/erikaandersen/2012/11/21/are-leaders-born-or-made/#36f1e07b48d5
24. SHRM, (n.d.) What is the difference between a furlough, a layoff and a reduction in force? Retrieved from: https://www.shrm.org/resourcesandtools/tools-and-samples/hr-qa/pages/furloughlayoffreductioninforce.aspx
25. Burjek, A & Kimmel, S. (18 March 2020) During Covid-19 outbreak, utilize internal communications in your company crisis plan. Retrieved from: https://www.workforce.com/news/during-covid-19-outbreak-utilize-internal-communications-in-company-crisis-plan
26. PwC. (n.d.) How today's response can position your business to thrive tomorrow. Retrieved from: https://www.pwc.com/us/en/library/covid-19/crisis-management.html
27. Ready.gov (n.d.) Crisis communication plans. Retrieved from: https://www.ready.gov/business/implementation/crisis

CHAPTER 10
Handling Human Resources

Case Study—Cooking Up a Culture of Excellence in Customer Service

Source: Used with permission from Joann and Bruce Harris.

Joann and Bruce Harris, owners of Ellensburg Pasta Company, know good customer service. They will only hire people with the same mentality. Prior to purchasing their restaurant in 2005, Bruce and Joann often spoke of doing so despite separate career paths. Joann was an elementary school teacher and Bruce was a Food Services of America sales associate. When the opportunity came to purchase the restaurant, Joann and Bruce seized it, knowing one of the most important aspects of their business would be customer service. A major challenge they faced in business was hiring employees with the same mentality.

Joann says their hiring process is typical, yet stringent. Potential employees are asked to drop off a résumé and, if there is time, Bruce and Joann spend a few minutes talking with the potential candidate prior to an interview. Joann says they always ask about availability. Employees are expected to commit for at least a year. In a university town, this can be a challenge. Once the prospective employee's availability and commitment to the restaurant are established, Bruce and Joann review their first impressions of that candidate.

After the selection process, new hires go through an orientation process covering such policies as "Where do I park?" and "What is the dress code?" The new hire is then paid for eight to twelve hours of training. This process is expensive; Ellensburg Pasta Company must pay the new hire as well as a fully trained employee to conduct the training.

After an employee has proven they are successful at bussing, they can move to a hosting position, then to a server position. At each of these levels, additional and extensive training is offered. Joann believes this type of training creates a harmonious environment in which employees are capable of providing the best customer service possible. This time commitment pays off, as Ellensburg Pasta Company is known around town as one of the best places to eat with the best customer service.

Joann sends new managers to professional training development off site. This helps employees be the best they can be. The skills developed through this training allow the employees to provide the best service around while teaching others how to do the same.

As with any business, there can be disciplinary issues. For example, not following specific polices outlined in the orientation will result in disciplinary action. Joann says all these actions, and discussions surrounding them, are documented.

Ellensburg Pasta Company has implemented successful Human Resources practices in their hiring, selection, training and management of employees. Human Resources is one of the biggest challenges facing entrepreneurs. Ellensburg Pasta Company seems to have it all "boiled down" to an effective recipe.

10.1 Recruitment, Selection, and Hiring Process

Learning Objectives

1. Discuss the process for hiring a new employee.
2. Explain the difference between a job analysis and a job description.

Once your business begins to grow, it is likely you will need to hire employees. There are three steps to the process of hiring: recruitment, selection, and hiring. **Recruitment** is defined as a process that provides the organization with a pool of qualified job candidates from which to choose. The **selection process** refers to the steps involved in choosing people who have the right qualifications to fill a current or future job opening. Finally, once you complete the selection process, you will go through the hiring process. That is the focus of this section.

Recruitment

The first step in recruiting is the development of a job analysis. The **job analysis** is a formal system developed to determine what tasks your employees will actually perform in their jobs. The purpose of a job analysis is to ensure the right fit between the job and the employee. The analysis also determines how employee performance will be assessed. A major part of the job analysis includes research, which may mean reviewing expected job responsibilities and researching job descriptions for similar jobs with competitors.

The job analysis ultimately is the basis for the job description you will need to write for the position. According to research by Hackman and Oldham, a job diagnostic survey should be conducted to diagnose job characteristics prior to any redesign of a job.[1] This type of survey allows you to gain information on what tasks someone in similar positions would do. You can then create your job analysis in the same manner. After you write the job analysis, you will write the job description.

A **job description** is a list of tasks, duties, and responsibilities for a job. Job *specifications*, on the other hand, discuss the skills and abilities the person must have to *perform* the job. The two are tied together, as job descriptions are usually written to include job specifications. A job analysis must be performed first. Then, based on that data, we can successfully write the job description and job specifications. Think of the analysis as "everything an employee is required and expected to do."

Job descriptions should include the following components:

- Job functions (the tasks the employee performs)
- Knowledge, skills, and abilities (what an employee is expected to know and be able to do, as well as personal attributes)
- Education and experience required
- Physical requirements of the job (ability to lift, see, or hear, for example)

---

recruitment

The process that provides an organization with a pool of qualified candidates from which to choose.

selection process

The steps involved in choosing people who have the right qualifications to fill a current or future job opening.

job analysis

A formal system developed to determine what tasks people will actually perform in their jobs.

job description

A list of tasks, duties, and responsibilities for a job.

How to Write a Job Description

Tips on How to Write a Job Description in 3 Easy Steps

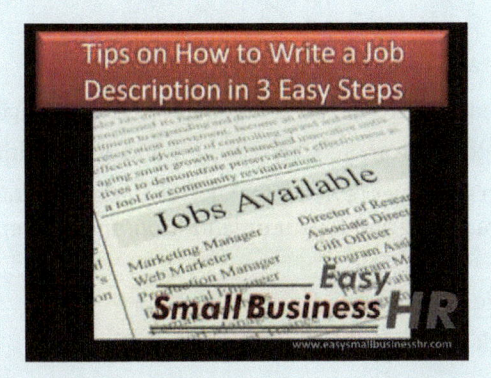

View in the online reader

After you have completed the job analysis and job description, you will begin the recruitment process. There are many ways to recruit for new positions.

Source: © Shutterstock, Inc.

What Would You Do?

Here are the important aspects to writing a good job description:

- Be sure to include the pertinent information: Title, Department, Reports to whom, Duties and responsibilities, Terms of employment, Qualifications needed.
- Think of the job description as a snapshot of the job.
- Communicate clearly and concisely.
- Make sure the job description will be interesting to the right candidate applying for the job. Avoid acronyms.
- Don't try to fit all aspects of the position into the job description.
- Proofread the job description.

Based on the information provided here, what do you think will be the most difficult part of the job description to write? Do you think job descriptions should be fluid and change over time? If so, how would you manage this process?

Check out SHRM.org and Monster.com for more resources on writing job descriptions.

Before you begin recruiting, it is important to have a recruitment plan—even an informal one—in place. This plan outlines where you intend to recruit. It also defines the expected timelines for recruitment, selection, and training of the candidate. Having a plan makes it easier to recruit from a variety of sources to ensure diversity. Lastly, consider the current economic situation. When unemployment is high, you may receive hundreds of applications for a single opening. When the economy is up and employment is low, you may not receive many applications. Consider using a variety of sources.

When recruiting, there are a few important considerations:[2]

- Ensure your recruitment ad uses inclusive language, that encourages diverse people to apply.
- Use social media as a tool to promote your company and also recruit.
- Review your ratings on employer review sites such as Glassdoor, and be aware of what current and past employees are saying about your organization, and be prepared to address any issues employees may find.
- Leverage your professional networks for recruiting.
- Use technology to track applicants, and the hiring process.

Many organizations, including smaller businesses, offer hiring bonuses to new workers, and you may find this is a good way to recruit new people, which was especially true after the lockdown during the COVID-19 pandemic. For example, Bartlett Plumbing and Heating, located in Michigan offers a sign-on bonus of $1,000 once a new employee stays for ninety days.[3] You as an entrepreneur may find you have a hard time recruiting people for particular jobs, especially those that are lower paying. This is one way to entice the right person to work for you.[4]

There are a number of sources you can use to recruit new employees. Table 10.1 contains some examples.

TABLE 10.1 Examples of Places You Can Recruit with Advantages and Disadvantages for Each Method

Recruitment Method	Advantages	Disadvantages
Outside recruiters, executive search firms, and temporary employment agencies	Can be time saving	Expensive
		Less control over final candidates to be interviewed
Campus recruiting/ educational institutions	Can hire people to grow with the organization	Time consuming
	Plentiful source of talent	Only appropriate for certain types of experience levels
Professional organizations and associations	Industry specific	May be a fee to place an ad
	Networking	May be time-consuming to network
Websites/internet recruiting	Diversity friendly	Could be too broad
	Low cost	Be prepared to deal with hundreds of résumés
	Quick	
Social media	Inexpensive	Time consuming
		Overwhelming response
Events	Access to specific target markets of candidates	Can be expensive
		May not be the right target market
SIG	Industry specific	Research required for specific SIGS tied to jobs

Recruitment Method	Advantages	Disadvantages
Referrals	Higher quality people	Concern for lack of diversity
	Retention	Nepotism
Unsolicited résumés and applications	Inexpensive, especially with time-saving keyword résumé search software	Time consuming
Internet and/or traditional advertisements	Can target a specific audience	Can be expensive
Employee leasing	For smaller organizations, it means someone does not have to administer compensation and benefits, as this is handled by leasing company	Possible costs
	Can be a good alternative to temporary employment if the job is permanent	Less control of who interviews for the position
Public employment agencies	The potential ability to recruit a more diverse workforce	May receive many résumés, which can be time-consuming
	No cost, since it's a government agency	
	2,300 points of service nationwide	
Labor unions	Access to specialized skills	May not apply to some jobs or industries
		Builds relationship with the union

Now that we have addressed the job analysis, job descriptions, and a variety of recruitment methods, we will discuss the selection process.

Selection

The selection process consists of five distinct aspects:

FIGURE 10.1 **The Steps in the Selection Process**

Criteria Development → Application and Résumé Review → Interviewing → Test Administration → Make the Offer

Source: Laura Portolese et al.

1. **Criteria Development:**

   The first aspect to selection is planning the interview process, which includes criteria development. Criteria development means determining which sources of information will be used to evaluate candidates and how those sources will be scored during the interview. The criteria should be directly related to the job analysis, job specifications, and job description.

   In fact, some aspects of the job analysis and job specifications may be the actual criteria. In addition to this, include things like personality and company culture fit, which would also be part of criteria development. This process usually involves determining which skills, abilities, and personal characteristics are required to be successful at the job. By developing the criteria before reviewing any résumés, you can be sure of exactly what you are looking for and how important each element is. This also allows you to be fair in selecting people to interview.

   You may need to develop an employment application as part of the criteria development process. Many employment applications are completed online and should include information about the candidate, their education, and their previous job experience.

2. **Application and Résumé Review:**

   Once the criteria have been developed, applications can be reviewed. There are different methods for going through this process, but there is also software that can search for keywords in résumés and narrow down the number of résumés that must be reviewed by hand. The software can also accept application materials and track candidates throughout the interview process. Depending on the size of your business, you may not need to implement this type of software, usually called talent acquisition software (typically part of a larger talent management system).

3. **Interviewing:**

   After you determine which applications meet the minimum criteria, you'll select people to be interviewed. You may choose to use phone screenings to narrow the field further, as most people don't have the time to conduct twenty or thirty in-person interviews. There may also be special circumstances such as the COVID-19 pandemic, which required all interviews to be conducted via video conferencing.

4. **Test Administration:**

   Any number of tests may be administered before a hiring decision is made. These include drug tests, physical tests (measure strength, endurance, and other physical requirements of a job), personality tests (used to measure attributes such as motivation and interpersonal abilities), aptitude tests (used to measure a candidate's ability to learn new skills), and cognitive tests (to measure intelligence). Some organizations also perform reference checks, credit report checks, and background checks. You may determine it is best to do a pre-employment test before the initial screening begins in earnest.[5] No matter when the employments tests are administered, it is important to establish the reliability and validity of a test prior to administering it. Some tests might affect prospective employees negatively, and some might even be illegal. (We'll discuss this issue in more detail in the next section.)

5. **Make the Offer:**

   The last step in the selection process is to offer a position to the chosen candidate, either through email or through a physical letter. There may be negotiation as part of this, which may be more formal than other stages of the hiring process.

Now that you have decided on the right person for the job, it is time to hire the employee. First, though, there are some legal considerations you need to take into account.

Types of Interview Questions for the Selection Process

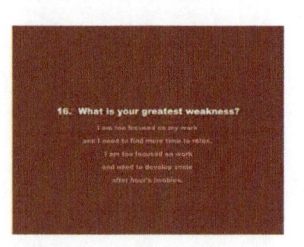

View in the online reader

FIGURE 10.2 Sample Candidate Evaluation Form

Job Criteria	Rating*	Weight**	Total	Comments
Dress	4	1	4	Candidate dressed appropriately.
Personality	2	5	10	Did not seem excited about the job.
Interview questions				
Give an example of a time you showed leadership.	3	3	9	Descriptive but didn't seem to have experience required.
Give an example of when you had to give bad news to a client.	0	5	0	Has never had to do this.
Tell us how you have worked well in a team.	5	4	20	Great example of teamwork given.
Score on cognitive ability test.	78	5	390	Meets minimum required score of 70.
Work sample rating.	5	5	25	Excellent work samples.
			458	

*Rating system of 1–5, with 5 being the highest
**Weighting system of 1–5, with 5 being the most important

Source: Laura Portolese et al.

Legal Considerations in Hiring and Beyond

There are certain discrimination laws you should be aware of in hiring, promoting, and compensating your employees. These laws are under the umbrella of The Equal Employment Opportunity Commission (EEOC), a federal agency charged with the task of enforcing federal discrimination laws. These laws protect employees from discrimination, assure equal pay for equal work, and ensure protection for the employee from retaliation should they file an EEOC compliant. The law protects employees based on the following:

- **National Origin:**

    It is illegal to treat people unfavorably because they are from a particular country or part of the world, because of their accent, or because they appear to be of a particular descent (even if they are not). The law protecting employees based on national origin refers to all aspects of employment: hiring, firing, pay, job assignments, promotions, layoffs, training, and fringe benefits. From an interviewing perspective, you cannot ask seemingly innocent questions such as, "That's a beautiful name; where is your family from?" This could indicate national origin, which could result in bias. You also cannot ask questions about citizenship, except to ask if a candidate is legally allowed to work in the United States. Questions about the first language of the candidate shouldn't be asked, either. However, asking, "Do you have any language abilities that would be helpful in this job?" or "Are you authorized to work in the United States?" are acceptable.

- **Age:**

    This law covers people who are age forty or older. It does not cover favoring an older worker over a younger worker, if the older worker is forty years or older. The law covers any aspect of employment such as hiring, firing, pay, job assignments, promotions, layoffs, training, fringe benefits, and any other condition or term of employment. From the interview perspective, you cannot ask someone how old they are. It is best to avoid questions that might indicate age indirectly, such as, "When did you graduate from high school?" However, asking "Are you over eighteen?" is acceptable.

- **Family Status/Pregnancy:**

    There are legal protections based on pregnancy and family status (such as married or not). In interviewing, you can't ask direct questions about marital status or ages of any children the employee might have. One alternative might be to ask, "Do you have any restrictions on your ability to travel, as this job requires 50 percent travel?"

- **Religion:**

    This part of the EEOC refers to treating a person unfavorably because of their religious beliefs. This law requires a company to reasonably accommodate an employee's religious beliefs or practices, unless doing so would burden the organization's operations. For example, allowing flexible scheduling during certain religious periods of time might be considered a reasonable accommodation. This law also covers accommodations in dress and grooming, such as a headscarf, religious dress, When interviewing, it is illegal to ask candidates about their religious affiliation or to ask questions that may point to a religion-affiliated school or university.

- **Disabilities:**

    The Americans with Disabilities Act (part of the EEOC set of laws) prohibits discrimination against those with disabilities and is enforced by the EEOC. Discrimination based on disability means treating a qualified person unfavorably because of a disability. For example, if someone has AIDS that is controlled, the employee cannot be treated unfavorably. The law requires an employer to provide **reasonable accommodation**. A reasonable accommodation is defined by the EEOC as any change in the work environment or in the way things are customarily done that enables an individual with a disability to enjoy equal employment opportunities, unless this accommodation would cause significant difficulty or expense for the employer. A reasonable accommodation might include making the workplace accessible for wheelchair use or providing equipment for someone who is hearing or vision impaired. When interviewing, you may not directly ask if the person has disabilities or recent illnesses. You can ask if the candidate is able to perform the functions of the job with or without reasonable accommodations.

- **Sexual Orientation and Gender Identity:**

    The EEOC set of laws protects people from being treated differently in hiring or promotion based on their gender or gender identity. When interviewing, avoid assuming someone is the gender they appear to be, and avoid asking questions about marriage and partner status.

- **Other Considerations:**

    Other questions you want to avoid asking includes questions about a criminal record, as it is illegal to ask these questions in some states. It is also a good idea to avoid asking personal questions, such as questions about social organizations and clubs to avoid accidently gaining information noted above, which could be illegal.

Besides these questions, any specific questions about weight, height, gender, and arrest record (as opposed to allowable questions about criminal convictions) should be avoided. Be aware of your own body language in an interview, too. Some habits, such as nodding, can make the candidate think they are on the right track when answering a question. Then there is the **halo effect** or **reverse halo effect**. This occurs when an interviewer becomes biased because of one positive or negative trait a candidate possesses.

Interview bias can occur in almost any interview situation. Interview bias is when an interviewer makes assumptions about the candidate that may not be accurate.[6] These assumptions can be detrimental to an interview process.

Contrast bias is a type of bias that occurs when comparing one candidate to others. It can result in one person looking particularly strong in an area, when in fact they look strong only compared to the other candidates.

A **gut feeling bias** is when an interviewer relies on an intuitive feeling about a candidate.

---

reasonable accommodation

A change in the work environment or the way things are customarily done that enables an individual with a disability to enjoy equal employment opportunities.

halo effect

This occurs when an interviewer becomes biased because of one positive trait a candidate possesses.

reverse halo effect

This occurs when an interviewer becomes biased because of a negative trait a candidate possesses.

contrast bias

A type of bias that occurs when comparing one candidate to others. It can result in one person looking particularly strong in an area, when in fact they look strong only compared to the other candidates.

gut feeling bias

When an interviewer relies on an intuitive feeling about a candidate.

generalization bias

When an interviewer assumes that how someone behaves in an interview is how they always behave.

similar to me bias

Results when interviewers have a preference for a candidate because they view that person as having similar attributes to themselves.

recency bias

This occurs when the interviewer remembers candidates interviewed most recently more than other candidates.

Generalization bias can occur when an interviewer assumes that how someone behaves in an interview is how they *always* behave. For example, if a candidate is very nervous and stutters while talking, the interviewer might wrongly assume that they always stutter.

A **similar to me bias** (which could be considered discriminatory) results when interviewers have a preference for a candidate because they view that person as having similar attributes to themselves.

Finally, **recency bias** occurs when the interviewer remembers candidates interviewed most recently more than other candidates.

Understanding both the legal aspects governing interviews, as well as your own potential biases, can make you a much better interviewer. This will in turn create better opportunities for your company. Your goal, after all, is to find the best person for the job.

Other laws relating to the recruitment and selection of candidates include The Immigration Reform and Control Act (IRCA), which was adopted by Congress in 1986.[7] This law requires employers to attest to their employees' immigration status. It also makes it illegal to hire or recruit illegal immigrants. The purpose of this law is to preserve jobs for those who have legal documentation to work in the United States. The implications for human resources lie in the recruitment process, because before inviting employees into the selection process (interviewing, for example), you must know if they are eligible to work in the United States. The I-9 form indicates a candidate's legal status to work in United States. It is normally filled out as a part of new-hire paperwork.

FIGURE 10.3 I-9 Tax Form

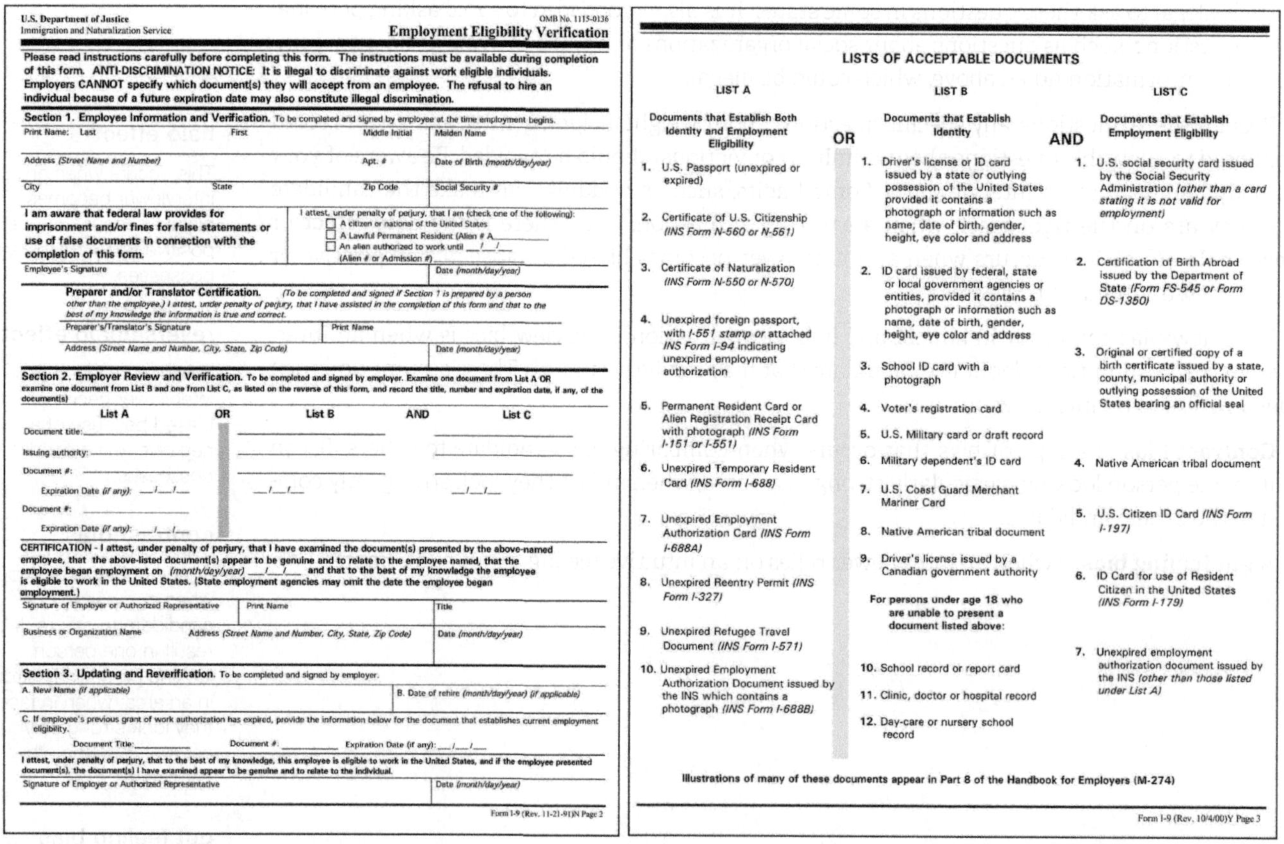

U.S. Department of Justice
Immigration and Naturalization Service

OMB No. 1115-0136

Employment Eligibility Verification

Please read instructions carefully before completing this form. The instructions must be available during completion of this form. ANTI-DISCRIMINATION NOTICE: It is illegal to discriminate against work eligible individuals. Employers CANNOT specify which document(s) they will accept from an employee. The refusal to hire an individual because of a future expiration date may also constitute illegal discrimination.

Section 1. Employee Information and Verification. To be completed and signed by employee at the time employment begins.

Print Name: Last | First | Middle Initial | Maiden Name

Address *(Street Name and Number)* | Apt. # | Date of Birth *(month/day/year)*

City | State | Zip Code | Social Security #

I am aware that federal law provides for imprisonment and/or fines for false statements or use of false documents in connection with the completion of this form.

I attest, under penalty of perjury, that I am (check one of the following):
☐ A citizen or national of the United States
☐ A Lawful Permanent Resident (Alien # A________
☐ An alien authorized to work until __/__/__
(Alien # or Admission #)________

Employee's Signature | Date *(month/day/year)*

Preparer and/or Translator Certification. *(To be completed and signed if Section 1 is prepared by a person other than the employee.) I attest, under penalty of perjury, that I have assisted in the completion of this form and that to the best of my knowledge the information is true and correct.*

Preparer's/Translator's Signature | Print Name

Address *(Street Name and Number, City, State, Zip Code)* | Date *(month/day/year)*

Section 2. Employer Review and Verification. To be completed and signed by employer. Examine one document from List A OR examine one document from List B and one from List C, as listed on the reverse of this form, and record the title, number and expiration date, if any, of the document(s)

List A	OR	List B	AND	List C
Document title:				
Issuing authority:				
Document #:				
Expiration Date *(if any)*: __/__/__		__/__/__		__/__/__
Document #:				
Expiration Date *(if any)*: __/__/__				

CERTIFICATION - I attest, under penalty of perjury, that I have examined the document(s) presented by the above-named employee, that the above-listed document(s) appear to be genuine and to relate to the employee named, that the employee began employment on *(month/day/year)* __/__/__ and that to the best of my knowledge the employee is eligible to work in the United States. (State employment agencies may omit the date the employee began employment.)

Signature of Employer or Authorized Representative | Print Name | Title

Business or Organization Name | Address *(Street Name and Number, City, State, Zip Code)* | Date *(month/day/year)*

Section 3. Updating and Reverification. To be completed and signed by employer.

A. New Name *(if applicable)* | B. Date of rehire *(month/day/year) (if applicable)*

C. If employee's previous grant of work authorization has expired, provide the information below for the document that establishes current employment eligibility.

Document Title:______ Document #: ______ Expiration Date (if any): __/__/__

I attest, under penalty of perjury, that to the best of my knowledge, this employee is eligible to work in the United States, and if the employee presented document(s), the document(s) I have examined appear to be genuine and to relate to the individual.

Signature of Employer or Authorized Representative | Date *(month/day/year)*

Form I-9 (Rev. 11-21-91)N Page 2

LISTS OF ACCEPTABLE DOCUMENTS

LIST A

Documents that Establish Both Identity and Employment Eligibility

1. U.S. Passport (unexpired or expired)
2. Certificate of U.S. Citizenship *(INS Form N-560 or N-561)*
3. Certificate of Naturalization *(INS Form N-550 or N-570)*
4. Unexpired foreign passport, with *I-551 stamp or* attached *INS Form I-94* indicating unexpired employment authorization
5. Permanent Resident Card or Alien Registration Receipt Card with photograph *(INS Form I-151 or I-551)*
6. Unexpired Temporary Resident Card *(INS Form I-688)*
7. Unexpired Employment Authorization Card *(INS Form I-688A)*
8. Unexpired Reentry Permit *(INS Form I-327)*
9. Unexpired Refugee Travel Document *(INS Form I-571)*
10. Unexpired Employment Authorization Document issued by the INS which contains a photograph *(INS Form I-688B)*

OR

LIST B

Documents that Establish Identity

1. Driver's license or ID card issued by a state or outlying possession of the United States provided it contains a photograph or information such as name, date of birth, gender, height, eye color and address
2. ID card issued by federal, state or local government agencies or entities, provided it contains a photograph or information such as name, date of birth, gender, height, eye color and address
3. School ID card with a photograph
4. Voter's registration card
5. U.S. Military card or draft record
6. Military dependent's ID card
7. U.S. Coast Guard Merchant Mariner Card
8. Native American tribal document
9. Driver's license issued by a Canadian government authority

For persons under age 18 who are unable to present a document listed above:

10. School record or report card
11. Clinic, doctor or hospital record
12. Day-care or nursery school record

AND

LIST C

Documents that Establish Employment Eligibility

1. U.S. social security card issued by the Social Security Administration *(other than a card stating it is not valid for employment)*
2. Certification of Birth Abroad issued by the Department of State *(Form FS-545 or Form DS-1350)*
3. Original or certified copy of a birth certificate issued by a state, county, municipal authority or outlying possession of the United States bearing an official seal
4. Native American tribal document
5. U.S. Citizen ID Card *(INS Form I-197)*
6. ID Card for use of Resident Citizen in the United States *(INS Form I-179)*
7. Unexpired employment authorization document issued by the INS *(other than those listed under List A)*

Illustrations of many of these documents appear in Part 8 of the Handbook for Employers (M-274)

Form I-9 (Rev. 10/4/00)Y Page 3

Source: U.S. Department of the Treasury. Internal Revenue Service. (2018). *Employment Eligibility Verification*. Retrieved from https://www.csuci.edu/academics/faculty/facultyaffairs/documents/hrforms/I9EmploymentEligibilityVerification.pdf

The **Equal Employment Opportunity Commission (EEOC)** is a federal agency charged with the task of enforcing federal employment discrimination laws. The EEOC's regulations must therefore be considered as part of the hiring process. The EEOC mandates the collection of data and investigates discrimination claims for organizations with more than fifteen employees. The EEOC's mandates may not apply to your small business (or may not apply *yet*), but as your business grows, they might. Under Equal Employment Opportunity (EEO) law related to the recruitment and selection process, employers cannot discriminate based on age (forty years or older), disability, genetic information, national origin, sex, pregnancy, race, or religion. In a job announcement, affected organizations usually include an EEO statement. Here are some examples:

- (Company name) is fully committed to Equal Employment Opportunity and to attracting, retaining, developing, and promoting the most qualified employees without regard to their race, gender, color, religion, sexual orientation, national origin, age, physical or mental disability, citizenship status, veteran status, or any other characteristic prohibited by state or local law. We are dedicated to providing a work environment free from discrimination and harassment, where employees are treated with respect and dignity.
- (Company name) does not unlawfully discriminate on the basis of race, color, religion, national origin, age, height, weight, marital status, familial status, handicap/disability, sexual orientation, or veteran status in employment or the provision of services, and provides, upon request, reasonable accommodation, including auxiliary aids and services necessary to afford individuals with disabilities an equal opportunity to participate in all programs and activities.
- It is the policy of (college name), in full accordance with the law, not to discriminate in employment, student admissions, and student services on the basis of race, color, religion, age, political affiliation or belief, sex, national origin, ancestry, disability, place of birth, general education development certification (GED), marital status, sexual orientation, gender identity or expression, veteran status, or any other legally protected classification. (College name) recognizes its responsibility to promote the principles of equal opportunity for employment, student admissions, and student services, taking active steps to recruit women and people who are minoritized.
- (Company name) will not discriminate against or harass any employee or applicant for employment on the basis of race, color, creed, religion, national origin, sex, sexual orientation, disability, age, marital status, or status with regard to public assistance. (Company name) will take affirmative action to ensure that all practices are free of such discrimination. Such employment practices include, but are not limited to, the following: hiring, upgrading, demotion, transfer, recruitment or recruitment advertising, selection, layoff, disciplinary action, termination, rates of pay or other forms of compensation, and selection for training.

In addition to including the EEO policy in the job announcement, you are required to post notices of EEOC policies in a visible part of the work environment (such as the break room).

Now that you have made an offer to the perfect candidate—and they've accepted—training and development is the next important step. We will address that in the next section.

> **Equal Employment Opportunity Commission (EEOC)**
> A federal agency charged with the task of enforcing federal employment discrimination laws.

Key Takeaways

- Recruitment is defined as a process that provides the organization with a pool of qualified job candidates from which to choose. The selection process refers to the steps involved in choosing people who have the right qualifications to fill a current or future job opening.
- Job descriptions should include the following:
    a. Job functions (the tasks the employee performs)
    b. Knowledge, skills, and abilities (what an employee is expected to know and be able to do, as well as personal attributes)

c. Education and experience required
d. Physical requirements of the job (ability to lift, see, or hear, for example)
- When you are ready to begin interviewing, you should develop selection criteria ahead of the interviews.
- There are many laws governing the interviewing and hiring of employees.

Interactive Activity

1. Consider a specific job for which you might hire in your business. Develop a job description for the position.

10.2 Training and Development

Learning Objectives

1. Discuss the steps to training a new employee.
2. Explain the advantages of training employees.

Training Steps

Even though your business may be small, most effective businesses have training in place to make sure employees can perform their jobs. Even the perfect candidate for a position may need training in how your company does things. Lack of training can result in lost productivity, lost customers, and poor relationships between employees and the business owner. It can also result in dissatisfaction, which can result in retention problems and high turnover. All these constitute direct costs to your business. In fact, companies that offer training and development see a 59 percent lower staff turnover rate.[8]

Generally speaking, there are four steps to effective employee training. First, the new employee goes through an orientation. Then they will receive in-house training on job-specific areas. Next, the employee should be assigned a mentor. As the employee becomes comfortable with the assigned job duties, external training may be appropriate. Employee training and development is the process of helping employees develop their personal and organization skills, knowledge, and abilities.

FIGURE 10.4 **Steps to Training Your New Employee**

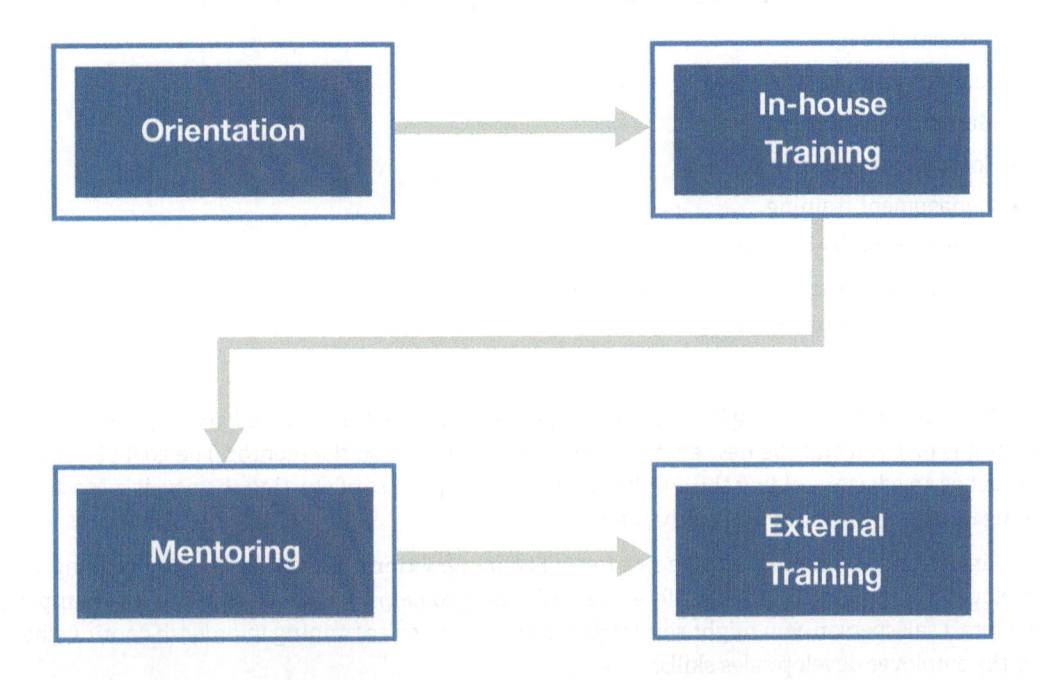

```
Orientation  →  In-house Training
                     ↓
Mentoring    →  External Training
```

Source: Laura Portolese et al.

The first step in training an employee is orientation. **Employee orientation** is the process used for welcoming a new employee into the organization. It helps employees gain an understanding of the company policies while learning how their specific job fits into the bigger picture. Employee orientation also involves filling out employee paperwork, such as I-9 forms. Some situations may allow for orientation to occur fully online or via video conferencing, as many small business owners needed to do during the COVID-19 pandemic.

employee orientation
The process used for welcoming a new employee into the organization.

The goals of an orientation are as follows:

1. **Reduce start-up costs:** If an orientation is done right, it can help get the employee up to speed on various policies and procedures so the employee can start working right away. It can also be a way to ensure all hiring paperwork is filled out correctly so the employee is paid on time.
2. **Reduce anxiety:** Starting a new job can be stressful. One goal of an orientation is to reduce the stress and anxiety people feel when going into an unknown situation.
3. **Reduce employee turnover:** Employee turnover tends to be higher when employees don't feel valued or are not given the tools they need to perform. An employee orientation can indicate organization values and provide tools necessary for a successful entry.
4. **Save time:** A well-executed orientation makes for a better prepared employee, which means it will take less time to teach and train the employee on the job.
5. **Set expectations and attitudes:** If employees know from the start what the expectations are, they tend to perform better. Likewise, if employees learn the values and attitudes of the organization from the beginning, there is a higher chance of a successful tenure at the company.

The next step is in-house training. **In-house training** programs are learning opportunities developed by your business. Often, they are ongoing. In-house training programs can be training related to a specific job, such as how to use a particular kind of software. In a manufacturing setting, in-house training might include an employee learning how to use a particular kind of machinery. For example, if you have hired someone in your screen-printing business, part of the

in-house training
Learning opportunities developed by the entrepreneur. Often, they are ongoing.

in-house training might be to teach the new employee how to use the printer. Other types of in-house training might include the following, depending on the size of your business:

- Ethics training
- Sexual harassment training
- Multicultural training
- Communication training
- Management training
- Customer service training
- Training to operate specialized equipment
- Training to do the job itself
- Basic skills training

The third step in training is mentoring. A **mentor** is defined as a trusted and experienced advisor. If it is just you and the new employee, obviously, you will be the mentor. The goal of a mentor is to act as an advisor, guiding the employee through the process of starting the new job. Most mentoring is ongoing, without a definitive end.

Finally, employees may engage in external training. **External training** involves sending your employee to seminars or other conferences and events to help sharpen their skills. For example, if you hire a salesperson, you might send that salesperson to sales training in order to continue helping the employee develop sales skills.

Training employees can help reduce turnover, but it may also help you gain valuable insight into you customers or products you offer. It can help grow your business, too. It is important to remember that much of this training can be done at an employee's own pace by implementing virtual training options. Virtual training options may be more cost effective, depending on the type of job.

Another way to retain valuable employees is through your compensation program, which we will address in the next section.

mentor
A trusted and experienced advisor.

external training
Sending your employee to seminars or other conferences and events.

Duncan Oyevaar: Turning an Employee into an Entrepreneur

View in the online reader

Key Takeaway

- Training your employees consists of four steps: orientation, in-house training, mentoring, and external training.

> **Interactive Activity**
>
> 1. Brainstorm a list of possible training topics you would need to provide to a new employee. How would you execute this training?

10.3 Compensation

> **Learning Objectives**
>
> 1. Effectively compensate employees.
> 2. Explain the reasons and goals of compensation.

Everyone wants to be paid fairly for their work. Compensating employees appropriately can have many benefits to your organization, while overpaying can make profit margins tighter. This section will address some considerations for paying employees.

Purpose of Compensation

There are several goals when you consider how you will compensate your employees. The compensation package should be positive enough to attract the best people for the job. If your company does not pay as well as others within the same industry, it probably won't be able to attract the best candidates, resulting in a poorer overall company performance. Once the best employees and talent come to work for your business, you want the compensation to be competitive enough to motivate people to stay with you. Compensation can also be used to improve morale, motivation, and satisfaction among employees. Dissatisfied employees can result in higher turnover but also in poor quality of work from those employees who do stay. A proper compensation plan can also increase loyalty within the organization.[9]

A paycheck is only one type of compensation we can offer our employees.

Source: © Shutterstock, Inc.

Considerations in Compensation

When determining what to pay your employees, there are some questions you should consider:

- From the employee's perspective, what is a fair wage?
- Are wages too high to achieve financial health in your business?
- Is your compensation good enough to retain employees?
- Are state and federal laws being met by your compensation package?
- Is your compensation package in line with labor market changes, industry changes, and organizational changes?

Asking these questions can help you determine the right wage for your particular city, industry, and job title. Salary.com is a good resource to determine the "going rate" salaries for your industry.

Types of Compensation

hourly wage
The specific amount an employee earns for every hour worked.

salaried employee
An employee who works for a set amount of pay in a given time period.

commission
An amount of pay based on some productivity factor, such as sales.

Employees may be salaried or paid hourly. An **hourly wage** means the employee earns a set amount for every hour worked. A **salaried employee** works for a set amount of pay in a given time period. Employees may also earn pay for performance. For example, if you run a retail store, you might pay an employee an hourly salary, but then also pay **commission** of 10 percent for every item the employee sells.

As an entrepreneur, you may decide you'd like to offer a hiring bonus.

Jobs may involve various benefits, some of which depend on the size of the business. Some factors to consider include the following:

- **The Affordable Care Act:**

    This requires companies with fifty or more employees to offer health insurance. Read more about the employer mandate here.

- **The Social Security Act of 1935:**

    This requires all employers to withdraw funds from workers' paychecks to pay for retirement benefits. This is called a payroll tax. All organizations are legally compelled to offer this benefit. After several revisions, we now call this OASDHI, or the Old Age, Survivors, Disability, and Health Insurance Program. To be insured, employees must work forty quarters, with a minimum of $1,000 earned per quarter. Once this money is put aside, anyone born after 1960 will receive benefits at sixty-seven. The OASDHI tax in 2011 was 4.2 percent on earnings for employees, up to $106,800 (and 6.2 percent for the employer up to the same limit). This covers both retirement income as well as medical benefits, called Medicare, once the employee reaches retirement age.

- **Unemployment Insurance:**

    Unemployment insurance is required under the Social Security Act of 1935 and is also called the Federal Unemployment Tax Act (FUTA). This program's goals include providing some lost income for employees during involuntary unemployment, helping workers find a new jobs, incentivizing employers to continue employment, and developing worker skills if they are laid off. The majority of this plan is funded by employers' payroll taxes, which account for 0.8 percent per employee. The rate is actually 6.2 percent of compensation, but employers are allowed a tax credit for these payments, which nets to 0.8 percent. The result is that employees receive unemployment benefits and/or job training when they are laid off or let go involuntarily from a job. Employees are ineligible to receive these benefits if they quit, however. As with Social Security, this payroll tax on employers is required.

- **Workers' Compensation:**

    Some employers also offer workers' compensation benefits. If employees are hurt on the job, they receive certain benefits, such as a percentage of pay. Jobs are classified into risk levels. The higher the risk level, the higher the cost of insurance. This is not a federally mandated program, but for some occupations in some states, it may be a requirement.

- **COBRA:**

    This applies only to companies offering health care to employees. The Consolidated Omnibus Budget Reconciliation Act (COBRA) requires companies to allow employees to extend their group coverage for up to thirty-six months if they leave the company. To qualify, there must be a qualifying event that would mean a loss of benefits, such as termination or reduction in hours. For example, if an employee works forty hours a week with medical insurance, but the schedule is reduced to twenty hours (no longer qualifying him or her for benefits), COBRA would be an option.

- **Incentive Pay Systems:**

    These are voluntary types of pay and might include commissions, bonuses, profit sharing, stock options, team pay, and merit pay. Commissions are usually calculated on the basis of a percentage and earned based on the achievement of specific targets that have been agreed on by the employee and employer. For example, many salespeople receive commissions from each item sold. Many commission incentive plans require employees to meet a minimum level of sales. They are then paid a commission on each sale beyond the minimum. A straight commission plan is one in which the employee receives no base pay; their entire pay is based on meeting sales goals. Many plans, however, include a base pay and commission for each sale. Base pay is the guaranteed salary the employee earns. Some organizations choose to reward employees financially when the organization as a whole performs well, through the use of profit sharing as an incentive. For example, if an organization has a profit-sharing program of 2 percent for employees, the employees would earn 2 percent of the overall profit of the company. As you have guessed, this can be an excellent incentive for employees to work as a team and also to monitor their own personal performance so as not to let down the team. For example, Southwest Airlines offers profit sharing to employees. While this is obviously a large business, companies that profit share—even small companies—perform statistically better in terms of turnover rate and overall profit.[10]

- **Employee Ownership:**

    This is a voluntary type of compensation, similar to profit sharing. In this type of plan, employees are granted stock options, which allow the employees to buy stock at a fixed price. If the stock goes up in value, employees earn the difference between what they paid and the value of the stock. With this type of incentive, employees are encouraged to act in the best interests of the organization. Some plans, called employee stock ownership plans, are different from stock options in that the employee is given stock as reward for performance.

Now that we have addressed some of the options you might want to consider when paying your employees, we will discuss other human resource issues.

Key Takeaways

- There are many considerations when compensating employees, including what an employee would consider fair pay and financial constraints of your business, to name a few.
- Employee benefits are also a cost consideration when compensating employees. These factors should be taken into consideration when putting together the compensation package.

Interactive Activities

1. For your business idea, what do you think is fair compensation? How will you determine this?
2. How much do you expect to pay for mandated benefits and other benefits for each of your employees?

10.4 Other HR Considerations

Learning Objective

1. Explain various employee issues and how to resolve them.

Once you have hired and trained new employees, you want the best work from them. You also want to keep them happy in the job so they will stay. This section will address some common human resource (HR) issues and give suggestions on how to resolve these if they arise.

Source: © Shutterstock, Inc.

Employee Performance Management

One of the most difficult parts of your position as an entrepreneur might occur when your employees underperform. Some common performance issues include the following:

- **Constantly late or leaves early:**

    This can be an issue with traditional working hours in all industries. The problem is exacerbated by the growing popularity of flexible scheduling, working from home, and other alternative work assignments. Some employees may take advantage of these benefits and, instead of working while at home, perform non-work related tasks instead. In addition, family issues cause an employee to leave early or come in late repeatedly.

- **Too much time spent doing personal things at work:**

    Most companies have an acceptable use policy concerning phones and computers. In most companies, some personal use is fine, but it can become a problem if employees are not spending their work time wisely.

- **Inability to handle confidential information:**

    Your business may require employees to handle important and confidential information. The ability to keep this information private for the protection of your company and others is important to the success of your business.

- **Drug and alcohol abuse:**

    The U.S. Department of Labor says that 40 percent of industrial fatalities and 47 percent of industrial injuries can be tied to alcohol consumption. The U.S. Department of Labor estimates that employees who use substances are 25 to 30 percent less productive and miss work three times more often than non-abusing employees.[11] Please keep in mind that when we talk about substance abuse, we are talking about both illegal drugs and prescription drugs. In fact, the National Institute on Drug Abuse says that 18 million Americans have taken a prescription pain reliever, tranquilizer, or sedative for nonmedical purposes at least once in the past year.[12] Substance abuse can cause obvious problems, such as tardiness, absenteeism, and nonperformance, but it can result in accidents or other more serious issues.

    Substance abuse can have a negative impact on employee performance.

    Source: © Shutterstock, Inc.

- **Nonperforming:**

    Sometimes employees just aren't performing to their potential. Some causes may include family or personal issues. Often, nonperforming involves motivational issues, lack of tools, and/or the ability to do the job.

- **Conflicts with management or other employees:**

    While it is normal to have the occasional conflict at work, some employees seem to have more than the average thanks to personality issues. These conflicts affect an organization's productivity and may even affect retention and morale.

- **Theft:**

    The numbers surrounding employee theft are staggering. The American Marketing Association estimates $10 billion is lost annually to employee theft, while the FBI estimates up to $150 billion annually.[13] This is a serious employee problem that must be addressed.

- **Ethical breaches:**

    This might include misuse of company time, altering a timesheet or not keeping company information private.

- **Harassment:**

    Sexual harassment, bullying, and other types of harassment must be dealt with immediately and, depending on the severity, may result in immediate termination.

- **Employee conduct outside the workplace:**

    Speaking poorly of the organization on blogs or Facebook is an example of conduct occurring outside the workplace that could violate company policy. Violating specific company policies outside work could also result in termination. For example, posting unsavory comments on social media might also violate company policy and prompt termination or disciplinary action.

While this list is not exhaustive, it provides some insight into the types of problems your company and its employees may experience. As you can see, some of these problems are more serious than others. Some issues may only require a warning or some coaching, while others can and should result in immediate dismissal. As an entrepreneur, it is your job to develop policies and procedures for dealing with such problems. Let's discuss these next.

Performance Issue Model

There are too many different performance issues to discuss handling each in detail here. Instead, we will present a model to help you develop fair, consistent policies around performance as your company grows.

FIGURE 10.5 Process for Handling Performance Issues

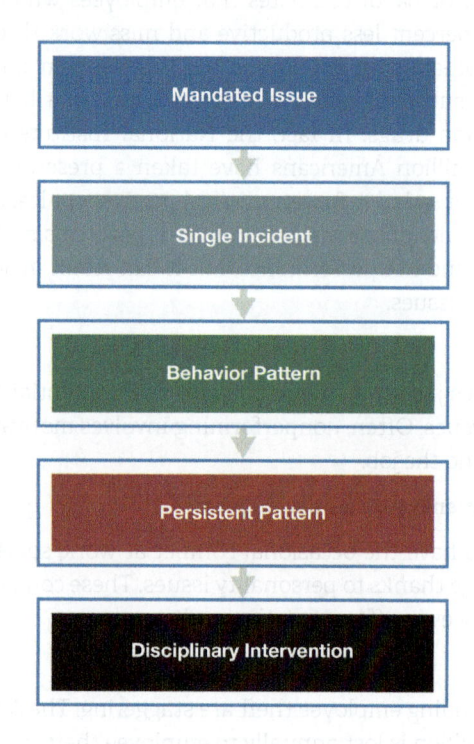

- Mandated Issue
- Single Incident
- Behavior Pattern
- Persistent Pattern
- Disciplinary Intervention

Source: Laura Portolese et al.

mandated issue
A serious performance issue and must be addressed immediately.

Performance issues can be viewed in five areas. First, the **mandated issue** is serious and must be addressed immediately. Usually, the mandated issue is one that goes beyond the company and could involve a law. Examples of mandated issues might include an employee sharing information that violates privacy laws, not following safety procedures, or engaging in sexual harassment.

Let's say a doctor's office employee posts something on his Facebook page that violates patient privacy. This would be considered a mandated issue (not to violate privacy laws) and could put the doctor's office in serious trouble. These types of issues must be handled swiftly. A written policy detailing how this type of issue would be handled is crucial. In this case, the employee could be fired or simply required to go through privacy training again after being given a written warning. Whatever the result, developing a policy for handling mandated issues is important for consistency.

single incident
A performance issue that happens once.

The second performance issue can be called a **single incident**. Perhaps the employee misspeaks and insults some colleagues. Perhaps the employee was over budget or late on a project. These types of incidents are usually best solved with a casual conversation to let the employee know that the behavior was inappropriate. Consider this type of misstep a development opportunity for your employee. Coaching and working with the employee on this issue can be the best way to preempt the problem before it gets worse.

When single incidents are not immediately corrected, they may evolve into a **behavior pattern**, which is the third type of performance issue. This can occur when the employee doesn't think the incident is a big deal. If the employee has not been corrected, or does not even realize there is a problem, that problem can and will reoccur. It's important to talk with the employee and let the employee know what is expected.

> **Leveraging**
>
> One of the biggest challenges entrepreneurs face when working with employees is performance issues. Most people avoid conflict. Avoiding performance issues, however, can cause the problems to get worse rather than simply "go away." Please take this quiz on conflict style and brainstorm ways you can better handle this type of conflict when you start your business.

behavior pattern
A performance issue that occurs repeatedly.

If the employee has been corrected for a behavior pattern but continues to exhibit the same behavior, we call this a **persistent pattern**. Often you see employees correct the problem after an initial discussion, then fall back into old habits. If they do not self-correct, it could be they do not have the training or the skills to perform the job. In this phase of handling performance issues, it is important to let the employee know that the problem is serious—and that further action will be taken if it continues. If you believe the employee just doesn't have the skills or knowledge to perform the job, asking them about this could be helpful in getting to the root of the problem. If the employee continues to underperform, you may consider using the progressive discipline process before initiating an employee separation. Investigating the performance issue, however, should occur *before* implementing any sort of discipline.

persistent pattern
Occurs when the employee has been corrected for a behavior pattern but continues to exhibit the same behavior.

By understanding how the policies and procedures you create for employees fall into each of these categories, you can begin to develop policies surrounding the rules you want employees to follow in your business. Remember that disciplinary actions should always be documented. The documentation should include the following information:

1. Date of incident
2. Time of incident
3. Location (if applicable) of incident
4. A description of the performance issue
5. Notes on the discussion with the employee on the performance issue
6. An improvement plan, if necessary
7. Next steps, should the employee commit the same infraction
8. Signatures from both you and the employee

This documentation helps both you and the employee know clearly the next steps that will be taken should the employee commit the infraction in the future. Once the issue has been documented, you and the employee should meet about the infraction. This type of meeting is called an investigative interview and is used to make sure the employee is fully aware of the discipline issue. This also allows the employee the opportunity to explain their side of the story. These types of meetings should always be conducted in private, never in the presence of other employees.

Performance Evaluations

Many small businesses provide performance evaluations to employees. An advantage of this is the fact employees will obtain formal feedback on how well they are doing. This allows us to document any performance issues. The performance evaluation should be based on the job analysis and job description, and performed on at least an annual basis. While you'll want to provide continuous feedback, the performance appraisal is more systematic. A deep dive on types of performance appraisal/evaluation systems is beyond the scope of this book, however, know that implementing a formal performance evaluation process can assist in handling performance issues with a fair, formalized process.

Remote Workforces

During the COVID-19 pandemic, small business owners had to pivot very quickly to move to a remote workforce. Some organizations provided equipment so employees could work at home, while others shut down entirely. Many entrepreneurs had worst case scenarios running through their minds with remote work, such as employees slacking off, and fears of poor communication. There are a few ways to handle a remote workforce:[14]

- Ensure your employees have the right tools to perform their jobs.
- Provide training on video conferencing platforms, and implement a culture that utilizes tools such as Microsoft Teams for communication.
- Make sure employees know expectations in terms of working hours and avaliablity.
- Avoid micromanaging.
- Develop specific goals for your employees to work toward.
- Consider operational and processes that can help facilitate remote work.

A remote workforce, however, doesn't just have to be during a pandemic. After the pandemic, many business owners have realized the advantages of a remote work force. For example, cost savings on office space (of course, depending on the type of work), more employee autonomy, and higher productivity. Many large organizations have switched to remote work, such as Apple, but the advantages can be harnessed for small businesses as well.[15] Small businesses that engage in a variety of services, real estate, and insurance lend themselves well to remote work. Other service businesses, such as landscaping businesses and pool maintenance businesses can operate remotely too. This can be done easily by allowing employees to take company vehicles home, and communicating daily on what customer jobs need to be completed. The cost savings and other advantages could be a great way to create higher productivity, and also motivate your workforce.

Key Takeaways

- Performance issues can come up, so it is important to have policies in place concerning how you will deal with each type of issue. These include mandated issues, single issues, behavior patterns, and persistent patterns.
- Performance appraisals can be a good way to give formal feedback to employees.
- Remote work can make sense for many types of businesses. In order to make remote work effective, there are several things that should be done, such as using a tool for regular communication and setting expectations.

Interactive Activity

1. Consider the possible discipline problems that could occur in your specific business. Write a policy for each of these issues, identifying the type of performance issue for each one. Address how you will handle such performance issues at each level (mandated issues, single issues, behavior patterns, and persistent patterns).

10.5 Test Your Skills: Applied Case

Shannon Lopez and Human Resource Planning

Two years ago, Shannon Lopez started a business out of her home. At first, she operated the business in her free time because she had another position, but the business has grown so much she's been able to quit her job and focus on the business full time. Her business is focused on designing and making specialty sized dog beds, with embossed, personalized names. She currently sells her products on Etsy, as well as on other sites, and has come to the point where she needs to hire two people in order to keep up with the high demand. It is her hope she can focus on the marketing of the business, and have the two new hires do the actual sewing, embossing, and shipping.

She isn't sure where to begin in terms of hiring people, interviewing them, and compensating them. Based on what you learned in this chapter, can you help her put together a human resources plan?

Source: © Shutterstock, Inc.

1. Draft a potential job description and job title for the positions discussed.
2. Develop five to ten interview questions that would be appropriate for this position.
3. Discuss the methods Shannon should use to train the new hires.
4. Compare and contrast the benefits to allowing these employees to work from home. What types of tools should she provide, and what is the best way to ensure they are meeting expectations as remote workers?
5. Should the new employees be paid hourly, a salary, and/or on commission? Discuss the rationale for your decision.

Endnotes

1. Hackman, R.J & Oldham, G.R. (August 1976). Motivation through the design of work: Test of a Theory, Organizational Behavior and Human Performance, 16(2) 250–79.
2. McConnell, B. (2021, June 30) Innovative recruitment ideas to help you beat your talent competitors. Retrieved from: https://recruitee.com/articles/innovative-recruitment
3. Sprockets. (2021, June 1) These companies are currently offering hiring bonuses. Retrieved from: https://sprockets.ai/hiring-bonus/
4. Hsu, A. (2021, July 6) A $500 sign on bonus to deliver pizzas? Retrieved from: https://www.npr.org/2021/07/06/1012344023/heres-what-you-should-know-about-that-eye-popping-sign-on-bonus
5. Society for Human Resource Management, (2018, September 10). Screening by means of pre-employment testing. Retrieved from: https://www.shrm.org/resourcesandtools/tools-and-samples/toolkits/pages/screeningbymeansofpreemploymenttesting.aspx
6. Verlinden, N. (n.d.) 11 ways to avoid interviewer bias in your selection process. Retrieved from: https://www.aihr.com/blog/interviewer-bias/
7. U.S. Citizenship and Immigration Services website. (n.d.) Retrieved from: http://www.uscis.gov/portal/site/uscis/menuitem.5af9bb95919f35e66f614176543f6d1a/?vgnextchannel=b328194d3e88d010VgnVCM10000048f3d6a1RCRD&vgnextoid=04a295c4f635f010VgnVCM1000000ecd190aRCRD.
8. Ottawa University, (2021 January). 5 benefits of training and development. Retrieved from: https://www.ottawa.edu/online-and-evening/blog/january-2021/5-benefits-of-training-and-development
9. Leonard, K. (2019, March 1) Importance of compensation in the workplace. Retrieved from: https://smallbusiness.chron.com/importance-compensation-workplace-38470.html
10. Blasi, J., Kruse, D.L., & Conway, M. (n.d.) Profit sharing and employee owned businesses make employees happier. Retrieved from: https://blog.careerminds.com/community/profit-sharing-and-employee-owned-businesses-make-employees-happier
11. United States Department of Labor, (n.d.) General Workplace Impact.
12. National Institute on Drug Use. (2020, June) What is the scope of prescription drug misuse? Retrieved from: https://www.drugabuse.gov/publications/research-reports/misuse-prescription-drugs/what-scope-prescription-drug-misuse
13. Net Industries. (n.d.) Employee Theft and Legal Aspects. Retrieved from: http://law.jrank.org/pages/1084/Employee-Theft-Legal-Aspects-Estimates-cost.html.
14. Tricarico, V. (2021, July 11) The step-by-step guide to managing remote employees effectively. Retrieved from: https://www.entrepreneur.com/article/374007
15. Courtney, E. (n.d) 30 companies switching to remote work. Retrieved from: https://www.flexjobs.com/blog/post/companies-switching-remote-work-long-term/

PART 4
Growing and Sustaining Your Business

Source: © Shutterstock, Inc.

CHAPTER 11
How Do I Grow My Business?

Case Study—Frankie's Pizza and Pasta

Frank Curtiss has long served in the food service industry. His career started at McDonald's, where he was an employee and ultimately managed two different restaurants. Eventually, he became well known in his community as the owner of Frankie's Pizza and Pasta. However, in October 2016, Frank had to close this successful restaurant because the owner of the building had sold the property to a hotel developer. Frankie's Pizza and Pasta no longer exists in brick and mortar form.

Source: Used with permission from Frank Curtiss.

When Frank first started the business, he was aware that there were very expensive Italian restaurants available—as well as lower priced, cheaper alternatives—but there weren't many alternatives between the two. His niche was the middle price point, which served him very well over the years. Most restaurants operate on small profit margins. Frank was very proud of the fact that his business carried a slightly larger margin than most.

Restaurants frequently go out of business during economic downturns. The tight margins on which they operate make it difficult for restaurants to weather slumping sales as foot traffic diminishes. Frank got through the economic downturn in 2008–2009 by making a couple of small increases in his menu prices. At the same time, though, he kept on eye on how much his ingredients were costing him. He was able to adjust and maneuver through that slump when other restaurants could not.

Change (refer to Chapter 9) can come from many sources. Sometimes the changes are not within your control, but how you choose to deal with them is. Frank dealt with change in his industry through multiple strategies. First, he let his employees and customers know very early on that he would be closing his doors. Next, he incentivized his employees to stay until the end as much as his budget allowed. Third, he leveraged his visibility within his community, invoking nostalgia so customers would experience Frankie's for as long as they could. Frank turned the close of his business into a celebration between himself and his customers. His final sales reflected this.

While Frankie's closed, Frankie's Pizza and Pasta went on as a brand. Frank is redefining it, exploring various avenues and leveraging his connections to the community. He has partnered with Microsoft campuses to plan menus for employees at local dining centers, for example. This opportunity was the result of his network of close friends and loyal customers. He has also partnered with a local sustainable living center, called 21 Acres, where he uses their kitchen to conduct cooking classes.

Frank still dreams of owning a property where he can one day teach cooking classes and food photography. He also wants to have his own garden to sustain the food preparation. One thing is for sure, though: Frank clearly demonstrates the creativity needed to be an entrepreneur. He also maintains a close eye on his business, carefully monitoring costs so his family can live the life they desire. Frank always puts his business plans down on paper so he can check his assumptions and the thinking behind his brand.

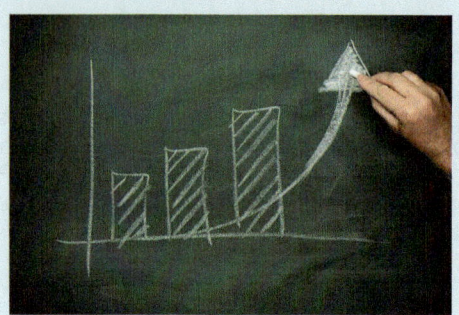

Source: © Shutterstock, Inc.

Frank's example demonstrates the importance of growth strategy, creativity, and the willingness to put your creative ideas in the marketplace. Through these, entrepreneurs can realize their business visions. Frank's best advice to anyone starting out on an entrepreneurial path is, yes, do what you love, but also be very clear about the kind of lifestyle you desire. According to Frankie, "There will always be things you love and things you don't" in running a business. Even though he never liked certain aspects of administration in his business, everything else balanced that out. Thanks to Frank's love of food and his community, there is no doubt that the next iteration of Frankie's is poised to succeed.

Many companies, big and small, seek to grow, although not every company does. Before Starbucks became a mega-corporation, operating worldwide, it was owned by three men who *only* wanted to sell coffee beans.[1] When Howard Schultz came along and wanted to sell coffee drinks as a way to expand the business, the owners reluctantly let him try . . . but they never liked the idea. Howard eventually left Starbucks to open his own coffee company. Ultimately, he purchased Starbucks when the original owners decided to sell. The rest, as they say, is history. Howard and his creative ideas started to work magic in growing the company. This chapter focuses on how you, like Howard Schultz, can grow your business.

11.1 External Sources of Growth

Learning Objective

1. Identify external growth opportunities for your business.

There are many reasons to want to grow a company. Your goal may be to dominate your market. This can serve you well if you are looking to build the value of your business so that it is attractive to a potential buyer when you decide to sell.[2] Companies may also seek to attract the best talent. A growing company is an attractive environment for potential employees. Regardless of the objective, there are multiple ways to grow your business. Often, as you grow, you can better weather financial and legal storms. Remember, though, that growth is a choice—and with it comes other challenges.

In this chapter, we explore multiple facets of growing a business, allowing you to make the choice that is best for you and your company.

Joint Ventures

Joint ventures are business agreements in which at least two companies come together to help each other grow. Each company retains its own legal identity.[3]

joint ventures

Business agreements in which at least two companies come together to help each other grow while retaining their own legal identity.

Source: © Shutterstock, Inc.

Let's say that you roast your own coffee products. You would like to expand your business but would like to have less overhead than would be required to open a new store. You could create a joint venture with a company that resells your product and share the profits with that partner.

Venture Capital

Venture capital is an infusion of money into your business through an investment of cash. There are different venture capital options in the marketplace. For example, some venture capitalists specialize in startup companies (refer to Chapter 8), while other venture capital firms seek to accelerate growth.[4]

For example, there are companies that invest in video game development (like this one).[5] If you are an online video game developer, you could start a business developing games for this company. This is one of the multiple ways that venture capital can assist you in a start-up or the ongoing growth of your business.

Venture Capital—What Is a Joint Venture?

View in the online reader

venture capital

An infusion of money into your business through an investment of cash.

Initial Public Offering (IPO)

An Initial Public Offering, or **IPO**, occurs when a company decides to sell stock to the public. If a company does not sell shares of stock, it is a private company, but once it sells stocks to the public, it is a public company.[6] One major incentive to conduct an IPO is the amount of cash this can generate for a business. Refer to Chapter 2 for information about different forms of business. Remember that if you decide to go public with an IPO, you will be required to supply financial information to the public.

Acquisitions

An **acquisition** is when you acquire another business or the limited assets of another business. Often, the acquisition will continue to operate as its own brand. One way this happens is to buy out a competitor, particularly one that is going out of business. You might also determine that another business has channels for selling products that you do not have, so you acquire it to gain access to these.[7]

When Starbucks acquired Seattle's Best Coffee in 2003, one of the big reasons they wanted to acquire the company was because of the grocery channels Seattle's Best Coffee used to sell product. The Seattle's Best Coffee brand continued to be sold as a part of the Starbucks family of products.

Eight Ways to Successfully Acquire a Small Business

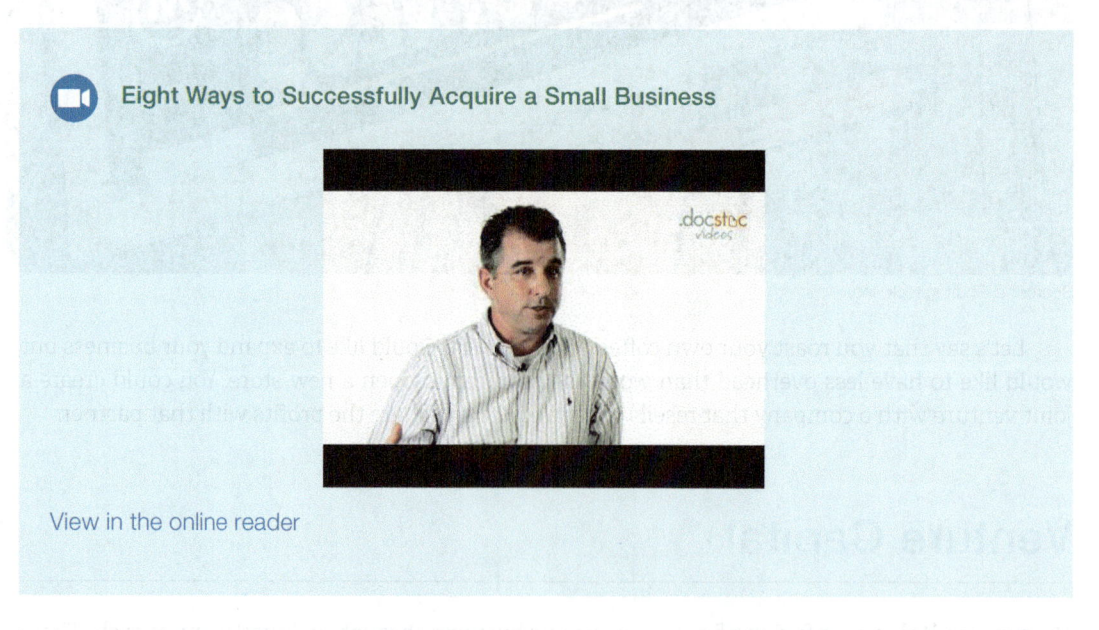

View in the online reader

Mergers

A **merger** is when you acquire another business or assets of another business and absorb them into your own company. A merger is a way to reduce production costs. It may also give you the ability to launch a new product that neither company would be able to accomplish as a separate entity.[8] In some cases, you may have to get a merger approved through either state and/or federal government entities. Your merger would have to be over a certain value in order for the Federal Trade Commission to get involved. You would not launch a merger without obtaining expert help in order to navigate this approval process.

Venture Capital Explained

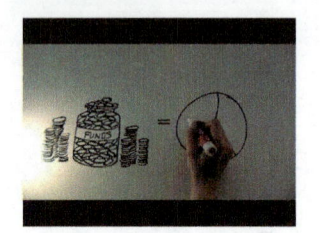

View in the online reader

IPO
When a company decides to sell stock to the public.

What Is an IPO?

View in the online reader

acquisition
When you acquire another business or the limited assets of another business. Often, the acquisition will continue to operate as its own brand.

merger
When you acquire another business or the assets of another business and absorb them into your own company.

There are several different kinds of mergers. The first one is a **conglomerate merger**. A conglomerate merger is one in which two different companies merge.[9] A good example of a conglomerate is General Electric (GE). GE started out in electricity production, but then expanded into financial services, aircraft, and household appliances (among other distinct products and services). These types of mergers are often approved because there is no real impact on the market share and there is no risk of a **monopoly**. A monopoly occurs when a company controls the supply of a commodity or service.

Another type of merger is the **vertical merger**. A vertical merger occurs when you acquire a supplier.[10] For example, if you manufacture a car, you may acquire a tire manufacturer. By acquiring the tire company, you can reduce the costs of purchasing tires for your automobiles and therefore expand your business. These types of mergers are usually approved, but there is a caveat. If you are trying to acquire the only tire company that other car companies use, the merger will likely not be approved.

Finally, you could attempt a **horizontal merger**. A horizontal merger is one in which you acquire a competitor.[11] It is tougher to get a horizontal merger approved because acquiring a competitor can give you a dominant position in the market (potentially creating a monopoly).

conglomerate merger
A merger in which two different companies combine.

monopoly
When a company controls the supply of a commodity or service.

vertical merger
When a company acquires a supplier.

horizontal merger
A merger in which a company acquires a competitor.

International Considerations

One of your goals may be to become a global entrepreneur, with locations worldwide. If you have never lived outside of your home country, there will be several things to consider. If you do add international elements to your business, be aware that you will likely need accountants that know how to consolidate your financial information. You will have to navigate the world of currency exchange. You'll also need to work with people who understand the legal and governmental landscape of working in another country.

Regardless of which route you take in growing your business through external sources, the truth of the matter is that the possibilities are endless. Through external sources, you can grow your business internationally. Next, we will examine how you can grow your business *internally*.

Key Takeaways

- Innovation requires cultivating creativity in your business.
- Lots of opportunities exist to grow a business.
- Growth can come from internal and external opportunities.
- Drop products that are no longer contributing to your gross margin.
- Encourage employees and customers to give you feedback concerning how your business can improve.
- Be sure to keep an eye on your infrastructure as you grow so that you are not losing operational efficiency.

Interactive Activities

1. Observe other businesses like yours. What are they doing to expand their products and/or services? If the company is publicly traded, look for their SEC reports online. What do you think could work for your business?

2. Southwest Airlines studied pit crews to find ways to minimize the time airplanes spend at the gate. How could another business or industry help inform you to leverage your business processes?
3. Experiment with your own habits in order to cultivate your own creativity. Here are some ideas to try (get creative and think of your own):
   a. Drive to work or school (or anywhere you frequent) by a different route.
   b. Sit in a different chair in a meeting room or classroom.
   c. Eat something different from your favorite restaurant menu.
   d. Change up your morning or evening routines.
   e. Notice which changes are easy and which ones are hard. Why are certain changes harder than others?
4. Search your LinkedIn contacts. Is there anyone among them who has ever completed a Joint Venture? Engaged in a licensing agreement? Opened a franchise? Invite them to coffee and discuss possibilities.
5. Find an accountant or business owner who has examined product profitability. How did they do it? What process did they follow to examine their profitability?

11.2 Internal Sources for Growth

Learning Objective

1. Identify internal growth opportunities for your business.

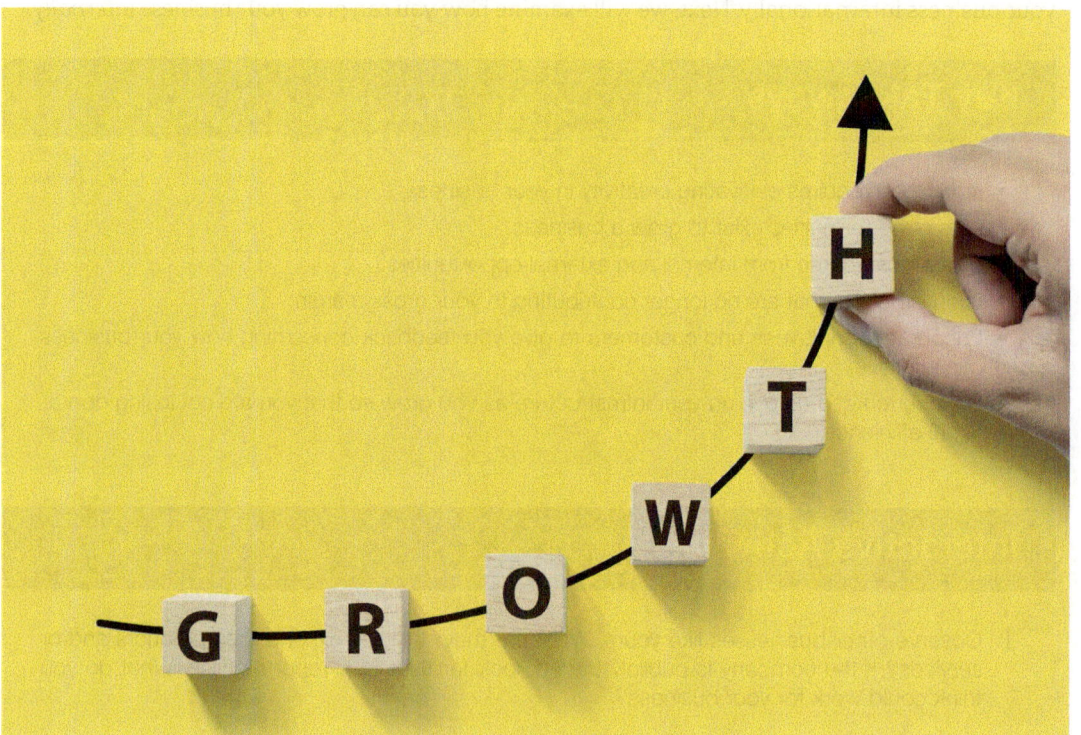

Source: © Shutterstock, Inc.

In the previous section, we looked at ways in which you can grow your business through external means. You can also grow your business internally. This requires you to pay attention to detail, surveying your customers, and tracking your profitability. Let's examine some ways you can grow your business through an internal examination of that business.

Expansion of Products and Services

One way to grow your business is to expand the products and services that you offer. When Howard Schultz bought Starbucks, the company was only selling roasted coffee beans. Schultz wanted to grow the business, and he did so by expanding the product lines offered to customers. Not only did Starbucks continue to sell roasted coffee beans, but it began selling coffee drinks, tea, merchandise, and food. This expansion of products also included ingredients in coffee drinks. For example, customers can now get regular milk, 2 percent milk, soy milk, and almond milk in their coffee drinks. Much of this change is attributable to market research conducted through traditional research methods, but Starbucks also formerly used the power of the internet to garner ideas and feedback from their customers at their website.

How do you check the pulse of your customers? Basically, you give your customers every opportunity to give you feedback, even negative feedback.[12] Customers can give feedback in many places—through your website, in your store, and on social media. You can also poll your customers through formal surveys, including having surveys print out on receipts. The goal is to find the trends in customer feedback that can yield ideas, not just for products and services, but for how your employees can and should interact with your customers.

Referrals and Subscriptions

A top strategy for getting new business is to ask for referrals.[13] Anyone in your business who comes in contact with customers should ask questions like, "How did you hear about us?" and "Do you know of anyone who could benefit from our products/services?" Questions like these can help you spread the word about your business (and let you know where your business is coming from).

One way to increase business and encourage repeat customers is to implement a **loyalty program**. Loyalty programs help you learn more about your customers and their buying habits while also encouraging them to do business with you again. This can also improve your cash flow through repeat business.

Subscriptions are another great way to expand your business. Consider the case of Steve's Plumbing, which we discussed previously. Steve implemented a subscription service that is a loyalty program. Through this program, customers pay a small fee each month to gain certain advantages. For example, the company normally charges a fee to make house calls for consultations. For members of the loyalty program, this fee is waived. The loyalty program also confers on members special pricing. This saves members while encouraging repeat business for Steve. It's a win-win for the company and for the Steve's customers.

loyalty program
A program that encourages repeat customers and generates more income while also providing you with data on your customers' buying habits.

Expand Your Market

When you start a business, you may be restricted to your local area or even your home. One way to expand that business is to open a new location or go online.[14] Approach the expansion as you did the opening of your original location; that is, you'll need a business plan. Some businesses may require a big cash outlay to open a new location (acquiring a storefront, investing in equipment, etc.), so going online may be the more cost-effective way to expand. With alternatives like the Amazon platform at your disposal to sell products and services, an online expansion might be easier and more cost-effective than you realize. For example, you can ship products to store in Amazon warehouses, or you can be a seller on Amazon and ship out of your own warehouses. There are other websites where you can sell products, like Etsy and eBay, so be sure to check out these options for opening up sales channels to reach new customers.

Cut Costs and Loser Products

Another option to consider is keeping an eye on your bottom line. This entails cutting costs and eliminating "loser" products.[15] In this context, a loser product is defined as a product that is no longer contributing a positive margin to your business (refer to Chapter 5).

> **markup**
> An amount of money you add to the cost of a product to determine your selling price.

As you set up your financial systems, it is important to analyze your products for profitability. For example, you must understand why you add a **markup** to products. (A markup is an amount of money you add to the cost of the product to determine your selling price.) If you buy a coffee mug, and you want to sell it as part of your product line, you would not sell it for the amount you paid for it. Therefore, if you buy the mug for $5, you might sell it for $10. That represents a 100 percent markup, because 100 percent of the cost is added on to the purchase cost to arrive at the sales price. In other words, $5 markup divided by $5 cost = 100 percent.

> **gross profit margin**
> The amount of money earned above the purchase price.

Do not, however, confuse the markup with the **gross profit margin**. The gross profit margin represents the amount of money earned *above* the purchase price. In this case, the gross profit margin is 50 percent. In other words, $5 gross profit divided by the sales price of $10 = 50 percent.

As prices rise, monitor gross profit margins. Over time, the gross profit of 50 percent can erode. If you are not paying attention, you could start losing money and be unable to cover your operating costs because the vendor costs are going up (in other words, it is taking more money actually to purchase products). This may mean, in certain circumstances, that a product simply is not profitable. Your customers simply cannot or will not pay a price that is high enough for you to make a profit, so you must stop selling it.

Consider having an accountant review your gross profit margins and keep you informed of any changes that are eroding your ability to pay bills beyond the cost of buying merchandise for resale. This is where an accountant can become a valuable asset to you and your business.

Duplicate Yourself

> **franchise**
> Setting up your business to be reproduced by business owners who purchase the right to operate under your brand.
>
> **license**
> Giving another business the right to sell your product while you share in the profits.

There are great alternatives for duplicating your business. For example, you can **franchise** your business or **license** your product.[16] If you have a business that you think you can repeat or reproduce, you may want to think about franchising your business (refer to Chapter 2). In this model, you develop training and other details so that the business can be repeated again and again. Franchising, however, may entail extra costs in developing the model.[17] There is also a lot of paperwork involved. You will want to find a good attorney that has experience in businesses like yours. The good news is that you set the rules for the franchise concerning how it operates and earns its franchise fee.

An alternative is to license your products to other businesses. There can still be legal costs associated with this approach, but you are basically giving another business the right to sell your product and give you a share of the profits. For example, when a Starbucks store opens in an airport, the airport vendor is *licensing* the product. Starbucks requires certain performance by the licensee. It also requires that the store meet certain appearance and cleanliness standards to make it compatible with the brand. Nevertheless, the employees running it and selling the products, are not Starbucks employees. They are employees of the franchisee.

What Would You Do?

You started your business with a product that was your heart and soul. Over time, other product lines have become much more profitable. Recently you discovered that your original product is losing money. Consider the following:

1. Review this Entrepreneur article. How would you use this information to expand a Google search on how to analyze your product line's profitability?
2. What other considerations might you need to assess?
3. How would you make sure your accountant can provide the information for your assessment?
4. How will you manage your emotional investment and attachment to the product line that started your business?

As you can see, growing your business requires both creativity and attention to detail. The possibilities are only limited by your ability to see opportunities around you. Next, we will look at how you can continue to innovate over the life of your business while managing your growth.

Key Takeaways

- Many different growth opportunities exist that can help you manage the risk inherent in growth.
- Building relationships is a crucial part of growth.
- Many growth strategies help you to reach international markets. You can reduce risk by leveraging others' knowledge of culture in the new market.

Interactive Activities

1. Examine a process in which you are involved. How could it be done more efficiently? Provide details concerning the following:
   a. Are there steps that are being repeated? Examine alternatives for eliminating the redundant steps.
   b. Are there manual steps that could be handled in a more efficient way, perhaps through technology? What technology is needed?
   c. Are there errors occurring in the process? How much do those errors cost in terms of time and labor to correct them?
   d. What are the total costs that could be saved?
2. Invite a business owner to coffee or lunch and talk to them about how they have designed referral programs. How do they track referrals? What kinds of referral rewards have they used to incentivize customers?

11.3 Models for Innovation and Growth Management

Learning Objectives

1. Create an environment for innovation.
2. Assess your business to ensure growth opportunities do not exceed your ability to support the new ventures.

Starting a business is a very creative process, but building the business can trap you in linear and non-creative thinking. Building processes and everyday operations produces a very step-by-step mentality. It is very important to keep creative juices flowing. You must tap the potential of your business even as you build business structures. In this section, we will discuss how to stay fresh in your thinking despite demands for repeatable procedures.[18]

Source: © Shutterstock, Inc.

Innovation Strategies

innovation
The process of developing a new product, a new method, or a new idea.

Innovation can be difficult to describe. At its core, it is simplicity in developing a new product, a new method, or a new idea. For example, as our opening case showed, Frankie built great relationships with his customers, his employees, and his community. Many opportunities can come from how you treat others and how you build those relationships.[19] Through all of the relationships Frankie cultivated over time, he was able to continue his business after closing his restaurant. Frankie succeeded because his customers did not just love his restaurant; they also loved *him*.

Developing creativity in your business does require some thought. For example, will you reward creative behavior? If a customer or an employee has an idea, will you be willing to hear it? Are you willing to change up things and experiment?[20] Your customers can tell if you cultivate creativity.

Consider the following scenario: You own a coffee shop and you have opened a drive-through. You have insisted that your employees ask how a customer's day is going. That is a fine directive and it shows good customer service, but what if your order window has no cover and the customer is getting drenched in rain? The customer could get very annoyed when asked how things are going in that situation. So, what do you do? You want your employees to be aware of the customer experience, not simply follow procedure no matter what happens. You want employees who can think for themselves and do the right thing to ensure a positive experience for the customer. Build in the ability for your employees to tell you what works and what does not. They are the ones on the front lines more often than not. Additionally, if a customer tells you that something is annoying, listen.

Experimenting with processes can be very creative. We are creatures of habit and that is *not* a bad thing. Habits can make us very efficient. They can also stop us from growing and learning, however. You must be able to insert new ways of doing things into your processes or you will get shut off from the creative process.

Use downtime as a way of rejuvenating your creative spirit. In fact, Stephen Covey says that one of the habits of successful people is their ability to "sharpen the saw"—to use downtime to give themselves a mental vacation.[21] One way that companies can do this is to use retreats and other downtime to help everyone in the company get out of their thinking ruts.

Much of your success in innovation will be tied to how you build your company culture. If you innovate, you have to have a culture that promotes innovation. For example, Amazon is obsessed with their customers—bringing new opportunities to their customers and providing any product at any time. Just because you start out small does not mean you cannot be innovative and grow. Amazon, Starbucks, and Google started small and are now worldwide phenomena.

Finally, even if an economy is struggling or other events like COVID-19 are occurring, you still may be able to start or grow a business in those conditions. The keys to success are to pay attention to contingency plans and to look for opportunities in all conditions.

Leveraging

As you think about ways to promote a creative mindset, consider other employment experiences you have had. Recall your business mentors and some of the creative approaches companies have used to remain innovative. Through whatever sources you have at your disposal, develop plans and ideas concerning how you will use the following tools to foster a creative mindset in your business:

1. How will you use performance reviews?
2. How will you use rewards?
3. How will you communicate successes? How will you communicate situations that have missed the mark?
4. How will you build in experimentation?
5. How will you use and encourage downtime or a new environment to encourage creativity?
6. How will you reward customers for their great ideas?

Regardless of what you try, your goal is to keep everyone in the company aware of changing conditions in the market. If you do that well, you can move and flow with the changing expectations of customers and employees. By staying creative and willing to experiment, you can remain competitive over the long run.

Growth Management

infrastructure
The physical and organizational structures that are needed to run your operations.

As you grow, managing that growth can become a challenge. There are many businesses that grew so fast they expanded beyond their **infrastructure's** ability to keep up. Infrastructure is the physical and organizational structures needed to run your operations. For example, you could easily run out of warehouse or office space as you grow (refer to Chapter 6). You may also need to restructure your business from an organizational design perspective as it gets larger (refer to Chapter 7).

As businesses grow, they can easily outgrow their systems and processes, too. For example, software that supports one location may not be suitable to supporting multiple locations. If you expand your business overseas, your software might not account for different currencies. There are many reasons why software that supports business processes may become obsolete.

Losing operational efficiency because you failed to manage your growth will affect your bottom line. You must know enough about your processes to understand when your employees are taking extra manual steps because there is no automated solution. You can lose great people if processes require a lot of manual work. These types of issues can really drag on morale and contribute to employee turnover.

Consider Starbucks again. The company has over 200 people working in its Accounting Department. How many accountants would Starbucks have to hire if it could not automate its thousands of daily transactions? If it did not have software and infrastructure in place to do this, it could not have grown to the size it is today.

When processes don't keep up with growth and manual steps are introduced, there are great risks incurred, too. If accounting transactions are being done manually, you could lose the ability to track them (refer to Chapter 5). This introduces risks ranging from theft and fraud to other situations that can cause losses on your financial statements. Even the largest companies can experience problems like these.

Even with its sophisticated software, for example, Starbucks could not track aging inventory. As a result, it was forced to write off over a million dollars in inventory in just one year. This was all because its software could not give it an accurate picture of aging and expired inventory.

While growth can be exciting, managing your growth is essential to maintain a healthy company. Unconstrained growth can take a toll on morale if your infrastructure cannot keep up. A healthy balance of growth and internal improvements is therefore essential to your long-term success.

Key Takeaways

- Develop creativity and innovation in your business by leveraging other tools, such as performance reviews and rewards systems.
- Be willing to leverage your contacts and professional networks for investors and joint ventures.
- Be willing to leverage other sales platforms, such as Amazon's seller program.

Interactive Activities

1. Invite a business owner to coffee or lunch and talk to them about how they have designed a subscription service. How did they design the value proposal? How did they price the service?

2. Search your business connections and see if you know anyone who works in mergers and acquisitions. Invite them to lunch to talk about why a company would acquire another company. Talk to them about what goes into these decisions and start making a checklist for yourself for acquiring a company to expand your business.
3. Do some research on publicly traded companies that have completed mergers or acquisitions. Go to their websites and search for financial information in their annual 10-K reports to see why they made these moves. You can find a 10-K in the "investor relations" sections of websites. Examine why the companies make these moves in order to know what may trigger you to do the same thing in your business.

11.4 Test Your Skills: Applied Case

Ebony's Dog Grooming Business

Ebony has started a dog grooming business and she has done quite well since her business started up four years ago. Now, she is itching to grow the business. Her sales margins are good and she has been able to save approximately $200,000. She could use some of that to possibly invest in another location. However, because of a recent health concern in her area, she has been having dogs dropped off and is not allowing owners to wait in the lobby as normal for their pets.

She is worried that she is not thinking of all of the possibilities when it comes to expanding her business. Her business is in a growth area, where the labor force is attracted to high technology and therefore salaries are higher than most places to spend on expenses such as dog grooming. She believes she could hire potentially very good people, at a competitive wage, but she is worried about not directly supervising someone's work. Thus, if she opened a second location, would another person be able to keep up her standards of grooming care?

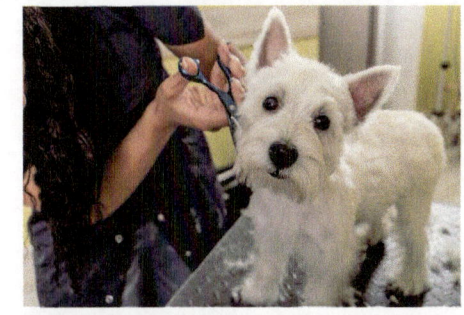

Source: © Shutterstock, Inc.

Given all of the variables here, consider the following questions that Ebony has about growing her business:

1. What else might Ebony be missing in terms of a growth opportunity?
2. Should Ebony only be thinking about *one* growth opportunity? Why, or why not?
3. Assess all of the possible opportunities that Ebony can use for her business. What are the pros and cons? (Hint: consider costs, psychology challenges for Ebony, risks, any other factors that can go into this decision.)
4. Finally, which opportunity do you think would be best for Ebony? How would you pitch it?

Endnotes

1. Schultz, H and Yang, D. J. (1997). Pour your heart into it. New York, NY. Hyperion Publishing
2. Community Futures, (n.d.). Business expansion" Why expand? Retrieved from: http://www.cf-sn.ca/business/business_expansion/intro.php
3. CFI. (n.d.). Joint ventures (JV). Retrieved from: https://corporatefinanceinstitute.com/resources/knowledge/deals/what-is-joint-venture-jv/
4. Deeb, G. (2016). What exactly is venture capital? Retrieved from: https://www.forbes.com/sites/georgedeeb/2016/07/18/what-exactly-is-venture-capital/#6e924c702501
5. Valentine, R. (2020). Bunch raises $20m toward multiplayer social platform expansion. Retrieved from: https://www.gamesindustry.biz/articles/2020-09-17-bunch-raises-USD20m-toward-multiplayer-social-platform-expansion
6. CFI. (n.d.). IPO Process. Retrieved from: https://corporatefinanceinstitute.com/resources/knowledge/finance/ipo-process/
7. Bloch, R. (n.d.). Buy, sell, or join forces? Retrieved from: https://www.thehartford.com/business-playbook/in-depth/business-acquisition-pros-cons
8. Sanders, M. (n.d.). What is a company merger? Retrieved from: http://smallbusiness.chron.com/company-merger-21903.html
9. Conglomerate Merger (n.d.). Meaning of Merger. Retrieved from: https://efinancemanagement.com/mergers-and-acquisitions/conglomerate-merger
10. Peavler, R. (2017). What are horizontal and vertical mergers? Retrieved from: https://www.thebalance.com/horizontal-and-vertical-mergers-explained-392846
11. Peavler, R. (2017). What are horizontal and vertical mergers? Retrieved from: https://www.thebalance.com/horizontal-and-vertical-mergers-explained-392846
12. Rampton, J. (n.d.). 9 ways to learn from your customers without spending a fortune. Retrieved from: https://www.inc.com/john-rampton/9-ways-to-learn-from-your-customers-without-costing-you-a-fortune.html
13. Ward, S. (2016). 10 proven ways to grow your business. Retrieved from: https://www.thebalance.com/top-ways-of-growing-your-business-2948140
14. Adams, R. L. (2021). 15 strategies for quickly expanding your business. Retrieved from: https://www.entrepreneur.com/article/306049
15. Ward, S. (2016). 10 proven ways to grow your business. Retrieved from: https://www.thebalance.com/top-ways-of-growing-your-business-2948140
16. SCORE (n.d.). The truth about franchising vs licensing in 3 minutes. Retrieved from: https://www.score.org/blog/truth-about-franchising-vs-licensing-3-minutes
17. Tice, C. (n.d.). Franchise your business in 7 steps. Retrieved from: https://www.entrepreneur.com/article/204998#
18. Henderson, T. (2017). Why innovation is crucial to your organization's long-term success. Retrieved from: https://www.forbes.com/sites/forbescoachescouncil/2017/05/08/why-innovation-is-crucial-to-your-organizations-long-term-success/#f816acd30986
19. Lund, J. (2021). The key to business success? Relationships! Retrieved from: https://www.superoffice.com/blog/business-relationships/
20. Gutierrez, L. M. (2021). Five practices to cultivate a creative mindset. Retrieved from: https://www.visualversa.com/five-practices-to-cultivate-a-creative-mindset/
21. Sovey, S. (n.d.). The seven habits of highly effective people: Habit 7 sharpen the saw. Retrieved from: https://www.stephencovey.com/7habits/7habits-habit7.php

CHAPTER 12
Planning for the Future

Case Study—Security Plus

What do you get when you mix cybersecurity expertise and a successful consulting business? You get a business called Security Plus, which boasts over fifty regular clients and a steady stream of new clients. The owner of Security Plus, Leon Crenshaw, has been in the cybersecurity business since the early 2000's when the internet and security needs were still new. However, Leon predicted a growing need for cyber consulting, and has grown his business for the past twenty plus years. The business focuses on advising large and small companies on how to secure their networks for employees and customers. The passion for his business—along with a steady stream of talented consultants on his team who have earned degrees in the various areas of IT (including cybersecurity)—has made it successful.

Source: © Shutterstock, Inc.

Leon, however, has decided he'd like to begin the process of retirement but is struggling with the thought of closing the business down completely. He has developed so many relationships over the years, many of which have turned into lifelong friendships, so he is worried about matching the quality of customer service his clients have come to appreciate and respect.

Much to his excitement, his son Desean has decided to major in cybersecurity. With only two years left of school, Leon is at a decision point: continue working in the business and transfer ownership upon graduation to Desean, or sell the business outright. For Leon, the advantages of turning the business over to his son are many. First, he'd like to maintain the family legacy of Security Plus. He also thinks this is a good option as he'd be able to work part time as Desean gets his bearings while he teaches him everything he knows about the business. However, selling the business outright has its advantages too. The cash gained from the business could help Leon take a two-month dream vacation and ensure he has a solid income during retirement.

Leon speaks with his son when he comes home for winter break. Desean has dreams of turning Security Plus into a franchise consulting business with established offices all over the world. While Leon never thought about growing the business in this way, he is interested and has faith in his son's abilities to grow Security Plus. And then . . . gets has an idea.

He proposes the business be transferred to Desean in three years. This will give Desean time to finish his degree and work for the business for a year before taking it over. After the three-year period, Leon would work part time with a few of his oldest clients and serve as an advisor to his son. In addition to the part-time income Leon would earn, he would take payment for the business over a period of ten years, rather than completely gifting the business to Desean. This plan has several advantages. First, it allows Desean to settle into the business prior to finally turning it over to him. It would also allow the staff consultants to get comfortable with the major organizational change. Simultaneously, Desean would be given the opportunity to grow and learn everything he can at a slower pace, knowing he will have a job waiting for him right after graduation. And as for Leon, this plan would allow him to continue earning a percentage of the company's income for a period of time while serving as his son's advisor.

Leon has papers drawn up with his attorney and he and Desean review them together. They are happy with this decision as it is a win-win for all involved . . . and the Crenshaw legacy, Security Plus, will live on.

12.1 Succession Planning

Learning Objectives

1. Discuss the reasons for succession planning.
2. Discuss considerations related to transfer of ownership, selling the business, and dissolving the business.

In Chapter 11 we discussed options for growing your business. Knowing how to grow your business is important, but there may come a time when you decide you no longer want to be in business. Perhaps you've decided to dissolve a partnership, or maybe you want to retire and transfer the business to your children. Whatever the reason, you must know how to transfer or close your business successfully. That is the focus of this chapter.

Why Succession Planning?

Succession planning is defined as the process of planning for the day a business owner decides to step down from a leadership role.[1] Although 66 percent of entrepreneurs do not have a succession plan, having such a plan is important for multiple reasons.[2] First, the succession plan will outline how the business should be run. For example, if it is a family business, will the kids take over the business? Which kids? What roles should they take? Perhaps you'd like your spouse to take over the business. All of this is addressed in the succession plan. It provides a clear path concerning what should be done with your business after you sell, leave, retire, or pass away.

Taxes are another reason to plan for succession. Should you pass away, there is a chance your successors will pay heavy estate taxes on your business. Planning a smooth transfer of ownership can make this process easier and less expensive for your heirs.[3]

Another major advantage of succession planning is the peace of mind it creates. Having a plan means you will be able to see the fruits of your labor extend past your involvement in the business.

There are a number of reasons why entrepreneurs do not plan for succession or are not successful in such planning. Consider the following:[4]

- **Driven people:** As an entrepreneur, it is likely you have a successful business because of your drive. It can be difficult for the entrepreneur to "let go" and let someone else take on the leadership role.
- **Loss of status:** Because entrepreneurs are often leaders in their communities, it can be difficult to successfully transition the business for fear of losing status.

Source: © Shutterstock, Inc.

succession planning
The process of planning for the day a business owner decides to step down from a leadership role.

- **"Go to" people:** Often entrepreneurs are the "go to" people in their businesses. To ask for help or completely hand over the business can create the feeling that the entrepreneur is admitting weakness.
- **Focus:** Because you've focused a lot of your life on this business, your skills may become very narrow. Handing over your business can create challenges revolving around self-worth and self-perception.

Although these challenges are real, it does not diminish the need for succession planning to protect you, the business, and your family. The next sections will discuss the various ways to plan for succession by selling your business, transferring it to family, or dissolving the business.

Reasons for Succession Planning

View in the online reader

Selling Your Business

There are three main types of ownership transfer. The first is an **outright sale**. In an outright sale, you transfer ownership immediately. The disadvantage of this type of sale is the fact you can't be sure the business will continue with your vision in mind. A cash influx for the purchase, however, is an advantage. There are several types of outright sales:

- **Sell to an Individual:** In this situation, you find an individual buyer or partners who would like to purchase your business.
- **Management Buy-Out (MBO):** This occurs when members of the management team within the business get together to buy the business. For example, if you own a restaurant, you could decide to sell to the chef and dining room manager.
- **Initial Public Offering:** This occurs when you sell stocks in your company to the public. This option is only viable for larger businesses.
- **Sale to Another Business:** This is the sale of your company to another company. For example, if you own a restaurant and another restaurant in town purchases it, this is a sale to another business.

Another option to transfer ownership is a **gradual sale**. In this type of situation, an agreement is made to sell a business over time. In some situations, the owner may be able to step away from the business, let the new owner run it, and still earn income while the new owner is paying off the business.[5]

outright sale
The selling of your business and transferring ownership immediately. You are paid for the assets of the business.

gradual sale
An agreement to sell a business over time.

lease agreement
Lending all assets and the business to a person for a specified period of time.

A **lease agreement** means you will lend all assets and the business to a person for a specified period of time. Once that time is up, you take the business back and continue to operate in full.[6] This may happen in situations where a person needs to be away from the business for an extended period of time. "Lending" the business to someone makes sense in that situation.

FIGURE 12.1 The Typical Process of Selling a Business

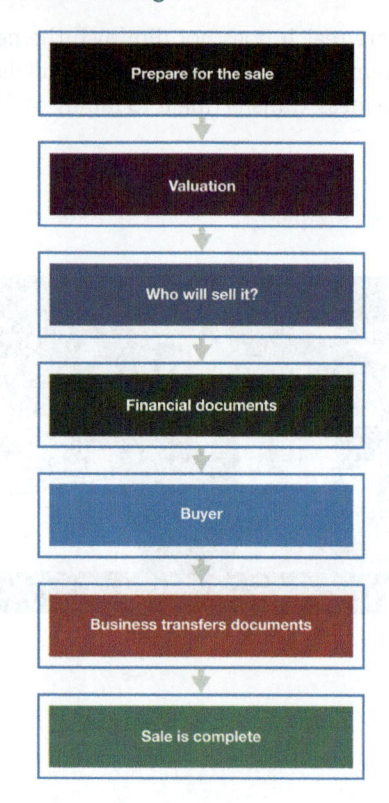

```
Prepare for the sale
        ↓
     Valuation
        ↓
   Who will sell it?
        ↓
  Financial documents
        ↓
       Buyer
        ↓
Business transfers documents
        ↓
    Sale is complete
```

Source: Laura Portolese et al.

business valuation
An expert's opinion on what your business is worth.

When you consider selling your business or transferring ownership, there are several steps you will want to take. First, prepare for the sale two years ahead of time. This gives you plenty of time to find a buyer and pull together all necessary paperwork. Next, obtain a **business valuation**. A business valuation is an expert's opinion about what your business is worth. The business valuation will help you set the price for your business. Next, you will want to consider if you will sell the business yourself or if you will employ a broker to help sell it for you. If you use a broker, it is likely that person will take a percentage of the sale, but they may have access to buyers you don't and can help you sell more quickly.

Next, you will want to gather the documents potential buyers will likely want to see. These include:[7]

- Profit and loss statements for two to three years
- Balance sheet
- Cash flow statement
- Tax returns for two to three years
- Insurance policies
- Lease agreement (if applicable)
- List of inventory
- List of assets
- Photos of business
- Business and marketing plan

After the documents are prepared, you might consider writing an executive summary and providing other information about your business to potential buyers. Once you have a buyer and have negotiated a deal, there is likely other paperwork to complete. For example, if your business is a corporation (refer to Chapter 2) as opposed to a sole proprietorship, there may be different documents to fill out. This is when it is wise to hire a lawyer if you don't already have one.

Finally, be aware of the tax consequences of your sale. A large influx of cash could have severe tax implications. A tax advisor can help you in this step.[8]

Transfer the Business to Family

Another option, rather than selling the business, is to transfer it to a family member. This is different from simply selling to a family member, which was addressed in the last section. Transferring to family gives you the option to keep the business stable and running under a vision similar to your own. There are some major advantages to transferring ownership to a family member:

- Emotional benefits of working together
- The ability to phase into retirement because the owner can stay as active as desired in the business
- Maintaining a family legacy

There are also disadvantages to transfer of ownership to a family member:[9]

- Children often desire their own career paths and may have little interest in the family business.
- You could sell the business rather than gifting it, which means by gifting it you are foregoing profit.
- It may be difficult to decide which family member gets the business.
- A business gifted to siblings might make it harder for those siblings to get along and run the business successfully.

What Would You Do?

Suppose you have started and have been running a new business, and now would like to gift the business to one or both of your children. One of them, Chad, has been working with you in the business since he graduated from college. The other, Angie, has worked in the business but is currently working for the sheriff's department in your town. Angie, although she doesn't have a lot of current experience in the business, has marketing savvy that Chad doesn't. What factors would you use to make the decision concerning who gets the business? If you transfer to both kids, how would you divide their duties?

Understanding the implications of gifting a business is therefore very important. Besides the financial implications, there are serious familial and emotional considerations. Should you decide to transfer ownership to a family member, you should hire a lawyer and an accountant to take care of the needed paperwork depending on your business structure.

If you can't or won't sell and you choose not to transfer your business to a family member, you might consider dissolving the company. We will discuss this in the next section.

Ten Factors Making Up the Succession Matrix for Transferring a Business to a Family Member

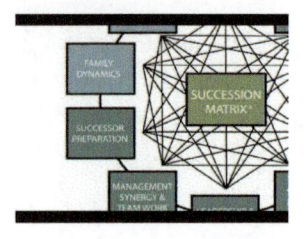

View in the online reader

Dissolving the Business

For a variety of reasons, you may decide just to close the business rather than trying to sell it or transfer it to a family member. Unfortunately, you cannot simply put up an "Out of Business" sign and lock the doors. There is a specific process to follow if you decide to close your business.[10]

FIGURE 12.2 Steps to Dissolve a Business

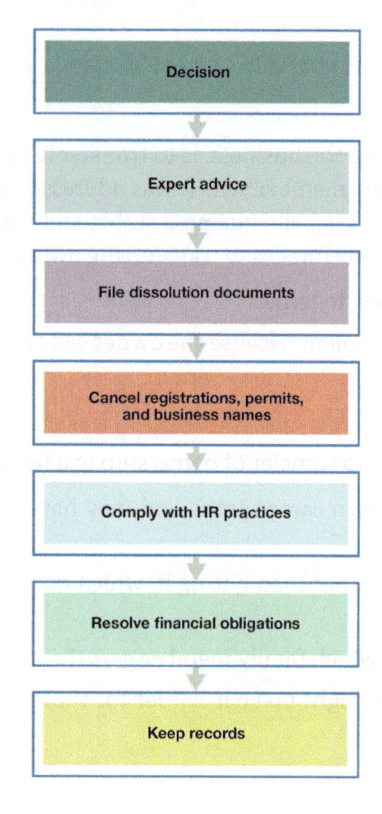

- Decision
- Expert advice
- File dissolution documents
- Cancel registrations, permits, and business names
- Comply with HR practices
- Resolve financial obligations
- Keep records

Source: Laura Portolese et al.

First, seek expert advice from your accountant and lawyer. Every dissolution is different, so we can't address all possible scenarios here. The lawyer and accountant will be better prepared to offer advice for your specific situation.

Once you have received advice, you will need to file dissolution documents with your state. Remember that state laws vary greatly. Next, any leases, permits, website registrations, and similar agreements will need to be canceled. After that, you'll need to make sure to follow all employee laws and regulations to make sure your employees get their final paychecks . . . and of course you'll have to inform them of the situation prior to closing your business.

Just because your business is closed doesn't mean you don't still have financial obligations. Determine what is owed and pay it off. Finally, make sure to keep financial records for at least seven years. It is not easy to make this decision, nor is the process to close a business any easier. It may still be the right choice for your situation, however.

If you find your debts are too great to manage, you may need to consider bankruptcy. Again, it is best to consult with a lawyer and accountant before making this decision. There are three types of bankruptcy we will discuss here. First, **Chapter 7 bankruptcy** is one in which all debts are cleared. Assets may be sold to repay creditors. This is the most extreme type of bankruptcy and can be used for corporations, partnerships, and sole proprietorships. The law, however, restricts who may file, so it is best to check with your lawyer.

Chapter 7 bankruptcy

A type of bankruptcy in which all debts become clear, but assets may be liquidated to help pay for debts.

> **Peter Kinsella on Bringing His Business Back from the Brink of Dissolution**
>
> View in the online reader

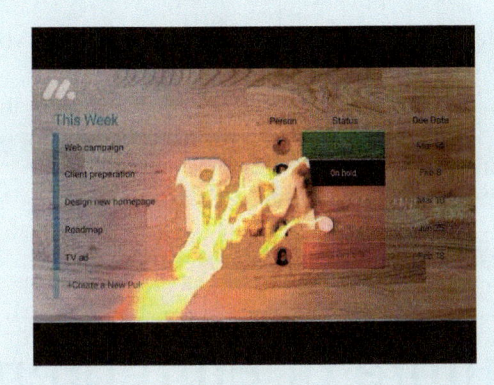

Leveraging: Bankruptcy Survival!

Many famous people have survived bankruptcy. Check out this article for some of the famous names who have prevailed even after going bankrupt. What are some ideas and philosophies you can implement in your business now to avoid bankruptcy? What mistakes and pitfalls should be avoided in your industry if you are to prevent bankruptcy?

Chapter 11 bankruptcy is a less extreme measure that allows the entrepreneur time to reorganize and restructure. Some entrepreneurs will use this strategy if they still believe they have a viable business plan but are threatened with lawsuits to pay debt. Chapter 11 can only be filed as a corporation or partnership. With Chapter 11, debts are reorganized and the company continues to operate. The court may order that it cut expenses or make other organizational changes.

Finally, **Chapter 13 bankruptcy**, also called a *wage earners plan*, allows the entrepreneur to pay debts over a three- to five-year period.[11] This is not an option for a corporation or partnership; it is only for sole proprietorships. Certain limits on debt and other requirements must be met in order to deem an entrepreneur qualified for Chapter 13.

Now that we have discussed ways to end your business, let's talk about some considerations in the future of entrepreneurship.

> **Chapter 11 bankruptcy**
> A type of bankruptcy that allows the entrepreneur time before paying debts to reorganize and restructure.
>
> **Chapter 13 bankruptcy**
> A type of bankruptcy, also called a wage earners plan, that allows the entrepreneur to pay debts over a three- to five-year period.

Key Takeaways

- Succession planning means determining how you will handle the business if you pass away or decide to leave it.
- There are a number of ways to sell your business, all of which should be done with the help of a lawyer and accountant.
- Certain considerations exist for giving your business to a family member.
- Dissolution of the business requires more than just "closing the doors." Entrepreneurs who decide to dissolve a business must complete necessary obligations.
- There are three main types of bankruptcies: Chapter 7, Chapter 11, and Chapter 13. Each type has varying requirements.

Interactive Activities

1. Research the elements you should include in a succession plan for your specific type of business (e.g., restaurant) and discuss them.
2. Research the specific requirements needed to apply for each of the three types of bankruptcy. If you had to file for bankruptcy, which type would apply to you? Why would you choose this type?
3. Create a succession plan for your business.

12.2 The Future of Entrepreneurship

Learning Objectives

1. Define and explain ethical decision making.
2. Define and explain the elements of social responsibility.

As you begin this venture, it is important to think about ethics and social responsibility as an entrepreneur. Social responsibility can give your business an edge, producing cost savings, improving customer perception, and generating a feeling of doing good for the community. Ethical, socially responsible entrepreneurs tend to be more successful.[12] **Social entrepreneurship** is the use of techniques by entrepreneurs to develop, fund, and implement solutions to social, cultural, and environmental issues—all while starting a small business.

Ethics

Making ethical decisions is a cornerstone of successful entrepreneurship. Entrepreneurs must make two types of ethical decisions. First, there is ethical decision making within your company—for example, choosing whether to promote an inferior product that you know has safety issues. Second, there is the way the entrepreneur treats people who work for that entrepreneur.

Ethics is defined as a set of values that define right and wrong when applied to decision making. The challenge, then, is in defining right and wrong. **Values** are defined as principles or standards that a person finds desirable. Therefore, we can say that ethics is a set of principles that a person or society finds desirable and that help define right and wrong.

People often believe the law defines what is right and wrong for us. To an extent it does, but there are many things that could be considered unethical that are not necessarily illegal. For example, discriminating against certain groups of people when hiring is illegal. However, something that may not be illegal, but is unethical might be exaggerating claims of your product or service to customers. This is the difference between something unethical and something illegal. You may not be breaking the law, but you might be doing something wrong nonetheless.

So what do ethics have to do with entrepreneurship? As an individual running a business, you have a responsibility to employees, customers, suppliers, and other stakeholders to make the right decisions. As a leader in your community, you are expected to do the right thing.

---

social entrepreneurship
The use of techniques by entrepreneurs to develop, fund, and implement solutions to social, cultural, and environmental issues—all while starting a small business.

ethics
A set of values that define right and wrong when applied to decision making.

values
Principles or standards that a person finds desirable.

A founder's ethics are shown through the ethics of an organization. The founder is the one who set the ethics to begin with, after all.[13] In other words, while we can discuss organizational ethics, remember that you, as the entrepreneur, are the one who will determine your company's ethics. If an entrepreneur can create an ethically oriented culture, the company is more likely to hire people who behave ethically.[14]

FIGURE 12.3 An Ethics Framework for the Entrepreneur

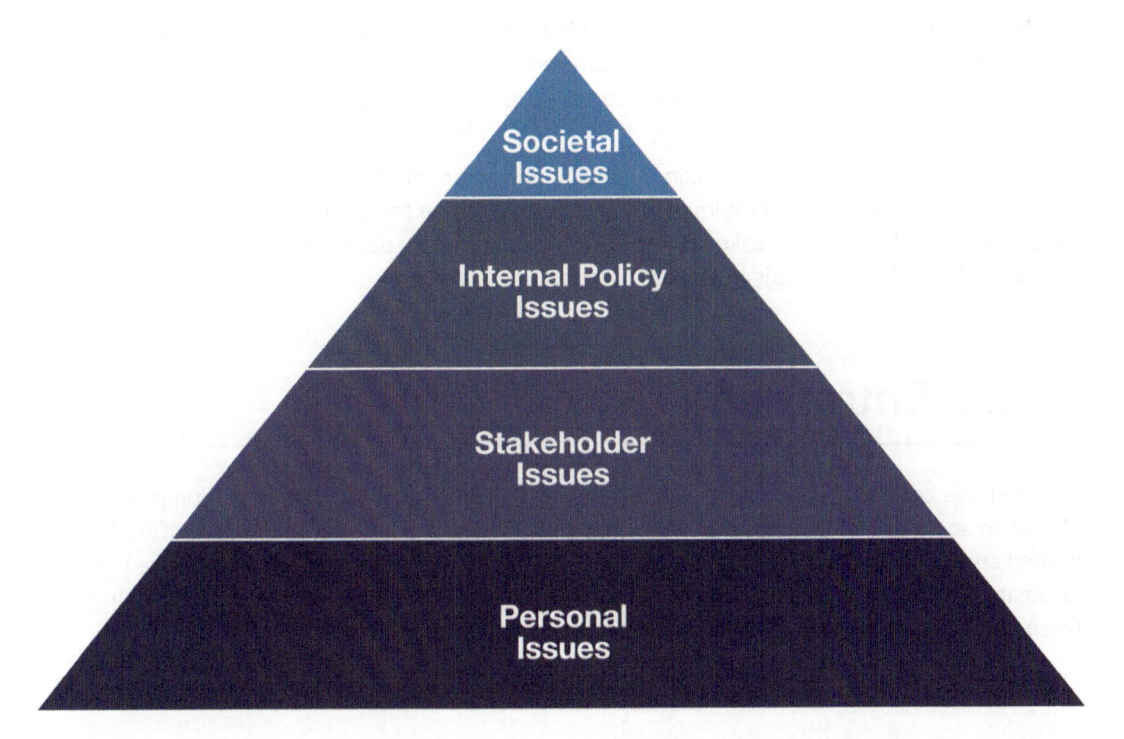

A pyramid diagram with four levels, from top to bottom: Societal Issues, Internal Policy Issues, Stakeholder Issues, Personal Issues.

Source: Laura Portolese et al.

There are four ethical levels within organizations.[15] The first level of ethical issues is personal issues. These deal with how we treat others inside and outside of the company. Showing favoritism toward one employee over another would be an example of personal issues in relation to ethics. Personal issues include "doing the right thing." Doing the right thing affects our credibility as an entrepreneur, both within our organization and in the community where we live.

The second level of ethics is stakeholder's issues. A **stakeholder** is anyone affected by a company's actions as we discussed in Chapter 9. At this level, businesses must deal with policies that affect their customers, employees, suppliers, and people within the community. For example, this level might deal with fairness in wages for your employees or notification of the potential dangers of a company's product.

The third level is internal policy issues. At this level, the concern is internal relationships between a company and its employees. Fairness in management, pay, and employee participation would all be considered ethical internal policy issues. You will have extensive control over this as the owner of the business. Creating policies regarding the treatment of employees relates to leadership—and the retention of those employees through fair treatment. It is in your best interests to create internal policies that benefit your company as well as the individuals working for you.

The last level is societal issues. These are the top-level issues relating to the world as a whole, which deal with questions such as the morality of child labor worldwide. Deeper-level societal issues might include the role (if any) of capitalism in poverty.

stakeholder
Anyone affected by a company's actions.

> **Leveraging: What Are Your Societal-Level Issues?**
>
> As the leader in your organization, you promote ethics through your actions. What types of ethical issues are important to you in terms of societal-level issues? How can you support these in your business?

Most companies do not operate at this level of ethics, although some companies, such as Toms Shoes, feel it is their responsibility to make sure everyone has shoes to wear. As a result, their "one for one" program gives one pair of shoes to someone in need for every pair of shoes purchased. Concern for the environment is another way a company can focus on societal-level issues.

While running a successful business, make sure your business ethics match your personal ethics. This trickles down to employees, producing a positive reputation. Ethics are also tied into social responsibility, in that it takes an ethical business leader to decide to focus on social entrepreneurship. This will be the topic of our next section.

Social Entrepreneurship

Consider the company 141 Eyewear. For every eyeglass purchase, the company donates a pair of glasses to someone in need.[16] Or consider Happy Blankie, which donates a combination blanket/stuffed animal to orphanages and children's hospitals when one is purchased. There are hundreds of organizations like these examples, which focus not only on making profit, but on making a difference. Review your business plan to see if your company is ethical in all four areas.

FIGURE 12.4 The Four Aspects of Social Responsibility

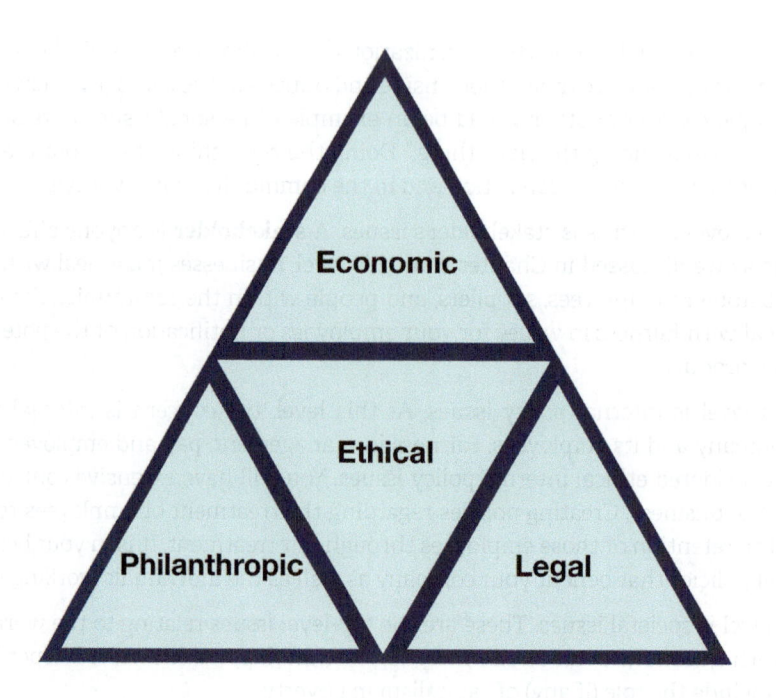

Source: Laura Portolese et al.

As depicted in Figure 12.4, the four areas include:[17]

1. **Economic aspects**

    Your business should maintain strong economic interests so you can stay in business. Being profitable and providing value to shareholders is part of being socially responsible.

2. **Legal aspects**

    As a business owner, you must follow the law. You have a legal obligation to do so. For example, if you open a business in a town that requires recycling, you should recycle. It is not just the law; it is the right thing to do.

3. **Ethical aspects**

    Acting ethically means going above and beyond the legal requirements and meeting the expectations of society. How can you go above and beyond the law to do the right thing for society in your business?

4. **Philanthropic aspects**

    This is the expectation that companies should give back to society in the form of charitable donations of time, money, and goods.

Changing the World Through Social Entrepreneurship

View in the online reader

Other Trends in Entrepreneurship

A major trend in entrepreneurship is the trend toward diversity of business owners. For example, women owned-firms make up 19.9 percent of all businesses, and that number keeps growing.[18] Similarly, entrepreneurs of color generate more than 1.4 trillion in revenue, and the growth rate for businesses owned by people of color is ten times faster than the overall growth rate.[19]

Co-working is also a popular trend for entrepreneurs, even after the COVID-19 pandemic.[20] Co-working refers to the rental of space or working environment by many people. Worker do not have their own offices, per se, but a collection of shared spaces they can use (together with the necessary equipment, such as copiers and phones, rented for a fee).

co-working

The rental of space or working environment by many people.

During the COVID-19 crisis, some employees were able to work from home. Do you think you'd enjoy working from home full time? Could you run your business remotely?

Source: © Shutterstock, Inc.

enterprise resource planning software (ERP)

Software used to help integration of company financials, supply chain management, and human resource activities, among other efficiencies.

customer relationship management (CRM)

A way to store customer information, manage marketing, track sales leads, and even send automated communication to potential customers.

Another trend is working from home or remote work. While for some businesses such as a retail store or restaurant this may not be possible, other businesses moved to a work from home model after the COVID-19 crisis. Remote work arrangements can be motivating to employees and boost retention due to time saved traveling to and from work, among other reasons. However, telecommuting full time can also cause employees to feel isolated, lonely, and anxious.[21] Some companies offer meditation programs, fitness classes, and remote games online to help keep employees motivated and productive.[22]

Technology is another consideration in entrepreneurship. Many small businesses use **enterprise resource planning software (ERP)** to help integration of company financials, supply chain management, and human resource activities, among other efficiencies. While ERP used to be focused for larger organizations, the more affordable nature of ERP today makes it a good choice for small business owners. Similarly, there are many types of software for **customer relationship management (CRM)**. CRM is a way to store customer information, manage marketing, track sales leads, and even send automated communication to potential customers. These types of technologies can help you, as a business owner, focus more of your efforts on growing your business, as opposed to resource and customer tracking.

Now that we have addressed some of the trends in entrepreneurship, we encourage you to consider how your business plan can affect your stakeholders, community, and the world at large in a positive way.

Entrepreneurship Trends

View in the online reader

Key Takeaways

- There are several trends in entrepreneurship. Ethical, socially responsible entrepreneurs position themselves for success.
- Other trends in entrepreneurship revolve around diversity, co-working, remote work, and the use of technology.

Interactive Activity

1. What elements of social responsibility would you consider implementing in your business—and why?

12.3 Test Your Skills: Applied Case

Noah Miles and Succession Planning

Twenty years ago, Noah Miles started a heating and air conditioning (HVAC) business in Las Vegas, NV. The business has grown over the years, and Noah prides himself on quick service and fair prices. Much of his business comes from referrals.

Source: © Shutterstock, Inc.

Noah, however, is close to retirement and wants to begin planning for what to do with his business once he retires. He had hoped his two kids would be interested in taking the business over, but they've moved away and work in other fields. He has several employees that would be cabable of owning the business, but he wants to make sure he looks at all options before selling the business to them. Can you help Noah determine the best way to plan for retirement?

1. What emotions and concerns do you think Noah likely has as he begins to think about selling his business?
2. Explain to Noah what his options are (besides giving the business to his kids) in terms of selling the business. What are the advantages and disadvantages of each?
3. Assume Noah has decided to sell. Explain to him the documents and information he will need for the sale.

Endnotes

1. Entrepreneur Magazine. (n.d.). Succession plan. Retrieved from: https://www.entrepreneur.com/encyclopedia/succession-plan
2. U.S. Trust (2014) 2014 U.S. Trust insights on wealth and worth survey. Retrieved from: http://www.ustrust.com/publish/content/application/pdf/GWMOL/USTp_ARGWF53F_2015-06.pdf
3. Kauffman Entrepreneurs, (2002, November 1) Understanding the fundamentals of succession and transition planning. Retrieved from: https://www.entrepreneurship.org/articles/2002/11/understanding-the-fundamentals-of-succession-and-transition-planning
4. Goldsmith, M. (2009, October 8) Why entrepreneurs sabotage the succession process. Harvard Business Review. Retrieved from: https://hbr.org/2009/10/why-entrepreneurs-sabotage-the
5. Small Business Administration (n.d.) Transfer of ownership. Retrieved from: https://www.sba.gov/managing-business/closing-down-your-business/transfer-ownership
6. Small Business Administration (n.d.) Transfer of ownership. Retrieved from: https://www.sba.gov/managing-business/closing-down-your-business/transfer-ownership
7. Handelsman, M. (2012, April 12). Selling your business? Get your documents in order. Inc. Magazine. Retrieved from: https://www.inc.com/mike-handelsman/selling-your-business-get-your-documents-in-order.html
8. Yuille, B. (2018, October 16). 7 steps to selling your small business. Investopedia. Retrieved from: http://www.investopedia.com/articles/pf/08/sell-small-business.asp
9. Key Bank, (n.d.) All in the family, Transferring a business. Retrieved from: https://www.key.com/kpb/our-insights/resources/all-in-the-family-transferring-a-business-to-the-next-generation.jsp
10. Small Business Administration (n.d.) Steps to closing a business. Retrieved from: https://www.sba.gov/managing-business/closing-down-your-business/steps-closing-business
11. United States Courts. (n.d.) Retrieved from: http://www.uscourts.gov/services-forms/bankruptcy/bankruptcy-basics/chapter-13-bankruptcy-basics
12. Allen, J. (2021, January 21) 5 reasons small businesses should adopt a CSR strategy. Retrieved from: https://www.charities.org/news/5-reasons-small-businesses-should-adopt-csr-strategy-how-do-it
13. Markkula Center for Applied Ethics. (n.d.) The role of the CEO in building an ethical organization. Retrieved from: https://www.scu.edu/ethics/focus-areas/business-ethics/resources/-role-of-the-ceo-in-building-ethical-organization/
14. Sims, R. R. (1991). The institutionalisation of organisational ethics. Journal of Business Ethics, 10(7), pp. 493–506.
15. Philosophy Question Library. (n.d.) What are the four levels of ethical questions in a business? Retrieved from: https://philosophy-question.com/library/lecture/read/328830-what-are-the-four-levels-of-ethical-questions-in-business
16. 141 Eyewear (n.d) Giving. Retrieved from: https://141eyewear.com/
17. Carroll, A. (1991, July–August). The pyramid of corporate social responsibility. Business Horizons. Retrieved from: http://cf.linnbenton.edu/bcs/bm/gusdorm/upload/Pyramid of Social Responsibility.pdf
18. US Census Bureau. (2021, March 21). Number of women-owned employer firms increased .6%. Retrieved from: https://www.census.gov/library/stories/2021/03/women-business-ownership-in-america-on-rise.html#:~:text=Women-owned firms made up,Annual Business Survey (ABS).
19. Small Business Majority (2021, July 2). The agenda for America's entrepreneurs of color. Retrieved from: https://smallbusinessmajority.org/policy-agenda/agenda-for-americas-entrepreneurs-of-color
20. Moreno, H. (2021, November 5) Top 13 coworking space trends. Retrieved from: https://www.andcards.com/blog/tips/coworking-space-trends/
21. Przystanski, A. (2020, March 26) RfH Insights: Great ways to support employees amid covid-19. Retrieved from: https://lattice.com/library/rfh-insights-great-ways-to-support-employees-and-yourself-amid-covid-19
22. Przystanski, A. (26 March 2020) RfH Insights: Great ways to support employees amid covid-19. Retrieved from: https://lattice.com/library/rfh-insights-great-ways-to-support-employees-and-yourself-amid-covid-19

APPENDIX A
Start Your Business Resources

A.1 Entrepreneurship Planning

Entrepreneurship Self-Assessment

One thing you can do prior to starting a business is to make sure you are ready—not just with a good idea, but personally ready to take on entrepreneurship challenges. Follow these links to take self-assessments to test your readiness to start a business:

- https://www.bdc.ca/en/articles-tools/entrepreneur-toolkit/business-assessments/self-assessment-test-your-entrepreneurial-potential
- https://eweb1.sba.gov/cams/training/business_primer/assessment.htm
- https://s3-us-west-2.amazonaws.com/oerfiles/WMBusiness/Entrepreneur-Self-Assessment-Survey.pdf

Start Your Business Resources

Here are some useful checklists for you to review before you launch your business:

- https://www.mycompanyworks.com/checklist.htm
- https://www.sba.gov/business-guide/10-steps-start-your-business
- https://www.xero.com/us/resources/small-business-guides/checklists/starting-a-business-checklist/

Business Model Canvas Template

A business model canvas template can be useful as you think about launching your business. Most business model canvases offer you the ability to explain your value proposition's, key activities, and customer segments, allowing you to have a clear picture of just where you want to go with your business. Check out the following resources to help build your business model:

- https://canvanizer.com/new/business-model-canvas
- https://www.strategyzer.com/canvas/business-model-canvas
- https://www.alexandercowan.com/business-model-canvas-templates/

Business Plan Templates

You already know that a business plan is necessary for a successful start to your business. Here are some links to templates you can use to develop your business plan:

- https://www.sba.gov/business-guide/plan-your-business/write-your-business-plan
- https://www.score.org/resource/business-plan-template-startup-business
- https://www.hubspot.com/business-templates/business-plans

APPENDIX B
Social Media Marketing

B.1 A Brief Look at Using Social Media to Market Your Business

What Is Social Media Marketing?

Chapter 4 discusses the preparation of a marketing plan and includes a discussion about market research, target markets, and demographics, as well as some traditional promotional strategies to market your business. Developing a marketing plan is an important step in determining the potential market for your business. However, promotional strategies have changed over the years. Traditional methods of print advertising, as well as radio and television ads still have their place for many businesses and business types. But social media marketing is another way in which businesses can reach specific target customers.

Social media is everywhere. Facebook, YouTube, Snapchat, Instagram, Twitter, and TikTok are just a few of the bigger social media platforms and each plays a slightly different role in providing social connections between platform users. The biggest difference between social media platforms and other forms of internet content is that all users of the platforms are both creators and consumers of the platform's content. While most social media users are happy to view content, many find a voice or a place where they are able to share their opinions. Those opinions can help a business flourish or flounder.

By developing a social presence for your business on several platforms, business owners can track reactions to new product releases and customer satisfaction with products or services allowing for a more immediate reaction. Businesses can take advantage of targeted advertising as well as real-time metrics that can help the business owner know if the ads are achieving the desired impact.

Advantages of Using Social Media Marketing

Marketing through social media can have several advantages. Billions of individuals use some form of social media daily and while your business may be a small, local bakery, it's possible to reach those target individuals through savvy social media marketing. Furthermore, social media lets you engage with your customers in ways that traditional advertising does not.

Cost: Business owners see a lower cost of advertising on Facebook and other social media platforms than traditional forms of media. In addition, business owners may find themselves or someone they employee to manage to maintain their social media presence as part of their job responsibilities.

Large target audience: Each social media platform has billions of users, yet each platform lets you target those users that meet your demographic requirements.

Instant feedback: Because of the nature of social media, business owners can receive instant feedback from actual customers. This opportunity allows businesses to make corrections or exploit positive feedback.

Portability: Social media users often carry their connections on their phones or other mobile devices. This allows business owners to reach customers regardless of where they are throughout the day.

Relationship building: Customer service problems can be resolved more quickly when they are known earlier.

#Hashtags: Social media's keywords that allow posts from all sources to be easily searched and found by interested users. The strategic use of hashtags can assure that your content reaches your target customers with a minimum of effort.

How to Leverage Social Media to Market Your Business

A good social media marketing campaign relies on understanding all that social media has to offer. Knowing the best choices for your specific business is important. Some forms of social media are better for recorded video or graphical representations while still others allow you to connect live with your customers.

- **Influencers**

    In the past, celebrity endorsements for your business or brand meant that you could expect positive impacts on your bottom line. Today, social media influencers offer similar services. An influencer is someone who has expertise in an industry and a significant following on social media where their voice has an impact. Influencers can help your brand with positive reviews or exposure. Positive reviews from influencers can cause your product to fly off the shelves. However, working with influencers can have drawbacks. A bad review can also have an equally devastating impact on your business. If an influencer is suspected of providing positive reviews for pay, they can lose credibility. While working with influencers can have a positive impact, using influencers should be part of a carefully planned social media marketing strategy.

- **Facebook**

    Facebook offers several ways in which a business may take advantage of the platform for marketing their goods or services. Creating a business page can increase awareness of your business. Depending on the business, fan pages or group pages can also have a positive impact. Through "Likes" and "Shares," posts become seen by more individuals. Additionally, businesses can buy advertising that appears for targeted users. This advertising can be used to increase awareness or advertise special promotions just for Facebook users. Depending on the business, using Facebook Live may help the business promote products or offer sale items to those watching live. Additionally, using CommentSold can allow users to register in advance of the Live event and purchase items for sale both during and after the live stream.

    For more information on using Facebook to market your business, visit their website here.

    For more information on CommentSold, visit their website here.

- **YouTube/YouTube Live**

    While selling products is often the goal of social media marketing, creating goodwill and a positive customer experience is another great way to consider using YouTube. Again, depending on the type of business, YouTube can be a good platform for hosting how-to videos, reviews, and live streaming events. In some cases, businesses use YouTube to host video libraries for their products.

- **Twitter**

    When Twitter first took the stage, users found themselves tweeting 140-character posts that creatively discussed what they were doing or answered questions. Today, Twitter has evolved into a platform that allows users to be far more creative with their curated content. Using hashtags, users can add links and photos to their tweets, allowing reposting of content from other sources. Businesses can exploit the use of Twitter by artful use of hashtags to promote their business that will assure target customers find their brand. Additionally, tweeting out flash sales and live events helps provide another way of connecting with mobile users.

    For more information on marketing on Twitter, visit their website here.

- **Pinterest**

    Largely a visual media, Pinterest can assist the business by creating visual content that demonstrates your products. Pinterest uses "pins" and "boards" to gather and share user-created content with other users. Users create pins that are then organized on boards, typically by topic. Users can follow other users' boards for ideas and inspiration.

    For more information on marketing on Pinterest, visit their website here.

- **Snapchat, TikTok, and Instagram**

    As with Pinterest, Snapchat, TikTok, and Instagram are visual forms of social media. TikTok and Snapchat allow users to post short videos while Instagram users can post both photos and videos. Using hashtags draws attention to the posts and allows for easy search. All three platforms allow businesses to create deeper brand awareness.

    For information regarding the rules of promotion on Snapchat, visit their website here.

    For information on marketing on TikTok, visit their website here.

    For information on marketing on Instagram, visit their website here.

Index

4Ps method
89

10-K report
106-107

Accounts Payable
112-114, 118-120

Accounts Receivable
106, 111-114, 118, 128, 172

accrual-based accounting
120

acquisition
214, 238, 248

active
31, 157, 219, 253

angel investors
174, 181

asset
35, 106-107, 135, 145, 173, 242

autonomy
29, 230

Balance Sheet
106-122, 128, 252

behavior pattern
229

benefits sought
87

board of advisors
149-150

board of directors
36-38, 149-151, 157

bookkeeper
121-128, 148-151

brand loyalty status
87

brand recognition
44-45

Break-Even Analysis
100, 121-124, 128

bullet points
179

bundle pricing
91

business income
35

business valuation
252

cash conversion
110-114, 118, 122

cash conversion cycle
110-114, 122

cash method of accounting
120

Certified Public Accountant (CPA)
125

Chapter 7 bankruptcy
254

Chapter 11 bankruptcy
255

Chapter 13 bankruptcy
255

clientele
13, 131-132, 169

co-working
259-260

collateral
173-176

commercialization
173

commission
106, 216-219, 224-225, 231

confirmation bias
159

conglomerate merger
239, 248

contingency plans
139, 245

contrast bias
217

cooperative
34, 38-40, 53

copyright
202

corporation
33-40, 46, 53, 105, 150, 158, 236, 255

cost of goods sold (COGS)
104-108

cost-plus pricing
90

credit score
101-103, 128

credit-reporting agencies
102

crisis communication plan
205

crowdfunding
102-103, 128

culture
136-138, 149-150, 155-162, 196-197, 201, 208-209, 214, 230, 243-245, 257

customer relationship management (CRM)
260

Days Payable Outstanding (DPO)
112

Days Sales in Inventory
111, 128

Days Sales Outstanding (DSO)
112

decline
70-72

demographics
79, 84-85, 89, 96-98, 130, 189-192, 198, 265

depreciate
135, 141

depreciation
135

direct labor
141-144

direct materials
141-144

discretionary income
84-86, 102, 128

disposable income
78, 84-85

disruptive technology
193

divisional
152-153

economic factors
191

economy
20-24, 34, 51, 188-191, 212, 245

elevator speech
102, 166, 177-180

employee orientation
221

employee turnover
137, 144, 221, 246

enterprise resource planning software (ERP)
260

entrepreneur
1, 7-8, 14-15, 19, 25-34, 43, 47-63, 68-74, 86-91, 98, 106, 126, 130, 144-146, 151, 162, 179-181, 205-206, 221-228, 232, 236-239, 243, 248-251, 255-257, 262-263

entrepreneurial ventures
18-20

entrepreneurship
2-266

Equal Employment Opportunity Commission (EEOC)
216-219

equity
106, 118-119, 128, 171-176

ethical/environmental factors
194

ethics
222, 256-258, 262

expenses
27-28, 35, 46, 55, 69, 84-85, 90, 96-110, 115-122, 128, 135, 169, 178, 247, 255

external influences
186-190, 196

external training
220-222

federal tax ID
202

fictitious business name
35

financial obligations
29, 254

fiscally responsible
167-169

fixed asset
106-107

fixed assets
104-107, 118, 128, 171

fixed costs
104, 110, 114, 122-123, 128

flat
9, 154, 162

foot traffic
129-130, 235

formal business plan
164-169

franchise
17-19, 34, 42-46, 50, 240-242, 248-249

franchisee
17-19, 32, 43-45, 243

franchisor
43-45

functional
152-155

funding
7, 18, 28-29, 33, 38, 43, 69, 100-105, 122-128, 164-180

furlough
205-208

general liability policy
137

General Selling and Administrative Expenses
117

generalization bias
218

gradual sale
251

grant
38, 43, 50, 170-181

gross domestic product (GDP)
22

gross profit margin
242

growth
23-25, 52, 57, 69-72, 134, 166, 178, 185, 236-247, 259

gut feeling bias
217

halo effect
217

hobby
13-17, 60-64, 74, 129

horizontal merger
239

hourly wage
148, 187, 224

idea generation
59-66, 71-74

ideation
65-68

in-house training
220-222

Income Statement
107-121, 128

incremental innovation
70, 74

independent contractor
46-47

industrial revolution
21, 25-26

inflation
191

informal business plan
165-166

infrastructure
25, 239, 246

innovation
19-26, 47-50, 69-77, 173, 193, 239, 244-248

innovative
7-8, 15-19, 47-50, 70-73, 77, 173-174, 232, 245

intellectual property
168, 179, 193, 202

interest
13, 47, 55-56, 60, 90-93, 106, 120-121, 148, 171, 177, 191, 197-200, 205, 253

internal influences
186, 196, 201

Internal Revenue Service (IRS)
61

internet
14-17, 21-28, 92, 105, 202, 212-213, 241, 249, 265

introduction
23, 32, 59, 69-72

inventory
17, 41, 106, 110-114, 118-121, 128, 134, 139-148, 171, 203, 246, 252

IPO
238, 248

job analysis
210-214, 229

job description
210-214, 220, 229-231

joint ventures
237, 248

knowledge-based jobs
21

leader
204-205, 256-258

lease agreement
252

legal factors
193

legal regulations
29

legal separation
35

liabilities
33-37, 43, 106, 118-119, 132

license
43, 193, 242

loan
29, 101-106, 110, 164-179

local ordinances
131-133

losses
29, 35-36, 61, 137, 246

loyalty program
241

malpractice insurance
137

manager
1, 58, 77-78, 150-153, 161, 174, 204, 251

managing relationships
199-200

mandated issue
228

manufacturing operations
132

market demand
57, 125

market research
78-82, 98, 212, 241, 265

market segmentation
83-89, 93, 98

marketing mix
89-92, 96-98

marketing plan
77-97, 167-168, 176, 252, 265

markup
119, 242

matrix
153, 195, 200, 254

maturity
70-72, 147

mentor
28, 103, 220-222

merger
238-239, 248

mind mapping method
63

minimum wage
187-188, 208

mix and match method
62

monopoly
239

monthly expense
107

non-disclosure document
150

North American Industry Classification System (NAICS) code
105

notes payable
118, 128

operating expenses
104-109, 115-117, 128

opportunity assessment plan
56, 66-68, 72

opportunity entrepreneurship
56

out with the old, in with the new method
63

outright sale
251

outsource
147-150

overhead
47, 141, 237

partnership
33-40, 46-47, 52-53, 139-140, 157-158, 162, 174, 250, 255

partnership agreement
157

passion
13-14, 27-28, 51, 60-64, 74-78, 98, 142, 179, 197, 201, 249

passive
157

patent
63, 134, 141, 180, 202, 207

penetration strategy
91

persistent pattern
229

PESTLE analysis
67-68, 190, 195-196, 208

political factors
191

power
8, 38, 74, 185, 191, 200, 204, 241

primary market research
80

primary research
66-68, 79-83, 91

principal
171

proactive
187-190

product liability
137-138

product-based businesses
34, 41-42, 53

product-producing
42

property insurance
137

proprietary
150

psychological pricing
91

radical innovation
70-72

reactive
187-190

reasonable accommodation
216-219

recency bias
218

recruitment
210-213, 218-219, 232

relationship management
201, 260

retained earnings
119, 128

revenue
35, 46-47, 61, 74, 93-96, 105, 109-111, 115-120, 124-128, 181, 191, 202, 208, 218, 259

reverse halo effect
217

risk
18-19, 25, 43-45, 52, 58, 101, 138-139, 157, 169, 178, 200, 225, 239, 243

salaried employee
224

SCAMPER method
63

SCORE
101-104, 126-128, 248, 264

seasonal demand
134

secondary market research
79-82, 98

secondary research
67-68, 79-82, 96

Securities and Exchange Commission (SEC)
106

selection process
144, 209-214, 218-219

self-managed
154-155, 162

service-based businesses
17, 34, 41-42, 53, 167

service-producing
42

silo mentality
155

similar to me bias
218

single incident
228

situational awareness
51

small business
8, 14-53, 92-93, 98-103, 110, 114-128, 143-150, 164-176, 181, 186-197, 201-204, 208, 219-221, 229-230, 238, 256, 262

Small Business Administration (SBA)
102-103

social entrepreneurship
256-259

social factors
192

soft skills
147-148, 204

sole proprietor
33-35, 136

sole proprietorships
17, 254-255

solve it method
62

stakeholder
197-201, 208, 257

Standard Industrial Classification (SIC) code
105

startup costs
17, 41, 102-107, 124-128

statement of equity
119

strategic plan
162, 195-196, 202

succession plan
156-160, 250, 256, 262

succession planning
159-162, 250-251, 255, 261

SWOT analysis
67-68, 95-97, 186-190, 196, 207-208

synthesis
81

tangible goods
41-42

target market
66, 78-97, 151, 168, 178, 212

tax deductible
27, 46

tax incentives
132

tax returns
35-36, 252

taxes payable
119

technological factors
193

terms
8-9, 15, 19-20, 24, 40, 45, 49, 53, 89-93, 97, 112-119, 150, 172-174, 179, 200, 211, 225, 230-231, 243, 247, 258-261

third party logistics providers
134

Timmons Framework of the entrepreneurial process
56-57

total product concept
90

trademark
202

unearned revenue
119, 128

usage rate
87

user status
87

values
86, 137, 195-196, 202, 221, 256

variable costs
109-110, 122-123, 128

vendor
23, 29, 35, 45, 50, 112-113, 118-120, 125, 150, 196-201, 208, 242

venture capital
171-174, 237-238, 248

venture capitalists
171-174, 181, 237

vertical merger
239

wages payable
119

what if you could method
62